PEOPLES AND CULTURES
OF THE MIDDLE EAST
VOLUME II

The Natural History Press, publisher for The American Museum of Natural History, is a division of Doubleday and Company, Inc. Directed by a joint editorial board made up of members of the staff of both the Museum and Doubleday, the Natural History Press publishes books and periodicals in all branches of the life and earth sciences, including anthropology and astronomy. The Natural History Press has its editorial offices at The American Museum of Natural History, Central Park West at 79th Street, New York, New York 10024, and its business offices at 501 Franklin Avenue, Garden City, New York 11530.

LOUISE E. SWEET received her training in anthropology and Near East studies at the University of Michigan and was awarded the doctoral degree in 1957. She has pursued ethnographic field research in Syria (1953–54), the Arab states of the Persian Gulf (1958–59), and Lebanon (1964–65), and has taught at a number of universities in the United States, Canada, and Lebanon. From 1966 to 1968 she served as the chairman of the Department of Anthropology at the State University of New York at Binghamton. She expects in 1969 to join the Department of Sociology and Anthropology at the American University of Beirut as Visiting Professor.

Dr. Sweet has written a monograph, *Tell Ṭoqaan: A Syrian Village*, and a number of papers in professional journals. She is currently engaged in research focused upon developing an ecological interpretation of the ethnohistory of the Druze people of the Levant.

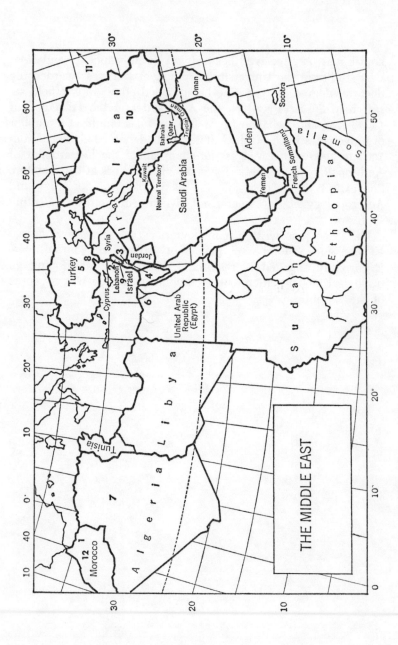

THE MIDDLE EAST

PEOPLES AND CULTURES
OF THE MIDDLE EAST

AN ANTHROPOLOGICAL READER

VOLUME II
Life in the Cities, Towns, and Countryside

EDITED AND WITH AN INTRODUCTION BY
LOUISE E. SWEET

NHP

PUBLISHED FOR
THE AMERICAN MUSEUM OF NATURAL HISTORY
THE NATURAL HISTORY PRESS
1970   GARDEN CITY, NEW YORK

The illustrations for this book
were prepared by the Graphic Arts Division of
The American Museum of Natural History.

Library of Congress Catalog Card Number 74–89112
Copyright © 1970 by Louise E. Sweet
All Rights Reserved
Printed in the United States of America
First Edition

Preface

The new nations and new and old kingdoms of the Middle East, from Morocco to Afghanistan, descendants of old kingdoms and empires and of the earliest civilizations, today face multiple threats in their struggles for survival and integration. These are of two major kinds. There are, first, those threats to continuity that are of internal origin, inherent in the resources of their lands, peoples, and cultural heritages. There are, second, those threats that advance openly against them from the outside, or that infiltrate slowly and establish footholds for pressure and dominance.

The list of internal threats is long and I suggest only a few: exploding populations; harsh environments with often meager and unevenly distributed resources in water supply, soil fertility, or minerals; the legacies of colonial occupations in the present irrational political boundaries, entrenched ruling elites, façade parliamentary political bureaucracies; well-developed armies and poorly developed economies; and ethnic, linguistic, and religious diversities exacerbated by contacts of dependency to external political powers of the modern world.

But in the face of these there are also inherent traits of resiliency and strength, of adaptability to diversity and adversity, of ancient stores of wit and wisdom, of values of honor and responsibility, and of modes of strategic compromise that will stand Middle Eastern societies in good stead. And in the discoveries of new resources of vast oil reserves and in the steady acquisition of industrial technology lie many hopes for survival and independence in cooperation with the world of nations.

To understand and appreciate more fully the Middle Eastern polities of today, close and detailed study of these and other aspects of the conditions for life and customs for meeting them of this vast area is an obvious requirement. In the main, anthropological perspectives on the cultural nature of the Middle East are presented in the selections in this *Reader*.

But the context of external threats to the integrity of these nations and peoples must not be forgotten. The Middle Eastern states face, as much of the world faces or has capitulated to, domination by the powerful, most fully industrialized nations or components of their systems, from the Americas, through those of Europe, to those of the Far East. The consequences of accepting dependency, or of resisting it even with force, or of attempting to industrialize their own economies, universalize their educational systems, and so on—and succeeding or failing—make the world's news headlines every day in one way or another, usually with very little perceptiveness.

Survival of these Middle Eastern polities will identify for the cultural anthropologist that process of adaptation to a world through which industrialized culture is spreading inexorably—as ten thousand years ago the domestication technology of the Neolithic Revolution began to proliferate inexorably from its earliest center of origin somewhere in the Middle East itself.

The selections compiled here will indicate, I hope, the extent to which the research of modern anthropology into the inherent attributes of Middle Eastern sociocultural systems in all their variety can contribute to a more accurate understanding of this part of the world of man.

Together, the two volumes of this *Reader* assemble studies that sample the full range in time and space of cultural adjustments to the conditions for human life in the Middle East, from archaeological and historical depth to the niceties of intercommunal and interpersonal relations in different situations from traditional systems of relative stability to scenes of disorienting current change.

Volume I comprises selections that present the depth of Middle Eastern cultural heritages from the Neolithic to the current scene, samples of major social institutions or customs characteristic of the whole area, and studies of communities of the most well known type of society if not the most prevalent in the Middle East, the nomadic pastoralists.

Volume II focuses upon two community types of the Middle East, rural agricultural societies and urban societies, and their interrelations. It is especially useful for students of "urbanization."

Two major criteria guided my selections from the enormous literature that is available on the Middle East: the scholarly presentation of empirical data and the sophistication of analysis. It is my first concern that old, stereotyped ideas of the Middle East and North African peoples and their cultures should be challenged by these studies drawn from some of the best literature of anthropology, geography, and history that I have been able to assemble.

Most of the selections have been previously and recently published as independent papers in professional journals, or as parts of books or symposia, and in the cases of Ibn Khaldun and Charles Doughty, from classics. A few are published here for the first time, and I am most grateful to those who responded to my request for a revised publication or a new article that would fit the plan of the whole. They are, in the order of their appearance: Volume I: Barbara B. Aswad, T. M. Johnstone, Safia Mohsen.

I am also grateful to a number of colleagues in teaching the anthropology of the Middle East who responded to my queries as to which of a very long list of selections would be most useful for their own instructional needs, and who, in some cases, offered ideas for better examples or organization than I had listed initially: Harold Barclay, Harvey Goldberg, John Gulick, Fuad Khuri, Robert Murphy, Dorothy Wilner, and Alex Weingrod.

—Louise E. Sweet
January, 1969

Contents

Introduction

Most of the peoples of this Middle Eastern "area" stretching from Morocco to Afghanistan are sedentary rural agriculturalists or urban dwellers, concentrated in the fertile interstices between the greater expanse of steppe and desert: hill and plateau peoples, coastal peoples, oasis dwellers. All of these are now most deeply affected by the process of "urbanization," endemic throughout the world, as industrial technology and production spread in the Middle East, locate most frequently in urban areas, and begin to drain the countryside for labor and service occupations. More sharply than in many of the selections in Volume One, the effects on the traditional pre-industry economics of the Middle East are to be seen in the literature assembled in this volume. Nevertheless, it remains important to recognize so far as possible the original systems of Middle Eastern life in order to understand their resistance and their response: we need to "know the territory" in order to comprehend the course of present events.

Especially characteristic of many areas of the Middle East is the "enclaving" of groups for whom no label is yet adequate ("tribe," or "confessional group," or "ethnic group" are among those used). It is an ancient phenomenon of the Middle East. While many such distinct polities have been called "tribes" (especially among the Berbers of North Africa or the Kurds), their structural organization is far more complex than this label usually means in general anthropology.

Part One of this volume, "Rural Peoples in the Middle East: Agricultural Enclaves and Villages," opens, therefore, with David Hart's study of the Berber Aith Waryaghar of Morocco, an ex-

ample of this form of dissident and distinct polity that as yet has
no explicit label of recognition.

There follows E. L. Peters' fine holistic description and analysis
of a Shi'a village in southern Lebanon. It reveals a social stratification and community type, with urban ties, hitherto unrecog-
nized in the rural Middle East where the stereotype of the
homogeneous, illiterate peasant village controlled by urban landlords has too long commanded the concept of Middle Eastern
peasant villages.

Alex Weingrod's and Henry Rosenfeld's papers, in particular,
show the impact of an industrialized state system upon kin-based
village society. Since both are concerned with the place of such
"nodule" communities in an essentially industrialized state system (Israel), the fact that neither the immigrant nor the indigenous communities were necessarily isolated settlements until
their incorporation into a powerful industrial state system is
overlooked, but implicit.

Finally, in both Paul Stirling's and Jacques Berque's selections
we see different aspects of the conflict between traditional organization and the foment of change.

Part Two gathers together a few of the few available anthro-
pologically oriented studies of urban scenes. The cities of the
Middle East are among the most ancient urban centers of the
world: Mecca, Fez, Cairo, Jerusalem, Damascus, Aleppo, Istanbul, Antakya (ancient Antioch), Isfahan, Shiraz—to name but a
few for which there are excellent historical studies. But the
"urban anthropology" of the Middle East has only begun. Besides
the work of Paul English (see selection in Part Two), another
recent study by an anthropologist, John Gulick's *Tripoli: A
Modern Arab City* (Harvard University Press: Cambridge, Mass.,
1967), is almost all that is available in the English language.
The few selections assembled here do not do justice to the older
literature that is available, nor to the diversity of urban types.
The oasis centers are represented by E. A. Alport's description
of the cities of the Mzab valley; social changes and sociological
persistences of traditional family structure in modern urban life
are discussed in Wolfram Eberhard's and Samih Farsoun's papers.
Two chapters from Paul W. English's *City and Village in Iran*
effectively present a polar type to the rural enclave of Hart's

Aith Waryaghar, the urban-dominated regional system. And, for urbanization protagonists, de-urbanization of a town in Afghanistan is presented in Louis Dupree's "Aq Kupruk," with a wealth of description of sports, food, and interaction of nomad, villager, and townsman. This will remind the student of Middle Eastern culture to some extent of the rich colors, flavors, excitements, and satisfactions for the participants in its traditions.

Lastly, since the tensions and recurrent fighting between the industrially powerful Israel and the industrially weaker Middle Eastern states on her borders have almost always been interpreted as ancient and inherent hostility between Arabs and Jews, Lawrence Rosen's fine paper illustrates how incorrect this view is. Nation-states at war with each other is a modern tragedy; the traditional relationships between Muslims and Jews is something very different indeed.

PART I

Rural Peoples in the Middle East:
Agricultural Enclaves and Villages

Editor's Note: Today there is a sizable literature on the villagers of the Middle East, although it is very uneven in coverage. Most of the people of this area are villagers, and the selections here are only a small sample of the literature that is available, old and new. I have particularly sought to emphasize certain very important features of rural life that have been neglected—the enclaving of polities, and the stratification of rural societies. Many other aspects of rural life also appear in these selections, and I hope they will send the student to other monographs that have not been sampled, for comparison.

DAVID M. HART

1. Clan, Lineage, Local Community and the Feud in a Rifian Tribe [Aith Waryaghar, Morocco]

I. INTRODUCTION TO THE AITH WARYAGHAR

This paper will discuss the social structure and territorial system, with special reference to the bloodfeud, among the Aith Waryaghar[1], a tribe of sedentary agriculturists (as are all their immediate neighbors) in the Moroccan Rif. Aith Waryaghar are the largest single tribe in that region, with, according to the Moroccan census of 1960, a population of 75,895. This population, if the Spanish figure for 1929—39,537—is correct (and there is no good reason to suppose that it is not) has almost doubled since effective Spanish occupation of the tribal territory (1029 square kilometers) in 1926. This followed the surrender in that year, to the French, of 'Abd al-Krim, Aith Waryaghar's most famous "native son." The population density, particularly in the northern lowland of this tribal area, is one of the highest in rural Morocco, with over 120 people per square kilometer.

The territory occupied by the Aith Waryaghar, which looks in

I am grateful to the author for permission to print this example of an "enclave" as an original contribution to this *Reader*. The research and writing were supported in part by a grant from the Social Science Research Council. [Ed.]

[1] I use the name, throughout this article and in all my other publications, by which members of this tribe refer to themselves in their own Rifian Berber language. Throughout, in the interests of accuracy, I retain all tribal and segment names in Rifian Berber, rather than in Arabic. I should add, however, that in Arabic the tribal name is Bni Waryaghal; French "Beni Ouriaghel" and Spanish "Beni Uriaguel" are not used here except in quoted passages. The orthography I have given will also distinguish the tribe in question from the small Arabic-speaking tribe of Bni Waryagil, located some distance southwest of the Rif proper, at Tafrant on the Wargha River. Aith Waryaghar disclaim any connections with this latter group, in any case.

outline like a lopsided sack with the heavy end at the southern bottom, extends into the back country behind al-Husaima (Alhucemas or El-Hoceima) and Adjir. Adjir was 'Abd al-Krim's old capital and since his time has been the principal seat of tribal administration, both under Spain, 1926–56, and under the Independent Moroccan Government since then. The tribal land can virtually be said to be framed on west and east by two rivers, the Ghis and the Nkur, respectively, although some of Waryagharland in fact extends west of the Ghis. On the north lies the Mediterranean, into which both rivers empty. This northern neck of the sack is made up of the alluvial plain (plus surrounding hillsides) of al-Husaima, which slopes gradually upward toward the south; the heavy bottom end of the sack culminates in the massive mountain knot of the Jbil Hmam, the Mountain of Doves (and doves do abound in it), rising to 1930 meters at its highest point. Here, too, is located the tomb of Sidi Bu Khiyar, a stranger to the tribe, but nonetheless its most important saint, at which an annual tribal pilgrimage is held on the day before the 'Aid l-Kbir.[2]

From the air, Waryagharland and that of its neighbor tribes looks like a crumpled piece of reddish-brown paper, with the crumpling heaviest and highest in the Jbil Hmam, and a slight and slender expanse of green in the northern plain. It is largely denuded of vegetation, and erosion has been extensive. Aith Waryaghar are farmers, and indeed good ones, considering their entirely traditional agricultural techniques; but in no corner of Morocco has the Malthusian law been perhaps so strikingly apparent as in their own. In the past, bloodfeuding tended to keep down the population, and even before the establishment of the protectorate over Morocco, Aith Waryaghar and their neighbors had established a pattern of labor migration to Algeria to work on the farms of French *colons* in the Department of Oran, where they became grape-pickers and "shotgun guards." This labor migration reached its heyday in the late 1940's and early '50's,

---

[2] Cf. David M. Hart, "An *'Amara* in the Central Rif: the Annual Pilgrimage to Sidi Bu Khiyar," *Tamuda*, V. 2, 1957, pp. 239–45. For more generalized ethnographic information, see David M. Hart, "An Ethnographic Survey of the Rifian Tribe of Aith Waryaghar," *Tamuda*, II, 1, 1954, pp. 51–86, and "Emilio Blanco Izaga and the Berbers of the Central Rif," *Tamuda*, VI, 2, 1958, pp. 171–237.

but came to an abrupt halt in 1955 with the advent of war in Algeria and the closing of the frontier. Nothing daunted, however, many young Waryaghar of the early 1960's have migrated to France and, even more, to West Germany to work in breweries and automobile assembly plants. The bloodfeuder of yesterday has become the migrant laborer of today.

For those at home, however, unemployment is a crucial problem, and infant mortality has in no way been sufficient to check the population growth. The relationship of the Aith Waryaghar to their land has always been an ambivalent one of love and hate; they never tire, for instance, of telling one, "We are poor and our land is worthless"; but on the other hand, the historical record, to be given cursory examination below, shows that on three separate occasions in the present century alone they have taken violent exception to invasion of their barren and eroded countryside by outsiders. And although they have had no firearms since the Spaniards confiscated them in 1926, the feud is only dormant among them—it is by no means dead. Infrastructures and the basic value-systems embodied in them are notoriously change-resistant; and the dispositions both to violence and to seclusion of their womenfolk, which are such characteristically Mediterranean traits, are high among the Aith Waryaghar.

The Jbil Hmam is claimed by all true Waryaghar as their point of origin; they say that from there they gradually radiated northward to the Mediterranean, and that it is only true Waryaghar clans and lineages which, living in the plain, have "brothers" (i.e., are replicated) in the mountains, and vice versa. As we shall see, the territorial structure of the tribe is a remarkably accurate reflection of this statement. The etymology of the tribal name is unknown to any of its members, probably an indication of tribal antiquity. All that *is* locally known is that the so-called Dahar Waryaghar, or Waryaghar Mountain, is an integral part of the Jbil Hmam (located in the present subclan territory of Aith 'Arus), as is Thawragh (in the subclan territory of Isrihan of the clan of Aith Yusif w-'Ari)—the similarity between the names Thawragh and Waryaghar is often invoked locally;[3] and

---

[3] *Awragh* (fem. *thawrakhth*) in Rifian means "yellow," but in this particular context such a meaning is either non-suggestive or has been lost.

thus *Aith* Waryaghar are "*the* people" from this particular region.

II. HISTORICAL SKETCH

It will be appropriate to preface the discussion of Waryaghar social and territorial structure with a brief historical summary, insofar as known, for certain points to be made here will have direct repercussions on what is to follow.

Firstly, the name *Aith Waryaghar* is very old indeed. The very first Muslim principality in Morocco was founded in 710 on the banks of the Nkur River in the clan territory of the present Aith Bu 'Ayyash. The town of Nkur which its founders built was completed in 760 and, no doubt not long afterward, its southeast gate (which would today have pointed toward the tribe of Axt Tuzin rather than toward Waryagharland, which is more properly due south and southwest) was labelled, in Arab chronicles, *Bab Bni Waryaghal.* Thus, since its inception, one might say, the tribe has had an Arabic name coexisting with an equivalent to its Rifian Berber one. But the Aith Waryaghar of that day were, in their fastness of the Jbil Hmam, the barbarians at the gates of the City of Nkur, and beyond the mere recording of their name, the medieval Arab chroniclers have nothing whatsoever to say about them. Their name remained, in Berque's phrase, "a pimple on the face of the local landscape."[4] At any rate, the Almoravids under Yusuf ibn Tashfin in 1080 destroyed the Nkur Kingdom for good—two previous attempts having only caused it, phoenix-like, to rise again. After this, one can only assume that the Aith Waryaghar rose and fell with the prevailing tides of Moroccan history as these happened to affect the Rif, a region which was both a backwater and, characteristically, one which only recognized the spiritual (as opposed to the temporal) authority of the Moroccan Sultan. It was *blad s-siba,* land of dissidence, par excellence, even though it had been Islamicized at the virtual dawn of Moroccan Islam. Its tribesmen, it seems safe to surmise, oscillated between feuding and truce-making among themselves

---

[4] Jacques Berque, "Qu'est-ce c'est une tribu nordafricaine?," *Hommage à Lucien Fèbvre,* I, Paris: Colin, 1953, pp. 261–71.

through the centuries until, at the end of the 19th century, the external pressures of wider politics began to bring them to the attention of both Morocco and Europe.

In the 1890's, the neighbors of Aith Waryaghar to the west, the Ibuqquyen, began to attack Spanish and French steamers passing by the Rifian coast. Official protests were lodged with the sultan of Morocco in Fez by the two governments concerned; and in 1898 a punitive expedition under Bushta l-Baghdadi was sent up from Fez to punish the pirates. He accomplished this task so well that his name is still remembered with horror and hatred in Ibuqquyen; and he was aided and abetted in his undertaking by some of the northern segments of Aith Waryaghar.

After this expedition, however, the Aith Waryaghar went back to their internal feuding for another ten years, when another external event united *all* of them for the first time in their recorded history: the invasion of the Rif by the pretender Bu Ḥmāra ("the man on the 'she donkey'") who in 1906 had set himself up in Qasba Silwan, near Nador, and had gained the support of all the tribes in the Eastern Rif. He then determined, in 1908, to cross the Nkur River and invade Waryagharland, but he made the great tactical error of entrusting this invasion to a Negro general. Not only were all Aith Waryaghar determined to resist this invasion, but they regarded the fact that the army commander was a slave as the ultimate insult; and on September 7 of the same year, they successfully mowed down Bu Ḥmāra's cavalry units as the latter attempted to cross the river below Imzuren. The remainder of the invaders fled east. The corporate tribal action initiated by the Aith Waryaghar (and who were assisted by their southern neighbors of Aith 'Ammarth in this undertaking) was emulated now by all the eastern tribes, who proceeded to attack Bu Ḥmāra's flanks until they drove him out of the Rif entirely.[5]

Aith Waryaghar now thought they were invincible. In this self-revelatory knowledge they returned once more to their own affairs of internal disputation and interminable bloodfeuding. However, the Bu Ḥmāra episode was only a local dress rehearsal

[5] An excellent and detailed account of Bu Ḥmāra's vicissitudes in the Rif may be found in Eduardo Maldonado, *El Rogui*, Tetuan: Instituto General Franco, 1952.

for what was to come thirteen years later. Beginning in 1909, the Spaniards had been gradually moving west into the Rif from Melilla; and the 1912 Protectorate Treaty, which allotted to the Spanish a northern slice of the country, was of course an invitation to them to occupy this region effectively. But, as it turned out, they were not able to do so until 1926.

'ABD AL-KRIM

In 1921, a remarkable man named Si Muhammad bin Si 'Abd al-Krim, from Ajdir of the Waryaghar clan of Aith Yusif w-'Ari, whose father had been a *fqih* or Qur'anic schoolmaster in Ajdir and who himself had been *qadi qudat* ("judge of judges") in Melilla,[6] took it upon himself to organize the Aith Waryaghar and others and to halt forcibly the increasing Spanish threat. He not only was able to obtain the adherence of all of his own tribe to his cause, but he quickly obtained the support of the neighboring Rifian tribes (Ibuqquyen, Thimsaman, Axt Tuzin, Aith 'Ammarth, Igzinnayen, etc.) as well. In July 1921, at Dahar Ubarran, on the tribal border between Thimsaman and Aith Wurishik, he inflicted on the Spanish Army the worst single defeat any colonial army had ever suffered anywhere up to that time—it is significant that Spanish history books tend to skirt the subject of Dahar Ubaran, and merely refer to it as being *de triste memoria.*

This is not the place to go into any more than the briefest possible résumé of 'Abd al-Krim's career, which I hope to discuss in some detail in a forthcoming work. Suffice it to say here that his victory at Dahar Ubarran established his unquestioned ascendancy over the Aith Waryaghar, and in turn their own unquestioned ascendancy over the other tribes of the Rif; for as Waryaghar then put it, the whole Rif has always danced to the sound of the Waryaghar tambourine. 'Abd al-Krim became the head of Dawla, a *Jumhuriya Rifiya,* or "Rifian Republic State," and selected ministers for it mostly from his own kinsmen and

[6] According to some informants 'Abd al-Krim's antecedents three or four generations back may have been *shurfa* or "descendants of the Qaraysh," from the clan of Asht 'Aru 'Aisa in the neighboring tribe of Igzinnayen to the south.

fellow tribesmen.[7] By 1923–25 the Rifian Republic State was at
the zenith of its power. Rifian forces overran and took control
of all the Ghmara and most of the Jbala to the west; and by the
spring of the latter year 'Abd al-Krim, a man who most effectively wielded both the pen and the sword, had begun to challenge the French as well as the Spaniards. For a number of
reasons too detailed to go into here, he suddenly moved into
and occupied the territories of certain tribes in the southern
Jbala, all within the then French Zone, and by the summer of
1925 even Fez was threatened. Marshal Pétain and a huge
French Army were hastily dispatched to Morocco to deal with
the situation. It was not, however, until after the combined
Franco-Spanish operations, leading to the Spanish disembarka-
tion at al-Husaima in the fall and the joint pincer movement the
following spring (1926) by both sets of armies, the Spaniards
from the north and the French from the south, in which the
subjection of Waryagharland was the primary objective, that
'Abd al-Krim capitulated to the French at Targist, May 27, 1926.
And in that final month of May, the fighting throughout Waryagharland was extremely heavy. Although their southern neighbors of Igzinnayen finally made the traditional act of submission,
ta'rqiba, by sacrificing one or more bulls to the French, the Aith
Waryaghar did nothing of the sort for the Spaniards; they merely
sullenly and resentfully turned over their guns to them.

Since that time 'Abd al-Krim has largely passed out of Waryagharland as such (he died in Cairo on February 6, 1963); but
he is very much a legend, and justifiably so, to this day. The
changes which he wrought in the Rifian social order were far-
reaching. Principal among them were the outlawing of feuds and
the extension of the *Shari'a* to all aspects of Rifian legal life.
Previously, only land, marriage, and divorce had come under the
jurisdiction of tribal judges; anything falling under the rubric
of "criminal law" fell under that of the clan or tribal *imgharen*,
the council-members of the *aitharba'in*.[8] Under the traditional

---

[7] This is *not* to be confused with the Rifian term *ripublik*, which means,
and very specifically, the period *prior* to 'Abd al-Krim, when bloodfeuding
was a dominant activity in the Waryaghar social order.

[8] I believe this term, in the Rif, to be derived from *aith-tarbi'in* (itself
from *tharbi'th*, pl. *tharbi'in*, "people"), literally, "people of the people"
and hence "representatives of the people," i.e., the governing body and, by

system also, as in most other Berber-speaking regions, the collective oath was the major mode of proof (though it never attained the refinements among Rifians which it did among the transhumant Berbers of Central Morocco).

In a word, 'Abd al-Krim decollectivized oaths, stamped out feuds, and finally Islamicized, remarkably thoroughly, the *qa'ida* (custom) of the Rifian tribes. But, of course, Rifians say that they have always followed the Shari'a and that they have always been the best of Muslims, and that 'Abd al-Krim only made them better ones. This may well have elements of truth, for such assertions are extremely difficult to assess objectively. The fact is, nonetheless, that 'Abd al-Krim had "acculturated" the "Berber" features of the Rifian social system (even though probing of the situation has revealed to me time and again that informants are evasive over the question, for instance, of whether daughters inherit, and how much) to such an extent that the Spanish administration from a *de facto* standpoint merely took over where 'Abd al-Krim left off. There were never any *tribunaux coutumiers* set up in the Rif; and the violent manifestations of Rifian "apartness" from the wider Moroccan society which culminated in the revolt of the Aith Waryaghar against the government of Independent Morocco in 1958–59 were based on essentially the same considerations as the Bu Ḥmāra episode and 'Abd al-Krim's war: that Aith Waryaghar like to be left to their own devices and dividedness, but that this dividedness disappears as though by magic in the face of outside threats or interference.

Aith Waryaghar history thus illustrates a first structural principle: that its members form indeed a single *dhaqbitsh*, a single tribe, if we take the standard anthropological definition of a tribe as the widest politically autonomous unit whose members act corporately within a kinship ideology of membership as our yardstick. It is also, of course, a tribe in a system of tribes, and in its own particular system, it is the dominant tribe. And now so much for history; let us turn to the facts of ethnography.

---

implication, government by consent of the governed. I think this etymology fits the facts far more closely than such arbitrary translations as "sons of the forty," forty in itself being a highly arbitrary number (except in the case of the Rgibat; cf. my article, David M. Hart, "The Social Structure of the Rgibat Bedouins of the Western Sahara," *Middle East Journal*, XVI, 4, 1962, pp. 512–27).

III. STRUCTURAL UNITS OF THE AITH WARYAGHAR

1. DESCENT GROUPS

Dhaqbitsh, khums (or *dhakhammasth*), *r-rba', dshar, dhar-fiqth* and *jajgu* are the Berber labels which, in descending order, Aith Waryaghar give their political, territorial and social units. These units are all interrelated social phenomena; and it is appropriate to realize at the outset that they are anything but conceptually rigid. Though each label has its own more or less exclusive radius of application, they all should properly be considered intercontextually, as referring to parts of a segmentary whole. Each segment of this whole on every level of segmentation, stands of course in the classical position of balance and opposition to other such segments of the same order. It will nonetheless be convenient to employ certain standard terms in the vocabulary of social anthropology to distinguish between certain kinds of segments at different levels. These terms are, primarily, *tribe, clan, lineage* and *local community;* and, secondarily, *"fifth," subclan* and *sublineage.*

By "tribe" (*dhaqbitsh,* pl. *dhiqbair*), I mean here the totality of Aith Waryaghar, or indeed the totality of any other such ceiling group as locally conceived which forms the highest politically autonomous unit in the region (other examples from the Central Rif are Ibuqquyen, Aith 'Ammarth, Igzinnayen, Thimsaman and Axt Tuzin; and as these all represent locally traditional structures, I refer to them as "tribes" and avoid mention of recently created administrative units which as often as not do not entirely correspond to them). In the Rifian context, as the reader may have surmised from the preceding historical summary, the question of descent, on this tribal level, from a putative common agnatic ancestor is quite irrelevant. The norm for Rifian tribes in general is rather that each tribe is an aggregate formed by a variable number (never more than five, however) of heterogeneous clans.

By "clan" (*ar-rba',* pl. *r-urbu'*), I designate the largest existing order of segment *within* the tribal framework whose members, by virtue of their clan name, implicitly or explicitly claim

a common agnatic ancestor or a common origin, but who lack or
have lost the genealogical knowledge or evidence to support this
claim. Thus, in a normal schematization based on levels, if we
consider the *tribe* as Level I, the *clan* would be Level II—but
alone of all the Rifian tribes, Aith Waryaghar shows certain complications even here, which will be discussed presently.

By "subclan" (also *ar-rba'*, indicating the fluidity of the Rifian
terminology), I refer to the segments in turn of a clan segment,
whose members are likewise unable to trace their genealogical
connections back even to the subclan ancestor or origin. And
here, under normal circumstances, we have arrived at Level III.
By "lineage" (*dharfiqth,* pl. *dharfiqin*), on the other hand, I mean
the largest effective social group whose members *can* and *do*
trace their ascent back to a common agnatic founder-ancestor.
Here we have arrived at any level from Level IV on up (or
down, depending how one looks at it; Rifians invariably start,
themselves, from the tribal or clan level and work down toward
the small units). And by "sublineage" (*jajgu,* pl. *ijujga*), I mean
a branch of such a lineage, generally constituted of the descendants of a single son of the lineage ancestor. Thus, if the effective
lineage is at Level IV, the effective sublineage will be at Level
V, or if the former is at Level VI, the latter will be at Level VII,
and so on. (See Figures 1-1 and 1-2.)

2. LOCAL COMMUNITY: THE DSHAR TERRITORIAL UNIT

It is well to point out here that *each of these units* has its own
name and its own territory within the framework of the tribal
territory as a whole. Thus by "local community" (*ad-dshar,* pl.
r-udshur), I refer to the *territorial unit* proper, also with its own
name. Generally this is a toponym in the Rif, but anthroponyms
are not uncommon, particularly if all lineage groups living in
this territory claim descent from a single ancestor, or if, as can
happen, one of them is dominant at the expense of the others.
This *dshar* or local community (I eschew the term "village" in
this Rifian context, even though in the Ghmara and Jbala to
the west the same word does refer to true villages) consists in the
Rif of widely dispersed individual households "like stars in the
sky," as Rifians say. If households are not dispersed individually,

they are grouped together only in minute clusters of two or three. The *dshar* acts as the unit of residence for a given number of *lineage-groups*. As each individual household is separated by at least 300 meters from the next, as was pointed out by Sánchez Pérez,[9] and as each, at any altitude below 1000 meters, is surrounded by barking dogs and an impenetrable clump of cactus (though of course, even though cactus does not grow above this altitude, dogs do), so the distance between one local community and the next is, of course, correspondingly greater. The reason is possibly to maintain seclusion of women—and all Rifians, especially Aith Waryaghar, are extremely jealous of their women, even though the latter seem to play no significant role in the segmentary system now under discussion.

3. THE "FIFTH": KHUMS, THE MAXIMAL POLITICAL UNIT BELOW THE TRIBE

By "fifth"[10] (*khums*, pl. *khmās*, or *dhakhamasth*, pl. *dhikhamasin*), I mean a special recombination, resorted to generally for political ends, of clans with other clans or with other subclans (even though the "fifth" does in some cases coincide with the clan itself) to be discussed below. Not only this unit, but before 'Abd al-Krim's time, Aith Waryaghar had also an extremely active system of mutually hostile dual factions (*liff*, pl. *lfuf*), though this was a consequence rather than a part of the segmentary and territorial system; and it, too, will be discussed later.

IV: ANALYSIS OF THE RELATION OF SEGMENTARY AND TERRITORIAL SYSTEMS

We may now examine the salient features of the segmentary and territorial systems in some detail. An appropriate point of

[9] Andres Sánchez Pérez, "Datos Históricos sobre Ciudades Rifenas," *Selecciones de Conferencias y Trabajos realizados durante el Curso de Interventores 1951–52*, Tetuan, 1952, pp. 29–47, esp. p. 32.

[10] This term has been coined by Carleton S. Coon, *Tribes of the Rif*, Harvard African Studies, IX, Cambridge, Mass.: Peabody Museum, 1931, pp. 91–92. I retain it because of its convenience and accuracy, although I do not accept the rest of his social unit terminology.

departure for this is contained in perceptive observation by
Robert Montagne:[11]

"La tribu des Beni Ouriaghel [i.e., Aith Waryaghar], divisée
en cinq 'khoms', présente une structure sociale assez compliquée, qui résulte à la jois de l'état de guerre permanent
dans lequel vivaient d'habitude des familles et de l'infertilité
du sol qui disperse les habitants. Chaque 'khoms' possède un
territoire principal en montagne et des enclaves en plaine
ou inversement. En outre, les marabouts forment un 'khoms'
supplémentaire dispersé dans tout le pays.

"Malgré cette confusion et en dépit de l'hostilité habituelle
des groupes familiaux à l'interieur du 'khoms' . . . , les
limites de chaque fraction restent parfaitement connues et
il arrive fréquemment que les querelles intestines s'apaisent
pour permettre à chaque 'khoms' d'entrer en lutte contre
le voisin.

"Seuls dans tout le Rif, les Beni Ouriaghel ont des 'khoms'
dont le territoire est formé de parcelles séparées. Partout
ailleurs, chez les tribus de Mtiwa, Beni Bou Frah, Beni Itteft,
Boqqoya, Temsaman, la division en 'khoms', très apparente,
découpe le pays en petites unités sensiblement égales en
force et en surface, quelles que soient les conditions géographiques de le vie."[12]

Author's translation:

"The tribe of Bni Waryaghal (= Aith Waryaghar), divided
into five *khmas* (sing. *khums,* "fifth"), presents quite a com-

[11] Montagne's fleeting analysis of Rifian social structure, and in particular
his labelling of the region as *"le Rif anarchique"* may otherwise be disregarded. The observation cited here is not to be confused with the notion he
develops elsewhere, of "organized anarchy" (cf. R. Montagne, *La Vie Sociale et Politique des Berbères,* Paris: Editions du Comité de l'Afrique Française, 1931, p. 74), and which was usefully applied and expanded by Emilio
Blanco Izaga for Aith Waryaghar, *Conferencia sobre Derecho Consuetudinario Rifeño,* Ms., Decembre 1935.

[12] R. Montagne, *Les Berberes et le Makhzen,* Paris: Alcan, 1930, note 2,
pp. 175–76. Montagne's labelling of the clan structure of the other tribes
which he mentions in this connection as *khums* is by no means entirely accurate, but this is not the point at issue in the present context.

plicated social structure, resulting both from the permanent state of war in which its [constituent] 'families' [read *lineages*] usually lived and from the infertility of the soil which brought about the dispersion of its inhabitants. Each *khums* possesses its main territory in the mountains and enclaves in the plain, or vice versa. In addition, the Imrabdhen form a supplementary *khums* dispersed over all the tribal territory.

"Despite this confusion and despite the habitual hostility of the 'family groups' [read *lineages* or *lineage groups*] within the *khums* . . . , the boundaries of each 'fraction' [read *clan* or *subclan*] are perfectly well known, and it frequently happens that internal feuds subside in order to permit each *khums* to enter into a [wider] struggle with a neighboring one.

"Alone in the Rif, the Bni Waryaghal (= Aith Waryaghar) have *khmas*, the territory of which is made up of blocs separated from each other. Everywhere else, among the tribes of Mtiwa, Bni Bu Frah, Bni Yittuft, Buqquya and Thimsaman, the division into *khmas* ['fifths'], very readily discernible, cuts the region up into little units of approximately equal strength and size, whatever the geographic conditions of existence may be."

Now, even though one may justly reproach Montagne for having failed to see the highly segmentary character of Berber social structures—and a character which had, even before E. E. Evans-Pritchard's well-known definition and elucidation of the problem, already been suggested by Emile Durkheim for the Kabyles[13] —the above statement really touches the core of the problem; and a systematic examination of this statement, and of the problems involved, is now in order.

Hence I shall discuss Aith Waryaghar social structure in the light of Montagne's statement, on a point by point basis, taking

[13] Emile Durkheim, *De la Division du Travail Social*, 1893 (1960 Edition), Paris: Presses Universitaires de France, 1960, pp. 150, 152, 153, 157 and 269. I am indebted to Magister Alv Alver for calling my attention to this point. Durkheim's sources were, of course, Hanoteau-Letourneux and Masqueray.

his statement apart, as one would a watch, and then putting it
together again.

1.   *"La tribu des Beni Ouriaghel . . ." "The tribe of Bni War-*
yaghal (= Aith Waryaghar) . . ."

From what I have said previously, the fact that Aith Waryaghar do indeed constitute a tribe should now be self-evident. It
is important to note here that under the Spanish protectorate,
the tribe was divided, on the suggestion and recommendation of
Col. Emilio Blanco Izaga in 1936, into three *qaidates* or territories controlled by a *qaid*. Utac, the northern one, for Aith
Yusif w-'Ari and Imrabdhen; Upper Ghis, the southwestern one,
for Aith 'Abdallah and Aith Hadhifa; and Nkur, the southeastern
one, for Aith Bu 'Ayyash and the mountain subclans of Aith
Turirth, Timarzga and Aith 'Arus. The "we-feeling" of the
group had become relaxed to the extent that a mountaineer could
speak of a lowlander as belonging to *dhaqbitsh n-waddai*, the
lower tribe, and the latter could speak of *him* as belonging to
dhaqbitsh n-dara or *dhaqbitsh n-innij*, the upper tribe (and there
were corresponding derogatory nicknames). This administrative
decoupage has been modified even more since Independence;
but the fact that all Aith Waryaghar think of themselves *as* a
single tribe, *as* Aith Waryaghar, was amply demonstrated in the
1958–59 revolt. Then, as on previous occasions, when under pressure or threat, it was the traditional structures and not the new
administrative ones which were invoked. (Though it may be
neither here nor there, I do not feel that the present rural
commune system has as yet made much impact on the traditional
social structure, or on the thinking behind it, of this tribal
group.)

2.   *". . . divisée en cinq 'khoms' . . ." ". . . divided into five*
khmas [*sing.* khums, *'fifths'*]"

Here we have reached Step I (and in fact Level II) of our
discussion of Waryaghar social structure. "*Nishnin zg-Aith Warya-*
ghar gharnagh khams khmas"—"We of Aith Waryaghar have
(i.e., are segmented into) five 'fifths,'" e.g., *khums*, pl. *khmas*, as

indicated above. This is the statement which invariably prefaces an old informant's discussion of tribal segmentation. It indicates three things: (1) the tribe, in this case *in particular,* is divided into five basic units of equal strength, or conceived to be of equal strength, even though sometimes individual informants may differ as to their composition (I give the most reliable version of the system below in Fig. 1-1); (2) each of these *khmas* or "fifths" forms a part (specifically, one-fifth) of the tribal whole, and that the total strength of the "five 'fifths'", expressed here, as in other parts of Berber Morocco, in segmentary terms, is a great source of tribal pride; and, (3) ideally, fines (*r-haqq*) levied by the *imgharen* (sing. *amghar*), or council-members, of the *aitharba'in* at their weekly meeting (*agraw,* pl. *igrawn*) in the market, from a murderer (only if he should commit his murder on market day and either in the market itself or on any path leading to or from it) are equally distributed five ways, among the *imgharen* of each "fifth." Lines of fine-collection and distribution, then, ideally follow those of segmentation; and market-day

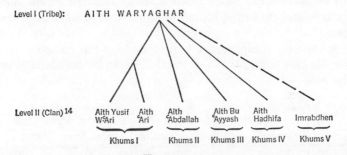

FIGURE 1-1

14 One extremely reliable informant, an old *qaid* who died in 1955, told me that in fact Level II really consists of only two rather than of five subdivisions: *Aith Khattab,* containing (on Level III) the two "fifths" of Aith Yusif w-'Ari/aith 'Ari and Aith 'Abdallah, and *Aith Bu 'Ayyash,* containing (on Level III) those of Aith Bu 'Ayyash Proper and Aith Hadhifa. The "holy" "fifth" of Imrabdhen is intrusive, as indicated by the dotted line in the diagram. This creates an intermediate segmentary level between tribe and "fifth" and gives a certain primacy to one or two vague and probably apocryphal origin traditions (such as the claim, supported especially by 'Abd al-Krim himself, that the Aith Khattab are descended from no less a personage than 'Umar ibn al-Khattab, the second of the "rightly guided" caliphs of Islam), but for present purposes it can be disregarded as having no real structural or functional significance.

was the one day of peace during the normal week of violence, murder, and feud. We shall return to this theme further on; but its keynotes of unity through fighting and dividedness through homicide have, I hope, now been established.

3. *". . . présente une structure sociale assez compliquée . . ."*
". . . presents quite a complicated social structure . . ."

Two of these structural complications are already apparent from Fig. 1-1. The first is that, as I have already said, a correspondence exists in the Aith Waryaghar between *khums*, "fifth," and *ar-rba*[c], "clan," but that this correspondence need not necessarily be complete and that two clans may be joined for political or other purposes to form a single "fifth." The case in point here is that *khums I* is formed by the clan of Aith Yusif w-'Ari *and* its brother clan of Aith 'Ari.[15] A further point in this connection is that under the total *liff* alliance system Aith Yusif w-'Ari and Aith 'Ari were also deadly enemies, indicating that the *liff*-structure on the overall levels tends to cross out that of the *khums* structure and the latter, rather, to follow that of the clan segmentation.

The second complication is provided by the presence of the intrusive clan—and "fifth"—of Imrabdhen, to be discussed in point 6 below.

4. *". . . qui résulte à la fois de l'état de guerre permanent dans lequel vivaient d'habitude les familles"* [read here lineages] *"et de l'infertilité du sol qui disperse les habitants." ". . . resulting both from the permanent state of war in which its [constituent] 'families' [read lineages] usually lived and from the infertility of the soil which brought about the dispersion of its inhabitants."*

At this point, I have no further comment other than that one could distinguish in fact *two* types of *liff* alliances in Aith Waryaghar and elsewhere in the Rif: (1) the "permanent" type, so to

---

[15] Tradition holds that Yusif w-'Ari and 'Ari w-'Ari were brothers, though no member of either clan could at the time of my fieldwork trace his descent back to his respective clan ancestor, or, indeed, anywhere near it, which proves the correctness of Coon's assertion to the effect that a "fifth" is bigger than a "fourth" (which is what *ar-rba*', of course, literally means).

speak, which split the whole tribe into two hostile factions, and
(2) the "temporary" type, operative *within* a clan, a subclan, a
local community, or even within a lineage itself, which mirrored
the overall tribal *liff* structure on a smaller scale. Ideally, at those
times when the permanent, upper-level type division was not
invoked, the temporary, lower-level one was in operation, and
vice versa. Informants all unanimously say that house-to-house
fighting was quite literally the rule (and often they have individual recriminations over this), and given the highly dispersed
character of dwellings and of the local communities to which
they belong, it is not difficult to see why. Feuds generally begin
over women on the one hand or over land and water rights on
the other. The endless sequence of "breach-counteraction-
breach-counteraction-breach-*ad infinitum*," as Paul Bohannan[16]
puts it, may be seen as the result of a number of factors, including pride, poverty, and population pressure. In the highly egalitarian social structure of the Aith Waryaghar, self-help is a first
principle.

5. "*. . . Chaque 'khoms' possède un territoire principal en
montagne et des enclaves en plaine ou inversement." ". . . Each*
khums *possesses its main territory in the mountains and enclaves
in the plain, or vice versa."*

We have now arrived at Step II (and Level III) in the
segmentary system of the Aith Waryaghar, which illustrates two
other cardinal and complementary principles: those of *territorial
discontinuity* and *territorial reduplication* on clan and subclan
levels. A perusal of the tribal map will show how this works when
the segmentary system (which exists, of course, in temporal
rather than spatial terms) is spread out on the ground to become
the territorial one; and Fig. 1-2 shows the relationships of the
clans and subclans concerned.

Explanations are nonetheless in order. In the clan of Aith Yusif
w-'Ari, the subclans Aith Ughir Izan and Isrihan are considered
closer kin to each other than either is to Aith Turirth; and hence
the dotted line leading to the latter in Fig. 1-2, a diagram based

16 Paul Bohannan, *Social Anthropology*, New York: Holt, Rinehart and
Winston, 1963, p. 290.

on the temporal principle of descent. Spread out on the ground of Waryagharland, however, Aith Yusif w-'Ari clan has no less than five separate and discontinuous blocs of territory: (A) a northern one, in which the local communities of Ajdir, Azghar and Izifzafen belong to Aith Ughir Izan, but in which Aith Mhand u-Yihya of the Plain (the flat-lying reduplication of Aith Mhand u-Yihya of the Mountain) is (though it is actually a stranger lineage) associated with Isrihan, (B) a smaller one to the southwest, Buhám, affiliated with Aith Ughir Izan, but which also contains a lineage called Isrihan n-Buhám, (C) Lower Thamasind, just north of the center of the tribal territory, affiliated with Aith Ughir Izan, (D) the Isrihan bloc on the north slope of the Jbil Hmam, comprising Isrihan Proper, Ikatshumen (or Ikultumen, which is also reduplicated in the Plain), and two stranger communities, the Mountain Aith Mhand u-Yihya and Aghridh, all affiliated with Isrihan, while 'Arnuq is affiliated with Aith Ughir Izan, and (E) *Aith Turirth* in the southeast, in the Jbil Hmam Proper, which consitutes a single and more or less homogeneous entity, even though some of its lineages, one of them a leading one (Imjjat, in l-'Ass, who came from across the tribal border in Igzinnayen), are "foreign."

In the clan of Aith 'Ari, (Fig. 1-2, Khums I) the story is the same, the development is parallel, and there are even more stranger lineages, most of which have come, according to tradition, from other neighboring or nearby Rifian tribes. Its subclans of Tigarth (largely composed of "foreigners"), Imhawren, and Aith r-'Abbas consider themselves closer kin to each other than any of them does to Timarzga; and hence, once again, a dotted line leading to the latter in Fig. 1-2. Once again, also, there are five discrete blocs of territory: (A) a northern one, facing the northern Aith Yusif w-'Ari, in which Tigarth "Proper" is of course affiliated with the subclan of the same name, in which Tafrasth and Imjjudhen (like Imjjat in the preceding paragraph, from Igzinnayen) are affiliated with Imhawren, and Aith Musa w-'Amar (again; mostly "strangers", as this word is locally conceived) with Aith r-'Abbas; (B) Bu Minqad (again, "foreigners"), just north of center with their main local community, though they are in fact reduplicated in not only one but two other spots in the tribal territory, and affiliated with Aith

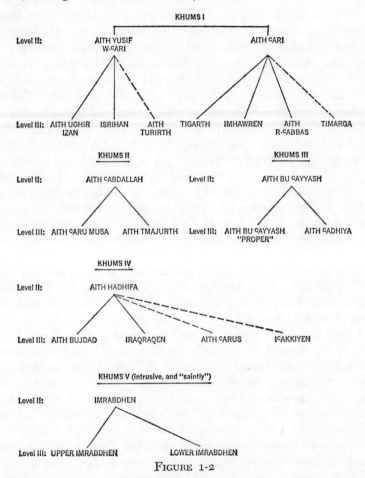

FIGURE 1-2

r-'Abbas; (C) Upper Thamasind, in the virtual center of the
tribal territory, and affiliated with Tigarth; (D) Iswiqen (once
again, "strangers"), on the northern slope of the Jbil Hmam (but
reduplicated in Aith Musa w-'Amar of the plain), and affiliated
with Aith r-'Abbas; and (E) Timarzga, forming a solid homogeneous bloc of—for once—entirely local Waryaghar origin, and
dispersed around the crest of the Jbil Hmam. And one lineage
group, Aith Dawud, though affiliated with or descended from
Tigarth, now resides in the clan territory of Aith 'Abdallah.

The clans of Aith Yusif w-'Ari and Aith 'Ari exhibit these features of dispersion and recombination in an extreme form, to be surpassed only by clan Imrabdhen. In the clan (and "fifth") of Aith 'Abdallah (Fig. 1-2, Khums II), the situation is considerably more homogeneous. Most of the western *communities* of this clan, such as Thariwin ("wells"), Aith Zkri (again, "strangers" from Igzinnayen, where they are reduplicated in Thariwin and Izikrithen), Aith Sa'id (from the eastern Rifian tribe of that name), Iqanniyen ("rabbits"), Uqrishen, Imarnison (locals, and not from the Jbalan tribe of Marnisa), and Ikiddaben ("liars"), are affiliated with its subclan of Aith 'Aru Musa; while most of its eastern *communities*, closer to the Jbil Hmam, such as Aith Ziyan, Ibunaharen, Tizi 'Ayyash, Tazaghindi ad-Dahar n-Zimmurth, Aith Dris, Bu Sarah, Bu Zdur, Ihwahwahiyen, Thimkiliwin, Thirkuzin and Marrui (though most of the two last-mentioned communities are again "strangers" from the neighboring tribe of Aith 'Ammarth), are affiliated with its subclan Aith Tmajurth. There is only one small enclave of this clan, I'ayyaden, outside of the main group, and here the affiliation is with the subclan of Aith 'Aru Musa.

The clan (and "fifth") of Aith Bu 'Ayyash (Fig. 1-2, Khums III), the biggest in the tribe (and indeed bigger than many whole tribes elsewhere in the Rif), indicates the same territorial homogeneity as Aith 'Abdallah, but as a "fifth," it shares an important characteristic in common with Aith Yusif w-'Ari. Aith 'Ari (whose alignments in the overall dual faction system were also reflected in the opposition between Aith Turirth and Timarzga): its two subclans of Aith Bu 'Ayyash "Proper" and Aith 'Adhiya were implacably hostile to each other. The dividing line between them on the map is therefore heavy, and intended to show this. Of local communities of this clan, Izakiren (all "foreigners"), Iryanen (partially "foreign"), Aith Tfarwin (entirely local), Isufiyen (entirely "foreign"), Aith Ta'a (entirely local) and Aith Bu Khrif (partially "foreign"), are affiliated with Aith Bu 'Ayyash "Proper": while Ighmiren (largely "foreign," with discontinuous segments in the mountain and in the plain), Igar w-Anu (largely local), Ajdir Bu Qiyadhen and ar-Rabdha (entirely local), Imnudh, and Aith 'Aisa and Aith Ruqmān of Tuzurakhth (all again largely "foreign") are affiliated with sub-

clan Aith 'Adhiya. Two other local communities which form part
of this subclan, Mountain Ighmiren and Igar w-Anu, are separated from its main body, while one lineage, Aith Bū Stta, has
even "infiltrated," as it were, into the territory of subclan Aith
Bu 'Ayyash "Proper," into Aith Bu Khrif community. As in Lower
Ighmiren and in Ikatshumen of Aith Yusif w-'Ari, this lineage
and other lineages in the latter communities claim descent from
the Merinids.

The clan (and "fifth")[17] of Aith Hadhifa (Fig. 1-2, Khuṁs IV)
is interesting in that it shows both homogeneity and dispersion.
The two subclans of Aith Bū Jdāt and Iraqraqen ("frogs") constitute Aith Hadhifa "Proper"; to the first belong the local com-
munities of Bū Jdāt "Proper," Mishkur, Ihadduthen, Bihban and
Aghzar 'Aisa; and to the second, Iharunen (reduplicated in Aith
'Arus), Thisimmurin, Bashkra, Yinn 'Amar u-Sa'id, and those
lineages in Zawith n-Sidi 'Abd l-Qadir which are not Imrabdhen
lineages. All are entirely local in origin. But now, once again,
Aith 'Arus and I'akkiyen occupy the same position vis-à-vis Aith
Hadhifa "Proper" as do Aith Turirth and Timarzga vis-à-vis Aith
Yusif w-'Ari and Aith 'Ari respectively (see Fig. 1-2), with one
difference: they were all in the same overall *liff* or faction. I'akkiyen (a community largely made up of tailors and butchers who
nonetheless fought hard amongst themselves), who "came from"
Aith 'Arus, are even territorially more discontinuous from the
latter than the latter in turn are from the mountain Aith Hadhifa,
whence they themselves "came." But there are, in Aith 'Arus,
only one or two "stranger" lineages; the rest, as perhaps befitting
the fact that it is in their territory that the original Waryaghar
Mountain is located, are locals. So are most of both Aith Turirth
and Timarzga; and it is perhaps in these three mountain subclans
which occupy the core of the Jbil Hmam that Waryaghar social
structure is most clearly displayed. I have even heard mountaineers from these subclans assert that the "five 'fifths'" of Aith
Waryaghar are Aith Turirth, Timarzga, Aith 'Arus, Aith Yusif
w-'Ari and Aith 'Ari; when for example one recalls to them the
existence of Aith Bu 'Ayyash or Aith 'Abdallah or Aith Hadhifa,
they shrug their shoulders and say, "Oh, they are just other ones."

[17] An integral "fifth," and by no means a nominal one, as Coon suggests,
op. cit., 1931, p. 106. See Figures 1-1 and 1-2.

At this juncture it will be useful to make a point or two about the names of some of the Waryaghar segments, on various levels. The clan names are all (save Imrabdhen, which is ascriptive of status) names of supposed individual ancestors, to whom, of course, no ascent can in any single case be traced. The same holds true for many, though not all, of the subclan names (Level III); and on this level descriptive or ascriptive names (Aith Ughir Izan, Iraqraqen, Aith 'Arus—the last one, "people of the bridegroom," although Aith 'Arus themselves have no knowledge of why they have their name, nor any legends justifying it; the neighbors of Aith Turirth and Timarzga say they had a Christian ancestress, an allegation they themselves hotly deny—and Timarzga itself, a supposed compound of Arabic *tamar wa zakah,* "dates and alms," with, again, no reason given) and simple toponyms (Tigarth, Aith Tmajurth, Aith Turirth—the last from *dha'rurth,* "hill" in Rifian, hence "people of the hill") creep in. On the level of the local community, however, toponyms predominate over anthroponyms almost at the rate of two to one. As virtually every physical feature or chunk of terrain in Waryagharland has a name, clusters of lineages living in these places are almost automatically called *aith,* "people (of)," followed by the place-name in question. Below this level, when we reach that of the local lineage group, the *dharfiqth,* anthroponyms in which the name of a lineage ancestor who *is* genealogically traceable now start to prevail.

Finally, on the levels of the higher segments, clans and subclans, which we have already discussed, we may note a phenomenon which, borrowing two everyday terms from genetics, I call *dominance and recessiveness.* In this situation, subclan X, for instance, gives its own name to clan A on the next level up, so that the same exists on two levels at once, whereas the name of its brother subclan Y of the same clan A exists only on one level, the lower one. In such a case, subclan X is dominant and Y recessive; and in this way, for example, Aith Bu 'Ayyash "Proper" is dominant over Aith 'Adhiya; Aith Hadhifa "Proper" over Aith Turirth; and Aith 'Ari "Proper" over Timarzga. But it should be added that dominance and recessiveness in this sense are onomastic rather than political; they are by no means necessarily a reflection of the numerical superiority or superiority in force of arms of the "dominant" clan or subclan concerned. Even so, such is the highly egalitarian and extremely competitive "dog-eat-dog" character of Waryaghar society that the "recessive" subclans have tried in fact to dominate the "dominant" ones, and (of course) the other way around, a fact which is well reflected in the *liff*-system.

All evidence now indicates that Aith Waryaghar originated in the Jbil Hmam and gradually pushed toward the Mediterranean; and the really startling reduplication of local communities from south to north strongly favors this argument. Clans Aith Yusif w-'Ari and Aith 'Ari, both existing in territorial chunks from the southern mountain border to the northern sea border, parallel each other all the way through the tribal area in their territorial organization; clans Aith 'Abdallah and Aith Bu 'Ayyash on the median west and median east, respectively, again show parallels; and in the southwest, clan Aith Hadhifa and their "brothers" of subclan Aith 'Arus in the central Jbil Hmam fill in yet other chinks. It is something of a patchwork quilt, *but not without its own internal order and logic.*

It now remains to fit the Imrabdhen (see Fig. 1-2, Khums), a whole intrusive "fifth," into a picture in which I estimate that some 44 percent of the existing lineage groups are already considered "foreigners," despite generations of local residence and despite the fact that most of them are from tribes neighboring Aith Waryaghar or from other parts of the Rif. In this sense, Aith Waryaghar is almost as purely "Waryaghar" in its present composition as America is Anglo-Saxon! Clans are thoroughly heterogeneous in their total make-up, infiltrated as they are by stranger accretions (a problem to be discussed later, at the level of the local community), and descent from common ancestors must be considered as largely fictive. The anthroponyms of clans and subclans is thus, in the Waryaghar case, primarily a kind of convenience for classificatory purposes; for the heterogeneity of these groupings is undeniable. Rifians like to tag labels onto people and things as much as we do, or more (and preferably derogatory ones); and as the Jbil Hmam *massif* dominates the tribal area physically, so it does also in contemporary and collective tribal recollections of their ultimate origins.[18]

6. "... *En outre, les marabouts forment un 'khoms' supplémentaire dispersé dans tout le pays.*" "... *In addition, the Imrabdhen form a supplementary* khums *dispersed over all the tribal territory.*"

Those whom Montagne labels "marabouts" form, of course, the fifth and final "fifth" of Imrabdhen. As I noted above, this name is one of status-ascription; it is the Rifian form of Arabic *mrábtin,* sing. *mrabit*—but the difference is that in Rifian, *imrabdhen* refers both to *Shurfa* proper and to *mrabtin* indiscriminately, even though Rifians themselves are well aware of the distinction.[19] The "fifth" (and clan) of Imrabdhen is sub-segmented into two territorially (but not genealogically) based subclans, and with the usual territorial discontinuity between them which we may now regard as the Waryaghar norm, Upper Imrabdhen and Lower Imrabdhen (*Imrabdhen n-Dara* and *Imrabdhen n-Waddai*). This territorial, as opposed to genealogical, factor is of course implicit in their names. With Upper Imrabdhen are affiliated the local communities of Aith 'Aziz, Aith r-Qadi, Aith z-Zawith n-Sidi 'Aisa and, discontinuous from the bulk of this group, Aith Kammun (located between Aith 'Abdallah and Aith

---

[18] This is quite apart from the traditions about Early Islamic caliphs and companions of the Prophet in Arabia, which provide locally convenient if somewhat implausible attempts at smokescreens. Apart from 'Umar ibn al-Khattab, mentioned in note 14, the same informant suggested Sidi Hudhaifa al-Yamani as ancestor of Aith Hadhifa, Sidi 'Abdallah ibn Ja'far for Aith 'Abdallah (both of whom actually lived, but were persons who, as Professor Philip Hitti once told me, had no connections with North Africa), and Sidi Ku'aish (probably mythical or nonexistent; no record could be found of him) for Aith Bu 'Ayyash. The Umayyad caliphs Mu'awiya and his son al-Yazid were also suggested by other informants in the Jbil Hmam as the ancestors of Aith Turirth and Timarzga, though perhaps the more local Amrabit Bu M'awiya, buried in the Eastern Rif (Mtalsa) was actually meant. My informants were not entirely sure.

[19] The major difference between these two categories of saintly personages is one of descent. *Shurfa* (sing. *sharif*) are descendants of the Prophet or are at least locally held to be so, whereas *mrabtin* acquire saintliness through the performance of miracles or even merely good works (although of course *shurfa* "proper" can and indeed do increase their local reputations by doing the same).

Hadhifa), Izarruqen and Bu Ghardain ("the possessor of rats"—the latter is within Aith 'Abdallah and the former on its northern border), and the Imrabdhen lineages of Aith z-Zawith n-Sidi 'Abd l-Qadar (between Aith Hadhifa and Timarzga, in the southwestern Jbil Hmam). Affiliated with Lower Imrabdhen, those communities of Aith Brahim, Igarrudhen, Aith z-Zawith n-Sidi Yusif (called the "lower *zawiya*" as opposed to Zawith n-Sidi 'Aisa, the "upper *zawiya*," even though Waryagharland contains no real *zawiyas* which function as such, in the true sense of the word, as a lodge of a religious brotherhood), Aith Misa'ud, Aith 'Amar u-Sha'ib, Ifasiyen ("those of Fez"), Idardushen, Aith 'Amar u-Bukar, and the Imrabdhen of Aith Hishim (of which the Iziqqiwen, descended from Sidi Mhand u-Musa who is buried there, and containing branches at Swani, on the Mediterranean beach, and at Tashtiwin of Aith 'Abdallah, are the most important), and of Aith Qamra.

But above and beyond these two subclans, there are little pockets of Imrabdhen, some affiliated with the one subclan and some with the other, scattered over the length and breadth of Waryagharland and even beyond (Aith 'Aziz, for example, have a branch in Tamjund of the Asht 'Asim clan of Igzinnayen, and Ifasiyen have one in Ighshamen of the Truguth clan in Thimsaman). The most important of these little pockets are the Dharwa n-Sidi r-Hajj Misa'ud, descended from Aith Kammun, found in community Aith 'Aru Musa of subclan Aith Turirth, the Imrabdhen of Marrui in Aith 'Abdallah (affiliated with Zawith n-Sidi 'Aisa), those of Iqanniyen in the same clan (affiliated with Aith 'Amar u-Bukar), those of Zawith n-Sidi 'Abd l-Qadar, and the Izziqiwen n-Sidi Mhand u-Musa, mentioned above.

Genealogically, these Imrabdhen claim to be Idrisid *shurfa*, and trace their descent back to the Prophet's daughter Fatima through Mulay 'Abd as-Slam bin Mshish (d. 1227–28, and buried in Bni 'Arus in the Jbala) and through Sultans Mulay Idris I and II. Their point of definition (as opposed to their actual point of fission) in the overall genealogy of *shurfa* in general[20] occurs at a point 27 generations down from the Prophet with a certain Sidi

[20] Cf. Georges Drague, *Esquisse d'Histoire Religieuse du Maroc*, Cahiers de l'Afrique et l'Asie, II, Paris: Peyronnet, 1951, genealogical charts, nos. 1 and 2.

Ibrahim al-A'raj, "the Lame," who, according to the *Maqsad* of 'Abd al-Haqq al-Badisi[21] came from the clan of "Banu Yammalak" (now nonexistent) "in the tribe of Banu Waryaghal," who died in Fez in 1284–85, and was buried there beside the Bab l-Gisa[22] and whom tradition indicates as being the first of the Waryaghar Imrabdhen. The point of fission of the Imrabdhen, however, only came eight generations later (and 35 generations from the Prophet) with Sidi 'Abd al-Krim ibn Aidi 'Abd al-Aziz, from whose two sons Sidi Ya'qub and Sidi 'Aisa all present-day Imrabdhen are descended. Only those at Zawith n-Sidi 'Aisa and the descendants of Sidi Hmid Marrui (in Aith 'Abdallah) are descended from Sidi Ya'qub; all the rest are descended from Sidi 'Aisa, who is buried in the *zawiya* which bears his name. And thus the genealogical record completely cross-cuts the territorial distribution.

This genealogical record, as I pieced it together, is remarkably good and remarkably consistent; but genealogy is not history, and a genealogical charter is not a historical document. Genealogies can only be employed in the reconstruction of historical time-spans if there is corroborative evidence from other fields. And as to Moroccan "saintly" or "holy" genealogies in particular, they are really rather the validation of the saintly status of a given "holy" clan or "holy" lineage existing at present, through genealogical linkage with the Moroccan and even generalized Islamic cultural past (to use Peters' term).[23] In the process of essentially oral transmission of events of "who begat whom," any given event, if agreed upon (informally) as important by those concerned, will be remembered, while others will be forgotten. The result is that, in just the same way that "history," in this

[21] *Al-Maqsad ash-Sharif, wa l-Manza' l-Latif, fi dhikr sulaha r-Rif* (Vie des Saints du Rif), trans. by G. S. Colin, *Archives Marocaines,* vol. XXVI, Paris: Honoré Champion, 1926.

[22] My own records, however, despite these dates, show a difference of eight generations between Mulay 'Abd s-Slam b. Mashish and Sidi Ibrahim al-A'raj.

[23] Emrys L. Peters, "Aspects of Rank and Status among Muslims in a Lebanese Village," in Julian Pitt-Rivers, ed., *Mediterranean Countrymen,* The Hague: Mouton, 1963, pp. 159–200. [Reprinted as Chapter 2 following.] The Waryaghar Imrabdhen—or at least a small but very significant percentage of them—are quite similar to Peters' "Keepers of the Culture" in Shi'a villages in Lebanon.

sense, becomes "telescoped,"[24] as it were, genealogies are equally liable to undergo the same foreshortening through time, a foreshortening which also tends to occur at precisely those points in the genealogy which have the least structural relevance.

I do not argue for the consistency here of the Imrabdhen genealogy, as there is not the space to do so; I simply state it as a fact. Even so, in terms of calculation of elapsed generations, from the Prophet to the present day, it appears a good two centuries too shallow; but for anyone to surmise on such ground that it is false is for him to misunderstand completely the nature of the problem. This resides in the manifest or latent acceptance of *imrabdhen,* of holy men, *as* such, *by* the *lay* (tribal) populations which surround them. As Gellner[25] has suggested, *Vox Dei* is in reality *Vox Populi;* and the bulk of the other four "fifths" of Aith Waryaghar do indeed, in one way or another, consider the Imrabdhen as somewhat apart from themselves.

There are, however, certain objections to the claim of the Imrabdhen to a holy genealogy, and these are particularly interesting in that they are all *extra*-genealogical (for the claim of the Imrabdhen *to* a "holy" genealogy is in fact integrally supported *by* that genealogy). These objections are six in number. (1) One is that it is in the *Maqsad* (see footnote 21) that only one of the Rifian saints mentioned in the work—and *not* Sidi Ibrahim al-A'raj—was a real and proper *sharif*. (2) There is the question of separating the sheep from the goats and the undeniable fact that some (a small percentage) of the Imrabdhen are certainly "holier" than the rest. (3) Although the Aith Waryaghar Imrabdhen *say* that they have a right to their share of the proceeds from the *sunduq* or box of Mulay Idris in Fez every year, they in fact never—and unlike "true" *shurfa* (such as the Shurfa n-Sidi Hand u-Musa of the Asht 'Aru 'Aisa, the neighbor tribe in Igzinnayen)—exercise this right; in the light of this their excuse that "Fez is too far away" appears somewhat lame! (4) There is

24 E. E. Evans-Pritchard, *The Nuer,* pp. 199–200. The Clarendon Press: Oxford, 1940.

25 Ernest Gellner, "Concepts and Society," *Transactions of the Fifth World Congress of Sociology,* Washington, D.C., vol. I, 1962, pp. 153–83. Gellner's data are derived from the Ihansalen of the Central High Atlas, but the concept behind them is valid for our Imrabdhen as well.

a very interesting sultan's *dahir,* cited by Maldonado[26] and dated
1771–72, which exempts them (and the rest of Aith Waryaghar)
from payment of taxes to the central government, which legiti-
mizes their descent, as it were, by sign and seal, from Sidi Ibrahim al-A'raj, and which implicitly urges the surrounding
populations to treat them as *shurfa* (an implication, if one reads
between the lines, that possibly some of them are only *mrabtin*
and that possibly parts of the genealogy have been cleverly faked
—though I doubt this). (5) With a few exceptions,[27] there is a
very marked lack of mythology about individual saints among
the Waryaghar Imrabdhen, and there is only a very generalized
collective group tradition concerning Sidi Ibrahim al-A'raj, Sidi
'Abd al-Krim and the group's installation in Waryagharland.
Most genuine *shurfa* are surrounded with a welter of traditions
regarding their abilities at curing, miracle-working and the like.
(6) Finally there is the fact that the most important saint of the
tribe, Side Bu Khiyar, is not one of the Waryaghar Imrabdhen

[26] Eduardo Maldonado (pseud. Et-Tabyi), "Los de Imerabten," in his
Retazos de Historia Marroqui, Tetuan: Instituto General Franco, 1955,
pp. 65–70.

[27] One of these is Sidi Mhand u-Musa, who died in 1838–39 in Aith Hishim
where he is buried in the so-called "Hillock of the Saints" (according to information I received from a *fqih* of his lineage). He is credited with (a) having mounted the Waryaghar guard on the mainland against the Spaniards
who since 1673 had occupied the Island of al-Husaima in the bay of the
same name (though Sánchez Pérez, *op. cit.,* 1952, says rather that the guard
was mounted from the time of Spanish arrival and persisted until the surrender of 'Abd al-Krim!), (b) with the ability of being in two places at the
same time, and (c) with having miraculously caused a heavy rain to re-
route the course of the Nkur River in Waryaghar favor at the expense of Axt
Tuzin, after a boundary dispute between the two tribes (the river then as
now having formed the boundary), and to have bested the Axt Tuzin saint
Sidi Bu Jiddain in this dispute. This last is a beautiful example of an "effective" saint's dual role as adjudicator and miracle-worker! (cf. an unsigned
Spanish administrative report, 1944).

Another such saint was Sidi 'Abd r-Qadar Agnaw, the ancestor of the
lineages of Zawith n-Sidi 'Abd r-Qadar, who was, as indicated by his name,
deaf-and-dumb, and who through leading an exemplary life was given the
gift of speech by God a year before his death (cf. Isaías Rodríguez Padilla,
Cofradías Religiosas en el Rif, Ceuta, 1930, p. 35). And Sidi Hmid Marrui
could walk on water. And Sidi Muhand n-Sidi r-Hajj Misa'ud, in Aith
Turirth, once flew to Mecca at the time of the pilgrimage and returned home
in the same day, accompanied by Sidi Bu Khiyar and the Igzinnayer saint
Sidi Hand u-Musa; they were seen performing their sacrifices at 'Arafat, but
nobody saw them in flight!

at all, but came, it is said, from Tlemcen in Algeria (where, Rifians say, the real *awliya* or miracle-working saints all came from).

There is not the space here to consider all these arguments in detail, but some of them can be briefly touched upon. The first objection with regard to the *Maqsad* is not relevant for present purposes, but the second one is. One criterion for approaching the "sheep-goat" distinction is to discover which Imrabdhen, out of all of them, are addressed as *Sidi* ("My Lord," or perhaps, "Sir"), which as *Si* ("Mr.," and generally a title accorded a *fqih* or anyone who is literate in Arabic), or merely by their names, without any title. These last, the rank and file of Imrabdhen (what Gellner[28] has termed "latent" as opposed to "effective" saints), form the great majority of Imrabdhen clansmen, probably over ninety percent. They dress, look, and act like any other Waryaghar; and they fought like them as well, and savagely, though generally among themselves rather than with the other clans or "fifths." In the overall *liff*-system, however, Imrabdhen was allied to Aith Yusif w-'Ari, for Sidi Mhand u-Musa had married a daughter of one of the major *imgharen* (councillors) of the latter clan, or so legend has it. The *Si*-group are the intermediates, and the *Sidi*-group contains the "effective" core (which is still a small portion of *them!*): those who possess *r-baraka,* the God-given power to work miracles for the benefit of their fellow men, and the charisma which derives therefrom.[29] Today there is perhaps only one man left who is considered to possess these traits, of the lineage of Dharwa n-Sidi r-Hajj Misa'ud resident in Aith Turirth; the Sidi-group also adjudicate interclan or interlineage disputes; they are exemplary in their observance of religious ritual; they are almost invariably endogamous in their marriage patterns; and they invariably wear white robes and turbans. Not only this; the pattern (at least among the Dharwa n-Sidi r-Hajj

[28] E. Gellner, "Saints of the Atlas," in Pitt-Rivers, *op. cit.,* pp. 145–57. [Reprinted at Chapter II, Vol. I, *Peoples and Cultures of the Middle East.*]

[29] I employ the Rifian version of the Arabic definite article here, for to say simply *baraka* would only imply the Moroccan Arabic (and Berber) word for "enough!" Gellner discusses the subject briefly but well in his 1962 paper, *op. cit.,* pp. 180–81; but the classic discussion remains that of Edward Westermarck, *Ritual and Belief in Morocco,* 2 vols., London: Macmillan, 1926, vol. I, pp. 235–61, on which nobody has yet improved.

Misa'ud, and in other "core" lineages as well) shows a distinctive division of labor and of power. No two such saints living at the same time possess *r-baraka;* in the same lineage, only one has it at a time; if one saint has *r-baraka,* another, generally lesser one (often his brother) acts as adjudicator in disputes. Ideally, the true *r-baraka*-possessor is freed from all worldly considerations; he stays at home, prays, fasts over and above Ramadan if necessary, performs his miraculous deeds and is in fact rarely seen by the rank and file, while his adjudicator brother settles disputes, always feeds and gives tea to those who come to see him, and acts as mediator between the lay public and his holier brother. (Of the two principal sons of Sidi r-Hajj Misa'ud, for instance, Sidi Muhand was the *r-baraka*-holder, while his brother Sidi Hmid acted as the top *amghar* of all Aith Turirth, and received one-fifth of the market fine in a murder case, all for himself. In other markets, too, it was usual to so compensate the core group of Imrabdhen in such a case.)

If, however, *r-baraka* is only held by one member of a holy lineage at a time, while his brother or agnate (in true Islamic fashion of non-dissolution of state and church) arranges disputes, treats for peace after intra-tribal feuds, and is in effect remunerated for these services, how does the selection of individuals who possess *r-baraka* occur, and how is *r-baraka* transmitted? Waryaghar, of course, say that only God knows on whom He will confer *r-baraka;* but the fact of the matter is that the neighboring lay tribesmen are very influential in the question of *r-baraka* attribution. It is really *they* who say just which saint has it and which one has not. Not only this, but among the Dharwa n-Sidi r-Hajj Misa'ud mentioned above, the same laymen unfailingly—and possibly without their own conscious knowledge—plotted a course of primogeniture in the inheritance of *r-baraka* in this particular lineage. In other lineages (Iziqqiwen, the descendants of Sidi Mhand u-Musa, for example) the transmission of *r-baraka* may skip around, from one saint to his brother, perhaps, and then to one of the latter's sons. Michaux-Bellaire has documented the same phenomenon for the Shurfa of Wazzan.[30]

[30] E. Michaux-Bellaire, *Villes et Tribus du Maroc,* tome IV: *Rabat et sa Région: Le Gharb (les Djebala),* Paris: Ernest Leroux, 1918, pp. 236–54, plus accompanying genealogies facing p. 254 and showing accompanying

When, in earlier contexts, I have spoken of "important" lineages of Imrabdhen, I have meant of course precisely these core lineages of the *Sidi*-category. I wish at this point only to introduce one further concept: that of *awliya* (sing. *wali*). These are a special category of saints, whether recruited from the ranks of *shurfa* or *mrabtin*, who possess *r-baraka* in abundance; they are, or were (for unlike the other kinds of saints, there are no living ones), all *ipso facto* miracle-workers and totally un-political and they represent the apex of Rifian hagiolatry. I mention them because of the Waryaghar Imrabdhen, perhaps only Sidi r-Hajj Misa'ud and his son Sidi Muhand (and *not* the adjudicating son Sidi Hmid) fall into this category, as do the stranger Sidi Bu Khiyar and the neighboring *wali* in Igzinnayen, Sidi Hand u-Musa.

To conclude this section: Sidi Bu Khiyar, the stranger but yet the most important saint in the tribal territory (to whose tomb an annual *'amara* is made on the day before the 'Aid l-Kbir, as I have said) is recognized as a real *sharif* and a real *wali*, as is Sidi Hand u-Musa in Igzinnayen (as differentiated from Sidi Mhand u-Musa in Aith Hishim). Sidi Bu Khiyar died without issue; but the descendants of Sidi Hand u-Musa, the Asht 'Aru 'Aisa (from whom 'Abd al-Krim may himself have been descended, though he is everywhere recognized as a fighter rather than as a holy man), automatically receive their share, annually, of the proceeds of Mulay Idris' "box" in Fez. The Imrabdhen of Aith Waryaghar, however, despite their impeccable genealogy, do not; rather, they collect annual *ziyara* or offerings from the surrounding lay "fifths" (and in Rifian opinion, only *imrabdhen* ask for *ziyara*, while true *shurfa* do not). Furthermore, despite the impeccability of their genealogy, they needed a sultan's *dahir*

---

passage of *r-baraka*. In the case of the Iziqqiwen of Aith Hishim, the descendants of Sidi Mhand u-Musa, according to my notes, *r-baraka* passed from Sidi Mhand himself to his grandson Sidi Misa'ud n-Siddiq, and then to the latter's son Sidi Hmid Bu Rjila. From this point, according to my informant, it reverted back to Sidi Hmid Bu Rjila's paternal uncle Sidi 'Abdssram, and from him down to his own son Sidi Muhand, to the latter's eldest son Sidi r-Hajj 'Amar (a qaid of Imrabdhen under Sultan Mulay 'Abd al-'Aziz), and then to *his* eldest son Sidi Muhand. As the last-mentioned Sidi Muhand was the elder brother of my informant himself, there may well have been a certain degree of self-interest here in arrogation of claims to "holiness"—but the Wazzan data show an equal degree of "leap-frogging."

to secure them in their position and to legitimize it. Why was this the case? Because, in the last analysis, the selection and election of saints depends upon the laymen who surround them; and in this case, the lay Waryaghar rationalized the situation to the point that the bulk of the Imrabdhen in their midst came to be regarded as collateral Idrisid nobodies. The fact, too, that they were homegrown further depreciated their value. They had a genealogy, but they lacked supporting traditions; and with only a certain very few exceptions (all, of course, supported by lay public opinion), they did not "make the grade."

7. *"Malgré cette confusion et en dépit de l'hostilité habituelle des groupes familiaux* [read lineages or lineage-groups] *à l'interieur du 'khoms' . . . , les limites de chaque fraction* [read clan or subclan] *restent parfaitement connues . . ."* Author's translation: *"Despite this confusion and despite the habitual hostility of the 'family groups'* [read lineages or lineage-groups] *within the* khums *. . . , the boundaries of each 'fraction'* [read clan or subclan] *are perfectly well known . . ."*

To illustrate this point, we may return to a theme briefly discussed earlier, in Point 2: *the division of tribal fines (r-haqq).* Prior to the Spanish occupation, Aith Waryaghar had what may be considered a central market, held on Sundays at Thisar (since then it has changed to Sundays at Thamasind, and has greatly dwindled in size and importance) in the exact center of the tribal territory. This market may not necessarily have been larger than some of the other major clan-level markets (such as Mondays at Aith Bu 'Ayyash and Aith Hadhifa, Wednesdays at Aith Turirth, and Saturdays at Imzuren), but it purported, at least, and given its size and central location, to serve the whole tribe. Council-members from every "fifth," clan and subclan generally attended the large weekly meeting, the *agraw*, of the *aitharba'in*, ("representatives of the people," or council) which was held under a large tree just off the market precincts, with the councillors sitting in an inner circle, and the Waryaghar at large, the *jma'th*, the "people," in an outer circle surrounding them.

And so it was that if one man should kill another on a path leading to or from this market, on market day (and in some markets the taboo on murder extended to the day immediately preceding market day and to that immediately following it), he had to pay, in money and/or in kind, the sum, crushingly prohibitive at the time, of 1000 duros hasani[31] to the assembled *imgharen.* Not only this, but the fine was doubled to 2000 duros hasani should the homicide be committed in the market itself, a fact which inevitably "broke" the market for that day. If the murderer could not pay this fine, the *imgharen* would exact it by descending on his house in a body, by burning it and his fruit trees down to the ground, and by making off with his livestock.

The murderer would of course almost never be present to witness this, for the council-members would in fact and in such a manner exact the fine from his agnates. If A had killed B, he had to flee immediately afterward as *adhrib* (from Ar. *tlib*, "enemy") to the territory of another clan, or preferably, that of another tribe entirely (a Waryaghar murderer might thus flee to Aith 'Ammarth or Igzinnayen, and vice versa), where he would be received at once upon his declaration of what he had done. The normal ritual was for an escaped murderer to go into a house in the new tribe, one where he was morally certain of being well-received, and to put his hand on the handmill. By so doing he ensured asylum for himself by putting himself under the protection of his host's wife, and by thus becoming *istihurm* ("seeker of refuge").

A murderer, however, had to flee alone, leaving his family and property behind; and both his victim's agnates and the council-members of Aith Waryaghar would naturally be gunning for him (the former, of course, more than the latter, unless one of the latter happened by chance to be a member of the former group). Thus it was up to the murderer's own agnates to make arrange-

[31] The problem of currency translation into modern terms here carries some pitfalls. A *duro* in Spanish is five pesetas, today, and implies a multiple of five, as does in fact the old Moroccan *duro hasani* and the present notion of *riyal;* but it goes further than this. The pre-protectorate duro hasani was in fact not five but fifty pesetas, as translated into the Spanish currency of the early and mid-1950's. Thus one thousand duros hasani was the equivalent of 50,000 Spanish pesetas (and 5000 Moroccan dirhams at the present time), and two thousand duros hasani, 100,000 Spanish pesetas (and 10,000 present-day Moroccan dirhams). The sum was one which, at the time, was effectively gauged to clean out the resources not only of one man but of all his lineage-mates as well.

ments for payment of *r-haqq* to the council-members, and for
payment of bloodwit (*d-diyith*, a variable sum ranging from 100
to 2000 or more duros hasani, in contrast to the *haqq*, which was
always fixed), to the agnates of the dead man, should, of course,
(and this was not often), the latter be inclined to accept it.

There was no fixed time that a murderer should stay away from
home, but it had to be a year, and generally two years, at the
very least, to allow for passion and rage to subside somewhat. If
the dead man's agnates became inclined to settle for bloodwit,
those of the murderer went to them, accompanied by an *amrabit*
(sing. of *imrabdhen*) or the *fqih* or schoolmaster of the local
mosque, and sacrificed a goat. After all present had partaken of
the sacrificial meal, the *amrabit* or *fqih* would open the peace
negotiations. And only after all the money had been paid, both
fines and bloodwit, to those parties reclaiming it, could a murderer return home. If not, he had to stay in exile for the rest of
his life, and in such a case he generally married or re-married
into the tribe in which he had sought refuge.

The reason for such a heavy fine was that market day was a
day of peace (*s-sulh*); and the interest of the fine itself lay not
only in that it acted as a deterrent to would-be murderers on
market day (although there was no question whatsoever of paying it on any other day of the week, when it was literally "open
season" for everybody on everybody else, and *la chasse a l'homme*
almost literally occurred as part of the daily routine—in several
corners of Waryagharland at once!), but in the fact that its division and redistribution followed and reinforced the segmentary
system. Although an occasion in which *all* the subclan and clan
councillors actually participated in *r-haqq*-collection and division
(and it is interesting to note that any clan whose councillors
failed to turn up or were late was automatically excluded from
participation) was probably quite rare, given the discontinuous
territorial system and the extent of the tribal area in general, the
overall distribution (perhaps a somewhat theoretical one) was as
follows:

The fine was divided into five equal parts, one for each "fifth"
of the tribe. After this initial division had been made, Aith Yusif
w-'Ari and Aith 'Ari (Fig. 1-2, Khums I) then split their joint
share of one-fifth of the total in half, with one-half for each of

them. Of the Aith Yusif w-'Ari share, one-fifth, in turn, taken off
the top, went to subclan Aith Turirth, and the remainder was
then split in half again for Aith Ughir Izan and Isrihan; and from
this point on down, each subclan divided its own share among its
own council-members in proportion to their own strength and to
that of the local communities which they represented. The same
was true for Aith 'Ari: one-fifth, first, for Timarzga, and then the
remainder into three equal parts for the three remaining subclans. Aith 'Abdallah split their share in half, for their two subclans, as did Aith Bu 'Ayyash and Imrabdhen for theirs, while
Aith Hadhifa gave one-third off the top to Aith 'Arus and I'akkiyen (of which two-thirds, in turn, for Aith 'Arus and one-third
for I'akkiyen), and then divided the rest in half between their
own two subclans proper.

The completely egalitarian aspects of this distribution of fines
are obvious, but, even so, it was quite normal for a given *amghar*
(sing. of *imgharen*) to try to claim more than his allotted share
at the expense of, say, those lower-rung council-members at the
level of the local community whose reputations for strength were
not sufficient to enable them to obtain a place in the *aitharba'in*
at clan level. Even so, by the time the fine had reached these
ultimate stages of distribution, the amount which each individual
councillor received was very little; and a notation (regarding
Aith 'Ari) which I have seen in an unsigned Spanish administrative report for 1928 to the effect that at the lowest levels, if
there was not enough money to go around evenly, matches were
bought, and the matches then were divided up, may be apocryphal—but it has a genuinely and authentically egalitarian ring.

Far more common, however, was for the division of fines to be
operative at the clan and subclan level, and the *r-haqq nj-suq*,
the market fine, at the Wednesday Market of Aith Turirth furnishes a typical example. It, too, was divided into five equal
parts, but their distribution was very different from that given
above. One-fifth, in its entirety, went to Sidi Hmud n-Sidi r-Hajj
Misa'ud, the adjudicating brother of the *r-baraka*-possessing Sidi
Muhand n-Sidi r-Hajj Misa'ud mentioned in Point 6; for Sidi
Hmid was the *amghar amqqran*, the top *amghar*, of the region.
(He used, I was told, to practice every summer, at harvest time,
what was known as *r-'aiwad nj-urbu'*, in which he travelled

around his constituent communities to put a ban on feuding, announced publicly by the market-crier on the following Wednesday, while the harvest was being brought in. He also collected his
annual *ziyara*—Rifian *z-ziyarth*—at the same time, as well. . . .
And in other Waryaghar markets, too, it was normal for the most
distinguished member of the locally "core" Imrabdhen lineage to
receive a portion from the top of the market fine.) The second
fifth went to subclan Aith Turirth, the third fifth to subclan Aith
'Arus, the fourth to Aith Bu Khrif of Aith Bu 'Ayyash "Proper,"
and the final one to the neighboring clan (Axt Tsafth) of the
tribe of Axt Tuzin, from whom the market site had originally
been more or less usurped. These subclans are all regular constituents of the market in question. But Timarzga, who are also
constituents, were excluded as, through the affinal ties of one of
their more important council-members, they collected one-fourth
of the *r-haqq* in a small neighboring market in the tribe of Igzinnayen. (Typically, however, they say that they had a right to
one-fifth of the share at the Wednesday Market at Turirth, and
that Axt Tuzin did not; and in any case, it is clear that the fifth
which the latter received was merely as a recognition of their
claims.)

What was lost on the swings was gained on the roundabouts,
as it were; and as virtually every clan in Waryagharland had and
has its own market (quite apart from the five special women's
markets which it still has, to which men are rigorously forbidden
access, and which are essentially a function of the extreme degree of sex-segregation which obtains here more than in any
other corner of Morocco)[32] the councillors who normally at-

[32] A. Sánchez Pérez, "Zocos de Mujeres en Beni Uriaguel," *Africa*, Madrid,
Mayo 1943, pp. 22–23, advances the theory that these grew up because, as
a result of incessant feuding, only women, theoretically exempt from feuds,
could carry on peaceful commercial exchange; and André Adam (personal
communication, February 2, 1965) thinks that as *some* women, each week,
are menstruating and hence are impure from a ritual standpoint, the reason
is to be found here. This, he thinks, is true even today, despite the fact that
a degeneration of custom has set in and that old women as well as poor ones
of any age may be seen at men's markets. Adam's theory is based on the
former existence of women's markets in the Sus.

Sánchez Pérez' idea is ingenious but wrong; for no matter how hot any
feud became, there was always the sanction of *r-haqq* fines present to deter
murder in a market attended by men (not that it always did so, by any

tended these quite naturally received most of their remunerations
from them. And *r-haqq* and its distribution, expressed in monetary as well as in fractional terms,[33] was a revalidation of the
segmentary system and an integral expression of the localized
clan limits to which Montagne refers.

8. *". . . et il arrive fréquemment que les querelles intestines
s'apaisent pour permettre à chaque 'khoms' d'entrer en lutte
contre le voisin." Author's translation: ". . . and it frequently happens that internal feuds subside in order to permit each khums
to enter into a [wider] struggle with a neighboring one."*

And here, once again, we return to the question of the *liff*-
alliance system of mutually hostile factions briefly discussed in
Point 4.

Montagne misunderstood how this worked in Northern Morocco, and the chessboard-like features of his Ghmara-Sinhaja
liff-map (Montagne; 1930, facing p. 208), representing a virtually
mythological war in which all the tribes of the north were "supposed" to have been involved, on one or the other side, ill accords
with his far more accurate statement as given above. It is indeed
ironical that the accuracy of the footnote presently commented
upon is so great while the text of Montagne's work abounds in
errors (at least regarding the Rif, for I am in no position to comment, except for certain reservations of judgment, on the sum
total of his achievement—and it was a considerable one—on the

---

means!). It is also of interest to note that in Waryagharland, women's markets exist only in the plain and in the median mountains; there are none in
the Jbil Hmam, and there never have been. Here the usual segregation and
dichotomy between the sexes is perhaps even stronger and more obvious than
elsewhere; and the highlanders, who keep their women rigidly shut in, look
upon the existence of women's markets in the lowlands sneeringly and as a
sign of weakness. I was told that a generation ago no women *ever* attended
the Wednesday Market of Aith Turirth.

There is one surviving women's market in Thimsaman, but it is just across
the Nkur River from the Waryaghar border, and its establishment there may
hence have been Waryaghar-influenced. Igzinnayen and Aith 'Ammarth are
said to have had women's markets in the days before 'Abd al-Krim, but
neither tribe has them today.

[33] Fines in the Rif have always been expressed in money, never in sheep,
as among Atlas Berbers. And by "fractional," I mean literally that, and not
fraction as the French use it to describe upper-level tribal segments.

Western High Atlas, the Sus, and the Anti-Atlas with which by
far the greater part of his book deals). Even though Robert
Montagne and the problems which he did his best to confront
may both be "out of fashion" today, I only wish to show here
that his quick and footnoted interpolation of Aith Waryaghar
social structure was an excellent overall gauge of the situation;
and I now continue to discuss it, after pausing only to agree
with Gellner that Montagne's work represents one of the two high
water marks of French protectorate sociology in tribal Morocco
(though I would also add the work of Michaux-Bellaire to the
list).[34]

The overall, "permanent" *liff*-structure in Waryagharland, that
which was invariably invoked in the event of a full-scale tribal
conflagration, represents, as informants have described it, an extremely interesting consequence of both the segmentary system
and the territorial system—but it is not a part of either. I give it
below, in Table 1, under the headings of Faction A and Faction B.

TABLE I

	Faction A	Faction B
Within *Aith Waryaghar*:	AITH YUSIF W-'ARI	AITH 'ARI
	AITH TURIRTH	TIMARZGA
	AITH HADHIFA "PROPER"	AITH 'ABDALLAH
	AITH 'ARUS	
	I'AKKIYEN	
	AITH BU 'AYYASH "PROPER"	AITH 'ADHIYA
	IMRABDHEN	
Outside *Aith Waryaghar*:	AITH 'AMMARTKH clan of IJA'UNEN	THIMSAMAN: clan of TRUGUTH
		AXT TUZIN: clan of AXT 'AKKI
		IBBUQUYEN: clan of IZIMMUREN

[34] The other such water mark, of a very different kind, in terms of the
problems dealt with (although the region itself is one of those discussed by
Montagne) is Jacques Berque, *Structures Sociales du Haut Atlas*, Paris:
Presses Universitaires de France, 1955. Cf. the dual review of both Mon-
tagne's and Berque's works by Ernest Gellner, "The Far West of Islam,"
British Journal of Sociology, 1958. A complete bibliography of the volumi-
nous output of Edouard Michaux-Bellaire is given in R. Gerofi, "Michaux-
Bellaire," *Tingu: Bulletin de la Société d'Histoire et d'Archéologie de
Tanger*, No. 1, 1953, pp. 79–85.

Several points emerge here. First of all, if we compare this information with that given in Figs. 1-1 and 1-2, we may see at once that the *liff*-structure does *not* correspond with that of the *khmās* or "fifths" (nor, to a lesser extent, to that of clan or subclan except in certain cases), but tends rather to cut across it, if anything, as shown in the case of the *khums* of Aith Yusif w-'Ari/Aith 'Ari, in which each clan is opposed to the other, as are Aith Turirth and Timarzga on the subclan level, in the mountains. The *khums* of Aith Bu 'Ayyash "Proper" opposed to Aith 'Adhiya, even the *khums* as such is a single block of territory, which Aith Yusif w-'Ari/Aith is not. Aith 'Abdallah on the other hand, *qua khums*, is such a unit, and stayed together in the total *liff* system, as did Aith Hadhifa (on the other side, and against Aith 'Abdallah), with their territorially discontinuous "brethren" of Aith 'Arus and I'akkiyen. Although there was no way of checking this at the time of field-work, it does not seem unreasonable to assume that the overall *liff* crystallized around disputes or fights between Aith Yusif w-'Ari and Aith 'Ari, between Aith Hadhifa and Aith 'Abdallah, between Aith Turirth and Timarzga, and between Aith Bu 'Ayyash "Proper" and Aith 'Adhiya, Aith 'Arus, I'akkiyen and Imrabdhen (who all fought internally), however, and all put aside their own internal squabbles to help Faction A.

This brings up a second problem, in terms of territorial distribution. The *liff*-heads are, of course, whichever clans or subclans one's informants may belong to. But aside from the fact that it is striking to note a general pattern of hostility towards one's immediate clan or subclan neighbor, within the framework of the tribal territory, one may also note a feature in the overall Waryaghar *liff* which, in all the Rif, seems to be quite unique, I believe. This is its basic *disequilibrium*, one which in fact defies the equilibrium theory behind *liff*-systems in general; and this disequilibrium is all the more interesting in that Aith Waryaghar themselves do not perceive it (or at least, they do not do so explicitly). The plain fact, which is in disagreement with *liff*-systems elsewhere, is that Faction A is undeniably bigger than Faction B. It is of course possible to postulate a previous equilibrium between the two before the advent of Imrabdhen on the scene; and, as we have seen, the latter were probably brought in upon

the side of Aith Yusif w-'Ari through the marriage by Sidi Mhand
u-Musa to a daughter of an *amghar* of the latter clan.

By such a reckoning, Imrabdhen then becomes a "fifth wheel,"
as it were, to add the extra weight on the side of Faction A
(which, in fact, informants say, generally did win most of the
intra-tribal wars which occurred). Thus two and two were added
up to make five. In an earlier publication,[35] I expressed the view
that the crucial determinant of the make-up of a given *liff*-system
was whether the number of primary segments, whether constituted by "fifths" or by "clans," was odd or even; and I argued that
in tribes that possess an even number of primary segments the
liff-affiliations were virtually automatically determined (as in Aith
'Ammarth, with four clans or *r-urbu'*, two were aligned against
the other two), whereas in tribes which possess an odd number of
primary segments, one of these tends to become odd man out,
and can either opt out for complete neutrality (as in Ibuqquyen
and Thimsaman) or opt in, and then become split down the middle (as in effect happened both in Igzinnayen and in Axt Tuzin,
though the actual details of each case are more complex and do
not concern us here). This argument was based on the assump-
tion of an overall equilibrium theory, and today and now, while
I do not reject it, I do not concede it the primacy which I did at
that time, in the light of re-thinking about the Waryaghar *dis*-
equilibrium. It is still a consideration, but a secondary one. The
Waryaghar *liffs*, on the overall level, remain *weighted*, in favor
of A.

Why was this the case? The Imrabdhen, the "fifth wheel," provide the answer, I think. Through their allegiance to Aith Yusif
w-'Ari, it was they themselves who created the disequilibrium,
and they did so, paradoxically, *despite* the fact that a certain few
of their individual lineages traditionally *restored* equilibrium
through peace-making (while the rest of their lineages might to
all intents and purposes have been or be "lay" lineages).

Looking again at Table 1, we can see that a certain attempt at
balance in the *liff*-system was looked for in alliances *outside* of
Waryagharland, with the neighboring clans of neighboring tribes,

[35] D. M. Hart, *op. cit.*, 1958, pp. 204–6, note 44.

to "remedy the situation," as it were. This brings up one or two more crucial points; and the principal one of these is: what were the *limits* of any given *liff*-system? As Gellner has argued,[36] permanent *liffs* in the Montagne scheme as presented for the Western Atlas were also *transitive,* i.e.; that if A and B were in *liff,* and B and C were also, it logically follows that A and C were in *liff* as well. Now this, in principle, is true for the *liff*-systems of the Rif, but only up to a point, for the system had well-defined limits. It was, in a sense, the chessboard which Montagne so liked to compare it to, but it was a very small chessboard, and perhaps rather a *series* of small chessboards, to the extent that this analogy can be pushed. I prefer to think of it rather *as a series of inter-locking and halved and/or bisected concentric circles,* each containing a core inner circle of a heavy line, representing the surrounding clans of neighboring tribes, which were all themselves likewise involved in their own similar *liff*-systems, but who gave "under-the-counter" aid, in arms and money, to the clans they favored (and to the moiety to which these clans belonged) in the warring tribe when they themselves were not at war.

This accounts for the presence, as indicated in Table 1, of a clan of Aith 'Ammarth on the side of Faction A, and of a clan of Thimsaman, one of Axt Tuzin and one of Ibuqquyen on that of Faction B. Fig. 1-3, below, indicates the general features of the Rifian *liff*-system, and Fig. 1-4 is a paradigm schematizing the *liff*-systems of all six of the Central Rifian tribes, more or less as they actually existed on the ground.

Each Rifian tribe had its *own liff*-system, on the overall level, in which neighboring clans of bordering tribes might sometimes be involved, or sometimes not, but *never,* to my certain knowledge, a whole neighboring tribe. And it is precisely at this point that we find the effective limit of the system. Each *tribal* circle, as it were, might be partially affected by one of its neighbors, but never totally. Thus, essentially, each wheel rotated independently of the others, though sometimes cogs might come together and mesh. In the Aith Waryaghar case, the issue was rendered somewhat more complex by territorial discontinuity of participant subclans and by the presence of Imrabdhen, which

[36] For the appropriate quotation, see Hart, *op. cit.,* 1958, p. 204, note 44.

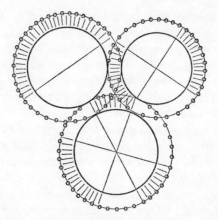

FIGURE 1-3 *Rifian Liffs: Interlocking, Bisection and Trisection:* The heavy inner circle represents a single tribal territory, the dotted outside one the clans concerned of neighboring tribes. White and black segments within a single tribal territory (i.e., within a single inner circle) represent the clans making up the opposed and hostile moieties, while shaded areas in the outer circles represent clans of the neighbor tribes which may be hostile in one context and/or friendly in another.

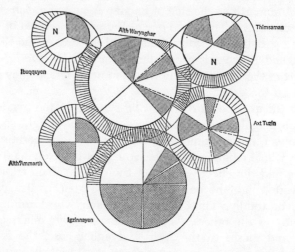

FIGURE 1-4 Paradigm of *Liff* systems of six central Rifian tribes. Dotted lines represent clans split in half by *liff;* N represents neutral clans.

created an imbalance in the system; but these factors do not obscure the way this system worked.

The "temporary" *liff*, however, operating within a clan, a subclan or a local community, could and did shift and change. We shall soon see that this is exactly what happened, in a brief survey, to follow, of local communities and lineages in the subclan territory of Aith Turirth.[37]

9.   *"Seuls dans tout le Rif, les Beni Ouriaghel [Aith Warighar]
ont des 'khoms' dont le territoire est formé de parcelles séparées."*
Author's translation: "Alone in the Rif, the Bni Waryaghal (= Aith
Waryaghar) have khmās, the territory of which is made up of
blocs separated from each other."

There is no need now to comment on this point, which has been adequately explained already in Point 5; see above.

10.   ". . . *Partout ailleurs, chez les tribus de Mtiwa, Beni Bou
Frah, Beni Itteft, Boqqoya, Temsaman, la division en 'khoms,'
très apparente, découpe le pays en petites unités sensiblement
égales en force et en surface, quelles que soient les conditions
géographiques de la vie."* Author's translation: ". . . *Everywhere
else, among the tribes of Mtiwa, Bni Bu Frah, Bni Yittuft, Buqquya and Thimsaman, the division into* khmās *["fifths"], very
readily discernible, cuts the region up into little units of approximately equal strength and size, whatever the geographic conditions of existence may be."*

Of these other tribes mentioned by Montagne, only Thimasaman is in fact segmented into "fifths," and in this case they coincide completely with the clan structure. Bni Bu Frah and Aith Yittuft each have four clans, Ibuqquyen has three, and Mtiwa appears to have seven (the last mentioned I have not empirically verified). However, the point is clear: that the territorial discontinuity of "fifths" and clans discussed at length above exists only in Aith Waryaghar.

[37] In this case, the shift in *liffs* will form a crucial part of the narrative history of a feud and its convolutions and ramifications, to be given in Section V.

V. LINEAGES AND LOCAL COMMUNITIES IN AITH TURIRTH, A SUBCLAN TERRITORY

Aith Turirth (Fig. 1-2, Khums I, subclan of Aith Yussif w-'Ari) say that their nine constituent lineages are descended from a common ancestor, 'Amar, and that they are therefore Aith 'Amar. Genealogical connections to 'Amar (said to have come from Aith Yusif w-'Ari) can be traced, but there is little doubt that the genealogy has been foreshortened. These lineages are (1) Aith Uswir, (2) Yinn ("those of") Hand w-'Abdallah, (3) Aith 'Aru Musa, (4) Dharwa ("sons of") n-'Ari Muhand Uqshar, (5) Aith Mhand u-Sa'id, (6) Aith Ufaran, (7) Aith Ikhrif u-Hand, (8) Ihammuthen (very few left today) and (9) Aith 'Amar "Proper." Of these lineages, only the last three have always lived on land belonging to Aith Waryaghar; the rest of them all bought their land from Igzinnayen across the tribal border to the south. Also, of these lineages, only Aith Uswir, Yinn Hand w-'Abdallah, Aith 'Aru Musa and Aith Mhand u-Sa'id (four out of nine) play any real part in what is to follow.

The subclan territory, however, also contains seven "stranger" lineages: two "holy" lineages, Dharwa n-Sidi r-Hajj Misa'ud of the Imrabdhen of Aith Kammun, and some minor representatives of the Shurfa n-Sidi Hand u-Musa of the Asht 'Aru 'Aisa subclan of Igzinnayen; and five "lay" lineages, Aith Hand u-Misa'ud (from Aith 'Ammarth), Aith Ya'qub (from Igzinnayen), Izna-gen (from Igzinnayen also), Ihawtshen (from Axt Tuzin), and Imjjat (again, from Igzinnayen). The story of how the last-mentioned lineage, Imjjat, came to be one of the two most power-ful ones in the subclan territory, and how it then subsequently disintegrated through a fight between two brothers and their descendants is a fascinating one. I tell it in purely narrative form in the next section, but reserve proper sociological analysis of it for a future publication.

Formerly, the tribe of Igzinnayen owned most of the present land of Aith Turirth; and the ancestors of the present lineages mentioned above gradually bought it from them. All of these lineages, as well as the first six "foreign" lineages (of the two holy ones, the first was installed in Aith 'Aru Musa and the second near l-'Ass, and Iznagen and Ihawtshen were both in Tigzirin), were already installed when, about 1860, Muhand n-'Ari n-'Abd r-Harim—and nicknamed the "Fqir Azzugwagh," the "redheaded lay-brother," as he was a member of the Darqawa brotherhood (and it was by his nickname that he came to be known, as oftens happens in the Rif)—scissioned-off[38] from his own lineage in Hibir, in the clan of Asht 'Asim of Igzinnayen,

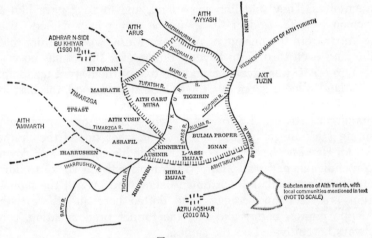

FIGURE 1-5

[38] What I call *scission* was an extremely common phenomenon in Rifian social structure. The fission of agnatic lineages has become an anthropological commonplace; but scission is a different matter altogether. What it involves is the physical act of individual or lineage A packing up its belongings and *moving* to locality B, which may be in a different clan of the same tribe or yet in a different tribe entirely. The name of the old lineage is, however, invariably retained in the new locality: thus we have Upper and Lower Ikatshumen, in Aith Yusif w-'Ari; Upper, Middle and Lower Bu Minqad in Aith 'Ari; and a host of other examples. The example which is pertinent here is that of the reduplication in just this fashion of the Imjjat lineage from Igzinnayen across the tribal border into Aith Waryaghar. The whole phenomenon of scission is one I plan to discuss in detail in a forthcoming work. I will say here only that the motives for it were generally twofold: (1) exile of murderers who broke the market "peace," and (2) population pressure which prompted emigration on the part of individuals in order to purchase land elsewhere.

It no longer occurs, of course, and has not done so since 1921 and the

and came to Waryagharland about 1852–53. It seems that the
reason for his departure was that he got into a quarrel with and
killed a *sharif,* no less (but not an important one), from the
neighboring Igzinnayen subclan of Asht 'Aru 'Aisa. It need only
be added that the remaining lineages of Imjjat still exist in Hibir,
and this physical move documents nicely how lineage reduplication can occur from one tribe to the next.

The Fqir Azzugwagh went to Bulma, above and east of the
Nkur River, where Yinn Hand w-'Abdallah had already installed
themselves. They sold him some land, and in 1953 gave him a
woman to wife. And at this point he met a man named 'Aisa
w-'Amar from the lineage of Aith 'Aru Musa, who told him that
the land even further up beyond Bulma (for Bulma has no water), in l-'Ass, was excellent; and the two of them went up there.
This land, 1400–1450 m. high, was indeed very good, the best in
Aith Turirth. There is always plenty of water in the small but
tumultuous stream of Saru nj-'Ass which rises from a mountain
spring (this allegedly gushed into being when one of the *shurfa*
of Sidi Hand u-Musa, who could also ride his horse up and down
perpendicular cliff walls, tapped the rock with his stick) to flow
into the Upper Nkur River down below; and even if the mountains are steep and craggy (and dotted here and there with
Aleppo pines), barley and rye, the former predominating, can
always be cultivated on the slopes.

So, at l-'Ass, both men jointly bought the land in question from
its immediately previous owners, Ihammuthen (who owned the
upper land) and Yinn Hand w-'Abdallah (who owned the lower
land); and they jointly built a house beside the stream, and,
nearby, an olive press. As the two of them shared expenses
equally in this venture, the division both of property and of
irrigation water (and of olive oil, also) among their present descendants is exactly the same as it was among them, even though
'Aisa w-'Amar had only one son ('Amar w-'Aisa w-'Amar)[39]

---

beginning of the 'Abd al-Krim regime. Reasons are: no more feuding, and no
more available land, wholly aside from the maintenance by the Spanish
protectorate of more or less of a post-pacification *status quo,* after 1926.

[39] It is very common in the Rif to name a man for his paternal grandfather and extremely rare to name him for his father. The latter only normally
happens if the father should die before the boy is born. And, under the same
set of circumstances, if the mother is left a widow, what Fortes has termed

and the Fqir Azzugwagh had four ('Amar Uzzugwagh, Mzzyan Uzzugwagh, Muh Akuh Uzzugwagh and Muh Uzzugwagh), as well as a daughter, whom he gave in marriage to 'Amar w-'Aisa, the son of his partner. The descendants of 'Amar w-'Aisa still have only one house, down below beside the stream and the joint olive press of the two lineages, and those of the Fqir Azzugwagh, in 1955 at the time of my original fieldwork, had four, all widely dispersed from each other in proper Waryaghar style, up above and alongside the grain-cultivated slopes. One of these houses had in fact just been completed when my first stage of fieldwork was finished.

LINEAGE COMPOSITION OF IMJJAT

In 1955, in these five houses, there lived a total population of 71 individuals. Of these, three *nubath* (sing. *nubth*) or nuclear families,[40] in the lower house, comprised the (sub)lineage group of Dharwa n-'Amar w-'Aisa (2 married brothers, their 2 wives,

---

"complementary filiation" (cf. M. Fortes, "The Structure of Unilineal Descent Groups," in Simon and Phoebe Ottenberg, eds., *Cultures and Societies of Africa*, New York: Random House, 1960, pp. 163–89) is also common. In this, a child is called by its mother's name, e.g., Muhand n-Fattush. This applies particularly if the mother remains a widow, and has to bring up her children on her own; and it also applies if she happens to be from another clan or tribe from that of her deceased husband, e.g., Muh n-Ta'rusth (with mother from Aith 'Arus) or 'Allush n-Tagzinnaith (with mother from Igzinnayen). (It may also act as a way to distinguish children, locally, in the event of plural marriages of their father, but this is rarer—and informants deny it.) But it serves only as a means of identifying and distinguishing agnates under the above set of circumstances; there are no corresponding rights or obligations on the distaff side.

[40] *Nubth* literally means "turn." It may also count for a young single man and his widowed mother as well as for a nuclear family *sensu stricto* of father, mother and unmarried children. The concept revolves around the collective maintenance by the local community of the *fqih*, the Qur'anic schoolmaster, in the local mosque, who is paid annually in barley for his services. In 1955 the *fqih* of the Bulma mosque, which serves l-'Ass, received 8–10 quintals of barley from the local communities of Bulma, Ignan and l-'Ass, each *nubth* having paid an equal share. Not only this, but each *nubth*, in turn (and hence the name), feeds the *fqih* every night, and the latter, every afternoon, sends out one of his students to the *nubth* concerned to pick up his dinner for him.

Irrigation is also parcelled out, within each lineage, on a *nubth* basis; see below, p. 52.

a widowed mother and her spinster sister, 3 unmarried sons and 4 unmarried daughters), with a total of 13 people. In the four houses above, ten *nubath* made up the lineage-group of Dharwa u-Fqir Azzugwagh, or Imjjat nj-'Ass, with a total of 58 people. These last were broken up into their three component sublineage groups (*ijujga*, sing. *jajgu*), descended from three of the four sons of the Fqir Azzugwagh, as follows:

(a) *Dharwa n-'Amar Uzzugwagh*, with 5 *nubath*—the first, of a man, his 3 wives, his widowed mother, the widowed sister of his father, his own unmarried sister, his unmarried son and 3 unmarried daughters, 1 male servant and 2 female servants (14 people); the second, of another man, the maternal half-brother of the first (their joint mother having successively married 3 brothers, of whom the first two had died by violence), his wife and 2 unmarried daughters (4 people); the third, of another man, paternal uncle to the first two, with his wife, 3 unmarried sons and 3 unmarried daughters (8 people); the fourth, of a patrilateral parallel cousin of the first two (it was he who had just built the new house alluded to above), his wife, his wife's unmarried son by a previous marriage, and his own two unmarried daughters; and the fifth, by a young unmarried man, the son of the deceased brother of the preceding individual, his widowed mother and 2 unmarried sisters (4 people—although, at the time, the widow in question and her son and daughters resided in her own lineage-group of r-Mquddam, of Yinn Hand w-'Abdallah, in the neighboring and larger local community of Bulma). Total for Dharwa n-'Amar Uzzugwagh: 35 people. (It should be added that the members of the first three *nubath* live in the only two-storied house in the region. However, the man of the first *nubth* owns in fact another house of his own, built by his father before the latter's death, which is not located in l-'Ass, but some 4–5 km. down below by the bank of the Nkur River; he himself, his widowed mother and his second and third wives and their children lived there regularly, while the first wife and her children resided in l-'Ass.)

(b) *Dharwa n-Muh Akuh Uzzugwagh*, with 2 *nubath*—the first, of a very old man (Muh Akuh Uzzugwagh himself, deceased as of 1956), his surviving wife, and 4 unmarried sons and 3 unmarried daughters (9 people); and the second, his married son, the latter's wife, and 1 unmarried daughter (3 people). Total for Dharwa n-Muh Akuh Uzzugwagh: 12 people.

(c) *Dharwa n-Mzzyan Uzzugwagh,* with 3 *nubath*—the first, of a man, his wife, his 3 unmarried daughters and 1 unmarried son (6 people); the second, of the man's younger brother, his wife and 1 unmarried daughter (3 people); and the third, of the unmarried male patrilateral parallel cousin of the first two men, and his widowed mother (herself a daughter of Muh Akuh Uzzugwagh) (2 people). Total for Dharwa n-Mzzyan Uzzugwagh: 11 people.

To the human population of Dharwa n-'Amar w-'Aisa could, at the time, be added an animal population of 2 cows, 1 donkey, 15 chickens, and 30 goats, as well as 20 days' worth of plowing and harvesting (of barley and rye—Rifians tend to make agricultural computations in temporal rather than spatial terms), 20 fig trees, 10 olive trees, 30 almond trees, 5 grape vines and 4 days of maize. To that of Imjjat (Dharwa u-Fqir Azzugwagh) could be added an animal population of 18 cows (though 6 of these were elsewhere at the time), 109 goats, 1 mule, 3 donkeys, some 40 chickens, and 2 cats, as well as 160 total days' plowing-harvesting of barley and rye (the barley, of course greatly predominating, but, again, not all of this at l-'Ass), 70 fig trees, 31 olive trees, 20 almond trees and 50 grape vines (both these last owned by a member of the lineage, but elsewhere in Timarzga).

The eight hectares of individually owned (*r-murk*) arable land (as opposed to the jointly or collectively-held *r-mishra',* the pasture land owned by the *jma'th,* all the land-owning male members of the community, and generally reserved for goat-grazing on the higher slopes) had originally been divided into eight parts by the Fqir Azzugwagh—because of his four sons—and 'Amar w-'Aisa; and of these, four belonged to Imjjat and four to Dharwa n-'Amar w-'Aisa. The breakdown on the sublineage level was as follows: 1 part for 'Amar Uzzugwagh and his sons, 1 for Muh Akuh Uzzugwagh and his sons, 2 for Mzzyan and Muh Uzzugwagh and the sons of the former (for the latter died violently, as did his only surviving son, without male issue), and 4

for 'Amar w-'Aisa. The daughter of the Fqir Azzugwagh, who
was married to 'Amar w-'Aisa, renounced—in very Rifian fashion
—her own share of the inheritance in favor of her brothers. And
water rights for irrigation were distributed in exactly the same
way: 4 days (96 hours) for Imjjat (Dharwa Uzzugwagh)—1 day
for 'Amar Uzzugwagh, 1 day for Muh Akuh Uzzugwagh, and 2
days for Mzzyan and Muh Uzzugwagh; and 4 days for Dharwa
n-'Amar w-'Aisa. (A day of irrigation in l-'Ass starts at 2000
hours in the evening, to continue until the same time the following evening.)

MARRIAGE PATTERNS

Effective living members of the Imjjat lineage are in some cases
three, and in some cases four, generations removed from the Fqir
Azzugwagh himself. Out of 42 recorded marriages in the total
agnatic genealogy (I have not counted out-marrying women in
this connection), 18 are those of individuals now living. There
have been 13 cases of plural marriages (with two or three, but
never as many as four, wives), 14 of secondary or successive
marriages, and 4 divorces. There have only been 3 instances of
lineage endogamy (2 of these involving marriage with true parallel cousins), for the prevailing marriage pattern is unquestionably one of local lineage exogamy: 10 women have gone out in
marriage to the lineages, respectively, of Aith Uswir (3),
r-Mquddam Hand w-'Abdallah (1), Iznagen (1), Aith Ufaran
(1), Aith 'Aru Musa (4—including the Fqir's daughter Fadhma
Uzzugwagh to 'Amar w-'Aisa in l-'Ass), while some 21 women
have come in, respectively, from Yinn bil-Lahsin Hanl w-'Abdallah (1—the Fqir's wife), Aith Uswir (4), Dharwa u-Mrabit
'Ari (2—this is a descendant sublineage of the Shurfa n-Sidi Hand
u-Musa of Igzinnayn but it is resident in Kinnirth, near l-'Ass,
in Waryagharland, and possessed of a certain prestige, if not of
r-baraka), r-Mquddam Hand w-'Abdallah (5), Aith 'Aru Musa
(1), Iznagen (3), Aith Mhand u-Sa'id (2), Ihawtshen (1), Aith
Ufaran (1), Yinn 'Aru Misa'ud Hand w-'Abdallah (1) and Yinn
Tufali Hand w-'Abdallah (1).

Local lineage exogamy is perhaps more marked in the Imjjat
case than in any of the other lineages just mentioned, and they

represent a fair "round robin" of the Aith Turirth lineages. The Fqir Azzugwagh and his sons wished to create marital and hence alliance links "around the clock," as it were, within Aith Turirth, among whom they were strangers, but where they had settled down.[41] Endogamous marriages in these other lineages only occur in a somewhat larger minority of cases, as my genealogical evidence shows. Marriage in Waryagharland tends to be within the clan or subclan, within which the given number of constituent lineages residing in a given number of local communities simply hand women around to each other in an endless succession, year after year; and if Lineage X (say, Imjjat) already has affinal links (is *idhuran* with, as Rifians say) with Lineage Y (say, r-Mquddam Hand w-'Abdallah, or Aith Mhand u-Sa'id), it tends progressively to keep these up and renew them in future.[42]

There has also been a certain amount, though more in recent years, of subclan exogamy as well: 2 women have gone out to Timarzga and 3 have come in from that subclan, as well as 2 from Aith 'Arus. On the tribal level of exogamy, 3 women have gone out to Igzinnayen (one of these to the Imjjat in Hibir), 1 to Axt Tuzin, 1 to Tafarsith, and 1 to l-Mtalsa, in the Eastern Rif. Marriages of this type thus occur at a somewhat higher frequency than endogamous ones within lineages, in the case under discussion; but in the other recorded Aith Turirth cases, this frequency is less rather than more. There have also been no fewer than 8 instances of widow inheritance (I call it such, following Evans-Pritchard's usage, rather than "levirate"), in which, when a man dies, his brother, generally a younger one, marries his widow but raises children to her in his own name rather than in that of his deceased brother[43] (and this style of "widow-

---

[41] The Imjjat in l-'Ass make no secret whatsoever of their "foreign" origin. All their personal marriage and property, etc., documents, drawn up in Arabic by the local *fqih* refer to the Fqir Azzugwagh and to each of his sons as *l-Gzinnayi aslan, wa-la l-Waryaghli daran*, "of Igzinnayen origin, but resident in Waryagharland."

[42] I have recorded also a small number of cross-cousin marriages, in some of the other lineages of Aith Turirth, although Imjjat had none. These are not the supplementary factor that they are among Cyrenaican Bedouins (cf. Emrys Peters, "Proliferation of Segments in the Lineage of the Bedouin in Cyrenaica, *JRAI*, vol. 90, no. 1, 1960, pp. 29–53. [Reprinted as Chapter 18, Vol. I, *Peoples and Cultures of the Middle East*.]

[43] Godfrey Lienhardt, *Social Anthropology*, London 1964, p. 138.

inheritance" is the Arab and Berber norm, quite unlike the true
levirate of the Ancient Jews and of Evans-Pritchard's Nilotic
Nuer). Coon[44] thought that the reason for this was to provide
for the widows of men who had died violently in feud; the
thought is attractive, but it only very partially corresponds to
the realities of the case. The real reasons, according to Aith
Waryaghar, behind *yarrit w-umas* ("she married his brother")
are far more utilitarian, as well as being based on pride and mistrust, and are three in number: (1) to ensure that any property
concerned remains in the hands of the agnatic lineage in question; (2) to prevent a man's brother's widow from losing status
by marrying an outsider; and (3) to prevent her children, if she
has any, from being brought up by an outsider. (Two cases in
fact involved *double* widow inheritance: in one of these a
woman, who is still living today, successively married *three* full
brothers, two of whom met sudden deaths—one by feud about
1920–21 and the next through a French-dropped bomb in the
Rifian War in 1925—while the third, who had been a *qaid* of 100
men under 'Abd al-Krim, became *shaikh* of Aith Turirth under
the Spaniards and died peacefully in bed in 1946. In the second
instance, a woman first married a man; then, when he was killed,
she married his male patrilateral parallel cousin, and upon the
latter's accidental death, she married the full brother of that
cousin.) The reverse side of the coin, the sororate (*iwi dhasrifth-
ines*, "he marries his wife's sister"), is also fairly common in
Waryagharland; but, although I have examples of it from other
genealogies in Aith Turirth, there happened to be none in the
Imjjat case. In the sororate, the question of property does not
apply, and there are only two considerations: (1) that a man's
widow's sister will take care of his children by his deceased wife,
and (2) that he himself will remain on good terms with his affines, by marrying her.

Dharwa n-'Amar w-'Aisa have all married women from their
own larger lineage of Aith 'Aru Musa, however, with two exceptions: the daughter of the Fqir Azzugwagh (who married 'Amar
w-'Aisa himself), and one living member who has a wife from
Aith Bu 'Ayyash. One instance of widow inheritance has been

[44] Cf. Eliot D. Chapple & Carleton S. Coon, *Principles of Anthropology*,
New York: Henry Holt, 1942, p. 311.

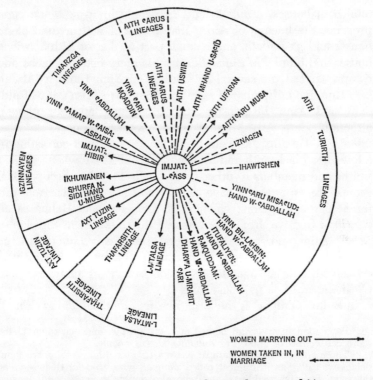

FIGURE 1-6 Local exogamy of Imjjat lineage in l-'Ass.

recorded (but since 1955); and this branch sublineage has thus retained strong links with its own original lineage-group located down below by the Nkur River.

OTHER COMMUNITIES AND LINEAGES OF AITH TURIRTH

In the overall subclan territory of Aith Turirth (total population, in 1952, 2690 people in 282 houses)[45] we find also the local communities and their membership of l-'Ass, Ignan, and Bulma "Proper," l-'Ass also includes, administratively, the lineage of Dharwa u-Mrabit 'Ari in Kinnirth, alluded to above and had a

[45] Figures kindly supplied by Capt. José Rodriguez Erola of the Spanish Army, at the time the *interventor comarcal* of Aith Waryaghar. The Moroccan census of 1960 indicates a total of 556 *nubath* and 3424 population.

total of 3 houses, 4 *nubath* and 23 people in 1955. *Ignan* compromises the lineage of Aith Mhand u-Sa'id with a total of 11 houses and 33 *nubath,* and a small part of that of Aith Uswir, 3 houses and 6 *nubath. Bulma "Proper"* is more heterogeneous and comprises: (a) the several sublineages of Yinn Hand w-'Abdallah: Itufaliyen, Ibutaharen n-Bulma, Yinn 'Aru Misa'ud, r-Mquddam and Yinn bil-Lahsin—total 18 houses and 37 *nubath,* although Yinn 'Aru Misa'ud have another 6 houses and 16 *nubath* in Tigzirin[46] as well; (b) a small remainder consisting of a low-class blacksmith and his son, from Axt Tuzin whence blacksmiths and members of other traditionally low-class occupational groups are supposed to have come;[47] and (c) two men from different parts of Igzinnayen. One of them came to Bulma as an *adhrib,* a fugitive, from Ikhuwanen (lit. "thieves") in the clan of Asht[48] 'Asim, and stayed there—total 3 houses, 7 *nubath;* all the above constitute a single local community, as administratively conceived, with an overall population in 1952 of about 450 people living in some 37 households.

In Bulma "Proper" is the local mosque (*thamzyidha nd-dshar*),

---

[46] Population in 1952, 36 houses and 521 people, and according to the Moroccan census of 1960, 117 *nubath* and 514 people.

[47] There are several such groups: *imziren* (blacksmiths), *imdhyazen* (musicians who play an instrument called *zammar,* who, paid for their services, sing and dance at weddings, and who also double as horse- and donkey-breeders to produce mules), *ikiyyaren* and *ibarrahen* (weighers and criers at markets), and *igizzaren* (butchers). Although there are many butchers in I'akkiyen, for example, their ultimate origin, like those of the members of the professions, is Axt Tuzin. These groups are all traditionally endogamous and propertyless; and they are considered to possess no "shame" (*r-Hashuma,* or *r-Hya*). And certainly, as Coon has pointed out (*op. cit.,* 1931, p. 92) all these trades require a certain self-exposure and publicity in crowds, and all involve noise-making. The 2 blacksmith *nubath,* father and son, in Bulma, however, have some property and have married into a Bulma lineage; but, even so, they are not only not respected locally, but are often the butt of jokes as well. . . . As I have said, Rifian society is extremely egalitarian, but some Rifians are more equal than others; and the tribe of Axt Tuzin in general is denigrated for having produced these occupational groups (which are almost, but not quite, "castes").

[48] *Aith, Axt* and *Asht* are all different local pronunciations of the same word, meaning "people (of)." *Yinn* means "those (of)," and *dharwa* (sing. *mimmi*), "sons (of)." Another form of lineage name is also common, the plural *I——n,* as in Ihammuthen or Ibutaharen, "the sons of Hammu" or "the sons of Bu Tahar." The reader will by now have seen these terms often enough to wonder about them; and I herewith explain them.

where a *fqih* teaches small boys to read the Qur'an while the larger "Friday Mosque" (*thamzyidha nj-khutbath,* or "mosque of the sermon"), which serves all of Aith Turirth, is located nearer to the Wednesday Market and employs 2 *fqihs,* one to deliver sermons at the noon prayer on Fridays and the other, lesser one to instruct the boys living in communities near the market itself. The local mosque of Bulma has no *habus* property (inalienable property belonging to and associated with mosques), while the subclan mosque has a little; but the local mosque of Tigzirin (lit. "islands"), on the other hand, has about 4 hectares of *habus* land.

So much, for present purposes, for this statistical attempt at a "community study." Bulma as conceived administratively today is a *dshar* (a "douar"), a local community, with a *mqaddim* (called *jari* in Spanish times, with a *mqaddim* heading the whole subclan of Aith Turirth); but within it, so also are Bulma "Proper," Ignan and l-'Ass (and even Kinnirth) *r-udhshur,* "local communities," on their own, given the spatial separation of one to three kilometers, uphill and downdale, of each one from the next. The nexus is the local community mosque in Bulma "Proper" (which as of 1961 became a "Friday Mosque" in its own right). But all who are truly serious about at least outward observances of religious ritual attend, every week, the subclan mosque of Aith Turirth. The Bulma community mosque has only a very minor saint (Sidi 'Abd r-'Aziz), who is in no way venerated, and a communal cemetery, divided into three lots for the lineage-groups in Bulma "Proper," in Ignan and in l-'Ass.

Within each of these *r-udhshur* or "local communities" are lineage-groups (*dharfiqin,* sing. *dharfiqth*): in Bulma "Proper," the various sublineages of the overall "founder"-lineage of Yinn Hand w-'Abdallah, plus a few incipient outsider groups; in Ignan, the two sublineages of Aith Mhand u-Sa'id (Ibutaharen n-Ignan—to differentiate them from Ibutaharen n-Bulma, of Yinn Hand w-'Abdallah—and Aith Mhand u-Sa'id "Proper"), plus certain *nubath* of Aith Uswir; and in l-'Ass, the two lineages, one now fully grown and the other still incipient, of Imjjat and Dharwa n-'Amar w-'Aisa. Given Aith 'Aru Musa themselves (who gave birth to Dharwa n-'Amar w-'Aisa) down below on the Nkur River, and the large remainder of Aith Uswir, near the Aswil Gorge where the Nkur rushes into Waryagharland from

Igzinnayen; and given, in Tigzirin, the stranger lineages of Iznagen and Ihawtshen (the last-mentioned group are mat- and
donkey-pannier makers, despised almost as much as blacksmiths
and musicians, a lineage whose members themselves never
fought, but who traditionally buried the dead of those lineages
that did), and of those Yinn 'Aru Misa'ud (Hand w-'Abdallah)
of Bulma who bought land there, the picture, is, as I pieced it
together, now more or less complete.

VI. THE FEUD IN IMJJAT LINEAGE AND ITS CON-
SEQUENCES

This article began with history; it will end with a tradition, a
local version of history, in an attempt to make a coherent narrative whole out of what, in the raw material stage, was a succession of anecdotes.

After the Fqir Azzughwagh was installed in l-'Ass, his sons
grew up and married: 'Amar Uzzughagh to a woman of Aith
Uswir, Mzzyan Uzzugwagh to one of Aith Mhand u-Sa'id, Muh
Akuh Uzzugwagh to another of Aith Uswir, and the wife of Muh
Uzzugwagh was the same woman as that of Mzzyan—she was
"widow-inherited" by the latter after the former's death by violence. The Fqir himself continued to live down below with 'Amar
w-'Aisa and his daughter (the latter's wife), while his sons built
their new houses on the upper slope. And with the support of
these sons (all of them, save Muh Akuh, excellent fighters), the
Fqir Azzugwagh, a stranger, became one of the two most powerful men in all of Aith Turirth.

There was only one other man strong enough to challenge him:
the Hajj Am'awsh of Yinn 'Aru Misa'ud (Hand w-'Abdallah),
in Bulma. And one fine day the Hajj and his agnates, along with
some men of Aith 'Arus and Aith Bu Khrif, all desirous of cutting
the Fqir down to size, came up to l-'Ass (which means "gardens"), with the intention of burning down his house. But the
the Fqir down to size, came up to l-'Ass (which means "gar-
sons that they would never be allowed to set foot in his house
again if they did not start shooting at the unwelcome visitors.
So, when the latter had reached the olive press on their upward

march, the Fqir's sons fired on them, wounding several, and the remainder then fled back along the path by which they had come.

Not long afterwards, a paternal uncle of the Hajj Am'awsh killed a man from Iznagen; an agnate of the dead man had wanted him (the dead man) out of the way and had promised the Hajj some land and a woman if he dispatched him. Thus Iznagen obtained the protection of the Hajj Am'awsh, some of whose descendants, as noted above, live in Tigzirin to this day. Hajj Am'awsh gave the woman in marriage to one of his sons.[49] Iznagen had previously fought amongst themselves, but not against any of the lineages to which they were now allied. Only Ihawtshen—who buried the dead of the fighting lineages—remained apart and outside. There was a repeat performance soon after, when another man of Iznagen wanted the Hajj Am'awsh to kill one of his agnates; and thus the Hajj gained even more land in Tigzirin.

At this point an event happened to make the picture more involved: Muh Uzzugwagh was killed in 1897 by one of those members of Imjjat lineage, one Muh n-Bu Yarij, who, unlike the Fqir Azzugwagh, had stayed in Hibir, the tribal area of Igzinnayen. Muh n-Bu Yarij fled as an *adhrib* to Iharrushen, again in Igzinnayen, where Muh Uzzugwagh's brothers 'Amar and Mzzyan rushed to seek him out. They were prevented from doing so by the people of Iharrushen, who came out and fired at them; Mzzyan Uzzugwagh escaped, but 'Amar was wounded in the leg and remained lame for life. He took refuge in the very same house where Muh n-Bu Yarij was hiding, and received the protection of the mistress of the house (through the ritual act of placing his hand on the handmill), under which he stayed until he was able to pay *r-haqq* amounting to 1000 duros hasani which the council members of Iharrushen had imposed upon him. A week later, however, he and his brother Mzzyan went to a wedding in Hibir; here they found Muh n-Bu Yarij whom, under cover of the wedding ceremonies, they dispatched with their

[49] In years to follow, Iznagen, whose women are reputed the most beautiful in Aith Turirth, were to follow the pattern now established: they gave three women to Aith Uswir, one to Yinn 'Aru Misa'ud, one to Imjjat (to 'Amar Uzzugwagh's son Mhand n-'Amar Uzzugwagh, as a second wife), and one to Aith Mhand u-Sa'id.

knives before returning to l-'Ass. . . . And now their father, the
Fqir Azzugwagh, died peacefully in bed.

Now, however, to shift gears again, the alliance between the
Hajj Am'awsh and Iznagen had become precarious. One day the
Hajj's agnates went to Tigzirin from Bulma to cut brushwood
there; they started doing so on Iznagen pasture land, and the
Iznagen protested. No shots were fired, but Iznagen, who began
to think that the Hajj's protection was becoming somewhat op-
pressive, went to l-'Ass to tell 'Amar Uzzugwagh what had happened. 'Amar had now become Imjjat lineage-head in l-'Ass
since his father's death, though his title was not to remain un-
contested for long.

For meanwhile, in l-'Ass, a rift had already developed between the surviving full brothers (by father and same mother)
'Amar and Mzzyan Uzzugwagh, over a woman and over a question of inheritance (that of the woman in question), in the following manner: when Muh Uzzugwagh, brother of 'Amar and
Mzzyan, was killed, his wife was taken over in proper widow-
inheritance fashion by his brother Mzzyan Uzzugwagh. This
woman had already had, however, a daughter, Fattush, by her
first husband, the late Muh Uzzugwagh. 'Amar Uzzugwagh
wanted to marry this girl to *his* son and her patrilateral parallel
cousin, Muh n-'Amar Uzzugwagh. Mzzyan Uzzugwagh, who had
become the girl's stepfather through having married her mother,
was in no way agreed to this. He thought that her share of the
inheritance would thereby escape him completely, and that it
would go entirely to 'Amar Uzzugwagh. So, therefore, he denied
his brother's request and married the girl off into the lineage of
Yinn 'Ari Mqaddim in Timarzga. By so doing, he kept her inheritance and gained new allies, at the same time. His brother,
'Amar Uzzugwagh, now furious, married his second son Mhand
n-'Amar to a girl of the same Yinn 'Ari Mqaddim lineage in
Timarzga, and then his third son 'Allush n-'Amar to another girl
in a neighboring lineage, Yinn 'Abdallah, which was hostile to
Yinn 'Ari Mqaddim. Thus, 'Amar seemed to check, but by no
means check-mate, his brother's moves toward lineage primacy.

Even wilder with rage and frustration than 'Amar was his
eldest son Muh n-'Amar Uzzugwagh, who was to show himself
the toughest member of a very tough lineage. If, he said, he

could not marry his parallel cousin, Fattush, he would never marry at all; and he was thus, aged nearly thirty-five, the only bachelor *amghar* in the *aitharba'in*. He gained a reputation as a "gunslinger," and everyone was afraid of him. He had also, perhaps, severe psychological problems as well, as he was his father's first-born child and all his younger brothers had married before him. He was reputed an excellent shot, and his excuse for carrying two rifles was that if the barrel of one got hot while he was blasting away in his *ashbar* or feuding pill-box, he always had the other! He was short, slight of build, and, for a Rifian, rather dark. Muh n-'Amar took, I am told, tremendous personal risks in feud-fighting, but was never so much as touched by an enemy bullet. In a region where everybody tries to become a personality, a cult of personality cannot exist (later, 'Abd al-Krim, who did away with feuding pill-boxes, was the only member of Aith Waryaghar to overcome this stricture—in his case one can even speak, and in no uncertain terms, of local-level and indeed national-level charisma); but even so, the name of Muh n-'Amar Uzzugwagh is remembered today by old men not only in Waryagharland, but in Igzinnayen and Axt Tuzin as well.

Finally, however, Muh n-'Amar married a daughter of the Mrabit 'Ari of the Shurfa n-Sidi Hand u-Musa (from Asht 'Aru 'Aisa in Igzinnayen, but resident in Kinnirth, in Waryagharland) —she was 14; he was 35. Ironically, he produced no sons, only two daughters, as a result of this marriage; one of these died in childhood, and the other is now married to a man in Aith Uswir. He had a premonition that he was to die by violence, even so, and he did not want his wife to be "widow-inherited" by any of his brothers. However, this is exactly what did happen, and not only once, but twice; it is the first of the two cases of double widow-inheritance referred to earlier. And the woman, still living, outlasted all three of her husbands, by all of whom, it might be added, she had children.

The Hajj Am'awsh, long waiting in the sidelines, was quick to take advantage of the breach between 'Amar and Mzzyan Uzzugwagh; he allied himself to Mzzyan by giving his granddaughter, Maryim Yighidh nj-Hajj Am'awsh, to Mzzyan's nephew Muh n-Muh Uzzugwagh (the only son of the late Muh Uzzugwagh,

who was killed while his wife was still pregnant). And the Aith
Uswir lineage, allied to 'Amar Uzzugwagh, became even more
so when one of the Hajj's sons, Dris nj-Hajj Am'awsh, in the
company of Mzzyan Uzzugwagh, ambushed and killed one of the
Aith Uswir men on a path leading to the Tuesday Market of Azraf
in Axt Tuzin. On another occasion, the Hajj and Mzzyan ambushed a man from r-Mquddam Hand w-'Abdallah and one
from Iznagen as they were returning from the Wednesday
Market of Aith Turirth (and no *r-haqq* was paid in either case).
Thus, these two lineages, already allied to 'Amar Uzzugwagh,
were now even more solidly in his camp. . . . At this point, the
Hajj Am'awsh, now very old, made the pilgrimage to Mecca and
died there. (It is odd that both he and the Fqir Azzugwagh
should have died of simple old age, when this was true of almost
none of the other actors in this drama.)

We may note here that in view of these events, the two *liffs* or
factions *within* Aith Turirth had completely shifted in membership. *Previously,* the Fqir Azzugwagh and his sons had been
against the Hajj Am'awsh and his; but *now* two of the Fqir's
sons, full brothers, 'Amar Uzzugwagh and Mzzyan Uzzugwagh,
were pitted against each other. All the other lineages of Aith
Turirth (Iznagen, Aith Mhand u-Sa'id, Aith 'Aru Musa, Aith
Hand u-Misa'ud, Aith Uswir, Aith Ya'qub, Ihammuthen,
r-Mquddam Hand w-'Abdallah, and Aith Ufaran) were on the
side of 'Amar Uzzugwagh, save that of the Hajj Am'awsh, Yinn
'Aru Misa'ud, as well as the other lineages (except for r-Mquddam Hand w-'Abdallah) of subclan Yinn Hand w-'Abdallah
(Yinn bil-Lahsin, Itufaliyen and Ibutaharen n-Bulma), and Aith
Ikhrif u-Hand (enemies of Aith 'Aru Musa), who were with
Mzzyan, as were also the Yinn 'Ari Mqaddim of Timarzga. Most
if not all of these alliances had been created through the establishment of affinal ties.

And as the Imjjat in l-'Ass were divided, so were those who
had stayed in Hibir in Igzinnayen; the lineages of Iqudhadhen
and Imrafen backed 'Amar Uzzugwagh, while Dharwa n 'Ari
(from which Dharwa u-Fqir Azzugwagh is an offshoot) was split
in half: Dharwa n-Mzzyan n-'Ari were with 'Amar Uzzugwagh,
while Mzzyan n-'Ari's own brother Azarqan ("Blue Eyes") n-'Ari

backed Mzzyan Uzzugwagh, as did Ibinhadduthen and Dharwa n-'Ari "Proper."[50]

And now Aith Mhand u-Sa'id in Ignan threatened 'Amar Uzzugwagh with war if he did not agree to kill his brother Mzzyan. Thus, 'Amar Uzzugwagh decided to send his sons Muh n-'Amar Uzzugwagh and 'Allush n-'Amar Uzzugwagh, aided by Muh n-'Amar w-'Aisa, who was his ('Amar Uzzugwagh's) sister's son (*ayyaw*) to deal with his own brother, Mzzyan, once and for all. Muh n-'Amar Uzzugwagh's hatred for his uncle Mzzyan was extremely great in any case, and he rejoiced at the thought that it was he who was going to put him out of the way. So the three of them went to the fruit trees in l-'Ass, where they waited for Mzzyan. When the latter came out of his house, he was accompanied by his deceased brother's son Muh n-Muh Uzzugwagh and by his *akhammas* (agricultural laborer who is traditionally paid one-fifth of the harvest for his services as the occupational label indicates). 'Allush n-'Amar Uzzugwagh, hidden, fired at Mzzyan but only wounded him in the leg; and Mzzyan escaped. And 'Allush, wanting to pursue his uncle, became tired after half an hour, and went home. . . . At the same moment, however, that 'Allush fired, his brother Muh n-'Amar Uzzugwagh fired the second shot, killing their cousin Muh n-Muh Uzzugwagh instantly; and the *akhammas* escaped.

While the noise of rifle fire echoed around the valley, Muh Akuh Uzzugwagh crept out of his house unobserved. He was on Mzzyan's side because his daughter was married to Mzzyan's son Muh Akuh n-Mzzyan Uzzugwagh, her patrilateral parallel cousin. And now, hidden, Muh Akuh Uzzugwagh saw 'Amar w-'Aisa come out of his house to see what was the matter; and he shot him down as soon as he reached the garden. A man of the Imjjat in Hibir (Igzinnayen) who was with Muh Akuh Uzzugwagh, and who was in full view of Muh n-'Amar Uzzugwagh was then shot by the latter. Muh n-'Amar Uzzugwagh had now killed two men that day, and he was not through yet.

During the fight, Mzzyan Uzzugwagh, wounded, hid himself

[50] This last sublineage was the one which produced the brothers Muh n-Bu Yarij and Aqshar—"Scabhead"—n-Bu Yarij. Rifians, and those of Igzinnayen in particular, are fond of nicknames; and these often turn into lineage-names, recording for posterity a physical trait or peculiarity of the lineage founder as well.

in a ravine. 'Amar Uzzugwagh himself passed by, and thinking that his son 'Allush was dead, as he had not seen him return home after wounding Mzzyan, called to his other son Muh, "Where is your brother 'Allush?" . . . And Muh n'Amar Uzzugwagh, who had seen that Mzzyan had fallen and that he was somewhere nearby, yelled back, "Father, be careful of Uncle Mzzyan!" At this very moment, Mzzyan, who still had his rifle, lifted it up with difficulty, took aim and drilled his brother 'Amar through the head. By so doing, however, he gave his position away to his brother's son Muh n-'Amar Uzzugwagh; and the latter, horrified at his father's death, rushed up to his Uncle Mzzyan and, with his two rifles, pumped eleven bullets into the latter's body. Then he left, thinking that Mzzyan was dead, but tradition has it that even with so much lead in his body, Mzzyan Uzzugwagh lay in that ravine for another two weeks before expiring. . . . And thus in one day, 'Amar Uzzugwagh, Muh n-Muh Uzzugwagh, Muh n-Si Muhand of Hibir, and 'Amar w-'Aisa all died; and Mzzyan Uzzugwagh was as good as dead, despite the fifteen days of semi-conscious life left to him. Muh n-'Amar Uzzugwagh had won a Pyrrhic victory, and the Ihawtshen came to bury the corpses in the Bulma cemetery.[51]

Now the vendetta began to ramify out in other directions, and the positions of the lineages in the two *liffs* became crystallized. Twenty-five men of Aith Uswir died violently, and this lineage remained solidly in the camp of the sons of 'Amar Uzzugwagh.

In point of time, World War I had now ended in Europe; but the grandsons of the Fqir Azzugwagh were at best only dimly aware, if even that, that a larger struggle than their own had just culminated in an Allied victory. They were more concerned with their own allies and enemies. Now Muh Akuh Uzzugwagh spoke to Aqshar ("Scabhead") n-Bu Yarij of the Imjjat in Hibir, whose brother Muh n-Bu Yarij had long ago been killed by 'Amar

[51] I realize that the repetition of names, and the endless recombinations of them, may at times be most bewildering to the reader; but this is what happens when one is dealing with a society in which there are only a limited number of names to go around! Parenthetically, *akuh* means "younger," in Waryagharland, so that if two brothers—such as Muh Uzzugwagh and Muh Akuh Uzzugwagh—have the same name, one is always, explicitly or implicitly, *amqqran*, "older," and the other is *akuh*.

Uzzugwagh. Muh Akuh gave the Scabhead[52] some money to kill Muh n-'Amar Uzzugwagh, who, after killing his uncle Mzzyan, had become the most powerful man in all of Aith Turirth. (The sons of the Hajj Am'awsh were no longer a real factor to be reckoned with.) And Muh Akuh Uzzugwagh was now the only important and effective member left of Mzzyan's family, as Mzzyan's own sons were still small boys.

Other things were happening in Hibir as well. Mzzyan n-'Ari, on the side of the sons of 'Amar Uzzugwagh, fled from there to l-'Ass as an *adhrib,* and was pursued and shot there by a brother, still living, of Muh and of Aqshar n-Bu Yarij, the scabhead alluded to above.

Muh n-'Amar Uzzugwagh had now, by 1920 or 1921, been married for three years to one of the daughters of the Mrabit 'Ari of Kinnirth; and one day he was invited by his father-in-law to eat with him. Aqshar n-Bu Yarij was invited also, and after the meal was over, he announced that he had to leave if he was to get back to Hibir before nightfall. So Aqshar left the house, but in fact hid himself behind a rock, with his rifle, not far away. Shortly afterward, Muh n-'Amar Uzzugwagh came out of the house at a call from his wife's sister's husband Muh n-bin Haddu, also of the same lineage (Ibinhadduthen) as Aqshar n-Bu Yarij in Hibir, and also in on the plot. Muh n-bin Haddu, up above the rock behind which Aqshar was hidden, called out, "Oh Amghar!" Muh n-'Amar Uzzugwagh paused in his stride, looked up and replied, "What?"—and Aqshar immediately shot him through the head. (Muh n-'Amar Uzzugwagh's father-in-law the Mrabit 'Ari had also been implicated, as Muh Akuh Uzzugwagh had given him money to invite Muh n-'Amar to his house.)

Muh n-'Amar Uzzugwagh was now dead, but he still had four surviving brothers. Of these, three, Mhand, 'Allush, and Hammadi, went to see the Mrabit 'Ari three months later. They told him to produce Muh n-bin Haddu, who had fled back to Hibir after the killing of their brother, or they would kill him. The Mrabit 'Ari was coerced into accepting; and so one day he brought Muh n-bin Haddu to l-'Ass to eat with Hammadi

[52] A victim of favus; and although Rifians joke a great deal about favoid individuals, they also say that they tend to be very courageous—I only note the existence of this "folk" correlation, but make no comment on it.

n-'Amar Uzzugwagh. After the meal, the Mrabit 'Ari said that he wanted to see his daughter (the fabled woman who was first the wife of Muh n-'Amar Uzzugwagh, then of 'Aisa n-'Amar [the fourth brother], and finally of Hammadi n-'Amar), and left. At this point, Hammadi n-'Amar Uzzugwagh grabbed a billhook (*r-hadida*); he struck Muh n-bin Haddu on the head with it with all his strength, and killed him. He then called his brothers to throw the body into the same crevasse where Muh n-'Amar had fallen.

Meanwhile, Muh n-'Amar w-'Aisa (the grandson of the Fqir Uzzugwagh's old partner) and 'Aisa n-'Amar Uzzugwagh were plowing together on the mountain slope, with 'Amar n-bin Haddu, the brother of the late Muh n-bin Haddu, and his son Muhammad. Hammadi n-'Amar Uzzugwagh sent a woman up to the field to tell Muh n-'Amar w-'Aisa that Muh n-bin Haddu was dead. Immediately on receipt of the news, Muh n-'Amar w-'Aisa dropped his plow, picked up his rifle, and shot both 'Amar n-bin Haddu and his son—both of the latter dropped in their tracks. And once again, the next day, the Ihawtshen took the bodies to the Bulma cemetery for burial.

The next incident: Hammadi, 'Allush, and Mhand n-'Amar Uzzugwagh called the people of Iznagen to come and take away the animals of Muh Akuh Uzzugwagh. But the latter heard what was going to happen and hid himself on the branch of an Aleppo pine; and when the Iznagen arrived, he fired on them and wounded two. At the same time, Mhand n-'Amar Uzzugwagh shot a woman, his own parallel cousin, Fadhma n-Mzzyan Uzzugwagh, and the goatherd of the late Mzzyan Uzzugwagh, both, with a single bullet, as they were standing in the doorway of Mzzyan's house. Thus, two for the price of one, as it were— even though women, under normal circumstances, were exempt from the male occupation and pursuit of bloodfeuding. (It may, however, be debated that this was a normal circumstance!)

But Mhand n-'Amar Uzzugwagh was soon to get his come-uppance. He was plowing his field on a hot day, and he made the great mistake of coming to the house of his uncle, the late Mzzyan Uzzugwagh, now dead a year, to ask Mzzyan's widow for some water. Instead, she gave him poisoned milk; and ten days after drinking it, he died in horrible agony.

Now the Yinn 'Ari Mqaddim of Timarzga, allied by marriage to a very powerful individual, the Hajj Biqqish of the tribe of Igzinnayen (of Ikhuwanen in Asht 'Asim), were to take a hand. 'Allush n-'Amar Uzzugwagh and his *asrif* (wife's sister's husband), Hammadi n-Zaryuhth of Aith Uswir, went together one day to Timarzga to help their affines of Yinn 'Abdallah, who were fighting against Yinn 'Ari Mqaddim. These latter were of course aided in turn by the Hajj Biqqish, for he had given his daughter in marriage to one of them; and he now came across the tribal border to be of assistance.[53]

'Allush n-'Amar Uzzugwagh and Hammadi n-Zaryuhth were in the feuding pill-box of Yinn 'Abdallah, when Biqqish called out to them, "Come out of there—it's not your fight, and nothing will happen to you!" So they came out and then Biqqish, in an aside, told his son-in-law to pick up his gun and shoot them both. His men grabbed their rifles, and the son-in-law of Biqqish shot 'Allush and Hammadi as they were struggling to break free (for a brother-in-law of 'Allush had previously killed his father).

Now Muh n-'Amar Uzzugwagh, Mhand n-'Amar Uzzugwagh, and 'Allush n-'Amar Uzzugwagh were all dead, and their brother Hammadi became family head and *amghar*. His first act was to kill Aqshar n-Bu Yarij, who had killed Muh n-'Amar Uzzugwagh; and the vengeance killing took place in Timarzga, at a wedding in Yinn 'Ari Mqaddim. Hammadi n-'Amar Uzzugwagh and his one effective remaining brother 'Aisa n-'Amar Uzzugwagh came to this wedding, which was given by the killer of 'Allush n-'Amar Uzzugwagh, with some men of Aith Uswir. They saw Aqshar n-Bu Yarij there and told their host that they would either take him or kill all the guests at the wedding. So their host gave Aqshar the Scabhead to them; they took him to the Nkur River, cut him down like a dog, and threw his body into

[53] Biqqish himself was later, late in 1925, poisoned by order of 'Abd al-Krim, of whom he had by then become an unsuccessful rival, in the Wednesday Market of Aith Turirth, after a period of captivity in 'Abd al-Krim's jail in Ajdir. Those of Ikhuwanen (Igzinnayen) and Timarzga (only Yinn 'Ari Mqaddim) in Waryagharland who had sided with Biqqish against the Rifian leader had their houses burnt by his irregulars from Aith 'Arus and Aith Turirth afterwards, for their pains. . . . It was Biqqish, incidentally, who had chased out of Ikhuwanen the old man from there who lived in Bulma in 1955; he had burned the man's house and killed his family. Biqqish was tough, but 'Abd al-Krim showed himself tougher.

the water. And, once again, there was more work for the under-
takers of Ihawtshen.

This state of affairs, no doubt, would have continued indefi-
nitely; but now the Rifian War broke out against Spain, and
'Abd al-Krim appeared as the *za'im* (Arabic) and the *mujahid,*
the "leader" and the "fighter," of the hour (and *not*, as some
would have it, the "Sultan of the Rif," for his government was
only a provisional one, during a war which in the end he lost);
his first act was to call an abrupt halt to bloodfeuds all over
Waryagharland and then all over the Rif in general.

And the new war, against the Spaniards, took its toll on Imjjat.
The eldest son of Muh Akuh Uzzugwagh was killed fighting
against them in Axt Tuzin; and then later in the war, 'Aisa
n-'Amar Uzzugwagh, who had helped to kill Aqshar n-Bu Yarij,
was himself obliterated by a bomb which a French airplane
dropped on the Friday Market at Ikhabbeben, in Igzinnayen, in
1925 or 1926, just as he was saddling up his mule to return to
l-'Ass. 'Abd al-Krim had appointed one Mzzyan n-Hmid of Aith
Mhand u-Sa'id as *qaid at-tabur* of Aith Turirth, with a *harka*
command of 400 irregulars; but this command was finally
switched and given to Hammadi n-'Amar Uzzugwagh, who distinguished himself for bravery in action. After the war was over,
and the Spaniards had, by the late summer of 1926, effectively
occupied the whole of the Jbil Hmam (the French had been
holding it and Aith 'Ammarth during the summer interval after
'Abd al-Krim surrendered), they nominated two shaikhs, Hammadi n-'Amar Uzzugwagh and Dris nj-Hajj Am'awsh, for Aith
Turirth—and old patterns of behavior nearly started to emerge
again. However, the new lowland *qaid* of Aith Waryaghar, another Spanish nominee who had also been with 'Abd al-Krim,
soon removed Dris nj-Hajj Am'awsh from the running: he had
him beaten to death before the year was up for having failed to
turn over two rifles to the Spanish authorities. And now Hammadi n-'Amar Uzzugwagh remained the *mqaddim* of all Aith
Turirth until his death in 1946. In 1938, in the company of
numerous other Waryaghar notables, he had made the pilgrimage
to Mecca and became the Hajj Hammadi. The Mrabit 'Ari had
died in 1936, Muh n-'Amar w-'Aisa died in 1942; and finally,
Muh Akuh Uzzugwagh passed away in 1956. And thus, in Imjjat

at any rate, the members of the older, feuding generation have all gone; their successors remember the foregoing events as recounted to them with a mixture of shame, pride, and regret. . . .

In the second half, the fight between the brothers, of this sanguinary chronicle, at least fourteen people died by violence: five on the side of 'Amar Uzzugwagh (e.g., 'Amar Uzzugwagh himself; his three sons Muh n-'Amar Uzzugwagh, Mhand n-'Amar Uzzugwagh, and 'Allush n-'Amar Uzzugwagh; and 'Amar w-'Aisa) and nine on the side of Mzzyan Uzzugwagh (Muh n-Bu Yarij, his brother Aqshar n-Bu Yarij, and Muh n-Si Muhand, of Hibir; Mzzyan Uzzugwagh himself, and his daughter Fadhma n-Mzzyan Uzzugwagh; Muh n-Muh Uzzugwagh; and Muh and 'Amar n-bin Haddu, and 'Amar's son Muhammad, again of Hibir). Five from nine leaves four, but, in view of the circumstances, only a stalemate had been achieved.

Living members of the Imjjat say, as a result of all the foregoing, that if their predecessors had stayed together as good agnates should do,[54] they would have become the strongest single lineage in all of Waryagharland—and a stranger lineage from the tribe of Igzinnayen, at that. (They are still "strangers," but

[54] As exemplified, for instance, in the collective oath (*r-imin* or *thzaddjith*), decollectivized by 'Abd al-Krim. In the Waryaghar version of this formerly generalized Berber phenomenon, any man accused of any crime short of murder had to swear with five of his agnates (making six cojurors, *yuxshin n-r-imin* or *izuddjen*, in all) in the "Friday mosque" on the Qur'an, and in front of both the plaintiff and the *fqih*, to his innocence. In a case of suspected murder, the accused had to swear in the same way, but with eleven agnates (i.e., twelve in all). And in any question involving men of different tribes, fifty cojurors (the accused and forty-nine others) were needed. In such a case, of course, many of the cojurors were merely fellow-clansmen or -tribesmen as well as agnates. Any male of age to fast during Ramadhan (who had, i.e., attained puberty) could swear; and women could not. Perjury at oath would produce dire supernatural consequences (the accused or any of his cojurors might be struck down by God); if the accused or any cojuror failed to turn up at the appointed time—on Friday, just before the noon prayer—the defendant had to pay the plaintiff. The testimony of witnesses (and twelve ordinary witnesses, or two *'adul* or notaries public, were needed), however, always overrode any denials by the accused or by his cojurors. Edward Westermarck (*Ritual and Belief in Morocco*, 2 vols., London: Macmillan, 1926, vol. I, p. 513) spoke of collective oaths among Aith Waryaghar (he referred to the phenomenon as "compurgation"), but his allusions to them, as well as his overall grasp of the nature of the problem, were fragmentary. Today, in the Rif, as a result of 'Abd al-Krim's reform, only the accused, without cojurors, can swear; women may do so as well.

"strangers *to* Aith Waryaghar" more than "foreigners *from* Igzinnayen"—there *is* a difference. And they are "strangers" who, for example, utterly unlike Ihawtshen—the morticians—attained a high political pre-eminence.) Their claim may be debatable, but it nonetheless illustrates the fact that they were fully aware, all along, that in their case at least, agnatic unity (so touted by social anthropologists) became a hollow mockery. And their case appears by no means to be an entirely isolated one, although they themselves self-reproachfully think it is. I know of at least four others (one in Aith Yusif w-ʿAri of the plain, two in Timarzga, and yet another case in Aith Turirth itself), in three of which there were killings by agnates of each other;[55] and in the fourth (in Timarzga), there was a complete and utter division of property between two full brothers, after one suspected the other of poisoning his wife. (I know both brothers; they would have been at each other's throats if the Spanish authorities had not been present, for in 1954–55 this case was a very lively one.)

Vengeance killings within agnatic lineage groups may indeed be considered utterly deplorable by the surviving members of these groups, or at least deplorable in the abstract (though often coupled with a note of regret to the effect that "our forebears were tougher than we are"); but the data from Aith Waryaghar show that such events have occurred too often simply to be dismissed as exceptions to the rule. And, as a North African (though not a Rifian) proverb has it, "Nobody hates like brothers." Ideally, "blood is not to be sold or mortgaged," as a Waryaghar proverb, to the contrary says: and this, again ideally, applies to

[55] In the Aith Yusif w-ʿAri case, a man shot his paternal uncle, and was then in turn killed by the son of that uncle, who then married the man's sister, his own parallel cousin; and that ended *that*. In the Timarzga case, a man killed his own brother over a question of inheritance; as he had heard that the brother was going to kill *him* over the same issue, he simply acted first. And the Aith Turirth case involved Yinn Hand w-ʿAbdallah, before the advent on the scene of the Fqir Uzzugwagh: three sons of Hand w-ʿAbdallah himself, Tufali, Misaʿud, and bil-Lahsin (all ancestors of present sublineages) ganged up on another son, their own brother, named Kakar, and killed him, again over his share of the inheritance. In punishment, however, they got none of it, and it was divided between the two remaining sons, Bu Tahar and Mqaddim (again both sublineage ancestors), for Kakar had conveniently died without issue. (Even though Bu Tahar did not participate in the actual killing, however, it is said that he tacitly approved Kakar's removal.)

the Aith Waryaghar as much as to any agnatically structured society anywhere. And, let us not forget, according to good solid segmentary principles, the sons of 'Amar Uzzugwagh stuck by their father against his brothers Mzzyan and Muh Akuh, at least. Nonetheless, the agnatic unit of vengeance here became, effectively, an agnatic *sub*-unit; and such cases of fragmentation, to my way of thinking, merit far more consideration than social anthropologists have given them in the past.

VII. REFLECTIONS ON AITH WARYAGHAR: A SYSTEM OF DISEQUILIBRIUM

In conclusion, we can only agree with Montagne's assertion that the Aith Waryaghar have a complex social structure; but I hope that this essay has adequately explained at least some of these complexities. From their point of origin in the Jhil Hmam, we have seen how the Aith Waryaghar proliferated and how their territorial units became reduplicated right down to the sea; we have seen how their organization into "fifths," again often consisting, on the ground, of territorially discontinuous units, was a shared collective response to payments of fines for murder on the tribal level; we have seen how the segmentary system corresponded in some ways to the territorial one, and how it failed exactly to correspond in others; and we have seen that on at least three occasions in its history the whole tribe acted corporately.

The above represents the warp of the social structure; while the woof seems to lie in the *liff*-system of two mutually hostile factions which cross-cut the segmentary and territorial systems. And here we have seen how, on a tribal level, these *liff*-alignments remained constant (or tended to do so), while on the local level they changed continuously. The effectiveness of the intrusive Imrabdhen as mediators and adjudicators was largely negated by the fact that so many of them, taking on a local color, as it were, feuded amongst themselves; and we have also seen that such mediators as there were among them tended themselves to be *imgharen* (though, of course, pacific ones!).

The incredible ramifications and convolutions which a single

feud could take have likewise been examined in detail, and alliance through marriage and hostility through inheritance (and
other reasons) have been duly considered as well. The bloodfeud
was an agent of decentralization and autonomy among local
lineage groups, while payments of fines and the threat of house-
burning were geared to have the opposite effect—to show a murderer that the collective *imgharen* were stronger than he was.
But usually, as we have also seen, an *amghar* too was a killer;
otherwise he would never have become *amghar!*

As Montagne himself pointed out,[56] the bloodfeud, in one way
or another, was the central feature of social life, and the
dispersion-patterns in settlement morphology (one house here,
another on top of that mountain over there, a third halfway up
another slope) of any local community in Waryagharland is a
constant reminder of this fact. All members of the tribe are in-
ordinately proud of being Aith Waryaghar, and for them the
rationale behind the notion of *khams khmas* amounts to a virtual
superiority complex; but the periodic push-together on the upper
levels of segmentation was almost constantly undermined by a
pull-apart on the lower ones, and vice versa.

Albeit constantly interrupted by internal discontinuity and reduplication, the clan, the lineage, and the local community in
Waryagharland (as, of course, elsewhere) all form what is essentially a single structure and territorial continuum; for Waryagharland, *in toto*, is after all a single block of territory. Within
this territory, the bloodfeud could either (1) be almost instan-
taneously turned off so that the whole tribe (or, if not, a whole
"fifth" or a whole clan) could be galvanized into corporate action,
as it was on three recorded occasions in its history, or (2) more
commonly, play itself out *ad infinitum* on the autonomous setting
of an inter- or intra-lineage stage which was set by the local
community, until whole subclans or even clans were involved—
or, indeed, here as well, the other way around. A theory which
seems to enjoy current favor among some anthropologists is that
segmentary systems tend to be linked with the concept of preda-

[56] Montagne, *op. cit.*, 1930, pp. 239–40. I have already discussed the case
history which he gives for Aith ᶜAbdallah in a previous publication (Hart,
op. cit., 1954, pp. 63–64).

tory expansion;[57] and it might even be suggested that as the Aith Waryaghar could not expand their territory beyond certain limits (i.e., the Mediterranean), they turned in on themselves and feuded. (Even so, their expansion was a very long and drawn-out process, and seems to have been accomplished just as much by purchase of land from neighboring tribes, as we have seen in the Aith Turirth case,[58] as by actual conquest.)

Like an accordion, the Aith Waryaghar could and did squeeze together to play in harmony; but, more often than not, the keys were damp, the stops pulled out full blast, the instrument was pulled and (finally) wrenched apart, and the music ended in a discordant screech. Wholly aside from any external conditions at the time, it was to the great credit of 'Abd al-Krim that he knew how to play this accordion (and indeed all other local tribal accordions as well)—but nobody else did. And the final result was

[57] Marshall D. Sahlins, "The Segmentary Lineage: An Organization of Predatory Expansion," *American Anthropologist,* vol. 63, pp. 322–45. The material in this article is primarily taken from E. E. Evans-Pritchard's ethnographic classic, *The Nuer* (Oxford: Clarendon Press, 1940), and from various publications by Paul Bohannan on the Tiv of Central Nigeria. The theory could be nicely adapted to fit the situations of certain Berber tribes in the Central Atlas and the Jbil Saghru (the Ait 'Atta are an outstanding example), and the solid historical evidence provided by Marcel Lesne (*Histoire d'un Groupement Berbère: les Zemmour,* Thèse complémentaire pour le doctorat ès lettres présentée à la Faculté de Lettres et Sciences Humaines à Paris, 1959) shows that this is unquestionably the case for the Zimmur as well; but the validity of the theory for, say, Berber tribes in the Western Atlas (for *all* Berber tribes have segmentary systems) seems questionable.

[58] Emilio Blanco Izaga, in his unpublished *Conferencia sobre Derecho Consuetudinario Rifeño,* 1935, refers to Waryaghar encroachments, all again through purchase, in the Buham region west of the Ghis River, on Ibuqquyen territory. These in fact became so frequent, Colonel Blanco says, that the Ibuqquyen finally decided not to sell any more land to the Aith Waryaghar. In the same work (which I have translated, along with his other work, published and unpublished, on Waryaghar social structure, and hope to publish under the title, *A Spanish Army Officer on the Social Structure of the Moroccan Rif*), Blanco refers to a kind of elasticity (existing within a basic framework of rigidity), regarding tribal boundaries, an elasticity which becomes more permanent when the boundary is a natural frontier, like the Upper and Middle Nkur River between Waryagharland and Axt Tuzin, and the Lower Nkur between Waryagharland and Thimsaman. Cf. also the Waryaghar–Axt Tuzin boundary dispute settled by Sidi Mhand u-Musa in Waryaghar favor, in note 27 of the present article; the fact that it was so settled is not really too surprising, as the Nkur River constantly shifts its course one way or another, after a heavy rain.

hardly that favorite of social anthropologists, a (virtually time-less) equilibrium system; it was, rather that paradox, a system of *dis*-equilibrium *in* equilibrium,[59] and a system in which, as I view the matter, in fact as opposed to theory, segmental opposition outweighed segmental balance, on virtually all levels of the scale.

ADDENDUM

I finished writing the above essay in April 1965. Early in December of the same year, I learned that the bloodfeud within the lineage of Dharwa u-Fqir Uzzugwagh had at long last had a "happy ending": for in August of the same year two marriages of classificatory (and cross-generational) parallel cousins took place to heal the breach (one hopes) once and for all: one of the youngest sons of Muh Akuh Uzzugwagh (who died in 1957) married a granddaughter of 'Amar Uzzugwagh; and a grandson of 'Amar Uzzugwagh married a great-granddaughter of Mzzyan Uzzugwagh. Not only is this the first (and dual) instance of marriage between the descendants of 'Amar Uzzugwagh on the one hand and those of Mzzyan and Muh Akuh Uzzugwagh on the other that has (except for one case) yet happened, but it also illustrates another principle: that an expanding lineage can occasionally afford to be endogamous. (An earlier marriage in 1957 between an older son of Muh Akuh Uzzugwagh—probably hastened by his father's death—and a slightly older great-granddaughter of 'Amar Uzzugwagh had possibly begun to pave the way for the exchange of 1965.) The rates of endogamy in the lineages of Yinn Hand w-'Abdallah, Aith Mhand u-Sa'id and Aith Uswir, for example (all lineages local to Aith Turirth), are certainly somewhat higher than the endogamy rate in the Imjjat lineage of Dharwa u-Fqir Uzzugwagh. The latter were late-

---

[59] As manifested throughout, on all levels, by the feud, and in the overall *liff*-system, by the fact that three does not equal two, for, in effect, three "fifths" were pitted against two; e.g., ½ of *khums I* (Aith Yusif w-'Ari plus Aith Turirth), ½ of *khuns III*(Aith Bu 'Ayyash "Proper"), all of *khums IV* (Aith Hadhifa plus Aith 'Arus and I'akkiyen), and all of *khums V* (Imrabdhen), all constituting Faction A, *against* ½ of *khums I* (Aith 'Ari plus Timarzga), all of *khums II* (Aith 'Abdallah), and ½ of *khums III* (Aith 'Adhiya), constituting Faction B. The overall *liffs* were of course conceived as two halves, but in fact they were not; and on the local level, the struggle within Aith Turirth, for instance, was equally weighted.

comers to the region, and not only did they need allies, but they needed them in a hurry. And now, at last, a certain stabilization seems to have been achieved. (The Imjjat still remaining in Hibir, in Igzinnayen, however, are still as divided as they always were, at least as of December 1965, as I write this addendum.)

EMRYS L. PETERS

2. *Aspects of Rank and Status among Muslims in a Lebanese Village*[1]

The main concern of this essay is with the ranked differences between people living in a Muslim (Shi'ite) village of the Southern Lebanon. One group of people is wealthier than the others, and dominates the political life of the village. A number of facts related to the sources of power indicate that this dominance is of an ephemeral kind. According to the rules of inheritance both the sexes are legal heirs, and women can and do alienate property from one family to another. There are no legal marriage bars between the Muslim groups. Peasants work both their own land and that of the power group, taking as the reward for this labour on the land of the power group half the crops produced. These facts appear to make for marked instability in the relationships between the groups. From the evidence I was given, however, the relationships as I observed them in 1952—and I must emphasise that this analysis does not include the events which occurred between that year and my second visit in 1956—had persisted for three generations and probably longer. This account is an attempt

Reprinted by permission of the author and publisher, Mouton & Co., The Hague, Maison des Sciences de l'Homme, from *Mediterranean Countrymen* (ed. J. Pitt-Rivers), Paris, 1963.

[1] The field work on which this article is based was carried out during the years 1952/53 and 1956. My first period of work was sponsored by the Treasury Committee for Studentships in Oriental Languages and Cultures, and the second period by the University of Manchester. I wish to express my indebtedness for their support.

This essay has been read as papers at seminars in the Department of Social Anthropology at Manchester University. I acknowledge with gratitude the comments made at these seminars. My thanks are also due to Miss Ann Lowcock of the Department of Geography, Manchester University for drawing the [original of the] map showing the disposition of groups in the village, and for copying the Arabic genealogy of the al-Hurr family.

at analysing the factors which have contributed to this persistency in relationships.

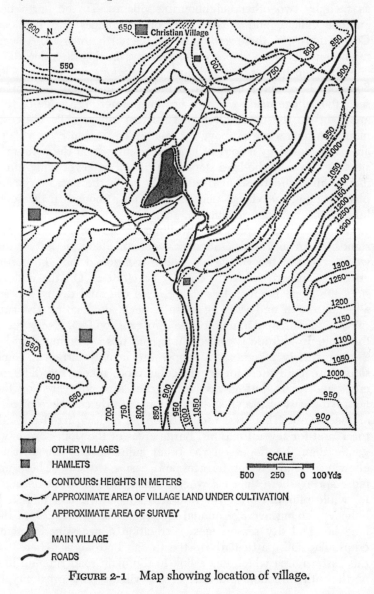

OTHER VILLAGES
HAMLETS
CONTOURS: HEIGHTS IN METERS
APPROXIMATE AREA OF VILLAGE LAND UNDER CULTIVATION
APPROXIMATE AREA OF SURVEY
MAIN VILLAGE
ROADS

SCALE
500   250   0   100 Yds

FIGURE 2-1   Map showing location of village.

The village is large compared with others in the same area. It is the main market centre for two nearby hamlets, and is used as such by two other neighbouring villages. To the north lies another village, and beyond this other villages and hamlets. Connections with these settlements to the north are weak. A deep ravine and its steep slopes make journeys in this direction difficult, but the barrier is chiefly one of religious differences. The Southern Lebanon is inhabited mainly by Muslims of the Shi'ite sect; the village discussed here lies on the northern edge of this area, and to the north of it lie Christian villages. To the east, mountain ranges tower above the village. To the south the village area is enclosed by a spur of land protruding from the mountain side. To the west the land slopes sharply off to lower lying hummocky hills, and these in turn tumble on to the narrow coastal plain, leaving the village perched high on a mound in the foothills of the Lebanon mountains.

The mound, on which the dwellings of the village are found, stands at an altitude of about 2,500 feet. Steep slopes on the western side of the village have been mentioned, but the northern and southern sides are equally precipitous. On the eastern side, the slope is much less steep. Here the land drops into an alluvial trough and rises again to a peak, dominating the surrounding landscape, at an altitude of over 4,000 feet. Everywhere the range in altitude is considerable, and this is accompanied by a great variety of crops. All slopes are heavily terraced. Some slopes are cultivated for a particular crop, others for different crops and so on, but an account of the crops cultivated on the land lying east of the village will afford a fairly complete picture of the variety. This area, too, is the most highly prized agricultural land for several reasons. Large areas of the slopes are more gentle than the slopes on the other sides of the village, thus allowing slightly wider terraces and easier working. There are more springs here than elsewhere; springs are an asset on land, for while rainfall during the rain season of November to March is heavy, giving average annual aggregates of 50 to 60 ins., the long hot and dry season makes irrigation a necessity for some crops. The soil, particularly in the trough bottom, is richer. It is this eastern area which has a link to the main road running in a north-south direction and east of the village, and proximity to the road gives land an added value. On this land the following crops were grown; tomatoes, eggplant, peppers, beans, peas, cabbages, a few oranges, potatoes, quince, radishes, lettuce, cucumbers, marrows and myrtle.

Immediately above the trough, on its western and eastern flanks, the land is steeper, terraces narrower and their walls higher. Many of the crops grown in the trough appear in reduced quantities on these slopes, but this is predominantly an area of fruit tree growing. Formerly, this area was largely given over to the mulberry bush, but since the decline of the silk industry, the mulberry, save for a very few bushes, has disappeared. The apple is rapidly taking the place of the mulberry. Two men, who had the capital and foresight to do so, converted some of their plots at these altitudes into apple orchards in the late thirties; although small, these orchards are now reaching maturity and bring in handsome returns. During the middle nineteen fifties more and more people were converting to apple growing. Higher altitudes, where land, formerly, was cheaper than elsewhere, have been found suitable for apple orchards, and land here and in the middle altitudes is appreciating in value. Peasants, some of them very poor, have been the beneficiaries of these windfalls, and already, one or two have sold such land and reaped profits sufficient to enable them to alter their position materially. While the spread of the apple was rapidly gaining momentum, the area of land it occupied was still small.[2] Large areas in these middle altitudes are still dominated by walnut trees, their whitish ghost-like forms giving an eerie touch to a landscape so frequently enshrouded in cloud during the bleak January days. In addition, plums, pears, figs, pomegranates, sugar cane and olives are widely grown. It is here, too, that poplars and oaks—both used as beams for the poorer houses of clay, stones and wood—are planted, some land owners having sufficient trees to sell a small surplus to timber merchants.

Higher still, on land which is drier, where there are few springs, but which has large stretches of level land, vineyards and cereal growing flourish; pear trees also appear here. Terraces are lower

[2] As late as 1956, when I last worked in the village, save for the two mature orchards planted before the Second World War, all the apple trees in the village were still in the nursery stage.

and therefore easier to maintain, although the run-off of water in winter is so severe that repair work is an annual chore; but this is offset by the availability in quantity of large stones, which are also of value for terrace work on the lower slopes and for house building in the village.

Beyond the vineyards, the land rises almost sheer. Here there is little opportunity for cultivation, because the soil cover is thin, the slopes too steep for terracing and run-off of winter rain is too severe. Here and there clumps of pine trees—the property of the village municipality—occur, and the few goats owned by the villages range the slopes nibbling the shoots of wild bushes.

Only the most characteristic products of the three areas have been included in this catalogue of crops, but sufficient have been included to illustrate the great range of products. Little, however, has been said about the sort of plots on which these products are grown, save that the width of the terraces differs at the various altitudes. In addition, the land is severely dissected longitudinally. Where the terrain is steep, and in a climatic environment marked by heavy winter rain followed by prolonged drought, the topography is characteristically diversified. Deep ravines, twisting this way and that, break it up into small blocks of cultivated land. The nature of the landscape together with the range in altitudes gives a multiple crop economy, and militates against compact estates. Plots are small, often only 400 sq. yds. or less, and the property of any individual landowner is scattered widespread over the altitude range.

A critical factor in this type of economy is not only that a broad subsistence basis is provided by the wide variety of crops, but that crops ripen in succession. A small labour force is all that is necessary, therefore, to manage a considerable number of plots conveniently. Unlike some other rural areas, where harvesting is a race against rain,[3] the productive unit of an estate does not presuppose a pool of reserve labour to gather in any of the harvests. Peasants, in a sense, constitute a reserve of labour for various purposes, but since the harvests are relatively small for each product, the concerted efforts of a large number of people are unnecessary. Small family groups of four to six persons manage each successive harvest, and the communal groups, such as those

[3] See Arensberg, 1968, Davies and Rees, 1960.

found in Wales and Ireland during haymaking, are absent. Multiple crops, coupled with a succession of harvests, render the formation of a large co-operating group unnecessary; landowners do not have enough plots in any one area growing one crop only to require a large labour force at a critical time of the year. Harvesting begins in June, when barley and a fodder crop are gathered. Wheat ripens soon after, and no sooner has this harvest been reaped than apricots are ready for picking—a pleasant task, for apricots are not grown in quantities for export and the picking takes the form of picnics in the gardens, families and their friends enjoying eating the fruit and leaving only a small quantity for jam making. Early July sees the beginning of the first big fruit harvest: plums. These are picked, boxed and exported to merchants in the coastal towns, to whom they are sold for cash. At about the same time, and while some members of the family are engaged in packing plums, chick peas, for animal fodder, are gathered by others. Towards the end of July, maize—grown only in small quantities for domestic purposes—ripens. The biggest single harvest in the calendar is the grape harvest. Several varieties are grown. Harvesting of grapes extends over several weeks, and because the period is not critically short, there is no need to call on a large amount of extra labour. All able-bodied members of the peasant families join in the grape harvest, beginning in a somewhat desultory sort of way towards the end of July by stripping the vines which are trained up the walls of houses, and picking the riper fruit from the vineyards. The labour involved in collecting the harvest is arduous. For many people it also means transporting the grapes from distant plots to the village square or to the house. Throughout the hot days of August men and women toil until sunset, and at the end of the day the menfolk are still left with the tasks of loading boxes on to donkeys and carrying a heavy load themselves; the women, in the meantime, have left for home to prepare the evening meal. But for all the hard work, the grape is considered a good crop to grow. It needs little attention; the returns are good; it provides quantities of jam for most households and most people grow a sufficient surplus to bring in a substantial income.

At the beginning of the grape harvest, but before serious picking begins, tomatoes and beans are collected. This is an easy task because both crops are grown near the village. Some of these crops are consumed immediately, and quantities of both are preserved for the winter. They are also good cash crops.

Throughout August, the eggplants and marrows ripen, but these again are grown nearby, and are managed easily. August is the busiest time of the year. Every member of the peasant families is fully employed. It is now that the strain of collecting crops, managing the household and performing various other necessary duties, is greatest. Relief is brought at this time of year by the addition of some 400 to 500 souls to the village population. Most of these summer visitors are kinsfolk of the permanent residents in the village. Some of them are women who have made over their village plots to their brothers and who in return reside in the village for the three months of high summer, together with their husbands and children. Others are people who have rights in plots of land; they may even own plots there, but are content to leave them in the keeping of relatives, providing they are given accommodation and a share of the products during their summer visits. A small number own plots, but have farmed them out to peasants on a yearly contract, and they are there to collect the contracted share of the products. Some have houses which have been occupied during the winter by either poor friends or relatives, who in summer live in bush huts built in trees in the gardens. Others move into houses of relatives, and reciprocate by allowing their country relatives to live with them in their town dwellings during the cold winter months. Only a small number of these summer visitors are relatively wealthy people from the coast, retreating from the humid heat into this mountain village, where they rent houses. The latter do not affect harvesting in any way, but kinsfolk, although grown too refined for the rigorous labours of full-scale harvesting after a few years of city life, nevertheless contribute significantly to the agricultural life of the village at this time of year. They help considerably in making jam and other forms of preserve; they deal with the daily routine of household chores and help with the picking of crops grown in the immediate vicinity of the houses. Compared with the work done by the permanent villagers their efforts may appear trivial, but their contribution is important in that the villagers are freed from routine tasks to proceed with the business of harvesting; at a time when the peasant labour unit is strained almost to breaking point, assistance of this sort is vital.

During the early part of September there are still some grapes to be gathered, and figs are also ready. The apple crop in 1952 was still small and concerned only two orchard owners, but it is in the first part of September that the two varieties grown locally ripen. Mid-September is still the period of the walnut harvest, above all else. Most people in the village have at least one tree; some have sufficient to export the nuts to coastal towns. Walnut picking and the gathering of beans continues into mid-October, when olives begin to ripen. Olive picking takes about a month, and after the fruits are collected, they are taken to be pressed for olive oil, all of which is consumed locally. As far as harvesting is concerned, the rest of November is a slack month, because the only fruit now ripening is the orange, but this fruit is cultivated only by one person in the village, since most of the area is unsuitable for it. November can be a busy month, however, if the rains begin then. As soon as the soil has been drenched, ploughing commences and wheat, lentils and fodder seeds are sown. Heavy rains after the long drought also mean that breaches are made in terrace walls and repair work for the peasants is heavy.

December and January, both wet and cold, with high winds whistling round the houses, are busy months for the peasants. Routine jobs such as ploughing, sowing and repairs to house and terraces must be completed during these months. Also, cabbages and cauliflower have to be cut and potatoes lifted. In the past mulberry leaves, food for the silk worms, were collected in February, but with the disappearance of the mulberry, there is now a lull in activities until March. Ploughing and sowing in March begin the new cycle of activities.

Throughout these winter months there is much coming and going between the village and the coastal towns where, climatically, it is much pleasanter. Wealthier people stay in the coastal towns for all or most of the winter. Younger people take it in turns to have a break from the monotony of the village. Only the 'land labourers' are tied to the village throughout the year, and even some of them manage a short visit to the coast when repair work is not urgent—a visit to which they look forward, because while in the towns they earn a small amount of money as casual labourers. Otherwise there is a demand for their labour in the village, and each morning, after daybreak, they congregate in the village square where people compete for their services.

Cows and goats are not reared in the village on a large scale, so that much of the meat consumed is brought from outside, either on the hoof or bought in the coastal towns.[4] Other imported foods are, mainly, rice, macaroni, and small quantities of flour. Within the village redistribution of products is carried on, either between individuals or through the small shops. In this way, people who have a surplus of one crop can either trade it to a shopkeeper for credit to his account, or exchange it with a friend or a relative for some other product. But most people aim at as broad a subsistence pattern as possible from their own plots; the emphasis in the first instance is on variety rather than a surplus of one crop, which might fail or not fetch a good price if there is a glut. A second aim is to have a series of crops ripening in succession, giving a well-balanced spread throughout the year, so that a minimum labour force can gather each harvest. The pattern of land holding, therefore, is that each head of household aims at an estate consisting of two or three plots in the lower altitudes, a similar number in the middle altitudes and a plot each for vines and cereals at the higher altitudes. Since the introduction of the apple as a cash crop some landowners have tried to concentrate their estates, but this was the pattern until 1953. By this time one wealthy man, who was the first to plant apple trees, and who had made every effort to concentrate his orchards, had only managed to increase his main orchard to just over an acre; this was of very irregular shape, and was divided into 11 plots, but it was the largest single orchard in the village. There are many reasons why it is difficult to concentrate an estate. People are unlikely to sell a plot at a given altitude unless they are confident that they have enough of the products grown there; neighbouring plots may be difficult to buy because it is recognised that kindred must have first preference, and after them, owners of adjacent plots—indeed one of the easiest ways of extending part of an estate is to marry a woman who is heiress, or likely to be heiress to an adjacent plot, and scores of marriage

---

[4] There are only 80 cows and 6 bulls belonging to the village, for example. No sheep are reared.

arrangements, which I recorded, attest to this fact. In addition, the topography itself is against the development of large compacted estates. The land is broken up by steep drops, deeply eroded gulleys and ravines, protruding spurs and a generally irregular surface.

In this area of small-plot cultivation, the big landlord, met with elsewhere in the Lebanon, is absent, for not only do individual owners aim at an altitudinal spread of plots, but the total estate owned by one person is relatively small. There is considerable discrepancy in the size and value of estates, but there is not a single individual whose estate is overwhelmingly large. Those who own a large number of plots argue that the more they own the greater the problem of supervision of the separate plots becomes. They grumble bitterly that they are cheated constantly by peasants who work their plots, not to speak of the petty pilfering that goes on. It is very difficult to supervise plots adequately during the harvesting of various crops, and for that matter at any time when the trees are in full leaf. It may be a relatively easy matter for one or two watchmen to guard a compacted estate, but it is difficult to guard plots distributed over a widespread area, and the costs of supervision would be prohibitive. Although there are no large landowners, estates vary both in size and the way in which they are managed. These variations closely follow differences of rank among the inhabitants, and it is to this matter that I turn my attention before discussing other aspects of land holding.

The total population of the village is about 1,100.[5] This figure represents, in round numbers, the number of people who are considered to be permanent residents of the village, together with those who spend some time in the coastal towns, and also, those who spend much of their time down on the coast, but who visit the village regularly throughout the year and who spend the entire summer there.

In this population there are four main categories of people: the Learned Families, as they style themselves; the shopkeepers, all of whom are petty traders as well; the peasants; and, lastly, the Christians. The population of the Learned Families represents

[5] The population varies greatly from season to season, and even within a season.

about one fifth of the total population. The men of these families
bear one of two titles—either Shaikh or Sayyid. The Shaikhs constitute about four fifths of the population of this Learned Family
group. Theoretically the title rests on the acquisition of religious
knowledge, over a very long period, at the Shi'ite Muslim University of Najaf in Iraq; only a very few earn it in this way, but it
is also accorded to a certain group of people by virtue of their
birth. Anyone considered to be descended from an historic figure,
one al-Hurr, who fought alongside the Prophet Muhammad's
grandson (Husain Ibn Ali Abu Talib) at the battle of Karbala
is also said to be an authority on religious matters, is addressed
as Shaikh and permitted to wear a white turban as a mark of this
distinction. Most of the Shaikhs are included in the al-Hurr stock
group. In addition to these Shaikhs, three men (one of them ex-
ceptionally wealthy) of different origin are included with them.
These three men claim a long tradition of religious learning for
their ancestors, they have inter-married with persons of al-Hurr
stock, and in 1954 they legally changed their family name to
al-Hurr in the hope, among other reasons, that it would be of
some advantage to them in an impending Municipal election.
Three other men and their sons have recently been accorded the
title, but their connection with religious learning is tenuous, and
has to be traced through lateral kin links to an elder who claims
scholarship and has in fact published a book and some articles.
In origin, these three men were of peasant stock, as their marriages, some fifty years ago, into poor peasant families clearly
indicate. By various means they have recently acquired relatively
large amounts of wealth, and have given their sons a Western
education in Beirut. Their wealth, their sons' education and their
elder's pretensions, together with their political influence in village affairs, have earned them the title of Shaikh, although there
was noticeable reticence among the villagers to accord them this
rank. They were, I was told, not 'religious Shaikhs, so to speak'
and they did not perform the traditional services of Shaikhs.
These services are performed by the al-Hurr Shaikhs who are
the recognised authorities on theological and legal matters.
They officiate at marriages and at funeral and mourning ceremonies; they conduct public prayers; when a person wills a 72
hour prayer to be said over his grave after his burial, it is they

FIGURE 2-2   Map showing the disposition of groups in the village.

who do it; they act as witnesses to wills and to property transfers; they effect divorce when required to do so; they are also available for advice on domestic matters and so on. In the past, they captured whatever administrative posts have been avilable in the village—mayor, *mukhtar,* municipal clerk—and all the teaching

posts in the village school, including the headship, have been in
their keeping. Traditionally literate, they have been the bearers
of Islamic culture in the village, living a relatively sophisticated
and leisurely life, enjoying a range of social experience outside
the village, and entertaining and vetting whatever distinguished
visitors appeared in the village from time to time. Their rank is
a source of income to them. Most of the services they give are
for payment, either in money, kind or favours. Among them
there is a rough division of labour. Those who hold administrative appointments do not perform religious services as a rule, but
surrender this monetary advantage to their kinsmen who are not
as well placed. In either event only very few of them fail to
derive income from their rank as religious and literate people,
and this income is significant in the maintenance of their status in
the village.

The Sayyids, who are distinguished by their green turbans, are
also considered to be versed in religious matters, are literate, and
function generally in much the same way as the Shaikhs. Yet their
authority rests not on their acquired religious knowledge, but on
the claim to be descended from Ali as-Saghir, the son of Husain
Ibn Ali Abu Talib. He was one of the few survivors of the battle
of Karbala and is counted as the fourth Iman of the twelve which
this particular sect of the Shia' recognise. By virtue of this
descent, the Sayyids are accredited with *Baraka*, which gives
them the power to bless.[6] Traditionally, they say prayers for the
dead; they are always present at religious ceremonies; they are
devout in their prayers and so on. Services given by the Sayyids
are supposed to be free, but they should receive the *Zikat*, or one
tenth of the fruits of the earth. Some peasants still give the Sayyids their religious dues—but nothing like a tenth—some make
payments in kind but a cash payment is nowadays the usual re-

[6] During my first visit, several evenings were spent in the roofless house of
a Shaikh debating the issue of whether Sayyids possessed *Baraka* (spiritual
blessing derived from their direct links with the Prophet Muhammad) or
Qadasa (holiness). Some thirty men of different social status in the village
would gather there on summer evenings to discuss points of theological
nicety, under the light of the moon, whilst the host conducted the 'seminar'
from his position in front of a samovar. Although a minority insisted that the
Sayyids were holy, the theological weight of opinion and the numerical majority were prepared to recognise only *Baraka* in the Sayyids.

ward.[7] The Shaikhs and the Sayyids, in addition to their religious dues, also owned relatively large areas of land in the village, but the discussion of this is better deferred until something has been said about other groups of people in the village.

The petty traders do not constitute as clearly defined a group as the Shaikhs and the Sayyids. All the senior men of this group wear the red fez, and although peasants in the village were not formally prevented from wearing it, very few of them did. Most of them also wear European-type suits and their womenfolk aspire to the habits and dress of the Shaikhly ladies, who wear the veil and black clothes and leave the house only in company or with an escort. As a group they are better housed and enjoy a higher standard of living than the peasants. They are distinct further because shopkeeping is confined almost exclusively to a small number of families. Of the twenty small general stores in the village, fifteen are businesses conducted by men of two patronymic groups: three contiguous shops are owned by four brothers, who all sell virtually the same goods, and all compete fiercely. The shopkeepers and their women and children constitute under one fifth of the total population.

The peasants traditionally wear felt hats, shirts and trousers with baggy seats and narrow legs; the younger men are turning more and more to wearing European clothes. Their womenfolk, gaily dressed in coloured clothes, are unveiled, walk about the village freely (except for the village square), gossip in little groups on corners and move freely to and from their gardens. The peasants and their women and children constitute more than three fifths of the total population.

Finally, a few Christians also live in the village. When I took a house to house census in 1953, they numbered only twenty-three in all, although a few had recently left, and some returned later. The relationships between the Christians and the Shi'ite Muslims present interesting problems; for example there is a bar which has the effect of proscribing their relationships in a number of fields. But the important fact in the present context is that, as a group, the Christian population appears to have remained static for the

---

[7] The Sayyids enjoyed minor benefits such as, for example, free rides on the bus and taxi which served the village.

past two or three generations; any increases of population seem to have been curtailed immediately by emigration.

The distribution of population among the various groups shows the Learned Families to be numerically weak in relation to the total population. Yet the land owned by this group almost equals that held by the peasants and petty traders together. I surveyed an area of a little over 31 acres for size of plot, type of crop grown and ownership over two, sometimes three, generations.[8] The Shaikhs and Sayyids together own 14.5 acres, and the peasants and petty traders own 15.3 acres. The Christians own 1.4 acres, but this represents practically all their land in the village, and it would appear that although they participate in local political life, the Christians are not strong enough numerically or economically to exert significant influence on it. I have introduced them to complete the account of the distribution of population and of land holding, and to indicate very briefly why I virtually exclude them from the particular problems of this essay. If the land held by them is therefore discounted, what is left is an area of just under 30 acres distributed almost equally between the group of the Shaikhs and Sayyids and the rest of the population.[9] In other words, half the village land is in the hands of a group which represents only a fifth of the total village population. This statement as it stands is an inaccurate representation of the situation, for the Learned Families do not work their own lands: their rank precludes them from doing so. Only one of them, a poor man married to a peasant woman and whose mother was also a peasant,

[8] Land in this part of the Lebanon had still not been surveyed as late as 1956. Consequently, I had to make a tramp survey of my own of some 300 plots, and if the area surveyed appears to be small, I can only comment, by way of apology, that the work had to be left until the winter months, when the weather was foul and the task of tramping through mud and climbing terraces was an arduous one. In addition to this detailed survey, I made similar enquiries about an area almost as large. There is nothing in this information to suggest that the conclusions I draw from the detailed survey are invalid. A number of reasons governed my choice of area for survey: there is greater competition for land here than elsewhere; the full range of crops are grown there; there is greater diversity of ownership than elsewhere, and I was able to get a fair representation of the distribution of land among the various families.

[9] I appreciate that this gives little idea of the difference in the capital value of land held by the two groups, but I was unable to arrive at any accurate figure for this.

worked his lands. A few others—and only the poorer—planted small plots of such things as tomatoes, and replaced fallen stones on the terraces, but even when faced with penury, some of them neither work their land at all nor collect any crops. Labour in the garden is considered undignified for the Learned Families. It is even more undignified for their womenfolk. I do not recall ever seeing a woman of the Learned Families assist in any way with work in the gardens; only rarely do they visit the plots and then the visit takes the form of a picnic in summer. These women suffer another disability as landowners. Their status precludes them from making arrangements with peasants to work their lands. The menfolk do this for them. So that in the event of a woman being left a widow with either small children or only daughters, or in the case of spinsterhood, the administration of her estate has to be controlled by one of her kinsmen. For these services the kinsman is given a share of the products, and, if the woman is a spinster, she rewards the kinsman for his services by making him her heir. Indications of property transfers of this sort can be readily picked up in the genealogies, for a man gives the name of his benefactress to one of his daughters, irrespective of his kin relationship to her. Such transfers of property occur among petty traders and peasants as well, and among them, if the heir nominated is either a niece's husband, a sister's son or a daughter's husband, this means the alienation of the property from the owner's patronymic group. The significance of land, therefore, is not the same for women of the Learned Families as it is for their menfolk, since if the working of land for men pre-supposes peasant labour, for the women it also presupposes a male who is prepared to make all the necessary arrangements for them.

Petty traders are not subject to the same disabilities in working their plots as the men of the Learned Families. They do what they can to their plots when they can spare the time. As the status-seeking group they do not plough themselves, but engage peasants to do this. If they do not collect all the harvests themselves, however, it is because a number of crops ripen during their busiest time of the year. These tasks are performed for them by peasants who buy from their shops, and the cost of the labour is set against accumulated debts or as credit against future purchases. Tied by debt to the shops in this way, peasant labour is more readily available to the petty traders than it is to the Learned Families, and this is important in a situation of increasing competition for their labour. Other arrangements between peasants and traders are also negotiated. A peasant, if his debts had increased too rapidly, for various contingent reasons, offers the entire crop of say, one vineyard, months in advance of the fruit ripening, on the understanding that he harvests it, and that part or the whole of his debt is liquidated. If the crop turns out, later, to be a good one, the shopkeeper gains; if it is poor or fails, the loss is carried by the shopkeeper. Petty traders also take into account the garden products which sell best in summer when the village population is at its maximum. Their pattern of land holding aims at conforming to this need. If they lack this or that product for sale in their shops on their own land, the deficiency can be made good, in part at least, by entering into an arrangement with peasants whereby the latter agree to hand over a negotiated quantity of a crop at a certain price either as liquidation of debt or as credit against future spending.[10] Debt relationships between shopkeepers and peasants are intricate, and since they are so largely in terms of garden produce in exchange for goods, they affect the general way in which the shopkeepers view their land holding, the areas they wish to increase, the type of products they aim at growing and, since marriage carries with it rearrangement and transfers of plots of land, the specific marriage links between them and the peasants.

The people best able to exploit the land to its maximum are the peasants. Men are not prevented by custom from performing any agricultural tasks, save that there is a certain amount of division of labour between the sexes; neither are the women restricted in their economic activities; they can visit their plots unescorted and work there without impediment. Within the general norms of propriety women are therefore unrestricted in working on the land, although if a woman is compelled through widowhood or spinsterhood to arrange for the working of her land, it would be improper for her to bargain with men for their services in public; arrangements of this sort are delegated to a

---

[10] Only rarely do the peasants enter into these arrangements with the Learned Families.

male kinsman of her choosing. Even so, such women among the peasants—unless incapacitated by ill-health or age—are better placed to enjoy more of the products of their land than are the womenfolk of the Learned Families. Peasant men are in the strongest position of all, for they work their plots themselves— ploughing, sowing, harvesting, repairing terraces and so on—and take all the products. More importantly, the proportion of the products the men of the Learned Families surrender in payment for labour goes to the peasants. The value of land, therefore, varies with the social position of the individual owner; it also varies with the sex of the owner.

This is of the utmost consequence in viewing the distribution of land between the two groups, since a considerable proportion of the products of the lands of the Learned Families are alienated to the peasants in this way. Numerous arrangements exist for the payment of labour, depending partly on the tasks required, the general condition of the plots, and the crops to be grown. Generally, the most favoured arrangement is that whereby a peasant takes over a plot of land, accepts responsibility for providing all that is required for working it properly (a team of oxen, plough, seeds, boxes for gathering and so on), gathers the harvest and delivers the correct share of the products to the owner. For this, the peasant's reward is half the products. This means that, in terms of yield, the Learned Families receive roughly one quarter of the total land produce, and the rest of the people receive three quarters of the total. The discrepancy between the products of land enjoyed by the Learned Families, and the proportion they represent of the total population, compared with products accruing to the rest of the population, is narrowed to the point which makes competition between the two inevitable. In other words, the margin between the two, in terms of the number of souls supported by the land products, is too narrow to enable the Learned Families to dominate the peasants completely, if land is their only source of wealth. The margin is narrowed further because parcels of land held by the Learned Families may lie fallow. There are two reasons for this. Among them, land disputes are chronic. All members of these families are intricately involved in inheritance, for reasons which will appear presently. Since they derive additional income from their reli-

gious and other services, the need to settle disputes over inheritance is not as urgent as it is among the peasants, some of whom
are so poor that failure to divide land or at least agree about its
use would mean starvation. Peasants must reach a settlement of
disputes summarily; the Learned Families wrangle among themselves for long periods over the disposal of this or that plot to this
or that brother or sister. One of the best pieces of land, bequeathed by a man of the Learned Families to his five sons, has
been lying fallow for some thirty years because the brothers have
failed to agree on its division; the dispute has cost them more in
litigation than the value of the land itself. Others among the
Learned Families attempt to solve the difficulty by leaving their
inherited estate undivided. In some instances these brothers have
not divided their father's house either, but occupy various rooms
of it as separate elementary families, their rooms facing a common courtyard. Such groups have all the appearance of joint families, but if joint families in other countries are constituted by
bonds which tie its members as kindred and for the expedient
management of estates, this is certainly not true of this village.
Joint families are bound here by hostility. It is because they cannot divide rather than because they wish to remain undivided
that they are held together. They are points of conflict in this system, not nuclei of cohesion. Further, while they may agree on the
use to which most of their plots are to be put most of the time,
they do not always agree on the use to which all their plots are to
be put all of the time. Consequently, in some instances an entire
estate is left to lie fallow and run to ruin.[11] When finally they
agree the land has to be restored to good condition and terraces
rebuilt. A peasant only does this if he is permitted to take all the
products of a number of seasons for the period he estimates is
required for full restoration; and what usually happens is that
the peasant begins by working hard to get the plots in full
production quickly, but for the last year of the arrangement he
allows them to deteriorate again in the hope that the arrangement will be renewed. Inheritance disputes among the Learned
Families therefore deny them a further share of the products of
their land.

[11] In one dispute I recorded brothers could not agree even on a picker for
their walnut trees, and thus denied themselves the fruit.

Land belonging to the Learned Families may lie unproductive for another reason. They have to rely on the peasants to work their plots and to grow the particular crops they require. These arrangements are made usually in late autumn when the peasants assemble in the village square shortly after dawn, and those requiring their services proceed there to try to persuade them to accept particular arrangements. The bargaining does not affect the proportion of the crop to go to the owner and peasant, but the crops to be grown and the plots to be worked. A Shaikh may find a peasant ready to work a plot for him a long distance away up the steep hills because the latter happens to have a plot in the same area, but they may not want the same crop grown. Plots near the village are always attractive but a Shaikh may find difficulty in interesting a peasant because the former may wish to grow eggplant and the latter beans. The interests of landowner and peasant do not always coincide. The aim of the landowner is to grow the full range of crops permitted by the distribution of his plots; the aim of the peasant is to make up the deficiencies of his own estate with products from the estates of the Learned Families. While the wants of the Learned Families remain fairly constant from year to year (save for rotation on some plots) the peasants' needs vary conspicuously from year to year. In one year he may, for example, decide to devote some of his plots to potatoes and green vegetables; this being so, he would not accept an offer from a Shaikh to grow more of these. The peasant may find he had too great a surplus of plums one year and will not be ready to take on the plum harvest for a Shaikh the following year. Changing needs, with a great proliferation of crops providing great latitude for permutations in relationships, is a situation not conducive to the development of enduring patron-client relationships between the Learned Families and peasants. My records show that it is unusual for a peasant to work for the same member of the Learned Families for more than three years in succession. Peasants, as a group, are tied to individual members of the Learned Families. The consequence of this, in the context of this discussion, is that a landowner may be unable to reach an agreement to work all his plots. In any given year, therefore, some of their plots may lie fallow, and the following year there

may be added to the cost of labour for growing a product the
expense of cultivating the plot anew.

When all the disabilities suffered by the Learned Families are
taken into account, it will be appreciated that the margin between them and the peasants with regard to the yields of the
land is delicately balanced.

Land is an area of serious conflict between the groups of the
village. It is certainly true that the competition for land is most
obvious within each group, between siblings, between heirs of a
man's several wives, and between nieces and nephews of spinsters. It is particularly obvious in the field of marriage when a
woman with property is available. Among both the men of the
Learned Families and the rest of the village there is abundant
evidence of ruthless competition for such women, one man taking
advantage of his first cousin's serious illness to steal his fiancée
from him; another man vying with his brother for the hand of a
girl, and so on. While not wishing to minimise these areas of
competition, the competition between groups is more relevant to
the present discussion. Disputes across these boundaries do not
break out simply because individuals of the groups are not as
frequently involved together in inheritance of property. One
group, however, sees the other as a threat to its interests. Peasants complain that the Learned Families aim to 'eat' all the village land. The Learned Families view the peasants as a group of
people awaiting the opportunity to buy up land from the poorer
of their members who want to sell. Peasants do not want their
land to pass to Shaikhs or Sayyids; the latter are anxious that their
property should not be alienated to peasants. The way in which
this is achieved will become clear through a discussion of some
aspects of marriage patterns, and the descent framework in which
these patterns are woven.

Among the Shi'ite Muslims there are no marriage prohibitions
arising out of differences in status or rank,[12] and in theory at
least, a man may marry any woman, having due regard to the

[12] Between Muslims and Christians a marriage bar does exist. Contraven-
tions do occur, and are followed by serious consequences. Most mixed marriages I have recorded are of Christian women marrying Muslims, a union
which is permissible as long as the woman is prepared to embrace Islam.
Discussion of marriage among the Christians is excluded from this essay because it does not have a direct bearing on the central theme.

prohibited degrees of consanguinity. It may be inappropriate for a Shaikh to marry a peasant girl or vice versa, but it is not wrong in law:[13] An analysis of marriages, however, shows that there are quite clearly delineated and different patterns for each group. I begin by considering the marriages of members of the Learned Families.[14] Of a total of 115 marriages contracted by the men, some 60.1% are with women of this group in the village. All these marriages will not be parallel cousin marriages,[15] which constitute only 36.6% of the total. Of this 36.6%, 40.5% are first parallel cousin marriages, although this figure would be much higher of course, if expressed as a percentage of the first parallel cousins available. In addition, another 23.5% of the total marriages are within the group. The remainder is made up as follows: 25.2% of the marriages are with women of other villages but of the same or similar status; 8.7% are with women of other places but not of the same status; 6% are with women of inferior rank in the village, but this figure includes marriages that have ended in divorce, and it therefore ought to be added that during 1952 only two men living in the village had wives who were not of their status. For women, marriage within the group is more pronounced. Out of a total of 84 marriages, 82.1% were within the Learned Families group. Parallel cousin marriages account for 49.8% of the total and first parallel cousin marriages for 40.1% of these. Only one of the marriages is with a man of inferior status from the village. The remainder is made

[13] See Fyzee, 1955, p. 92, for the legal position on this point.

[14] I have used both my house to house and genealogical censuses for information on marriage. If the house to house census alone is used the incidence of internal marriages is disproportionately high, for particulars about people who have left the village altogether (particularly those of the generation now dying out) may not be given. Figures based on this census only for marriage within the Learned Families, for example, are about 18% too high. I suspect that some of the exceedingly high figures given for what are called endogamous or parallel cousin marriages in the literature on Arabs in general would be significantly reduced if full weight were given to this point.

[15] Unless otherwise stated 'parallel cousin' refers to persons related through males only. It is hardly necessary to point out that many of these will be cross cousins also. Throughout, I have included as parallel cousin marriages only those where an actual genealogical link can be traced, and I have excluded marriages which merely happen to fall within the patronymic group.

up of marriages to men living outside the village but of similar
status.

In brief marriage is, in the main, within the group, and this
results in such a bewildering complexity of ties between the
members of the Learned Families that, if they are to be unrav-
elled at all, they have to be limited to two generations or three
at most. The Learned Families constitute a genealogically defined stock group; they also constitute a closely knit kinship
group exhibiting practically all possible permutations in relationships. Vis-à-vis the shopkeepers and the peasants they are almost
wholly autonomous; they have strong connections with their
equals in other parts of the country and it is largely through these
links that they have been able to enjoy a range of social experience unequalled by the other village groups. It is equally important to appreciate, however, that many men have married
women of lower status outside the village and that women have
made permanent links outside, albeit with men of equal status.
Both kinds of marriage point to the fact that there is a pressure
for a proportion of both sexes to move out of the village. Further
aspects of these marriages will be discussed when dealing with
the significance of genealogies.

The patterns of marriage for the shopkeepers are significantly
different. The details for men are as follows: out of 50 marriages,
9 were to first parallel cousins (a proportion of the total about
equal to the Learned Families); 7 married within their patronymic groups, but it would be erroneous to regard these as parallel cousin marriages since patrilineal links are lacking, and most of
them are clearly cross cousin marriages; 2 were to women of a
different shopkeeper patronymic group living in the village; and
16 were to peasants in the village, and an equal number with
women of other places. Neither men nor women married into the
Learned Families. The marriages of women show a similar pattern. Of the 48 recorded, 9 married their first parallel cousins,
and 7 within their patronymic group; 2 were to men of a different
patronymic group; 18 married peasants in the village and 10
peasants living elsewhere; and finally 2 married traders living
on the coast. The general pattern is that marriage with close
cousins mainly on the father's side runs high; between these close

relatives and more distant ones there is a conspicuous gap across which lines are thrown into peasant families or outside the village altogether. Save for the latter, these general directions taken by marriage connections are, it will be seen, repeated with certain modifications for the peasants.

Patronymic groups among the peasants vary in population to such a degree that average figures for all the groups taken together would be misleading. Some of the larger of these groups show a high first parallel cousin marriage figure. Some of the very small groups show great variation from none at all to a high figure—one very small group for which information on four males was recorded showed three of them married to their first parallel cousins. Obviously, if the group is very small, and assuming a desire to marry first parallel cousins, the rate will be very erratic since it depends on the contingency of one man having daughters for his nephews to marry. A better picture of the peasant marriage pattern appears when individual patronymic groups are examined, and for this reason I propose to give the details of two here.

	GROUP A		GROUP B	
	Males	Females	Males	Females
Total Number of Marriages	49	46	15	10
1st Parallel Cousin	4	4	2	2
Other Parallel Cousin	4	4	—	—
1st Cross Cousin	1	—	—	—
Other Cross Cousin	1	1	1	—
Within Patronymic Group	11	11	—	—
To Shopkeepers	2	1	—	—
To Other Peasant Patronymic Groups in Village	20	20	10	8
To Peasants of Other Places	7	5	2	

Close parallel cousin marriage is still high, but outside this range there is a conspicuously low rate of marriage with cognatic relatives. An outstanding characteristic of the peasant pattern is the large number of marriages to other peasant patronymic groups in the village. It should be added these are not concentrated on links with only one or two such groups, but with many. The 20 such marriages shown for Group A (Males) are with women of 14 different peasant groups; for some other groups this figure reaches the maximum. This pattern of marriage provides a widespread dispersal of links among the peasant groups.[16] Peasants do not, however, reckon patrilineal descent beyond two or three ascending generations as a rule. Consequently many of my marriage records show no relationship between the spouses which, if in their descent reckoning they included one or two more ascending generations, would appear as third or fourth parallel cousins or cross cousins of similar degree.[17] This will become clearer in the discussion of genealogies which follows, but before beginning this it is necessary to make some brief remarks about the inheritance of property.

The laws relating to the inheritance of property are complicated; practice complicates matters even further. Any brief statement, therefore, can be no more than a general guide. First and foremost, it must be emphasised that the Muslims of the village are of the Shi'ite sect and follow Shi'ite law. Of cardinal interest in this context is that Shi'ite law places relationships through men and women on an equal footing. Secondly, while women inherit among Sunni as well as Shia', they can and do become sole heirs among the Shia' of this village. Moreover, since they inherit property they can alienate it from their patrilineal or patronymic group. In one way or another, women come to accumulate large amounts of property. On marriage a land settlement is made on them, and until the terms of a settlement have been agreed, the marriage is not legal.[18] This settlement remains the property of the wife, and is not included in the share of her husband's property to which she is entitled if he pre-deceases her. On her husband's death her share of the inheritance varies with the circumstances. She takes one quarter if there are no children, an eighth if there are, and if she is the sole surviving heir she may take all. As a daughter she inherits with sons in the proportion of one to two. Women can also affect the distribution of

---

[16] I have examined over 300 marriages contracted by men and over 200 by women of the peasant group. The general conclusions offered here are confirmed by this wider analysis.

[17] If the figures were based on statements of relationships given by the people themselves the figures would not be substantially different. They count only the closer relationships.

[18] The settlement takes the form of land in most cases. Sometimes a cash sum is included with land and only occasionally is the settlement entirely in money.

property in other ways, some of which will be mentioned later. In practice a woman may not, for various reasons, receive her legal entitlement, or she may relinquish it, although when this occurs she usually acquires rights to the services of those who benefit. What I wish to make quite clear here, however, is that women accumulate property and can and do alienate it from their father's group. This being so, then clearly property considerations will significantly influence marriage patterns.

These patterns are also affected by the mode of descent reckoning. The discussion will now concern this matter, to be followed subsequently by an assessment of the combined effects of marriage patterns and descent reckoning on the rank and status differences which exist in the village.

People of any group in the village are prepared to assert that members of the Learned Families have a long ancestry. This is true, but it is also true of the peasants or of any other people the world over. What people of the village assert in effect, is that the awareness of this ancestry is important for the Learned Families, but not for the shopkeepers and peasants. This is so because the rank enjoyed by the Learned Families is based on birth in a particular line of descent. Few of the men of the Learned Families knew all their genealogy, but one of them did, and it was this person who was generally acknowledged to be the authority on the history of families, on theological problems and on religious law. Each generation seems to have produced one such leading scholar or Keeper of the Culture, as I will refer to him. In 1954, an eminent Shaikh, who had served his generation with distinction in this role, and who had a published theological thesis to his credit, died. Some years earlier, because he had become senile, his place had been taken by another Shaikh in his late fifties, who had already published several articles dealing with the history of local distinguished families. He was also grooming a younger man of the Sayyid section to succeed to his position. Both this Keeper of the Culture and his novice were anxious to give me their genealogy. They began by drawing up a document entitled 'The Relationship Between The Learned Families', in which they were concerned to give me the marriage ties within the group, to show that, 'We are like one family, because we are of one weave, and this is knowledge'. What they did, in addition, was to draw up a list of the mature men who were to be included in the genealogy. They began, that is, with the base of the genealogy, the contemporary group. Various changes affect the group from time to time. Some lines peter out through lack of heirs; others proliferate over-rapidly, causing some people to leave the village for other places in the Lebanon or to migrate to neighbouring countries, to the Americas, or to West Africa. Other people included in the contemporary group may be the descendants of men incorporated into the group a few generations ago, some of whom are included in the genealogy even though they are known by the living to be of different origin. In the first stage of constructing the genealogy, the past history of those to be included was irrelevant. Their next step was to cluster these people into small groups of males related to each other through a common grandfather or great-grandfather. These clusters the Keeper of the Culture wrote on separate pieces of paper, and when he had finished the result was a number of unconnected clusters, any one of which did not differ significantly from the form of peasant genealogies which I recorded. I have no reason to doubt that the jottings on the separate pieces of paper were completely accurate statements of patrilineal kinship for the several separate family clusters. After completing this task the Keeper then began setting out the genealogy proper, placing the first name he wrote, the ubiquitous Muhammad, in the centre of the page.[19] From Muhammad, the Keeper then drew two lines into the bottom half of the page, and enclosed the two sons, Sa'aid and Ahmad, in circles. Two very old living men were the grandsons of Sa'aid and Ahmad, and on their evidence, they can be accepted as genuine historic persons. There have, however, been many Sa'aids and Ahmads in the past, and whether these two particular persons occupied the position attributed to them in relation to the genealogy in general, is another matter. Further, these two men contracted four marriages between them, one of which was a leviratic marriage. As a result of these marriages, these two men begat four sets of children. Two males among these children

---

[19] This Muhammad is shown on the Arabic genealogy of the al-Hurr family for 1956 in the circle which is bisected by the line dividing the cultural past from the contemporary families. The genealogy included here is a replica of that made for me by the Keeper of the Culture.

THE GENEALOGY OF THE AL-HURR FAMILY
1956

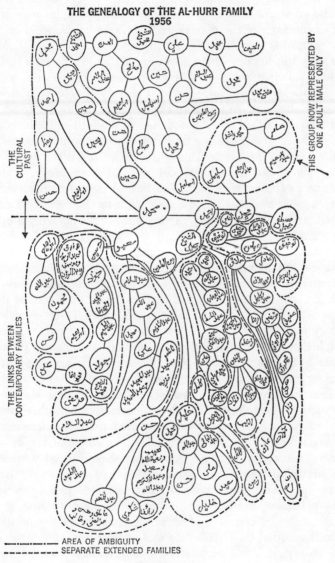

AREA OF AMBIGUITY
SEPARATE EXTENDED FAMILIES

FIGURE 2-3

married two of the females, and in addition others married within
the Learned Families. The result is a highly complex network of
ties in this area of the genealogy. The exact relationship of their
descendants is a problem for most members of the group, and it
was only the Keeper of the Culture and his novice who had the
temerity to claim that they knew the solution to the problem. All
the small clusters of families which already had been drafted on
separate sheets of paper were now written on to the genealogy
and linked to Sa'aid and Ahmad, and through them to the central
Muhammad, giving them a nodal ancestor some five generations
removed from the living. This completed, the Keeper of the Culture then added the upper portion of the genealogy, which I
refer to as the cultural past. The Sayyid novice constructed his
genealogy in exactly the same way, with the help of the Keeper.
When completed its form was very similar to that drawn up for
the Shaikhs.

Peasant genealogies differ significantly from those of the
Learned Families in two important respects. They lack a long
descent line connecting them with the remote past; they also
lack a nodal ancestor. Instead, their genealogies tie living males
only to a grandfather or great-grandfather. Their genealogies
closely resemble the small clusters of patrilineally related males
which the Keeper of the Culture drafted on separate pieces of
paper before putting them together on his genealogy. But the
peasant clusters are left unconnected, ending abruptly after two
to four generations. Patronymic groups of various sizes—some
with a total population of only a dozen persons, others with a
total of well over 100 persons—exist among the shopkeepers and
peasants, but, of the forty separately named groups, only eight
showed a connection to a single ancestor, and in all these cases
the maximum number of generations was only three. In the
larger of these groups, men bearing the same patronym would
deny patrilineal relationship. I doubt very much whether people
of these groups conceive of their relationships in the patrilineal
form I recorded them. If left to reckon their kin without prompt-
ing, they gave complex bilateral connections within a range of
some two generations. In short, the groups in terms of which they
habitually thought were bilateral kin groups, not patrilineal descent groups.

Men of the Learned Families, it might be argued, remember their ancestors better than the shopkeepers and peasants because of differences in the use of names. The mode of address in speaking to a male of the Learned Families is to preface his personal name with the title of Shaikh. Among the shopkeepers and peasants the mode of address is to prefix his first born son's name with 'father of'; the use of his personal name would amount to insult.[20] Only after a man of either of these groups has made the pilgrimage to Mecca is his personal name used, prefaced in this case by *Hajj* (pilgrim). What is certainly true is that men of, say, two or three generations ago are better remembered as 'father of so-and-so' rather than by their personal names. This usage, however, cannot account for the difference in length between the descent lines of the Learned Families and the others, since there is no reason why a continuous descent line of many generations could not be remembered for the peasants from the names included in the mode of address they use. On the other hand, the use of the personal name does tend to fix individuals of the Learned Families, unlike the merging of generations implicit in peasant usage. Among the peasants, a man has lost his individual identity once his wife has borne him a male heir. I was told that when a man becomes father to a son he has fulfilled his purpose, 'he is finished; it is as if he is dead'—and the same applies to a woman after she has borne a male child. Among the Learned Families men ought to distinguish themselves as individuals in the field of scholarship, or leadership or as wise counsellors, so that they may be remembered for their individual qualities after their death. The Keeper of the Culture, in his account of members of the Learned Families which he wrote for me, added frequent glosses to men's names: the gifted scholar; the faithful servant; the honest slave (of Allah) and so on.[21] The insistence is in giving men a distinguished individuality; the distinction for

20 A mature man who fails to have male children is addressed by his father's personal name, prefixed by 'father of'; e.g., a man named Muhammad, and whose father's name was Ibrahim, would be called 'father of Ibrahim' if he had not begotten a male heir. This practice is consistent with the custom of naming a man after his grandfather.

21 One gloss—to my astonishment—made a neighbour of mine out to be a 'lamp of knowledge'; he hid his light under a bushel, while I resided in the village, most successfully.

a shopkeeper or a peasant is to create an individual, and in doing this his own individuality is lost.

While there is this insistence on the significance of individuality of each male who has survived to maturity among the Learned Families, not all males are included in the genealogies. The shape of the genealogy in the first five ascending generations up to Muhammad is a clear indication of this. The first two ascending generations, reckoning from adult males, include a large number of names, the third many fewer, the fourth only two, and the fifth only the one man, Muhammad. Changes of various sorts have occurred. Some left the village never to return, and their names are no longer recalled except when the older men are prompted to give them. Others have not left issue. At the same time the group has incorporated new members. The line Yahiya-Husain-Yahiya, placed on the genealogy in what I refer to as the area of ambiguity, is openly admitted not to be of the al-Hurr stock. It is included because two men of the line married into the Learned Families; the second of them died without leaving any children, but left substantial wealth which was inherited by several members of the stock group after his widow died.[22] Again, three living men, affinally and matrilaterally connected with the al-Hurr group, legally adopted the name al-Hurr in 1954 (see p. 86). In short, some men of the Learned Families who are unable to make ends meet in the village, are sloughed off to other towns or villages locally or to other countries, while at the same time new members—wealthy people in all the cases I have recorded—are recruited into the group.[23] There was, therefore, a certain amount of mobility into and out of this seemingly rigidly fixed stock group of the Learned Families. Its composition changes over a period, and these changes must be comprehended

[22] The position of this line changed between 1952 and 1956 on the genealogies drawn up by the Keeper of the Culture. In the 1952 version their descent line was lengthened to show them among the living or recently dead; at this time the disposal of the property left by the last of the line was a live issue. By 1956, the property dispute had been finally settled and the line was relegated to what I have shown on the genealogy as the area of ambiguity.

[23] It ought to be pointed out that my evidence shows these recruits to have come into the village from elsewhere with a claim, at least, to traditional religious learning. The three men who were incorporated in 1954 claimed, in addition, that they were of the same stock as the al-Hurr group in the remote past.

by the genealogy. A genealogical statement of descent is fixed and rigid and cannot, if it is to remain historically authentic at every point, comprehend social reality. It was for this reason that the Keeper of the Culture began his work of constructing the genealogy with the contemporary reality of small extended family groups. These men had to be included, even though it necessitated manipulation of past ancestors on the genealogy. They also had to be linked up to the nodal ancestor. This point in the genealogy was, it will be recalled, the first position to be fixed. It is in this linkage to a nodal ancestor that the genealogy of the Learned Families differs critically from that of the shopkeepers and peasants. It conceptually made of the former a united stock group; the peasants and shopkeepers appear as fractionised extended families, with emphasis on affinal and cognatic links. It remains now to compare genealogies tied to a nodal ancestor with those showing multiple ancestral points.

In the first place, a linkage through a nodal ancestor provides a ready frame of reference for the regulation of marriage. Whether they marry patrilineal parallel cousins, matrilateral cross cousins, or affinal relatives, they are marrying within their own group and in a sense all their marriages are with parallel cousins, as they themselves point out. Though, as has been stated, women inherit and transmit property, as long as marriage takes place within the stock group, its lands are not alienated. Thus connections through marriage are fed into the field of property, giving great complexity in the rights to land, and making the task of unravelling them very difficult. Another aspect of this complexity is the intense competition among males of the Learned Families for women who happen to be holding relatively large amounts of property. I give as an example a brief description of some of the events concerning the marriage of A and B, and C and F, shown in Figure 2-4; the diagram shows only a part of the complexity of the kin relations which were involved. During the middle forties, F was betrothed to E. Subsequently, and before the marriage took place, E, who had been ailing for some time, suffered a serious illness from which he died. During his last illness, G pressed H to break the betrothal between F and E, proposing instead that F should marry C. This proposal was accepted by H, and C married F forthwith. C himself was known to be in love

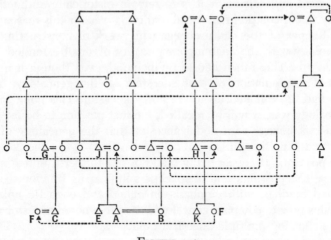

FIGURE 2-4

with another of his cousins, but his father's (G) will prevailed.
J was greatly angered that the betrothal of F to his son E should
have been broken, particularly at a time when his son was seriously ill, and claimed that this mean act had hastened his death.
G and C had a small shop from which J, naturally, bought; he
promptly revoked his custom and has not bought from them
since. Later on, in the early fifties, K became engaged to B, but
almost immediately afterwards left for South America. His plan
at the time was to spend two or three years there, accumulate
savings and then return to the village to take B as his wife. While
he was in South America A began negotiating for the severance
of the betrothal between B and K. His ally in this scheme was
L. At the time the latter began to enter local politics and came
forward as a candidate for the office of mayor; but he was a poor
speaker, whereas A, although still young, had a reputation for
oratory. L very much wanted A on his side. A agreed to make
speeches and L, for his part, agreed to press for the severance
of the betrothal between B and K. The pretext used for this was
that K had promised to return within three years but had not
done so. L wrote to K saying that B could not be expected to
wait any longer and that if he did not return immediately, he, L,

would sever the betrothal—as a senior Shaikh he had every right to do this and knew that if the matter went to court he would be upheld. K protested saying that he would be returning very soon, that his absence was not unduly long and that it was not the custom to break off betrothals in this way. His pleas availed him nothing. The betrothal was broken and B was promptly betrothed to A. In 1956, they married. K's father, H, who earlier had so angered A and his father, J, by agreeing to break a betrothal between his daughter F and A's brother, had the tables turned on him for his son now was made to suffer a similar fate. I must emphasize that I have isolated only a part of the relationships involved, and I have reduced the number of people mentioned to a minimum, for had I analysed all the various components in the situation it would have been necessary to have included all members of the Learned Families. This remark would be equally true for a discussion of any of the marriages among people of this group.

While there is thus a great deal of internal conflict built into the relationships of members of the Learned Families, as long as the bulk of marriages recur within the genealogical framework of the group, the threat of alienation of property is removed. Marriage therefore is strictly controlled. If the men and women of the Learned Families married solely for love, the whole structure of their position in the village would collapse.

Marriage with the peasants and shopkeepers would lead to the alienation of the property of the Learned Families and constitute a threat to their position as a land owning group. Loss of status is usually given to account for the small number of such marriages between them and other groups in the village. It is a serious matter for one of their menfolk to marry a peasant girl, but since status and rank are carried by the male, the children of such a union remain Shaikhs although they will have kin of inferior status. If a woman of the Learned Families marries a peasant, the matter is much more serious because she then has to assume the role of a peasant woman, work in the gardens, abandon the veil, change her style of dress and mix with the peasantry. With regard to the movement of property, reference may be made briefly to two family histories, those of the two surviving men of the Learned Families married to peasants. One

married his wife after first impregnating her, so that an heir
within the family was ensured in advance; the land settlement
was small, but in any event it was secured for the group by an
heir. The second man, the son of a peasant mother, himself married a peasant; he had been poor but was improving his lot,
and although he carried the title of Shaikh he lived a mode of
life akin to the peasants, tending his plots himself and doing all
he could within the limits of his skill, strength and equipment—
the only member of the Learned Families who lived this sort of
life. His daughter, who had relationships with the peasantry
through her mother, married a peasant against her father's wish,
and caused general consternation among the Learned Families.
Whether or not this daughter had heirs, there was a strong threat
that property from the Learned Families would move through
her to the peasants.

There is not the same threat of alienating property of the
Learned Families when marriages occur outside the village.
Many of these marriages have been contracted by men who have
left the village for good, who have either sold their property in
the village, or who have been disinherited, or who have traded it
with a close kinsman for the right to enjoy summer residence in
the village at this man's expense. In any event whether it is a
male or female who goes away to marry the likelihood is that the
property will be sold to a kinsman, or surrendered in exchange
for other rights or given as an outright gift, because, unless it
can be looked after by the owner it is of little value. A woman,
by chance however, may become sole heir to property, and thus
be able to alienate the land or its cash value to a man of similar
status in another village. In some of the cases for which I have
evidence, women have relinquished their rights to property in
the village to their kinsmen. Men control the marriage of their
womenfolk, and, obviously, arrangements of this sort can be
made part of the bargain. Moreover, in response to this problem,
the spinster rate is high: about one spinster to every five married
women.

The genealogical framework, with its nodal ancestor, is, I suggest, critical to the marriage and property arrangements of the
Learned Families. The absence of a genealogical framework, and
particularly the lack of an apical ancestor to their descent lines,

is of equal importance when relationships among the remainder of the village are considered.

The fact that peasants lack an elaborated genealogy means that when the forms of marriage characteristic of the Learned Families occur, they have a different significance. First and second parallel cousin marriage among peasants is as high as it is among the Learned Families, but the incidence of third or fourth parallel cousin marriage is very much lower—and this is bound to be so, since the genealogical framework for conceptualising these more distant cousins is absent; the peasants, like members of the Learned Families, also marry cross cousins; they also employ other forms which appear among the Learned Families. Any marriage within the Learned Families, however, assists in maintaining the lands of the group intact; cross cousin marriage among the peasants shifts property from one patronymic group to another. The significance of a particular marriage form lies not in the form itself but in the frame in which it is set. The same form can make an estate or break it. A nodal genealogical ancestor ensures that any marriage within the framework of which he is the apex retains property within the general estate; the multiple ancestors of the peasant patronymic groups ensure that some forms of marriage will necessitate a transfer of property from one group to another, but in both cases, the incidence of close parallel cousin marriage is high. This can be viewed partly in terms of individuals attempting to enlarge part of their estates by marrying women who have plots of land near theirs in this or that area. Indeed, viewed in terms of the acquisition of property by individuals parallel and cross cousin marriages represent attempts to expand the total land holdings of an individual or to extend a particular plot or plots at a certain altitude. The shopkeepers and peasants, lacking an extended lineage, are concerned only with the individual estate. Among the Learned Families individual acquisition is compatible with the maintenance of the property of the group as a whole. Since women inherit, the marriage forms, and the property movement which accompanies them, critically affect the pattern of land holding, giving marked differences between the pattern of the Learned Families and the others. These two different patterns are best illustrated by two examples, one from the Learned Families and one from the peasants.

I begin with the example taken from the Learned Families. When A married B, eight parcels of land were brought together. The girl B was the only surviving child of her parents; she captured the property of both of them. Her father had married before he took B's mother, and B acquired the property inherited by her father from this wife. B's mother's sisters were spinsters and, after her betrothal to A (their matrilateral relative) they made B their sole heir. A was the only surviving son of his parents. He had three sisters one of whom married, went to live in Palestine and surrendered her share of her parents' land. A second married a Shaikh who had indulged in extramarital relations with a peasant girl whom he married and then divorced after she had borne him a child; he was fortunate to be given A's sister as a wife, and agreed to her surrender of her share in her parents' land. A third had married well and was apparently willing for her brother to succeed to her share of the property. These arrangements were accepted largely because A remained at home until both parents died, nursing first his elder brother through a long illness until his death, then his mother through years of illness and his father for several months.[24] In addition he had also looked after the property of his father's sister; in 1953, she had already made over her property to him on condition that she should be allowed to continue to enjoy the products of her lands for the rest of her life. A's marriage to B reassembled the property of eight people, which in previous generations had undergone many vicissitudes—fractionisation of plots, expansion here or there, contraction in other places and so on.

Not all marriages are affected by the same property contingencies as affected the marriage of A to B. Differences, however, are only in detail, for such is the complexity of relationships that each and every marriage carries with it a property dispute and a reshuffle of plots within the land holding of the group. Some marriages effect a reassemblage of plots to constitute a bigger

[24] For a number of reasons, the sisters wished to revive the whole issue of inheritance after the death of their father in 1954, and during my second visit to the village in 1956, a dispute of a kind so familiar among the Learned Families was well under way.

estate than the parents of either spouse enjoyed. At the same time other marriages represent, in terms of property, less of an estate than that enjoyed by either of the parents. In the succeeding generation the pattern may undergo a kaleidoscopic change. This, of course, includes only one part of the total land held by the group; other parts are experiencing similar vicissitudes but at different times, the one part dovetailing into the other, and resulting in a highly intricate pattern.

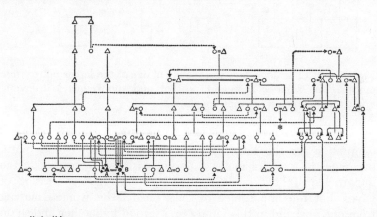

FIGURE 2-5

The peasants, by contrast, display a significantly different pattern. The genealogical diagram below (Figure 2-6) shows the actual details of marriages (and hence of property movements) for a portion of one of the larger patronymic groups. Characteristically property moves out of one group of origin into several others. At the same time the group of origin receives from many others. In short there is a high degree of circulation of property among the peasant groups. The vehicle of mobility in property can be cross cousin marriage, but it only becomes significant as such when a nodal genealogical ancestor is lacking. Other links can also have a similar effect: they can be affinal links of various sorts, or sometimes they are links created by the movement of a divorcée from one husband to another or a woman contracting

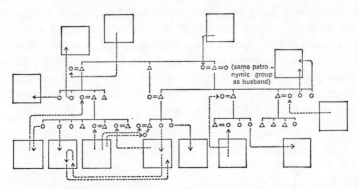

FIGURE 2-6   The genealogy is a section of one of the larger patronymic groups. The squares represent peasant and shopkeeper patronymic groups with which it has marriage links.

successive marriages due to the death of her spouses. There is temptation for the investigator to think of divorce and plural marriages in terms of males. I do not wish to underestimate the importance of links made by one man having a succession of wives, but the importance of links created by women moving from one husband in this family to a second in another and so on must be given full weight also. Many marriages which at first sight appear to have no social significance, become intelligible when the marital histories of both men and women are known. Thus a woman may give her first husband a son, pass on to a second, third or even more husbands, giving each of them children. The son by her first husband, through his mother, will have relations with all the children she bears for her various husbands, and in addition will be permitted social relations with the daughters of his mother's husbands by other wives. In this way a man comes to have social access to unrelated women which otherwise he could not enjoy. Moreover, through his mother again, he will have property relations with these children.[25] And it is these

25 At this point, I wish to make my view on the relationship between marriage and property quite clear. Marriage necessarily contains a property relationship because it is instituted by a settlement on the bride which usually takes the form of land. This is not the same as saying that property relationships are always decisive in determining a match. The starting point of any marriage is an agreement between two fathers on the desirability of

links which provide the motive for some peasant marriages. I give below an example of the sort of thing I mean (Figure 2-7).

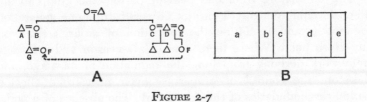

FIGURE 2-7

G, the heir of A and B, married, in 1953, F, the heir of D and E. The strips to which there are heirs are shown in Figure 2-7B.[26] Their marriage resulted in the fusion of the four separate plots a, b, d and e. Neither is heir to C, but I was told that C might be offered another plot in exchange for the one she now holds as her marriage settlement and which lies between B and D. Nothing was being done at the time lest C should predecease A, in which event D (since both his sons by C were small children) could do much as he liked with the plot. In any event, there are various forms of pressure that can be put on person owning plots in positions similar to C's, to sell out to the owner of plots on

a union, and it is after this that discussions about the disposal of plots of land are commenced, not the other way about. The desire for a particular union arises out of social relationships, and these are often formed in a whimsical manner. For example, women making the pilgrimage to Mecca are conducted there and instructed in the rituals by a guide, who is a native of the village, and who is required to enter into a special form of marrriage with relatives of the women (usually very young girls or babies) in order to establish a kin relationship with the pilgrims, so that he may have free social access to them. Similar marriages often occur between men who have merely become friends, so that they may enter each other's houses without having to wait for the womenfolk to retreat from view. Many people are thus fortuitously linked through this special kind of kinship, and indulge in unhampered social relationships, just as a woman passing from one man to another in successive marriages, generates social relationships between people. Such links occur outside the context of property, but may give rise to marriage. The stress in this essay is on the reshuffle of property which occurs after a marriage has been made; had I been dealing with problems of kinship, other aspects of marriage would have been given precedence. For this reason I wish to stress that the reduction of marriage to property relationships is not merely an oversimplification, but a fundamental error.

26 The diagram of the land involved was drawn for me by the informant himself.

either side. Whether the link is cross cousin, affinal, or of the sorts described above, the effect on property movement is the same; it is kept circulating from one peasant patronymic group to another, levelling out the disparities in wealth from one generation to another and inhibiting the formation of a large estate at any given point. Where there is a nodal ancestor and a lineage framework deriving from him, the regulation of marriage, and therefore the control of property movement can be effected within the boundaries of this framework. The absence of a nodal ancestor and the consequent disappearance of a lineage framework, means that the conceptual framework for keeping an estate among kin is lost. Short unconnected descent lines facilitate the transfer of property among people for whom land is scarce; nodally connected lines restrict property movements away from people of rank.

The presence or absence of a nodal ancestor is crucial not only in the context of marriage arrangements. It is through this ancestor that the Shaikhs are able to conceptualise their separate parcels of land as constituting an undivided group holding. They themselves speak of all the land having come to them from Muhammad (the nodal ancestor) and that they are involved in each other's property for this reason—they are certainly deeply involved jointly in the land but on account of their bilateral connections rather than of their descent from Muhammad. This notion that the total group holding belongs to them all, through their ancestor Muhammad, has important practical consequences. They can see themselves as a group and act as one in situations when their common interests are affected. Thus, in 1955 all the male members of the Learned Families met to discuss the recent sale of relatively large areas of land by one of their number. The man guilty of this was reminded that this land was not his to do with as he liked, but to care for and hand on to his son who in turn could increase his holding by marrying a daughter of one of his kinsmen; he, it was said, would be the first to complain if, when his son married, the wife would have no property to add to his; if he went on doing this sort of thing, the whole group would be relegated to the status of peasants. Under the symbol of a common ancestor the entire group can rally together against the threat of peasant encroachment on to their land. The peasants lack the unifying sentiment of common descent, and although the Learned Families are clearly defined for them, the idiom in which they speak is of the threat to this or that individual's property, not to the land of the group.

The sentiment of common descent from a nodal ancestor of five ascending generations remove, is not the only bond which holds the Learned Families together. Beyond him, in time, their genealogy shows a series of other ancestors. Save for those in the area of ambiguity, the names in this part of the genealogy are those of the revered leaders of early Islam or of the Prophets. It is of course true that these names are currently in common use in the village, but there are many others also. It seems doubtful that in the past only these names should have been used, and the repetition of names increases these doubts—the name Muhammad occurs seven times, the name of Husain four times, the name of Hasan three times, and all the others twice. But there is no need to debate the accuracy of this part of the genealogy; the Keeper of the Culture gave his genealogies first to my wife in 1952 and to me in 1956; what is referred to as the 'Cultural Past' area of the genealogy showed considerable differences in the two versions. Inaccuracy was of little consequence, however, since what the Keeper wished to demonstrate was that the Learned Families have a long line of distinguished and scholarly ancestors which carries this history deep into the past. Neither did these lines link up with their ultimate ancestors. The Keeper saw no need to do this when everyone knew them to be descendants of Islam's early heroes. Shaikhs, as everyone in the village knows, are descended from the noble al-Hurr Ibn Yazid al-Tamimi, who fought with Husain at Karbala; they know too that the Sayyids are descendants of the same Husain, the Prophet's grandson, who gave his life at that battle for the true religion of Islam.

The long line of ancestors is important not for its accuracy as a statement of descent but as an indicator to a past from which the present Learned Families derive their contemporary position in the village. The rank of these families, while it rests heavily on the amount of landed property in their possession, is strengthened and validated by their claim to be the representatives of the true Islam, learned in its ways and committed to it by descent. This connection with the past gives them, too, their pre-eminence in the major celebration of the village—the Miracle Play of Husain. They sponsor it, they control the casting of the parts, they hold the script, they collect the funds for it, and are in complete charge of the proceedings on the day it is performed. No discussion of social differentiation in the village would be complete without a reference, however brief, to this Play. I was told about it soon after my arrival in the village in 1952, and for several months before its performance it was discussed daily. It occupied universal attention in the village; it required long hours of rehearsal for many men; it was costly for the people—practically everybody contributed some money to the cost of hiring camels and horses and equipment. Its performance was watched by everyone who could walk or who could be moved up the hill to the village common ground which served as a stage. Yet this Play is not compulsory even for Shi'ite Islam, and there are some Shi'ite scholars who hold that it should not be performed at all. It is the only non-compulsory religious festival of the village. All other religious celebrations are major festivals common to Sunni and Shi'ite Islam alike. There are no first fruit ceremonies or harvest festivals in this village though they have a long history in this land and are held in many villages today.[27]

The Muslim festivals which are celebrated annually in the village are general to Islam, and have no connection with the seasons; they are tied to a lunar calendar, and therefore fall at different times of the year over a period of time. These festivals belong more to pastoral Islam[28] and, in a sense, are incongruous in the setting of this village. They are not in their historical origin, nor in the form they take, nor in their timing, intimately linked to a peasant way of life. But they are compulsory whereas the Play is enacted in very few places, in the Shi'ite world only. Yet, in this village, the people have chosen to hold it—and the word chosen is used deliberately here because, in 1952, they were consulted by the Shaikhs before the matter was decided. The argument, then, is that while Islamic festivals have to be celebrated whether or not they have any social referents, since the Miracle

[27] See Tannous, 1949.

[28] I can vouch, from my experience among the Cyrenaican Bedouin, that among pastoralists they are different both in the form they take and in the significance given to them.

Play is optional for people of the Shi'ite sect and the people of this village have chosen to celebrate it for as long as anyone could remember, it will display consistency with some aspects of the social life of this particular village.

In other parts of Islam, festivals are held which bear a direct relationship to the economy of the people. Among the Cyrenai-can Bedouin, for example, one of the major festivals is sheep shearing, which is not a festival prescribed by Islam. In this village where so many people spend so much of their time working on the land, and where the land moulds so many social relationships, it is not made explicit in any of the rituals or ceremonials. Perhaps the local economy does not lend itself to celebrations. Harvests are ranged in succession over most of the year. There is an absence of a definite opening and closing to the harvest season; harvesting begins in a desultory fashion and trails off at the end of the season. The same is true of the individual harvests. There is no definite time of the year which can be referred to as, say, the grape harvest, because harvests overlap to a marked extent. It is difficult to evaluate one crop higher than another, because although the rating of crops in terms of their cash value can be ascertained, this rating may not correspond to a rating in terms of sentiments attached to crops; what is an important crop for one man may not be for another, and a man's evaluation of his crops may change from year to year in any case. Finally, and most importantly perhaps, a large communal labour force is not necessary for gathering the harvests. These factors taken together are, I suggest, associated with the absence of rituals and ceremonials directly related to the land.

The Miracle Play of Husain is concerned with political manoeuvres during the early history of the Caliphate, and the schism between the Sunni and the Shia'. It commemorates the historic battle of Karbala, fought by Husain Ibn 'Ali Abu Talib, and a small band of his followers, against the armed forces of the Caliph Yazid (whom the Shia' regard as a usurper), on 10th October 680 A.D. During the battle Husain was slain and his supporters almost completely annihilated. Of the few survivors, one of importance in this discussion is Husain's son, Ali The Younger (otherwise known as Zain al-Abidin); he is important because the Sayyids of the village claim to have descended from him.

Of the participants in the battle on Husain's side, al-Hurr needs special mention because the Shaikhs claim to be his descendants. According to local popular belief, all the members of the Learned Families group are thus linked historically with the early founders and defenders of Shi'ite Islam. Their early ancestors were bound together by a common aim and purpose: the defence of the true Islam against the desecrator Yazid, 'who made permissible all that is forbidden'. As descendants of these early founders the present-day members of the Learned Families carry the responsibility of perpetuating the religious and moral values for which their forebears gave their lives. This link with the past is made abundantly clear in the performance of the Play. The Sayyids and the Shaikhs took the parts of Husain and his supporters only. Not one of them has ever taken one of the enemy parts. These were taken by shopkeepers and peasants, the shopkeepers playing the parts of generals and the peasants constituting the bulk of the army. The part of Shimr (meaning 'traitor') was played in 1952 by a most unsavoury character who had served a prison sentence, and the previous year the part was played by a man who, among other faults attributed to him, had committed the grave offence of striking his father in the village square. During the enactment of the Play the Learned Families were ranged on one side, and on the other the overwhelming army of shopkeepers and peasants; the defenders of the good life, of ordered living, were ranged in battle against the forces of ignorance and evil. On the battlefield evil triumphed, and drunken with success the barbarous army ran amuck, slaying even a small babe, and finally the blasphemous Shimr severed the head of Husain, the grandson of the very Prophet himself. The battle over and the Play ended, the victors marched in a procession to the village square led by the captive, Ali as-Saghir, Husain's son and the only male survivor of the vanquished. But the victors in battle, during this last march, flayed themselves with chains, beat their foreheads with swords, thumped their bare chests and wept in anguish for the deeds of horror they had perpetrated. The true Islam triumphed over all in the end.

The action on the battlefield was not a reversal of roles such as occurs in some rituals—even though in real life, the peasants do not flout the authority of the Shaikhs. What the Play did was to give the vast audience a glimpse of the kind of world they could anticipate when evil triumphs. What was depicted was a world of madness, a world of complete unreason, a world without order of any sort. It did not depict a revolutionary situation of one group supplanting another—indeed, the peasantry could never supplant the Learned Families in this sense, for the peasants are far too numerous. What it showed was the chaos that would result if the Learned Families lost their control of village affairs.

I am not attempting a full analysis of the Miracle Play here. Its meanings are so complex and relate to so many aspects of the life of these people, and to their religious beliefs and sentiments, and to their relations with other branches of Islam, that such a task would be impossible in a general essay of this sort. I am aware too that the Play is performed in other countries, and accounts of it have been given by Pelly, Morier, von Grunebaum, Donaldson and others.[29] The Play and all it contains is part and parcel of the Shi'ite world and has its roots in historical facts. These historical details must appear in the Play, but the precedence given in this essay is to the local context in which the Play is performed. It is this context which accounts for the casting of the parts, the importance given to this or that character,[30] and the stress of meaning given to the Play as a whole. My suggestion is that the choice of the Miracle Play as the major non-compulsory religious festival in the village is of critical significance to an analysis of rank, and may also be associated with the absence of rituals relating to the land.

The religious position of the Learned Families is derived directly from the historical event of the battle of Karbala, and since the battle is so bound up with Shi'ite religion itself, their religious position is accepted as axiomatic. As a derivative of this position, the authority of the Learned Families is also accepted in the general field of morals. What is considered as the field of religion

[29] The details of these works are given in the bibliography of this article in the original publication.

[30] A Christian, for example, takes part. All he is required to do is to listen to Husain briefly explain his plight, espouse his cause and die fighting with Husain's men. But in this village, where there is a Christian minority, the Christian is made conspicuous by his trilby hat, his European clothes, his sunglasses, and he is given a mount; he circles the field of the Play, doffing his hat to the spectators as he rides along.

and morals, however, is almost as extensive as the entire range of social relations; conjugal disagreements, adultery, land disputes, acts of violence, drinking, gambling, norms of behaviour between the sexes, the proper modes of behaviour for women and so on, all fall within the field. The authority possessed by the Learned Families is religious in the first place, but in practice it ramifies to capture a whole sphere of social behaviour.

The rank of the Learned Families is taken for granted and is clearly stated. For this reason it can be included and made explicit in ritual. While granting that numerous factors can be adduced which militate against rituals explicitly associated with land, it is also important to appreciate that the relationship between the Learned Families and the rest of the people of the village with regard to land is not clearly stated and has no basis in religious history. The balance between the two groups in the exploitation of the land is delicate. This is a field of social relationships characterised by intense competition. Relationships which are characteristically competitive, which are burdened with stress and strain, which constitute an area of conflict, are excluded from rituals. Where there is certainty in relationships, they can be given expression in ritual form; where they are conspicuously uncertain, this cannot be. It follows from this that ritual, since it validates only relationships which are certain, appears where it is redundant; it merely states the obvious. The acceptance of what is made explicit, however, comprehends other sets of relationships which are not overtly fed into the Play. Just as the religious authority of the Learned Families is extended to cover multiple sets of social relationships, so too the acceptance of their rank implies its extension into economic relationships. It gives them the power to perform a variety of duties from which they earn a substantial income; their traditional literacy—also closely linked to their rank—has enabled them to capture administrative and teaching posts in the village and elsewhere. It is this income which has freed them from the labour of tending their plots, and it is important in the maintenance of their estate against competition. The products of their land alone would not give them the economic dominance they have enjoyed until now. The additional income they derive from their position as religious leaders is critical, and vitally affects their control over

a large acreage of village land. By stressing their religious pre-
eminence in the Play their position as landowners is also but-
tressed. The weight given to relationships which are certain
tends to hold in balance those which are uncertain. The uncertainty arising out of competition is displaced on to an area which
is free of competition and is accepted. Ritual, by stressing what
is certain, conceals the uncertainties, and in so doing ensures that
they are contained within fixed limits. In short, so much is in-
capsulated in rank that this major festival of the Miracle Play
secures a wide range of relationships, including those which are
not made explicit in it.

The main concern in this essay has been to discuss power relationships in a Lebanese village. Land has been given prominence throughout the discussion, for it is the main source of
wealth there. Potentially, anyone in the village has the chance to
accumulate plots of land, and establish himself in a position of
power. But power has remained in the keeping of a relatively
small number of people. The focus of power has not changed
haphazardly from one group to another; it is not whimsical in
the sense that any individual or group, through the rapid accumulation of wealth, can seize and lose it easily, for the path
to wealth is rough and its retention is difficult. Power has remained the prerogative of a defined group. The ecological description, the account of land holding patterns, the discussion of
marriage arrangements, and the exposition of the genealogical
ordering of groups, were given to indicate the play of competition between the Learned Families and the rest of the village in
relation to the maintenance of estates in land. This competition,
considered in isolation, leads to an uneasy and delicate balance
between the two main groups and offers a serious and urgent
threat to the position of the Learned Families. It is the rank accorded to them which weighs down the scales in their favour.
Land is a commodity for which they have to struggle along with
the rest of the village inhabitants, but their rank enables them
to dominate successfully the economic and political life of the
village. The importance of the Miracle Play is that it secures their
rank for them. Rejection of the Miracle Play and all that it em-
bodies would leave them stripped of their rank, and with only
the vestigial reverence due to their connection with the early
heroes of Islam remaining in their keeping.

3. Change and Stability in Administered Villages: The Israeli Experience

Considerable interest has recently been focused upon questions of community stability in situations of rapid change. The major issue may be phrased as follows: under what conditions does a community adopt major technological or organizational innovations without becoming disorganized? The best documented recent study of stability in change is Margaret Mead's *New Lives for Old.*[1] In her re-study of a New Guinean community Mead describes how the sudden intrusion of Western technology and ideology lead, in the course of a generation, to a far-reaching transformation in the socio-cultural organization of a once isolated people. Moreover, Mead shows how this Manus community retained its viability in the course of change. A number of other studies—in particular, Vanstone and Chance's Eskimo reports, Redfield's re-study of Chan Kom, Nash's monograph on industrialization in Cantel, and Epstein's study of two villages in India—reveal similar developments: in each of these instances rapid change takes place, yet the community retains its internal cohesiveness.[2]

Studies such as these offer a somewhat novel view. Rather

This study is published here for the first time by the courtesy of the author, Dr. Alex Weingrod, Brandeis University.

[1] Margaret Mead, *New Lives for Old* (New York: Mentor Books, 1961).

[2] James Vanstone, *Point Hope: An Eskimo Village in Transition* (Seattle: University of Washington Press, 1962); Norman Chance, "Culture Change and Integration: An Eskimo Example," *American Anthropologist*, Vol. 67 (1960), pp. 1028–44; Robert Redfield, *A Village That Chose Progress: Chan Kom Revisited* (Chicago: University of Chicago Press, 1950); Manning Nash, *Machine Age* (Glencoe: The Free Press, 1962); T. S. Epstein, *Economic Development and Social Change in South India* (Manchester University Press, 1962).

than insisting upon the necessity for gradual change, or the presumed "natural reluctance" to accept innovations, or the disorganization changes bring to "functionally integrated" societies, these studies indicate that extensive changes may indeed be possible, and that they may be accompanied by community-wide integration. While this view may be realistic and congenial, it too raises additional questions. Why does rapid change take place in some circumstances, and not in others? What factors influence community stability?

In generalizing from their own research experience, authors such as Mead, Redfield, Nash and Chance have framed a series of hypotheses regarding change and stability. For example, these authors agree that rapid change becomes possible when "people . . . want to change rather than merely submit to being changed."[3] The desirability of the innovation from the "people's point of view," as well as autonomy in making choices, are also said to be major variables. Mead makes the additional point that rapid change is possible when it is total and complete: partial change leads to constraint and conflict, whereas more encompassing changes permit a new and different integration to emerge.[4] Redfield and Mead also lay stress upon the role of community leaders; Redfield in particular places heavy emphasis upon the importance of village leaders in change situations.[5] In regard to community stability, Chance lists a series of conditions which influence a community's cohesiveness: these include the general acceptance of new norms, maintenance of primary group ties, the possibility of successfully realizing new goals, the ability of traditional leaders to retain their influence, and the absence of generational factionalism.[6]

Israeli conditions are particularly well suited for further clarifying these hypotheses. In particular, Israeli immigrant villages, or *moshvei olim,* provide an excellent opportunity for studying problems of community stability under change conditions. Rapid change is a distinctive feature of these villages—the immigrants have undertaken wholly new social, economic and political roles.

[3] M. Mead, *op. cit.,* p. 320.
[4] *Ibid.,* p. 322.
[5] Robert Redfield, *op. cit.,* especially pp. 168–69.
[6] Norman Chance, *op. cit.,* pp. 1033–36.

For example, in almost all of the villages farming represents a new occupation for the settlers; many of the immigrants formerly lived in urban or semi-urban communities, rather than in small, relatively isolated villages; and the cooperative format of these communities also defines a new type of political and economic context. Faced by these new conditions, some immigrant villages have become relatively well-integrated, stable communities, while others are more disorganized and conflict-ridden. These variations between villages permit some refinement in hypotheses regarding change and stability. Is choice, for example, a precondition for rapid change, and are primary-group continuity and the acceptance of new norms conditions for community stability? How does factionalism affect community cohesion? These are some of the general problems posed in this article.

THE MOSHAV AND THE SETTLEMENT SYSTEM

Israeli immigrant villages are communities modelled after the older *moshav ovdim,* or cooperative village. Briefly described, the *moshav* is a small cooperative farming community, in which the participant families live in their own homes and farm on lands leased to them, while also joining in cooperative purchasing and marketing activities.[7] *Moshav* cooperative practices include the joint marketing of crops, investment and credit arrangements between village members, the purchase of heavy equipment or agricultural supplies (seed, water, fertilizer) by the community as a whole, etc. Community government is also fully democratic—elected committees are responsible for managing the village's cooperative economy, as well as directing educational, cultural or technical activities. Thus, although the individual nuclear family is the basic unit of production and consumption, major economic and political issues are determined on a community level. The degree of family interdependence is

[7] Descriptions of the *moshav* are contained in S. Dayan, *Moshav Ovdim* (Tel Aviv: Palestine Pioneer Press Library No. 6, 1947); Y. Talmon "Social Differentiation in Cooperative Villages," *British Journal of Sociology,* Vol. IV (1952); and A. Weingrod, "Reciprocal Change: A Case Study of a Moroccan Immigrant Village in Israel," *American Anthropologist,* Vol. 64 (1962), pp. 115–31.

therefore very high. Agricultural resources—such as land, water and credits—are also distributed equally between community members and hiring labor is formally prohibited. These *moshav* principles have the effect of minimizing the formation of separate class or interest groups, and emphasize the egalitarian structure of these communities.

Seventy-two *moshavim* had been established prior to the creation of Israel in 1948. The post-state mass immigration lead to a greatly intensified colonization program: between 1949 and 1957 an additional 274 immigrant *moshavim* were formed. Although similar in format to the pre-state cooperatives, immigrant *moshavim* are distinctive for their inclusion of unselected, untrained immigrants, and for their dependence upon government agencies. Indeed, they can best be thought of as "administered communities"; these are villages "whose social, political or economic development is directly determined by outside agencies."[8] Dependence and outside controls are major features of these communities.

The system of settlement may briefly be described as follows. Groups of immigrants were dispatched, immediately upon reaching Israel, to small farming communities, where homes and agricultural work were provided them. In some instances the immigrants chose to move into these *moshavim;* in many cases, however, they had little choice, and were brought directly to a village. Each new community usually contained between sixty and eighty families; in most instances they included members of a single ethnic group, although in some cases they were composed of two or more ethnic groups (see Tables I and II). Since the new settlers generally lacked agricultural background or training, teams of Israeli agricultural and managerial instructors were assigned to each village. These experts—typically young men and women—were entrusted with teaching farming techniques to the immigrants, as well as training them in community management skills. Village instructors were, in turn, directed by the regional and national administrators who were responsible for implementing this massive colonization program. Extensive

[8] Alex Weingrod, "Administered Communities: Some Characteristics of New Immigrant Villages in Israel," *Economic Development and Cultural Change*, Vol. II (1962), p. 69.

TABLE I[9]

New Villages According to Administrative Area

North	58
Central	85
Hill	66
Lachish	31
Negev	34
TOTAL	274

TABLE II[10]

New Immigrant Villages According to Largest Ethnic Group

Country of Origin	Number of Villages
Iran	17
Iraq	25
Yemen	32
Morocco	57
Tunisia	15
Tripoli	13
Poland	14
Hungary	22
Rumania	31
Israel	12
Others	36
TOTAL	274

funds were channeled into the villages by the administrators: for example, the directing authority (primary responsibility was given to the Jewish Agency Settlement Department) built the village homes and roads, installed irrigation systems, made tractors and other equipment available, extended credits, etc. Outside administrative control therefore extended to major areas of village life; in time, however, some villages became increasingly autonomous, as settlers began to adapt to the new conditions, and also as village leaders began to assert greater authority.

[9] *Source:* Statistical Department of the Jewish Agency, "Settlements Directed by the Settlement Department" (in Hebrew), mimeographed, April 1959, p. 2.
[10] *Source:* J. Goren, "The Villages of the New Immigrants in Israel, Their Organization and Management," [in Hebrew] (Tel Aviv; Ministry of Agriculture, 1960), pp. 38–41.

OREN: A STABLE COMMUNITY

Oren and Shikma, two villages in the central Negev, provide an excellent opportunity for examining problems of stability in change.[11] The comparison between these villages is nearly ideal. The two villages border upon one another, and thereby share the same environment. Both were settled at approximately the same period of time, and both are composed of immigrants from Morocco. The villages also include a comparable age-distribution. Yet, with these factors in common, the two villages developed in much different ways: Oren has emerged into a period of relative stability and economic growth, while Shikma was characterized by internal crises and minimal agricultural development. Comparing these two communities therefore permits a preliminary identification of factors which influence stability in change.

Oren was first settled in 1954, when a group of thirty families moved into the village. This initial settlement group was comparatively homogeneous: nearly all of the settlers were from Morocco, and, in addition, twenty-seven families were from Moroccan villages and smaller towns, while only three families had formerly lived in urban centers. Almost all of the settlers had formerly been small tradesmen, peddlers or artisans. The urban members of the group had probably been more affluent, and were also better educated; in general however, the group was characterized by minimal formal education, and limited financial means.

Migration into and from the village was comparatively heavy in the period between 1954 and 1957. Sixty-two homes had been built at Oren, and, with homes available, new groups and individual families entered the village. These newcomers were culturally similar to the first settlers; they were nearly all from

11 Oren is described more generally in my article "Reciprocal Change: A Case Study of a Moroccan Immigrant Village in Israel"; my information regarding Shikma comes from N. Nevo's study "Shikma: A Moshav in the Western Negev" (stencil). I am indebted to Nevo for making this material available to me.

Moroccan towns or rural zones, and in Morocco they had been
employed in traditional Jewish occupations. Cultural homogeneity was therefore maintained. Unlike the original group, however, many of those who later joined the village had relatives in
the community: the first settlers had been artificially thrown together by the settlement authorities, but, in a type of "chain
migration," the newer settlers were drawn to the village by
their kinsmen.[12] Several small clusters of kinsmen also became
members of the community; these clusters were composed of
several brothers, cousins, or in-laws. In addition, two larger
groups of kinsmen migrated to the village. One of these groups,
the Dehans, included fourteen related nuclear families, and the
other, the Levi families, numbered ten nuclear families.

The family composition of Oren is summarized in Table III.

TABLE III

Family Groups at Oren (1958)

Type	*Number of Families*
Small kin groups (2–4 members)	21
Dehan group	14
Levi group	10
Extended family	4
No kinsmen	8
Empty homes	5
TOTAL	62

Table III shows that only eight families were without kinsmen,
while all of the other families were members of small or large
kinship units. Given this type of social composition, kinship became the critical factor in most social, economic and political
relations. Kinsmen formed leisure-time groups, visiting one another in the evenings and on the Sabbath; in the context of a
relatively isolated Negev village, this relationship was important
psychologically. In addition, the various kinship groups also functioned as cooperative economic units; relatives often assisted

[12] For a discussion of "chain migration," see C. Price, "Immigration and
Group Settlement," in *The Cultural Absorption of Immigrants,* edited by
W. Borrie (Paris: UNESCO, 1959).

one another during harvesting or planting, and they sometimes also made joint capital investments. These social and economic ties were advantageous, and families without kinsmen felt themselves isolated and without support. Personal relations sometimes focused upon other criteria—age or friendship, for example— but the most closely linked groups were the kinship units.

Kinship ties also provided the basis for village political organization. The two large kinship groups each formed the core of a political faction, and both groups contested for control of the village: the Dehan families supported one another in village politics and so too did the Levis. Since these groups were large, they had a natural advantage in the election of village officials. Moreover, the other villagers tended to support one of the two factions; although sporadic attempts were made to form other factions, these attempts were usually short-lived. Shifts in allegiance sometimes took place, but these were minor changes, and the size of the dominant factions was relatively permanent.

The most authoritative, powerful persons in the village were the two leaders of the dominant factions. Each was a young married male; both were the eldest brothers in the families which lead the factions. Their authority rested mainly upon their political skill: these men interpreted events to their kin and other followers, and also advised them in regard to the recurrent problems of village life. Both possessed unusual managerial skills, and they quickly learned to cope with the new problems encountered in *moshav* living. Although other men were also influential in village affairs, and the leadership of these two was sometimes challenged, no other political authorities emerged at Oren. None of the other settlers was influential enough to form another faction, or to successfully challenge the heads of the two factions.

SHIKMA: AN UNSTABLE COMMUNITY

Shikma was established in 1953. The original settlement group was composed of twenty-six Moroccan families, most of whom met for the first time while emigrating to Israel. While unrelated socially, these families did share a common cultural background:

twenty-three of the families came from urban centers (such as Casablanca, Fès and Marrakech), while only three were from rural zones.

Shortly thereafter, however, Shikma's social composition changed drastically. Following 1953 the population came increasingly to include many persons stemming from rural regions. For example, of the forty-four settlers who joined the village between 1954 and 1961, twenty-four came from rural areas, and twenty from cities or towns. Moreover, during this same period there was a general exodus of urban settlers: of the twenty-eight families who left the village between 1953 and 1961, twenty-six were "urban" families. This selective migration movement—both to Shikma, and from the village to other communities—resulted in a community equally divided between persons with rural and urban backgrounds: the population in 1961 included twenty-four families from rural regions, and another twenty-four from cities. Shikma therefore became increasingly heterogeneous in regard to origin and culture.

Moreover, this change in personnnel also involved changes in the social composition of the community. Nineteen of the twenty-four urban settlers did not have family or kinship ties in the village; on the other hand, all but three of the rural villagers were members of kinship groups. In addition, ten of the rural families belonged to a single large kinship unit, while other eleven related rural families included several smaller groups of kin (brothers or in-laws). Family isolation was therefore related to urban origins, and kinship affiliation to rural background. It is also important to note the large number of persons lacking in kinship ties; these included twenty-two of the total of forty-eight families.

The family composition of Shikma is summarized in Table IV.

TABLE IV

Family Groups at Shikma (1961)

Type	Number of Families
Small kin groups	16
Large kin groups	10
No kinsmen	22
TOTAL	48

Shikma's political organization was complex and fluid. The village included four different factions. The numerically largest factions were composed of fourteen and seven members each. In both of these the core-unit was based upon a set of kinsmen; not all of the factions' members were related, but the groups' permanent core included persons bound by kinship ties. The leaders of these factions were young or middle-aged males. In general, however, their influence was limited to the faction itself: that is, within the faction these leaders held sway, but they had relatively little influence upon the rest of the villagers.

Two other factions were differently organized. These groups were organized around powerful leaders, rather than being based upon kinship or other social ties. Two powerful personalities, Machlouf and Daniel, succeeded in gaining adherents and joining them together into political groups. The permanent membership of the factions they lead was small—one numbered four families, the other seven families. Yet although their permanent following was small, both Machlouf and Daniel were extremely influential in the village. Their administrative ability, energy and persuasive talents enabled them to join persons and groups together into larger political blocs. Both men had served as village secretary, and each had previously represented the village to outside agencies. Their own interpersonal relations were usually stormy; they intrigued against one another for community dominance and control.

These four factions were fairly stable units. They did not, however, include Shikma's entire population: the factions numbered only thirty-two families, while another sixteen families were not aligned with any group. These latter villagers—almost all of whom were isolated, urban families—formed a loose, floating body that did not pledge regular allegiance to any faction. In many cases their support was crucial in village politics—they formed the balance between the contesting factions.

This combination of forces—numerous factions, aggressive factional leaders leading small groups, and a large body of unattached persons—produced a highly volatile situation. No single faction was large enough to dominate the community and its councils: although the kinship-based factions were comparatively large, neither group possessed a leader who was sufficiently attractive or strong enough to control affairs. On the other hand, both of the powerful personalities were not supported by a large, permanent core of followers. A never-ending process of politicking followed from this situation: factions temporarily joined one another, Machlouf and Daniel recruited members for their "parties", and each faction head sought to attract the third of the village that had no permanent affiliation. The confederations that were formed were short-lived, and tended to break and re-form periodically.

OREN AND SHIKMA COMPARED

Comparing Oren with Shikma indicates that the social and political organization of these adjoining communities is much different. Oren is more culturally homogeneous than Shikma: whereas almost all of the Oren settlers were from rural Moroccan regions, Shikma was equally divided between urban and rural settlers. Moreover, there were important contrasts in the social composition of the villages. At Oren, only eight families did not have some kinsmen in the village (16%) while at Shikma, twenty-two families were without kin (46%).

Oren and Shikma also differ in regard to the number and size of their factions. Shikma was split between four factions, while at Oren, two larger groups contested for power. In addition, the factions at Oren were numerically larger than those at Shikma. For example, the Dehan group at Oren included twenty-eight families: fourteen of the members are kinsmen, and the others were families tied to the Dehan's by friendship, common interest and obligation. The Dehan and Levi factions together included all but nine of Oren's fifty-seven families. Membership in these groups was relatively permanent, and the factions were therefore able to institute long-term political control.

There are also differences in the authority structures of the two communities. At Oren, the dominant village figures were also the leaders of the two large kinship groups. These men found their primary support from among their kin, and more widely from within the faction. Generally speaking, they were guaranteed a large, stable base of support. At Shikma, on the other hand, the powerful leaders did not have a guaranteed constituency. Paradoxically, neither of the two kinship-based factions had leaders who were able to assert village-wide authority; while both persons who had leadership abilities did not have the support of broadly based groups.

Thus far we have seen how Oren and Shikma differ in internal composition and organization. In addition, the villages' patterns of development also differed systematically. Indeed, the socioeconomic growth of these villages took diametrically opposed directions. More families migrated from Shikma than from Oren: between 1953 and 1961, twenty-eight families left Shikma; while between 1955 and 1961, nineteen families migrated from Oren. More importantly, migration has been relatively continuous at Shikma—there the exodus continued through 1961, whereas Oren's population has hardly changed since 1957. One may therefore conclude that, in regard to population movement, Oren is a more stable community than is Shikma.

There are also differences in the proportion of persons employed in farming. All of the settlers at Oren were engaged in farming; indeed, the level of agricultural activity there was intense. At Shikma, on the other hand, nineteen of the forty-eight settlers did not work their farm plots—more than a third of the villagers (39.5%) were employed in non-farming tasks. Substantial areas of farm land were left idle, since these settlers did not undertake sustained farming. Those Shikma settlers who did farm often received crop yields similar to those at neighboring Oren: in both villages some farmers received excellent yields, while others had more average crops. Yet the villages are clearly differentiated in regard to the numbers of persons actively engaged in farming.

Shikma and Oren may also be contrasted in regard to the permanence of community-wide institutions. At Oren, committee elections were held once a year; for example, between 1959 and 1961 three committees were chosen, and each served a year's term. Political controversy was often intense during this period, and various internal crises led to prolonged crises; yet some measure of consensus was established, and village-wide activities were maintained. During this same period at Shikma, however, seven different committees were elected: political conflicts led to a continuous realignment of forces, and community-wide activities tended to be spasmodic. Shikma was an inchoate, sharply divided community, while Oren developed relatively viable community institutions. In brief, Oren represents a village successfully adapting to new socio-economic conditions, while Shikma's adjustment is more limited and tenuous.

CHANGE AND COMMUNITY STABILITY

Let us return now to the problems originally posed: how does the Israeli experience contribute to understanding rapid change? What is the relevance of the Israeli data for a general view of community stability in change situations?

"Stability" in this case is measured by two variables—migration from the village, and the relative permanence of community-wide institutions. As we have seen, Oren and Shikma differ systematically in regard to these features. Two factors explain the higher migration rate at Shikma: the absence in the village of extensive primary groups, and the greater concentration there of persons with urban backgrounds. As was remarked earlier, primary group ties are important psychologically, and they also have important economic and political advantages. Given these advantages, members of primary groups were less likely to migrate than were the other socially "isolated" villagers. Since primary-group ties were absent for many of the Shikma settlers (in contrast with the immigrants at Oren), a greater proportion tended to migrate.

Moreover, adopting to *moshav* conditions presented especially acute problems for immigrants from urban regions: for these immigrants the problems of adjusting their status image to *moshav* conditions necessitated a major re-orientation. Many of those who did not make successful adjustments have migrated. Shikma included a greater proportion of persons with urban backgrounds—and the presence there of persons who were both "urbanites" and were without primary-group ties lent the village its greater "instability." These conclusions tend to support Chance's hypothesis that community stability depends upon persistent primary-group relations, as well as the acceptance of new norms. Immigrants with urban backgrounds appear to have had more difficulty in adopting the new *moshav* norms—and the absence of primary-group ties removed a buffer of emotional and economic security. Both of these factors appear to be relevant to community stability in change.

What of the contrasts in the viability of village public institutions? At Shikma, it will be recalled, the village committee was continually reshuffled, and intergroup hostility was constant, while at Oren the committee had greater permanence, and group conflict was muted; at Oren, the settlers were able to arrive at consensus on crucial community issues, whereas at Shikma group division made village cooperation much more difficult. These contrasts between the villages are closely related to their different authority systems: that is, to the differences in the relative size of factions, the number of factions, and the relations between leaders and constituents. The two large kinship groups at Oren offered a dependable base of power—either one of the two factions dominated village affairs, or the two groups joined together in a coalition. Since the major village personalities were also members of these groups, the two factions were themselves strengthened. On the other hand, at Shikma, since authority was suspended between many small groups, and since the major village personalities did not have dependable sources of support, power in the community was fractured and consensus difficult to achieve.

Community stability would thus seem to depend upon group alignments, and the ways in which local village forces become balanced. While variables such as factional size or relations between leaders and constituents are important in maintaining community stability under most conditions, they become particularly crucial in situations of change when ambiguity and uncertainty are magnified, and where decisions regarding new types of problems need to be made. In the Israeli case emphasis is given to such variables as factional size, the number of factions, and relations between "leaders" and "followers." Although the circumstances will differ between situations—for example, the type of factionalism may be varied—these variables are likely to be pertinent in a wide range of cases. From this perspective, the importance of what are essentially fortuitous circumstances is also emphasized. That is, whether factions are large or small, and whether powerful leaders have dependable constituencies, may largely be matters of chance. For example, the factional organization at Chan Kom, as reported by Redfield, was determined by the chance numerical superiority of one of the leading families.[13]

CHANGE AND "WISHING TO CHANGE"

The analysis thus far has concentrated upon questions of community stability. Let us turn next to an analysis of change: what variables are important in rapid change, and how is the immigrant village experience relevant to theories of change?

One of the striking contrasts between Oren and Shikma is in the different proportions of persons engaged in farming: almost all of the Oren settlers farm, while a substantial number of the immigrants at Shikma have not become farmers. Once again, these contrasts are related to differences between the villages in regard to previous life-style, and to differences in the extent of primary-group attachments. Both variables are important in adopting a farming career: immigrants from rural zones probably adapt more readily to farming, and primary-group cooperation also has benefits in pursuing new agricultural and village activities. This conclusion lends support to the widely held hypothesis that primary-group persistence is advantageous for adopting new technological or organizational skills: the maintenance of family ties may be functionally adoptive for taking on novel skills and successfully managing new types of situations. Security in personal contacts allows, as it were, for greater flexibility in undertaking new roles.

Although the contrasts between Oren and Shikma are certainly marked, what is most distinctive about the villages is the substantial degree to which members *of both communities* have adopted new types of behavior. What is striking is the fact that the immigrants do farm their fields, and that both communities do function, to a greater or lesser degree, as cooperative villages.

[13] R. Redfield, *op. cit.*, especially pp. 3, 93.

Certainly these changes were hardly predictable in advance; that they have happened at all seems truly remarkable. Margaret Mead's hypothesis regarding "total change" seems relevant in explaining why these—and other—new patterns were adopted:

> The alternative . . . if there is to be purposeful change [is when] the whole pattern is transformed at once, with as little reminder of the past as possible to slow down the new learning, or make that learning incomplete and maladaptive. . . . A people who chose to practice a new technology or enter into drastically new kinds of economic relationships will do this more easily if they live in different houses, wear different clothes, and eat . . . different food. . . . The speed with which European immigrants adopted to American life [was influenced by] the transforming experience of entering a world where everything was different.[14]

The very scope of the changes that transformed the immigrants' lives do seem to have contributed to their adopting new behavior patterns. Consider the immigrants' "past" and their "present." In Morocco, the settlers were independent tradesmen, artisans or peddlers, living in small towns and cities; they were sheltered in closed communities, and lived in multi-family dwellings; the zone of Jewish concentration—the Moroccan *mellah*—was restricted to Jews, and even though the post-1912 French Protectorate had improved their political and economic position, Morocco's Jews were historically subservient and dependent upon the Muslim majority. In stark contrast, in Israel the immigrants became farmers, they lived in small communities, their homes were new and each was a separate dwelling, they learned a new language and wore different clothes, and they became members of the dominant Jewish society. The changes, therefore, were "total"—one entire pattern of living was replaced by another, much different one. Indeed, the separate aspects of the new pattern supported one another, the new clothing or new language symbolized the totality of the shift. The extent to which

[14] M. Mead, *op. cit.*, pp. 372–73.

these new behavior patterns were accepted attests to the gen-
eralizability of Mead's formulation.

While the immigrant village data supports Mead's hypothesis
regarding total change, it also appears to contradict the more
widely accepted hypothesis linking "change" with "choice" or
community autonomy. The immigrants *did* become farmers, they
did cooperate in a series of new activities—but, at least initially,
most did not choose these new roles. On the contrary: the village
situation was imposed upon them, and their communities were
managed from outside rather than being autonomous. What,
then, is the relationship between "change" and "choice"?

For one thing, the previously described total change in conditions may be important for understanding why imposed patterns were accepted. Moving to a new and relatively unknown
situation, the immigrants possessed a sense of the inappropriateness of their previous patterns; cut off from their traditional culture, many felt that new types of behavior were required. They
were predisposed to accept new types of political organization,
or even new occupations; what had been relevant in a Moroccan
village or town was clearly not meaningful in an Israeli *moshav*.
Given this orientation, many immigrants were also prepared to
accept direction: so many features of *moshav* life were new and
different, and the administrators appeared to have such superior
knowledge, that compliance and dependence seemed the most
reasonable course. The village instructors were often perceived
as models of the new, and proper, modes of conduct: their
prestige and power was patently real, and many immigrants
sought to emulate them. This is not to say that there were not
conflicts between settlers and administrators, or that significant
differences did not exist between the settlers in their readiness
to accept new behavior patterns; yet, in general, the widespread
sense of a "new beginning," and the inappropriateness of traditional behavior, lead many to accept direction.

Moreover, the immigrants had few alternatives to adopting the
imposed behavior patterns. Given a situation of extensive government control—particularly over immigrant housing—the settlers had few options other than to farm. Some resisted the prof-
fered farming career and sought to leave the community; even
though migration from the village tended to be a long and

arduous process, some immigrants did seek this option (as the migration statistics show). Migration was, of course, selective—those who most strongly resisted farming and village life left the village, while others who were more pliant remained, or even migrated to the village. Thus, over time, migration to and from the village may have led to communities composed of persons more positively attuned to the new conditions.

In addition, the settlers adopted the imposed patterns since the new system had many tangible rewards: not only were there few other choices, the farming option itself held out important benefits. The directing agencies assumed economic responsibility for the villages: the settlers, who migrated with little resources, were continuously subsidized by the planning groups. Homes, equipment, credits, subsistence loans, capital grants—these were all made available by the administrative authority. Even though the system often operated inefficiently, and disappointment and crises regularly shook village life, the settlers were quick to realize that their situation had certain advantages. So long as rewards continued to be available, the settlers were able to tolerate the system. Moreover, the settlers were also able to alter and affect the system—to a considerable degree they were able to manipulate the administrators.[15] Receiving rewards and economic guarantees, and also able to alter some features of the system, they became increasingly "engaged" within their new way of life. They began to accept the settlement authority's norms, and therefore to adopt major reorganizations in their traditional patterns of behavior.

A contribution of the Israeli experience is therefore to suggest that, given a predisposition to change, limited alternatives and regular rewards, changes may be imposed upon communities. Of course, over time many villagers opted for the new patterns: as a majority of the settlers began farming, outside direction and control were limited and the villages grew increasingly autonomous. It is no longer relevant to speak of "imposed change"—most of those who reside in the village live there by choice. Still, during the initial period imposed change and outside direction were influential in the adoption of new behavior patterns.

[15] See A. Weingrod, "Reciprocal Change: A Case Study of a Moroccan Immigrant Village in Israel," *op. cit.*, especially pp. 128–29.

CONCLUSION

Certainly the Israeli experience represents a "special case"—
mass migration, an imposed cooperative farming system, migration to a "Jewish" society, are among the special features of this
experience. But then, all cases are special, and comparing the
Israeli data with other material helps to clarify some of the conditions underlying community stability in change situations. It is
important to re-examine some of the traditional anthropological
concepts regarding these problems, and the Israeli data makes
possible some testing of hypotheses. More specifically, the conclusions drawn from this inter-village comparison lend support
to the proposition that change is not necessarily incompatible
with community stability. Additional comparative research, both
in Israeli communities and in other contexts, should provide further tests of some of the propositions discussed in this article.

4. From Peasantry to Wage Labor and Residual Peasantry: The Transformation of an Arab Village

The peasantry inhabiting the area that was formerly Palestine developed out of a particular type of feudal conditions. Using data collected on economic-occupational groupings covering the years 1920 to 1963 in an Arab village in Israel, we trace the transition of a peasantry into a rural-dwelling proletariat. However, along with this radical transformation and within a non-feudal state, a form of what we call "residual" peasantry still characterizes the village. We shall attempt to offer a causal analysis for this development.[1]

THE FEUDAL PAST

Peasantry is an ancient phenomenon in the Near East and in the territory that was formerly Palestine. The particular productive system and the relations between overlords and peasants, which we here designate as feudal, go back for at least a thousand years and more. (See, for example, Prawer's brief discussion of rural villages during Crusader times, 1963: 405–18.) It did not

Permission to reprint this paper is gratefully acknowledged to the author and to the publisher. It originally appeared in *Process and Pattern in Culture: Essays in Honor of Julian Steward*, Robert A. Manners, ed., Chicago: Aldine Publishing Company, 1964, pp. 211–34.

[1] This paper, in slightly altered form, was read before the Mediterranean Sociological-Anthropological Conference held in Athens in July, 1963. I wish to thank the sponsors of the Conference, the Social Sciences Centre, Athens, and its scientific director, J. G. Peristiany, for inviting me to participate. This paper was prepared while working on a grant from the Research Institute For The Study Of Man through the Center for Anthropological Research (Israel). I wish to thank Shulamit Carmi for her comments on this paper.

undergo a fundamental change until the late 19th and early 20th centuries, despite repeated wars and conquests. Space limits our presentation of data to the period of the 19th century. The sparse Palestinian population reached 300,000 in 1800, about 450,000 by 1882 (Abramovitz and Gelphat, 1944: 3–4). With the exception of two or three ports carrying on limited commerce with Europe, a few seasonal ports trading goods to Egypt and Syria, and some underdeveloped market town administrative centers, this population was essentially rural and settled in some hundreds of villages.

Nineteenth century Palestine was an agrarian society. Land constituted the main capital (Abramovitch and Gelphat, 1944: 13). Extensive tracts were either in the hands of the government or of large landowners. Government lands, when settled by peasants, yielded land use, property, capitation and other extraordinary tax returns of no less than one-third the crop (Burckhardt, 1822: 299–300; Robinson and Smith, 1841: II, 323–24; Bergheim, 1894: 197–98). Large estates, owned predominantly by urban or towndwelling landowners, exploited the existing nucleated villages (Waschitz, 1947: 38) by draining off surpluses through rentals in kind. These landowners were recruited, especially in the second half of the century, from a class of merchants in Beirut, Damascus, Jaffa and other localities who, through privileged connections with the Ottoman government (Shimoni, 1947: 166; Granott, 1952: 37) purchased, cheaply, whole valleys and plains, together with their villages (Poliak, 1940: 96; Abramovitch and Gelphat, 1944: 15), or imported poverty-stricken and landless elements to work unsettled land. Merchants, high officials, officers and Bedouin sheikhs (Waschitz, 1947: 19) bought tax-farming tithe rights from the Government, and through extreme taxation which commonly demanded more than one-half the crop (Volney, 1798: II, 243; Bergheim, 1894: 197–99; Granott, 1952: 57), advances in goods given for the future crop on the threshing floor (Volney, 1798: II, 245; Wilson, 1906: 297; Waschitz, 1947: 38), and money lending at usurious rates (Volney; *ibid.*) often deprived private owners of land, forced others into tenancy (Granott, 1952: 58), and even drove a wedge into the collectively-operated village land system (Abramovitch and Gelphat, 1944: 24–25). These tax farmers operated with Government sanction but also possessed a private militia which, when on the move, was fed and housed by the villagers (Volney, 1798: II, 245; Burckhardt, 1822: 291; Wilson, 1906: 291). After 1858, individual land registration was demanded, but many peasants failed to register, fearing both taxes and conscription (Granott, 1952: 75). In many instances merchant–money lenders and notables succeeded in registering the land in their own names, thus alienating the peasants from the land, and creating patriarchal relations between dominant landowner and dependent tenant (Baldensperger, 1906: 193).

In many mountain areas village land was owned individually by the peasants themselves (Robinson and Smith, 1841: II, 387; Baldensperger, 1906: 193; Granott, 1952: 69, 174). Much of the plains land was used in communal fashion, *masha'* where field plots (but not building sites, vineyards, orchards or gardens, which were individually held) were redistributed every two years or so (Granott, 1952: 174, 197, 213–40; Klein, 1883: 43; Post, 1891: 105; Patai, 1949: 438). Although the peasants had usufruct, legally the land belonged to the Ottoman state (Robinson and Smith, *op. cit.*). Many villages were tenant villages whose land was owned by absentee landlords or town merchants. Tenants took a portion of the crop, depending on their contribution in plough animals, seed, etc., while the owner took his rental in kind (Shimoni, 1947: 166). No matter what the form of ownership or use of land in the villages, feudal property relations existed in regard to land, and in all instances taxes were ruinous. Mountain villages, however, less dependent on grain crops alone and growing a greater variety of crops, were generally better off than plains and valley villages (Robinson and Smith, *ibid.*; Poliak, 1940: 75). The latter, due in part to their ecological positions, seem to have been more liable to pressures by their overlords to produce grains for taxes in kind. It is on the villages where grains constituted the major crops that we shall focus in this discussion.

All villages remained backward in their use of tools and land (Volney, 1798: II, 246). No technological improvements were instituted, and agriculture remained extensive (Abramovitch and Gelphat, 1944: 22; Waschitz, 1947: 22). What irrigation there was existed only in areas where natural possibilities encouraged it. The method of redistributing "communal" lands, while underwriting a minimal level of subsistence for the peasants, was a creation of the feudal regime (Rosenfeld, 1958: 1132). Its purpose was to keep people on the land, fix a two or three field wheat and/or barley and durra seed cycle and serve for the orderly collection of taxes and rentals in kind (Robinson and Smith, 1841: II, 387; Grant, 1907: 135). The redistributive system existed also in many tenant villages where it similarly prevented agriculturists from gaining fixed rights in land or building on or improving plots (cf. Bergheim, 1894: 192).

Peasant production was mainly for use and for taxes or rentals in kind; little went to markets (Volney, 1798: II, 246). These were often no more than local affairs (Robinson and Smith, 1841: III, 236). In some areas Bedouin tribes, often in alliance with the pashas, felt free to pillage and exact tribute from settlers (Burckhardt, 1822: 301–2). Many taxes fell upon the villagers collectively, remaining fixed even when the number of inhabitants was severely reduced (Volney, 1798: 243–44; Burckhardt, 1822: 300–1; Robinson and Smith, 1841: II, 146, 388; Wilson, 1906: 291). The amount of land individually exploited by peasants was a function of animal power at hand (Klein, 1883: 43; Baldensperger, 1906: 193–94). Poverty was extreme (Volney, *op. cit.*; Burckhardt, 1822: 299); vast areas of land remained unsettled and uncultivated (Robinson and Smith, 1841: III, 183; Macalister and Masterman, 1905: 342; Granott, 1952: 35); peasants often moved from village to village looking for the least drastic relationships of dependence or seeking work as sharecroppers (Burckhardt, 1822: 221, 225). Others—probably artisans faced with the absence of any industrial opportunities—dispersed to towns in order to avoid taxes or conscription (Volney, 1798: II, 247; Granott, 1952: 55). Still others became nomads (Robinson and Smith, 1841: II, 177). Servitude, in which people were forcibly tied to the land, probably existed formerly in some transient form, but had been abolished by the early 19th century (Poliak, 1940: 85; Abramovitch and Gelphat, 1944: 14; and cf. Volney, 1798: II, 242). Yet there were no opportunities for occupational mobility (Granott, 1952: 34).

If we follow Wolf's definition that "the peasant aims at subsistence, not at reinvestment" (Wolf, 1955: 454), the Arab peasants certainly existed at a subsistence level. Even in 1930,

80% of all crops were produced for home consumption (Johnson-Crosbie, 1930). The villagers operated a household economy—a natural economy—in that they supplied, essentially, their own needs (Volney, 1798: II, 258; Abramovitch and Gelphat, 1944: 13–14). And, following Kroeber (1948: 284), Redfield (1960: 20) and others, we may take note that these subsistence peasants formed a class segment of a larger society (Sjoberg, 1952). What is definitive for us, however, is that the subsistence level and this peasant class segment were determined by the particular set of productive and social relations perpetuated by feudal rulers, military governors, tax farmers, merchants and landlords whose interests were solely concerned with taxes and rents.

The backward economy of Palestine underwent few changes until the terminal period of the Ottoman Empire. But the transition from feudal relations to a form of pre-capitalist relations (which we cannot detail here) had their effect on the Arab village. In a partial attempt, for example, to modernize its administration, make for greater centralization, and emphasize individual tax responsibility (Wilson, 1906: 290) (rather than collective village responsibility exemplified by the *masha'* system), the Empire instituted, in 1858, the individual registration of plots mentioned above. This was not conclusive, for at the end of the Empire in 1918, 70% of the land remained *masha'* (Waschitz, 1947: 46). In 1930 it was estimated that half the land was still held under this form of use (Johnson-Crosbie, 1930: 45).

Although France held commercial interests and later concessions in the area as early as the 17th century, it is only with the growth of subsidized religious, medical, educational and charitable institutions backed for political and commercial ends by various foreign powers in the late 19th century (Hurewitz, 1953: 103–4) that we encounter an increase in trade in Palestine (Granott, 1952: 34). A more direct effect on the internal economy in its transition out of feudalism was exercised by the growth of Jewish immigration and the appearance of Jewish capital. The Jewish population rose from 24,000 in 1882 to 85,000 in 1914. In the five years following the end of World War I, 40,000 additional Jews entered the country. (By the end of World War II there were 650,000 Jews in Palestine; approximately 1,200,000 Arabs. Today there are over two million Jews in Israel and about 250,-

ooo Arabs.)[2] Capital entered Palestine both through Jewish national organizations and with individual Jews. Cities grew, market
centers for Arab crops expanded, land values increased, the
number of laborers went up, tenants became hired workers. The
British Mandatory period brought on changes in law and taxation. Health and service agencies, in part Jewish, affected the
villages. The population grew, transportation facilities increased:
the developing money economy began to invade Arab villages
(Abramovitch and Gelphat, 1944: 24–29; Waschitz, 1947: 22–24).

FEUDAL RELATIONS WITHIN THE VILLAGE

The internal political and social relations within the villages,
which we can only touch upon briefly, were an expression of the
feudal economy. Many of these relations persist today within the
non-feudal economy of Israel. Seventy-five per cent of today's
Arab population is rural, living in 104 villages. It is true that
feudal landlords and tax farmers no longer exist. There are no
industrial enterprises within the villages and the use of land and
wage labor are the means of livelihood. Land today is basically
private property; about four-fifths of the peasants own the land
they work (Israel, 1958: 43). The *masha'* system and tenant villages are no longer present. Individual plots, however, are small
and, at least in part, due to the former *masha'* system, fragmented
and scattered throughout the village, hence unsuitable for modern agricultural methods (Poliak, 1940: 87). There are landless
rural dwellers and villages with little land. In some instances this
condition is old; elsewhere it is the result of land confiscations
prompted by security considerations of the State. As we shall see,
with the Arab inheritance system and population growth, plots
held by heirs are reduced in size each generation. Although the
amount of land cultivated in the Arab sector has increased by
almost one-third and productivity has doubled since the establishment of the State of Israel in 1948, the value of agricultural
produce per *dunam* of cultivated area among Arabs is only one-

[2] According to the Israel Government, between 615–630,000 Arab inhabitants of what is today Israel left the country due to the Arab-Israel war; about
145,000 remained (Israel, 1958:10).

fourth of that among Jews. Ninety-seven per cent of Arab farming is still extensive. Crops are non-diversified, and unresponsive
to new and changing market demands and prices. They are non-
commercial crops largely similar to those grown generations ago
(Flapan, 1962: 24–27). The village family was extended in structure and patriarchal in the distribution of authority with regard
to the ownership and use of the major means of production,
such as land, work animals, or flocks. Grown sons did most of the
necessary physical work and large families would attempt to
channel their labor power into as many diversified occupations
as possible. Ideally, sons remained with their father until his
death when property was to be divided equally among them.
Since fathers were often poor or landless, sons had to become
share-croppers or tenants. For this reason, and because of contradictions in property, inheritance and work relations, the ideal
could not always be realized in practice (Rosenfeld, 1958: 1130).

Extended families were further linked together in the patrilineal line into *hamayil* (*hamule*), or patrilineages. These patrilineages persist to this day. *Hamayil* combined against each other
(Macalister and Masterman, 1905: 344; Shimoni, 1947: 175), and
often competed as factions, openly and violently, in a struggle
for security and political position within the village. On the one
hand, the lack of any great economic differences between individuals and families inhibited the growth of class distinctions,
and made for a rough equality of status, honor and prestige. At
the same time, economic weakness lent emphasis to the common
struggle for survival, spurring the formation of larger groups for
its successful prosecution. On the other hand, local governors,
wealthy merchants and landlords sparked the factional potential
of the *hamayil* (either within or between villages) in order to
maintain their own control system and the status quo. They
would give recognition, minor privileges and limited authority to
one *hamule* or faction to underwrite its role in preserving the
established order, meanwhile supporting a developing faction,
balancing one against the other and achieving general compliance for the overlords (Rosenfeld, 1959a: 16–17; 1961: 45–46).

Only some two decades ago *hamayil* often maintained ties of
dependency, involving reciprocal obligations with some wealthy
or powerful urban dweller.

The basis for this tendency in most instances lies in economic dependency and in traces of the feudal order. The person or the family to which the *hamule* is connected are in many instances the landowners in the area or wealthy persons on whom the village depends in one form or another (trade, loans, debts, etc.). A dominant family such as this is obliged —and this also is a remnant of feudal ties—to defend the *hamayil* that are connected to it. . . . (Shimoni, 1947: 174)

The internal solidarity of the *hamule* and factions formed by a number of combined *hamayil* was achieved largely through the marriage system, which is also characterized by many feudal overtones in spite of its concern with kinship. Solidarity was a necessity not only due to the internal power struggles stemming from this economy. It was fostered as well by the feudal state for its own purposes of control and because it wished to deal with individuals collectively, as representatives or members of a larger blood group. *Hamule* members, in turn, had to maintain solidarity in the face of the alien state.

Preferred marriage was among paternal cousins, within the *hamule*. Marriage between individuals of different *hamayil* within the village served also to build factions. *Hamule* and faction gained increased solidarity through endogamous marriages; secondarily such marriages satisfied social and welfare needs and obligations, especially pronounced among kinsmen. The closest *hamule* relatives had first rights as to the disposal of a man's daughter in marriage, her child-bearing and work capabilities (Granqvist, 1931: 133–34). But within the feudal property system the father or brother exploited the value of the daughter or sister by receiving the major part of her bride price, *fed* or *mahr*. The bride received a part in gold coins, clothing, etc. (Rosenfeld, 1957: 47–50). Thus while *hamule* patrilineage rights were recognized and kin units built up upon them, patriarchal property rights received equal recognition.

ECONOMIC-OCCUPATIONAL TRANSFORMATIONS IN AN ARAB VILLAGE

Exact data on the economic and occupational groupings of Arab villages covering the period before 1930 are not available. However, the general evidence for the nineteenth century and the early years of the present century shows that we are dealing with villages wherein almost all working individuals were restricted to activities connected with agriculture and herding. Men and youths were either farmer-owners, share-croppers or tenants, part-time workers in the seasonal round of agriculture, cameleers mainly occupied in haulage from the village fields to the threshing floor, and shepherds. In many areas local artisans were nonexistent, with the family doing its own house building and tool making, milling and olive-pressing or clothes making (Volney, 1798: II, 258). Elsewhere there were masons, potters, part-time carpenters, plough-repairers and lime-burners (*ibid.*). Often there was a village religious functionary; barbers and/or circumcisors and smiths were commonly itinerant; a village guard or two and a prayer-caller would in most instances complete the list. Undoubtedly there were a few local village merchants in the 19th century Palestinian Arab village. Perhaps some individuals working as cameleers in haulage also tried their luck in transporting goods on a commercial basis; or some persons bought and sold animals or seed.

Let us now turn to a detailed consideration of the changes in the economic-occupational groupings of one Arab village from the early 1920's until today. These changes are radical and emphasize the effect on the village of a developing economy and its transition from peasantry to wage labor outside the village.

The village chosen for detailed investigation is a typical Arab Moslem–Christian village in the lower Galilee of Israel. It is characteristic in that fields are not irrigated. Its population today is about 2,250 people (as opposed to probably less than 800 about forty years ago). This population occupies about 12,500 *dunams* of land (3,125 acres) not all of which is cultivable. The village today has numerous olive trees and flocks of goats but the main agricultural economy was based on its winter subsistence crops of wheat and barley, horse beans, lentils, etc., and its summer market and subsistence crops of sesame and watermelons, melons, chick peas, bamya, tomatoes and other vegetables. It was, in the past, relatively isolated from contacts other than those with other Arab villages like itself; it took five or six hours of travel by donkey or camel to reach its main market center, Acre. Today it still lies within the main area of concentration of Arab villages in Israel, but—with modern transportation—within a half hour's travel from the Arab town of Nazareth and an hour or two from the largest Jewish cities.

In the early 1920's, nearly all economic activity remained centered in the village. Subsistence was based on agriculture and in no case was any individual cut off from some role in agriculture, or isolated from its effects. With the influx of Jews in these years, some villagers began to work for Jews outside the village as agricultural laborers or construction workers. Within the village, others turned—at least in part—to the extraction of lime and charcoal burning, spurred mainly—though not entirely—by Jewish building needs. But occupational categories often remained fluid. This was true forty years ago when village artisans were also part-time farmers, while many farmers and cameleers worked in lime extraction in their free time, or a man might work as sharecropper one year and as a hired shepherd the next. The same phenomenon continued to characterize the 1920's, both due to the type of agriculture practiced and due to the transitional character of the larger economy.

Rapid changes in economic-occupational groupings within the village took place in the early 1940's of the British Mandatory period. During these years many villagers found work in British Army camps, or, for instance, as supernumerary police. Industry in Palestine, which had developed slowly, gained additional impetus due to such catalysts as war contracts, and a few villagers began work in industrial plants. With definite wage possibilities present many sons of farmers worked outside the village and fields were left idle. Share-cropping farmers declined in number. Some individuals, especially Christian Arabs, took the first steps toward urbanization. A number of young men entered secondary schools.

The economic-occupational changes following the establishment of the State of Israel have been radical. The number of individuals seeking work outside the village has grown tremendously. Most seek work in the Jewish sector. The market demand for unskilled workers, together with the pressures of industrial and agro-technical development, which do not stem organically from the village, are causing major economic and occupational realignments. The peasant type agricultural economy is such that the impact of these factors only serves to intensify its existing surplus labor, the basic condition for the transformation of the groupings.

Two organic factors reinforce this growth of surplus labor in the Arab village. One of these is the type of land inheritance practised in the Arab village where sons inherit their father's land equally. With any one individual's land holdings also fragmented into small parcels over the entire cultivated area of the village, in a few generations many persons are reduced to small holdings. Either these cannot support the family, or they are too small to provide full work-time, or they are more economically left to hired workers, hired tractors, etc. Many such "reduced" farmers are potential laborers. The second factor is tied to the first. Agricultural labor in extensive farming is seasonal. There are idle periods after the summer harvests and often long idle winter periods. Under such circumstances, today, every mechanical advance such as the introduction of tractors, or ploughing and harvesting machinery, frees additional people from the absolute necessity of contributing agricultural labor. In the past, with simple technology, the labor of all family members was important at least during the active seasons, like harvesting. While today many persons continue to work in family agriculture and many laborers combine family farm work with outside wage labor due to lack of permanent jobs outside the village, their labor is less necessary, and never requested in the case of permanent wage earners.

However, any inheritance system based on small private property would produce such surplus labor, and the introduction of agricultural machinery would itself produce the same effect. It is mainly traditional extensive agriculture, with its lack of diversification coupled with the lack of village industry that accentuates this internal surplus labor and will continue to do so.

The crops grown up to only 10 or 15 years ago were subsistence crops and varied enough to supply the basic needs of the family. Today agriculture has become a branch of the larger economy and is secondary, in regard to income, to wage labor. There are only a handful of family heads with over 100 *dunams* (about 25 acres) of land. No one can supply his subsistence needs from farming alone. The tendency has been to reduce the number of crops grown to wheat, barley and sesame, to sell these crops, and to purchase needed food. People continue to supply some of their eggs, milk, cheese, olives, oil, vegetables, flour. But even these must be purchased in most cases or at some time. Food needs have also changed; thus meat is now eaten fairly often. It is mainly wage labor outside the village that provides the means to buy food and cover other needs.

Table I represents a breakdown of economic-occupational groupings of the village for the years 1920–25, 1956–57 and 1963.

The economic-occupational groupings may seem arbitrary, and require explanation. This arbitrary character of the terminology stems from the fact that we see these groupings in transition. What was true forty and more years ago is no longer true today. The agriculturists, share-croppers, agriculturists-laborers, shepherds, cameleers, miscellaneous village workers and, in fact, many of the manual laborers and merchants, were all essentially peasants. Further, these categories of forty years ago do not represent differences in means of livelihood, all of which came from agriculture, nor differences in occupational tasks, since all were dictated by agricultural demands. We may therefore look upon them as groupings of peasantry divided mainly by ownership chances. For example, "agriculturists" designate those small proprietors who worked their own land. "Share-croppers" include those who were landless or practically so, or sons who became share-croppers or temporary tenants of others within the division of labor operating in their father's extended family. Sons might become cameleers, or shepherds, etc., and then, on receiving their inheritance, become proprietors. Ownership chances might determine temporary economic position; life chances, while fluid (one year a cameleer, next year a share-cropper), bound all to being economically, occupationally, peasants. The economic-occupational groupings which are difficult to differentiate for the

TABLE I

Economic-Occupational Groupings of an Arab Village in Israel* (Males over age 14–15)

Groupings	1920–25		1957		1963	
	Moslems	Christians	Moslems	Christians	Moslems	Christians
Agriculturists	34 18%	13	30 8%	10	16 4%	9
Share-croppers (Agriculturists)	26 12%	5	4	—	—	—
Agriculturists-Laborers	20 11.5%	10	68 18%	20	32 6.5%	8
Shepherds	25 19%	4	53 16%	—	34 8%	—
Cameleers	43 23%	17	4	—	—	—
Miscellaneous village workers	5	2	8	5	4	3
Non-workers	7	3	23	10	31	12
Merchants	2	4	20 5%	6	46 9.5%	12
Manual laborers and village artisans	11+5 12%	20+2	99+6 32%	68	246 56%	73
Non-manual laborers	—	—	7	6	7	7
Secondary school	—	—	3	10	13	8
Live outside village (permanently)	—	—	6	23	4	43
TOTALS	178	80	331	158	433	175

* Percentages do not include individuals who live permanently outside the village.

period forty years ago, take on definite form with the inclusion
of the village in the general economic system. For example,
manual workers become a permanent group economically and
occupationally determined by market demands.

We can now follow, in some detail, the character of the transition of these economic-occupational groups to the status of wage
laborers, living in the rural area. We shall discuss in turn each
of the categories that appear in the chart.

AGRICULTURISTS: By agriculturists I mean men who were exclusively or almost entirely active peasants on their own land. Thus
approximately in the early 1920's, 18% of the villagers or their
sons were peasant-proprietors or agriculturists. The percentage
of active agriculturists in 1957 was 8%; in 1963 it was only 4%.
Cultivable land in the village has actually increased over the last
ten years, and most people have some, if little, land, even though
the male working population today is approximately two-and-a-
half times that of 1920. Two tractors were first introduced in the
village in 1953 but most villagers continued to employ their oxen.
Only during the last few years when village surplus labor began
to encounter growing work opportunities in the Jewish sector did
it become economically realistic to utilize farm machinery. In
1963 the major ploughing and harvesting (with a number of exceptions in regard to wheat harvesting) was done by some ten
hired tractors and harvesting machinery. Twenty years ago there
were some one hundred oxen in the village; today there are about
forty. Only a few agriculturists use plough animals exclusively
for major work tasks although vegetable plots, vineyards or olive
groves are, in most cases, still ploughed with animal power. The
agriculturists of forty years ago were mainly young men working
for their fathers within the structure of the extended family. Today they are mainly middle-aged men whose sons are wage earners occupied outside the village. Only two or three farmers
operate at what can be considered profits. I do not believe that
any agriculturist netted $1,000 for a year's farming of his own
land, though one or two may have done so by renting land in
addition to their own. Comparative figures for Arab and Jewish
farming for 1960 estimate the annual income per person employed in agriculture at 3,123 I£ in the Jewish sector and 1,700 I£

in the Arab sector. The average wage in Israel is 3,180 I£ per year (about $1,000) in the Jewish sector. Such figures indicate that Arab agriculture is essentially at the below-subsistence level. Nevertheless, this agriculture yields some food for each family, though it is now wage labor which largely underwrites the standard of living.

SHARE-CROPPERS (AGRICULTURISTS): The share-croppers worked for other landholders in the village and received one-fifth of the crop. In 1920 they represented 12% of the population, in the 1940's about 3%, in 1957 less than 1%, and today there are none. These share-croppers worked the land of others with the plough animals and seed of the owners. The great number of share-croppers in the past probably reflected the great poverty of the population and the inability of many to obtain or use land and/or plough animals and seed of their own. Today they are non-existent as a class due to the opportunity for wage earning both within and outside the village; agricultural workers are paid in money.

AGRICULTURISTS-LABORERS: One definitive group for our understanding of the transitional processes within the economic-occupational groupings of the village is that of the agriculturists-laborers. In 1920 the majority of these individuals worked in lime extraction; others worked as harvesters in the village and surrounding villages for either part of the crop or wages, when not farming on family land; some combined farm work with a craft. In all cases their work was within the village or within another Arab village. While this same category existed in 1957 and continues to exist today, there has been a marked change. Forty years ago such individuals began to seek wage labor, when free from family agriculture. Later laborers without fixed work outside the village returned to help out at farming especially during the harvest season. At first this group showed a marked growth. In 1920 there were 11.5% in this category; their number increased to 18% for 1957. During the last six years, however, wage labor outside the village has become definitive, for today 6.5% only are in this combined grouping. Extensive farming, which is seasonal, and formerly commanded the labor and part-time aid of all persons has been left, to a high degree, to middle-aged people and machinery.

SHEPHERDS: In 1920 the shepherds worked within the village. Many of them worked mainly for their own families; some worked also for other households where they were paid in kind, receiving part of the newborn flock, milk and measures of wheat. Most shepherds were Moslems. Christian shepherds were rare in the Arab village; over the last 15 years at least there have been none. This may be due to the fact that Christians had fewer flocks; low status was attached to the work; the most young shepherds are removed from school early or have not attended school, a rarity in the Christian community. Our figures thus relate to the Moslem component of the population. Fourteen per cent of the Moslems were shepherds in 1920, 16% in 1957. Again there has been an important socio-economic shift. In 1957 one-third of the shepherds worked for wages as shepherds outside the village and a number worked for wages within the village. Today, in 1963, only 8% of the Moslems are shepherds; almost all are family shepherds or take care of flocks for others in the village. Thus, between 1957 and 1963, many of the low-paid shepherd youths became laborers. Moreover, herding has become an important branch of the economy with many shepherds being helped by fathers or brothers. Flocks have grown in size and while many own small flocks for household needs, the tendency is to concentrate small flocks and to entrust them to the care of a number of flock-tending families. With the rise in meat prices in the general economy, and with more people eating meat, a business interest has developed in herding, especially over the last five years. About six families, or cooperating brothers, can be classified as herders netting a profit from their own flocks and those of others. Today, hired shepherds receive part of the newborn flock (one-third instead of one-fourth as formerly), some money for each goat's care (instead of the former payment in kind, of wheat) and Thursday's milk.

CAMELEERS: Camel transport and haulage was the village means of conveyance forty years ago: sixty men, 23% of the villagers, were cameleers. Camels were utilized for hauling grain from the fields of the village, and from those of neighboring and even distant villages, with cameleers taking measure of wheat in payment; for hauling lime; bringing goods back and forth from the Acre market, etc. Some of the cameleers were also merchants in lime and charcoal. The great number of cameleers in the village in the 1920's seems to relate not only to increasing possibilities for trade but even more to the fact that in the peasant economy with its seasonal agricultural demands, villagers tended to fill every possible work opportunity both within and outside the village. The family allocated its labor resources as rationally as was possible, at this level of the economy: one son became a farmer, another a shepherd, a third a cameleer or merchant. With altered commercial and trade systems, with trucks and modern transportation, only four men worked as cameleers in village haulage in 1957. Today in 1963 there are no cameleers or camels remaining in the village, although there are still numerous donkeys.

MISCELLANEOUS VILLAGE WORKERS: This category includes village watchmen, village criers–servants, priests, a Moslem prayer-caller, a Moslem religious head. Previously, I included in this category part-time carpenters, woodworkers, plough repairers, shoemakers, a saddle maker and barber (Rosenfeld, 1959*b*) because of their organic and traditional connection with the village and because they were commonly paid in kind. The craft-artisans among them now work for money payment only; the watchmen are paid wages by a local council; the barber is paid both in money and kind. In the period under consideration, village artisans, paid in kind, have given way to artisans and laborers who receive money payment and who have joined the labor force seeking work outside the village. For this reason they have been added to the manual laborer and village artisan category.

NON-WORKERS: Many of the non-workers today were non-workers six years ago when they were in their fifties. Today almost all of the 43 men in this group are over 60 years of age. In the past more men with grown sons probably stopped physical work at an earlier age than today. Some of these men may do some part-time work during the harvest season when they help in threshing or guard their vineyards. On the whole they are now supported by sons. Many of the men enjoy small sums through National Insurance. In 1963 they constitute slightly more than 7% of the male population over age 15, as they did in 1957. In at least seven instances these men are either members of the local council or lineage heads. Thus these older men fall into two categories: a category of leaders, usually land owners, wealthier men, who have sons working for them; and another grouping of individuals who may perform simple tasks, often on their own land, or who are totally inactive, but whose sons are now responsible for the operation of the household. In 1920, the ten non-workers were almost all family or lineage heads—land owners with others working for them.

MERCHANTS: The handful of merchants of 1920 traded in seeds, lime, animals and olive oil. Their number has increased greatly only over the last five years: from 5% in 1957 to 10% in 1963. The term merchant is a catch-all for individuals engaged in trade in many different ways. Often they are little more than marginal types, exploring every possibility for trade that will allow them to step into the higher prestige category attached to earnings without physical labor. More than a dozen men trade seasonally in village manure: they have their own trucks and hire workers for loading. Others contract to take village women for agricultural work on Jewish plantations and settlements. Still others are truck owner-drivers or part-owners. There are eight animal merchants, a few seed merchants. With the great increase of food purchases, especially over the last five years, new shops have opened, about ten people are shopowners. A number of merchants are in partnership with other Arabs or with Jews. There are today twenty-seven truck or car owners in the village, almost all of whom have appeared over the last eight years. The increased and general contact with cities and markets, the great movement of workers about the country has given vehicle owners an opportunity to discover various commercial possibilities, especially those connecting the Arab village with the broader Jewish sector. The wealthiest people in the village are among the merchants and, while some are also large land owners, agricultural income is secondary for them, many hiring their land out to others.

MANUAL LABORERS AND VILLAGE ARTISANS: In the 1920's manual laborers worked almost exclusively in lime and charcoal extraction on the mountain behind the village. At best they represented 12% of the male population and most combined this work with harvesting for others; some few combined it with a craft. These individuals were among the first wage workers in the village. World War II marked the revolutionary change in the village work patterns. For a brief time some 42% of the villagers (56% of the Christians) found work outside, but with the end of the inflationary period (and then with the Arab-Israel war) the majority returned again to the village. Some ten years after the establishment of the Jewish state, the trickle of villagers looking for work in Jewish towns and settlements had again expanded greatly and is now a permanent feature in the economy of Israel. By 1957, 35% of the male population living in the village could be regarded as manual laborers commonly working outside the village (33% of the Moslems, 50% of the Christians). Six years later their number is 56% (about 58% of the Moslems and 55% of the Christians). The number of persons who formerly combined agriculture and wage labor dropped considerably over the six year period: the direction is towards wage labor alone. If we combine the agriculturists-laborers, the non-manual laborers and the hired shepherds, all of whom work at least part-time for wages, with these increasingly full time laborers more than two-thirds of the villagers, or 67%, are wage workers. It is reasonable to say that over sixty years ago there were no wage earners in the village; that forty years ago, and at best at the height of a season, not more than 25% of the men might have been gaining some part-time wages. At the present time, according to my estimate, 90% of those between ages 15–45 seek wages.

Space does not permit us to dwell on a total breakdown of the type of work performed by these laborers over the years. We shall do so, in brief, only for the year 1963. The overwhelming number of Moslems worked as non-skilled agricultural laborers in Jewish villages and settlements, non-skilled manual workers in

Jewish cities, manual laborers for village merchants, or dish-washers in urban restaurants. Not more than 20% qualify as skilled workers, such as plasterers, masons, tractor drivers, truck drivers, mechanics, cooks. Not more than 20% of the laborers have permanent work; most average 15 work days a month over the years. Here the Christian Arabs contrast markedly with the Moslems. More than one half of the Christian laborers have trades, they are mainly plasterers, but also carpenters, masons, plumbers, tractor drivers, skilled cooks and bakers. A relatively larger number of non-skilled Christians are permanently employed. In general the Christians have a higher educational level than the Moslem Arabs, a history of mission schools and a long history in the crafts.

NON-MANUAL WORKERS: Eight of those living in the village today are teachers (in addition to two women), two are policemen and four are clerks, government employees, local council personnel. Thus only two per cent of the male villagers can be considered non-manual workers.

I wish to discuss, in brief, the secondary school students in the village and those who have left the village permanently. Neither are economic-occupational groups, but by including the students we complete the picture of all the males over age 14 in the village and gain a perspective on future occupational trends. Those who have left the village are discussed, because they high-light a world-wide process which, in this instance, has affected only one part of the village community.

Although there are individuals who attended secondary school during the late Mandatory period, they were exceptions and limited in most cases to a year or two of additional schooling. In the 1920's there were no secondary school students. In 1957 there were thirteen. In 1963 twenty-one attend secondary or vocational school. The overwhelming majority of youths pass into the labor force of the unskilled, work with fathers or brothers on the land or become shepherds. In 1957 Christians outnumbered Moslem students while today the latter show the greater absolute number in the village. This reversal is due to the fact that 43 Christians have moved permanently to the city and many of their children are students. In general the country's Christian population has

placed greater emphasis on education and has been able to utilize church and Mission educational facilities.

Within Israel as a whole, as well as in the village, Christians
and Moslem Arabs present marked contrasts. Even before the
Arab-Israel war, a higher proportion of all Palestinian Christian
Arabs than Moslems lived in the northern cities of Nazareth and
Haifa. Many of these Christians have remained in these cities
after the war, their number increasing steadily due to immigration of Christians from the villages. Two-thirds of the Christian
Arab community in Israel is now urban. One-fourth of the Christian inhabitants of our village have taken up permanent residence
in urban centers, though most still retain ownership of at least
some small parcel of land in the village, and a majority visits
there from time to time. At the same time, a larger proportion of
Christians than Moslems in the village investigated has permanent
work in cities. All have relatives in town. More stable work op
portunities and greater urbanization among the Christian Arabs
have further reinforced their greater utilization of educational
facilities.

In contrast, the Moslem Arab population of the village—now
constituting about 75% of the total village population—remains
essentially rural in ties. Relatively more Moslem Arabs seek work
outside the village than do Christians, under present circumstances, yet none have left the village permanently. Almost all
Moslems are unskilled workers. Arab cities—in southern Israel
—once contained larger Moslem populations. Today, however,
they are either non-Arab, or lie outside the borders of Israel. Thus
major Arab urban centers which could absorb rural migrants no
longer exist. Moreover, the Military Government of Israel, both
for security reasons and in order not to flood the market with
cheap and largely unskilled Arab labor, at one time severely
restricted the movement of Arabs from one part of the country
to another. Any Arab urbanization in the future would depend
on two factors: the ability of Arabs to gain permanent jobs as
skilled workers in urban centers on the one hand, and a radical
change in economic, social and political relations with the Israel
Government and the Jewish population on the other. Neither
of these changes appears imminent. Meanwhile almost 80% of

all laborers return to the village every day while about 20% return once a week or less frequently.

THE PERSISTENCE OF A "RESIDUAL" PEASANTRY

Thus the Arab villagers have been transformed from a village-dwelling peasantry to a proletariat living in villages. When at least 60% of the males of a typical Arab village earn wages mainly outside the village, one may no longer call them peasants. While they dwell in villages, they operate economically in a wage market, tied to the Jewish sector of the economy.

Not only do wage earners working in the Jewish sector now predominate, but traditional work patterns have also altered, work for payment in kind has ended, modern transportation has removed the cameleer, and a growing number of merchants reflects the changed pattern of production and distribution. The Christian Arab community has changed radically, not so Moslem Arabs: their population has increased greatly, but they remain rural dwellers.

We have said that a bare four per cent of the male working population can be called agriculturists today; another eight per cent are shepherds. In 1920, 72 per cent were agriculturists, share-croppers, shepherds or cameleers. Yet, the fields are not idle. Nearly all are cultivated, even though the major tasks are now done in many cases by agricultural machinery. Agriculture remains a major concern. Many wage workers continue to help in family farming during periods of idleness, even though the number of persons occupying full-time agricultural roles has decreased.

Other features of the traditional culture also persist. The extended family continues. The father owns the land, and sons are formally landless until his death. The marriage system has not altered. In the village studied, over the last four to five generations more than thirty per cent of all marriages were paternal cousin *hamule* marriages. Another forty per cent were marriages within the village (Rosenfeld, 1957: 46). During the last decade close to 60 per cent have been paternal cousin marriages and another 25 per cent of all marriages have taken place within the village. There exist large *hamayil,* whose growing numbers make such marriages possible, where eighty per cent of all marriages are endogamous within the *hamule.*

This tendency towards increased endogamy may be due in part to the absolute decrease of the Arab population as a consequence of the Arab-Israeli war. Yet this can hardly constitute the major cause of this phenomenon, since endogamy increased in the village studied, together with an absolute increase in the village population. The continuation of the pattern, in a situation in which the overwhelming majority of young men seek work outside the village, appears paradoxical. Yet it may be explained in part by the particular social attitudes and relations prevailing between Jews and Arabs and, in part, by the continuing depressed position of Arab village women. Men are free in their movements and actions outside the village, while women are not. Women have taken to working in groups for wages, outside the village, especially in agricultural tasks. They nevertheless remained severely restricted and confined. Male prerogatives in owning and using property continue unchanged. To obtain personal security, women forego their formal property rights in order to enjoy kinship rights (Rosenfeld, 1960). As long as men do not grant their women freedom, they must marry them themselves. At the same time, each *hamule* seeks to guarantee a marriage for every *hamule* son or daughter. Pressure is still placed on young men and women to this end.

Similarly, bride price continues to flourish (Granqvist, 1931; Rosenfeld, 1957: 47–50), especially among Moslems. Laborers and intellectuals both bemoan the high bride prices. But the institution draws continued strength from its association with patriarchal control. Sons are tied to their fathers until they marry —their dependence is a function of their obligation to pay bride price. Thus, bride price remains the key in determining when a person marries and whom he may marry. Disappearance of the bride price would seriously impair both patriarchal control and *hamayil* structure.

Such a population—largely dependent on wage labor, yet maintaining contact with the land, and cleaving to the traditional social relations based on control of land—we may term a "residual" peasantry. The persistence of such a peasantry, product of the feudal past within a society with advanced agriculture and advancing industry such as Israel, presents a paradox. This remains true even though progressive health, welfare and educational facilities have been provided to villagers by the government of Israel. The paradox is maintained by two interrelated sets of conditions. One of these underlying complexes is internal to the village: it consists of the traditional property system within the village. The other set is external: it derives from the relation of the State of Israel to the Arab village.

The traditional property system, tied to the traditional alignments of kin, inhibits the development of a more advanced form of agriculture. Agricultural plots are small and scattered throughout the village. With each new generation, plots are subdivided still further upon inheritance. Given a growing population, this form of peasant proprietorship creates its own labor surpluses. It also maintains the unproductive character of Arab cultivation.

The subsistence character of agriculture, characteristic of the feudal regime, continues unaltered. Farming involves the cultivation of small plots, and remains extensive, dry, and non-diversified. With only a few differences, the subsistence-tax crops grown forty years ago and 140 years ago (Burckhardt, 1822: 296, 323; Robinson and Smith, 1841: III, 25, 265) are still grown today. What has altered is not the character of subsistence agriculture, but the subsistence level of the Arab villager. Because of growing wage labor, he no longer lives at the level provided by his traditional form of cultivation. It was the economic, social and political relations of the feudal regime which defined the subsistence level of the agriculture and the social organization of this peasantry. Therefore, the second and, I believe, the definitive condition for the existence of a "residual" peasantry is the relation of the State to Arab village production and to its social organization.

Thus Arab agriculture lags behind Jewish agriculture, even though improved agricultural prices here and there are stimulating an increase in agricultural productivity and spurring the introduction of machinery, together with irrigation. Three per cent of Arab cultivated land is now irrigated. Yet, as mentioned, the annual income per person employed in Arab agriculture remains half that of the annual income per person employed in agriculture within the Jewish sector, and the value of agricultural produce per *dunam* of cultivated area among Arabs is only one-fourth of that among Jews. Forty per cent of the total Jewish agricultural area is irrigated (Flapan, 1962). A further development of Arab agriculture, whether capitalist or Socialist, would require both the introduction of larger sums of capital and the wholesale reorganization of existing property relations. In either case we would not consider the rural dwellers a peasantry.

Furthermore, and despite the establishment of local councils and the introduction of elections for local representatives to such councils in one-third of the Arab villages, the *hamule* system continues in force. It continues to be supported by the State of Israel, much as it was supported in more extreme form by the British Mandatory government and the Ottomans. In the past, *hamayil* representatives or the civil heads or heads of the village, the *muhtar*—usually the representative of the most powerful and prestigious *hamule* in the village—were usually in league with the tax farmers and money lenders against their own fellow villagers. Today, the feudal elite has disappeared; but the *muhtar*, as well as lineage heads and others, still receive special privileges if they can guarantee the cooperation of their kinsmen. The Israeli authorities let it be known that these go-betweens are "their men", and that such a role brings advantages to the occupant. Actual violence between *hamayil* in any one village is not as common today as it was two decades ago. Yet its occasional recurrence indicates the persisting tendency to factionalism within the village structure. The larger number of Arab laborers working for wages outside the village, the growing number of merchants throughout the country, form groups which crosscut *hamule* ties, and signal the development of classes. Yet the state continues to emphasize its ties with the *hamayil*, generated during the feudal regime. It thus upholds and reinforces the traditional structure of the village through its maintenance of a form of paternalism which makes use of social groupings and their leaders that are tied to the economic and political organization of the past. The Arab villages thus remain economically and politically isolated from the larger economic and political system of the state. Wage labor has bridged this isolation, since the market was receptive to the influx of cheap, unskilled and temporary workers, derived from the reservoir of surplus labor created by the backward productive system of the villages. At the same time the persistence of this productive system, together with the shoring up of traditional social groupings by the State, has restricted the process of proletarianization and underwritten the continuation of a residual peasantry. The resolution of this contradiction awaits a complete change in the economic and political order.

5. A Death and a Youth Club: Feuding in a Turkish Village

The primary aim of this paper is to describe two events which occurred during my second field trip to Turkey,[1] to offer some analysis of them, and to raise one or two general questions. The analysis requires also a description, which I have sought to make complete, if brief, of the patrilineal groups found in these villages.

Folkhead, the village in which I lived on this trip, was fairly large—about 1200 people, living in about 215 households. One afternoon in November, one of the wealthier villagers had invited me to drink coffee in his own guest room. Most of the middling and more prosperous households have a room, usually well away from the family part of the house and the women, which is specially reserved for the men of the household; it is generally known as *oda*, the ordinary Turkish word for *room*. Here the men sit and talk, and entertain their guests. As we finished drinking coffee, we heard a child crying grievously outside. We went out of the room on to the stone platform at the head of the outside staircase which leads up to it. A girl was running into the courtyard of the next house shouting out, "Çocuk vurdular." Literally, this might mean "They have struck a child," and I did not at once realize what she meant. "Dead, dead," shouted the

Reprinted by permission of the author and by the editors of *Anthropological Quarterly*, from Vol. 33, pp. 51–75 (1960).

[1] In 1949 and 1950, I spent about nine months in a village of central Turkey of roughly 100 households, and 640 people, which I here call Blackrock. In 1951, I spent three months in a second village, not far from the first, here called Folkhead, to which I returned for about six weeks in the summer of 1952. Blackrock was fairly remote and poor; Folkhead was richer, more sophisticated, and larger than most villages in the area. I paid a further flying visit to both villages in the summer of 1955.

girl as she disappeared into her house. She had been telling us that a young man had been shot.

The victim, head of a household and father of a young family, had recently returned from military service. He had been shot by a young neighbor, and had died within a few minutes, right outside the guest room of the current village headman.[2] Women were wailing and screaming and gesticulating wildly round the corpse, while a solemn group of men stood by watching, and occasionally trying fruitlessly to restrain them. The murderer had made off; apparently countershots had been fired, but unsuccessfully, and by this time no one seemed concerned to pursue him —that was left to the authorities.

After a while, we retired to the headman's guest room which was close by. The dead lad's father sat in grim silence, while the father's brother sobbed and trumpeted, shouting the name of the dead youth. A younger brother was also crying violently, and for a short while even a woman who had refused to leave the body was brought in to calm down.

In spite of these disturbances, conversation proceeded. The men sitting round discussed what had happened, and when the doctor would come. They praised the excellence of the young man—only his friends and kinsmen were present. There was a marked sense of shock—"A vile and outrageous act," they said. It was so sudden. "If only there had been a quarrel, insults flying, and fighting," they kept repeating. Nevertheless, the blame was not put on the murderer's shoulders. In the villages they were used to this sort of thing. "A barbarous people." "Our life is rotten." People condemned their village freely. They saw the killing as a part of the village way of life.

The next day, a doctor and other officials arrived and carried out a formal inquiry, and the corpse was buried. The young murderer was arrested in a day or so in another village, and put in jail. He was eventually sentenced to ten years imprisonment. For a day or two the atmosphere in the village was tense with fear of reprisal, but things slowly returned to a sort of sombre normal, and three years later no reprisal had taken place.

Acts of violence in Turkish villages are fairly common. People

[2] Headmen are elected every two years, and very rarely stand for office for a second term.

are quick to resent insult, and most adult men are armed with knives or revolvers. I heard of many cases during my field work. In this village another fight took place shortly after I left, and led to shooting, though the victim recovered. In Blackrock, between my first visit in 1949 and 1953, there had been to my knowledge two killings and three woundings. Reports from other local villages and from other parts of Turkey indicate that these two villages are by no means exceptional. The description and analysis of this particular quarrel may therefore throw some light on a more general problem, namely the social conditions which lie behind these acts of violence. But first I must outline village social structure.

Everyone in the countryside in this area must be a member of at least two kinds of groups—village (*köy*) and household (*ev* or *hane*). Villages are distinct clusters of houses, separated from each other by anything from half an hour to two hours' walk over bare, unfenced fields,—often broken by rocky, sharp escarpments or even mountains. Each village is composed of patrilineally organized households. Normally, married sons live in their father's household so long as he is alive, and brothers often remain together for a while afterwards. Men rarely migrate from village to village.

Within the village, the men of these households form patrilineal kinship groups, which with hesitation I call lineages. They are not of very wide span—the effective group usually consists of households whose heads acknowledge a common ancestor two or three generations above the senior living generation. In Blackrock, with about 100 households in all, the largest effective lineage was twenty households strong. Seven others, ranging from four to ten households strong, showed some solidarity. The remaining thirty-four households had no agnatic affiliation beyond a fraternal household or two. For Folkhead where my information is less comprehensive, the situation, proportionate to size, was similar. AY lineage, of which I give the details below, was the largest lineage at nineteen households.

These lineages have no formal constitution. They are not legal or jural persons,—they own nothing in common, they have no common ritual corresponding to totem or ancestor worship, and they are not exogamous. They do have names, and there is a village word for this type of group—*kabile*, the Istanbul Turkish word for a tribe, taken from Arabic,—but they have no other symbols of unity. It has been suggested that the term 'corporate group' is a tautology,[3] and in strict logic this makes sense. Yet it also makes sense to say of these groups that they are not corporate,[4] but depend rather on the duties which the individual members owe each other as patrikin. These duties are many and complex, but one overrides all the others—a man must support all members of his lineage in any quarrels and fights in which they are involved. Other duties, such as help in times of economic crisis or in sickness, or help with marriage arrangements and expenses, may be given to near kin who are not members of the lineage, but the obligation to fight on each other's behalf is confined to lineage members. Of course, any men present at a fight are clearly liable to join in, but if they do so, then it is ad hoc, out of friendly zeal or passing anger, and not a matter of duty; and they risk embroiling their own lineage in the quarrel.

If a man is in trouble with his neighbors, his patrikin will come to his aid, and in doing so, will be acting together as a group. But it is not only at times of open fighting that this situation occurs. Quiescent hostility is normal in the villages. For this, the villagers use a word 'küs,' by which they mean a sort of mutual sulking. It implies the state of mind of Achilles in his tent,—one has been wronged or insulted, and broken off normal social relationships. The negative of *küs* is 'to speak to each other'; to say "We are speaking to each other" (*konuşuyoruz*) may sometimes mean "We have been reconciled." Any self-respecting lineage is more than likely to be *küs* with at least one other similar group.

The lineage exists to defend its members. When in Blackrock, I once suggested migration to distant parts of Turkey as a solution to land poverty, they at once said: "But if we quarrelled, who would come to our aid?" But at the same time, the existence of the lineage depends on its having enemies against which to defend its members; since it has no other occasion for corporate

[3] Remarks of Professor Daryll Forde in a seminar.
[4] See Fortes (1953:25) for a discussion of the "corporate" nature of unilineal groups. Evans-Pritchard (1940:203) remarks, however, that Nuer lineages are not corporate.

action. A lineage at peace with its neighbors would lose the main point of its existence.

Not all households are effective members of lineages, and not all lineages take their solidarity seriously. In societies where unilineal groups are more important than they are here, it may be impossible to survive without the support of a powerful lineage to defend one's rights. But in these villages, many households are isolated. This isolation may result from one or more of a number of causes; namely the dying out of collateral branches, genealogical remoteness from, or simply lack of interest in one's agnates, active quarrelling with them, or migration to a new village.

Households which have lost all their close agnates may become relatively prosperous, by inheriting a sufficiency of good land; though prosperity also depends on the size and industry of the household. Sometimes a poor or slow-witted man will ignore agnates if they are not very close, or they will ignore him. Quarrels between very close agnates, though common, do not usually become permanent, especially if the lineage is under pressure from outside. I did record one case where a man, claiming membership of a large lineage with which he had quarrelled, was left to shoot it out with another large lineage supported only by his own sons.

Most migrants between villages move into their mother's village, and marry her brother's daughter or other close kinswoman, and in these cases sometimes seem to be regarded more or less as full members of her lineage. In Folkhead, there were two immigrant households which had no local kin ties at all, and there were also about fifteen households of refugees from eastern Turkey, who had been living in the village at least since the Russian invasion in the first World War. Among these are now groups of households whose heads are brothers, and the whole group is sometimes spoken of as 'the refugees.' Most of them live in the same quarter, and tend to intermarry rather more with each other than with the old established village households. But they are not equivalent to a lineage, although they contain the beginnings of several separate lineages.

It is mainly poor households which seem to avoid lineage responsibilities and do without lineage support. Many poor households belong to small groups of brothers or brothers' sons, and one or two lineages of considerable size whose members are all poor and of low social rank do not appear to take their lineage membership seriously. On the other hand, large and effective lineages always seem to include a number of middling or poor households, clustered round and supporting close agnates of greater power and wealth.[5]

To say that the effective group normally has a common ancestor no more than three generations above the senior living generation is not to say that they do not know of more remote agnatic links. AY and AX (see Figures 5-1 and 5-2), for example, are part of a common patrilineal stock, which they claim now numbers more than sixty households in all. In several other cases, I was given a list of five or so ancestors above the living, going back to the man who had come to the village and founded the patrilineal stock. But this information was often difficult to get, and clearly not felt to be of much importance.

The large stock A is typical in everything but its unusual size. It contained 48 households without question, according to my census of the village. Although some branches had moved away to the outskirts, the original quarter of the village which belonged to it still contained the majority of its member households. AY, though I have called it one effective lineage, was divided into two segments, one AYp, consisting of eight households, and the other, AYq, of ten. The group seemed to be led mainly by the brothers AY1 to AY4, and all AYp seemed to support them. Many members of AYq also associated closely with them, but not all—the estimate of nineteen households is based on genealogical completeness, not on certainty that all these people would in fact fight for AY in a quarrel.

AX's genealogical link to AY1 I did not discover, and though it was fairly close, they were very definitely distinct social groups.

Besides these two main segments, there were a number of other small groups. One set of two well-to-do brothers, plus a son separated from his father, and a brother's son, appears to have been FFFSSS to AY1, but seemed fairly aloof. There was another group of five households, consisting of three fairly poor brothers (who had been brought up by their mother's brother), their

---

[5] The reason for this lies in the effects of household fission and egalitarian inheritance rules. This matter will be dealt with in a future publication.

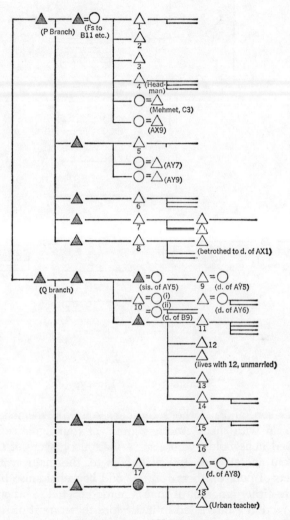

FIGURE 5-1 AY Lineage

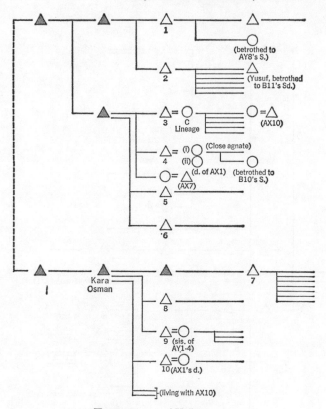

FIGURE 5-2   AX Lineage

brother's son, and a father's brother's son who seemed to have
little to do with them. Another group of four agnatically inter-
connected households, who also seemed aloof, were of the same
patrilineal ancestry as, and neighbors to, the main group. Two
other sets of poor brothers and one odd household also belonged,
but were either ignorant of their agnatic link to the other groups,
or else were not interested in it. Besides these, a set of six households claiming close and definite agnatic connections between
themselves, were said by some to belong and by others not to
belong to the same stock. The evidence was contradictory, the
statements of informants being clearly influenced by current relations of friendship or hostility. In any case, no one was greatly

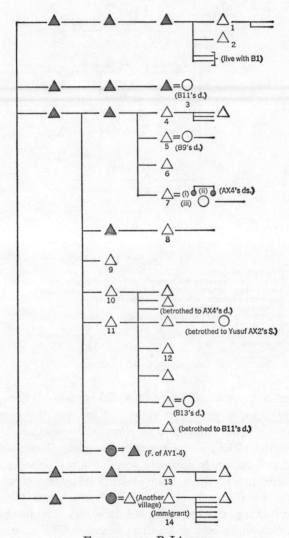

FIGURE 5-3 B Lineage

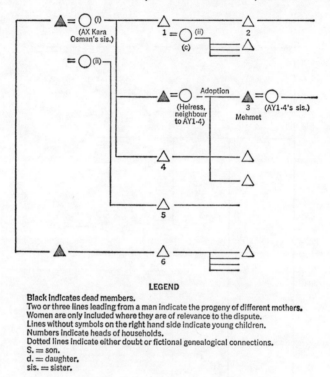

LEGEND

Black indicates dead members.
Two or three lines leading from a man indicate the progeny of different mothers.
Women are only included where they are of relevance to the dispute.
Lines without symbols on the right hand side indicate young children.
Numbers indicate heads of households.
Dotted lines indicate either doubt or fictional genealogical connections.
S. = son.
d. = daughter.
sis. = sister.

FIGURE 5-4   C Lineage

interested in the matter. These fifty odd households then did not
constitute a social group, in spite of their agnatic connections,
and many of them belonged to no effective lineages at all.

The segmentation, and ultimately complete fission, of agnatically related groups is normally gradual. Since lineages have no
formal constitution, there is no definite criterion by which one
can say that a former lineage has now become two. Clearly segmentation along the genealogical lines is normal—that is, a
lineage with three sets of brothers who are FBS to each other
would tend to operate as three related groups rather than as one
undifferentiated group. Increasing genealogical distance, physical separation due to change of house sites, and the non-
occurrence over a period of events in which all have a common

interest or duty all weaken lineage ties, and in the end lead to total fission. Specific quarrels such as that between AX and AY cause a sudden and more definite break. But in most cases I came across, quarrels between agnates, however common, were unlikely to be accepted as beyond hope of reconciliation unless the genealogical distance was such as to justify total fission.

So far, I have said only that the main duty of lineage members to each other is that of fighting on each other's behalf. To observe exactly who fights on a given occasion would be extremely difficult, and in any case, I never actually witnessed a fight. My estimate, therefore, as to who acknowledges lineage loyalty and who does not is bound to be impressionistic. Since people may in fact feel mutual loyalty without showing much mutual cordiality, this is not always reliable, but sufficient of these estimates are based on good evidence adequately to support my general argument. Only those households who are themselves sufficiently important to contend for power, or who are agnatically close to such households, constitute effective lineages engaged in more or less continuous quarrels.

Defence in quarrels is not the only mutual duty of agnates. Lineage members are expected to help each other in distress from sickness, crop failure or other disaster. They attend in force at each other's weddings and funerals, and assist with the expense and chores. They are often close neighbors, and associate informally, especially in sitting together at seasons of leisure in the guest room of one of the better-off members of the lineage. At religious festivals, they often do their visiting, sacrificing or entertaining together. But in none of these respects does the lineage act as a body. The group which is helping a man to celebrate a wedding, or bury a corpse, or help an ailing man out with his harvest will contain, besides a core of near agnates, other kin and neighbors.

Agnates are expected to give each other their daughters in marriage. As in many other Islamic societies, FBd is said to be the preferred marriage partner, and people sometimes talk and behave as though a man had a right to the first option on his FBd. But in these villages only about 10% of the marriages of which I hold records were with a FFBSd or closer agnate. Such marriages are both a symptom and a reinforcement of lineage solidarity. The effect is to overlay existing relations with even more intimate ones. Hence the overall structural consequences of a small percentage of marriages within the lineage is slight. On the other hand, marriages outside the lineage, which either create new links with other lineages or re-establish old ones, establish a network of ties between lineages very much as do marriages in societies with exogamous lineages.[6]

A senior member of a lineage may have considerable influence —indeed, it is plain that such a group must have some kind of leadership. But outside the authority of an elder brother over his juniors, which is sometimes very marked, lineage leadership is informal, and divided counsels may be unresolvable. The dispute in AX lineage over the betrothal of AX1's daughter in the story which follows is a good example.[7] Moreover, a well-to-do man in Blackrock who did not have the support of a large lineage, built up a body of rather less committed supporters from among his matrilateral and affinal kin, a process which in turn weakened the lineage affiliation of those supporters. Notably, he claimed to be a man of peace, who quarrelled with no one. Could he afford to?

To sum up, then, lineages are groups of households which will combine for mutual support in serious quarrels and fights. The genealogical range of membership is variable, but the group is always united. The members, in view of their agnatic kinship, owe each other many duties besides this support. But it is quarrelling which maintains the lineage, not because quarrels are the only situations where lineage ties are active, but because they are the only occasions when lineage ties are active to the exclusion of all other ties, and when failure to carry out obligations is tantamount to rejection of lineage membership.

Each of the four lineages involved in the quarrel I am about to describe fits the general description I have just given. Each has a central local cluster, each has a guest room where most members of the lineage can be found foregathered on a winter evening, each is involved in quarrels, each contains one or two households of wealth and consequence, and each looks after its own in trouble.

[6] See e.g., Fortes (1953).
[7] See p. 184 below.

On the attached genealogies I have only put in marriages where these are known to me to bear directly on the relationships between the lineages, or where they are within the lineage. Since my information on marriages in this village was far from exhaustive, I cannot say that all marriages of these two classes are included, but most of the marriages which I have not noted can be assumed to be with people not directly concerned in this particular matter, very often with people from other villages.

The frequency of visiting and co-operation which resulted from the existing intermarriages between the various parties to the quarrel naturally declined as a result of the open breach, but they were not forgotten and were felt to make matters even more deplorable. Both sides pointed out to me the connections between AX and C, and also that B11 was mother's brother to AY1 to 4.

Some kind of quarrel between AX and AY seems to have been going on for years. The evidence is scrappy, and some of what follows is perhaps 'conjectural history,' but I have sought to indicate clearly the degree of confidence I feel in the statements I make.

The village has several stories of great men of the past, men who have been in charge of the district of which the village is still the administrative centre. One of these was the father of B11, who spent his wealth going on the pilgrimage to Mecca and died poor, leaving his heirs with very little. The last of the great men was Kara Osman. I met him when he came from his own village to visit some pilgrims who returned from Mecca to Blackrock during my first field trip. He was said 'to have held the whole district in his hand.' I gather he was a sort of semi-official boss of the immediate area during the disturbed period after the 1918 peace. He died, unfortunately, just before I arrived to do field work in his village.

The poor of the village spoke well of him, and he was quoted as having simplified some details of the village marriage customs merely by setting the example himself. His house was far and away the most pretentious in the village, and he was rich by village standards. He had acquired far more land than anyone else in the village simply by ploughing it when a large village whose lands lay adjacent to his own was evacuated by its Christian population during the exchange of population with Greece (1923 onwards). He is said to have employed much labor in former days. He also bought farm machinery when it was still very rare in this part of Turkey, and each year used to take it and hire it out in the fertile and early harvested Cilician plain south of the Taurus. People often said to me, that, after him, the village had no real *ağa*, but only half a dozen or so pretenders to such standing.[8]

Part of the dispute between AX and AY was to do with the revolt against his power—at least that is my reading of the events. My reason for believing this is partly based on national politics.

Up to 1946, Turkey was ruled by a single party, the Republican People's Party. Elections did take place, but all candidates were members of the party, or at least approved by it. At this stage, most villagers did not understand the ideology of the revolution, and were not at all keen on being made to use the infidel script and wear the infidel hat. But they accepted as inevitable the acts of government, and they had deep respect for Atatürk, the Holy Conqueror of the invading Greek forces in the War of Independence (1919–22).[9] Once they had accepted the new government, their previous experience of government led the people to assume that all officials must be members of the ruling 'party,'[10] and accordingly all headmen claimed to be supporters of the R.P.P. After 1946, an opposition party was allowed to form, and this began to organize in the villages, calling itself the Democratic Party—now in power in Turkey. In some villages, for example, in Blackrock, people regarded this new choice as a personal matter, and brothers and neighbors took opposite sides quite openly. But in other villages, of which Folkhead was one, existing factions took on party labels. The headman in office was usually R.P.P., because he and the village assumed it was necessary that he should be, and thus his supporters became R.P.P., while his opponents in the village, for local rather than national reasons, declared themselves supporters of the D.P.

[8] *Ağa* (pronounced in Turkish, roughly, 'ah') is often, as here, used to mean a man of substance and importance. But it has many other uses; for example, it is a common form of address in the villages for any adult man.

[9] See especially Toynbee (1923); and Stirling (1958).

[10] This was the first time most people had heard of political parties, and they used the word *parti*, which to the villagers at first meant *the rulers*.

In Folkhead, the headman in office in 1952, AY4, and his predecessor, were on good terms with each other, and were both supporters of the R.P.P. The village D.P. is led by the other side, B11 and AX2. These facts fit the above interpretation. Previously, B11's eldest son had been headman. During and before his tenure of the office, villagers had been ploughing up village pasture on a large scale. The lands are extensive, but only recently did improved transport and fixed prices lead villagers in large numbers to seek to plough more land than they needed for their own subsistence. In village custom, ploughing village pasture conferred the right to its use; nowadays, after twenty years, this right becomes legally confirmed. My informants describe something of a land rush about the time of the end of the war, which ended in fighting when a section of the village, including AY, objected to the loss of pasture for village animals, and tried to prevent their neighbors, who included AX, from encroaching any further. My surmise is that the split between AY and AX goes back at least to this trouble, and that AY and supporters succeeded in wresting the headmanship from Kara Osman and his faction at this point. At any rate, more fighting took place, with AX on one side and AY on the other, at the 1950 election for headman, when AY4 was elected. At or about this time, AX10 knifed AY3, in a general fight.

C lineage, as far as I know, was not tied up with this struggle. They had ties by marriage with both sides, and have a reputation for aloofness. True, they also appear to have acquired a comfortable sufficiency of land at this point, by the same means, but then so did most village households which had men and oxen available to expand their normal activities. Successful acquisition would not necessarily involve their joining a dispute about the restriction of ploughing up pasture.

So much for the general background. Now let us turn to the immediate series of events. I have already mentioned the fighting at the election for headman in May 1950. In the autumn of that year, apparently, the main incident which led to the killing took place. Mehmet, the victim, was away on military service at the time. His wife and Yusuf (AX2's son) quarrelled over the washing of grain at the fountain. Yusuf struck the girl, and immediately her lineage took reprisals on a woman of his lineage.

A general fight followed. In the spring, apparently, another fight had broken out, also, according to informants, started by Yusuf. No casualties occurred, it seems, on either occasion.

Soon after this flare-up, the District Officer[11] brought the elders of the two sides together in his room, to eat a meal and make peace. Everyone shook hands, but the general relationship of *küs*[12] seems to have continued. However, the atmosphere did relax, and conciliation was under way. AX1, a senior member of his lineage, took the very great step of responding to overtures for marriage from AY8, and promised his daughter to AY8's son. (See Figure 5-1.) If it is true that marriage ties do not prevent the development of feuding relationships, it is also true that to negotiate a marriage one must be at peace, and be expecting the peace to continue.

In the meantime, Mehmet returned from military service, about one month before his death. He is said, with probability, to have told Yusuf what he thought of him, and to have threatened to take revenge for the insult to his wife. Yusuf would certainly have no grounds for supposing that such threats were purely empty. One way of communicating one's feelings on this kind of subject is to abuse with strong language any animal that is within range in the hearing of one's enemy. The hearer cannot take exception without admitting the cap fits, but he and everyone else knows quite well for whom the insults are intended.

Three days before the murder, AY8 and his kin paid a formal betrothal visit to AX1. On their departure, Yusuf was lying in wait, and fired shots—not, it was said, with intent to kill, but simply into the air in the general direction of the departing guests, to indicate strong disapproval of the proceedings.[13] I was told by members of his lineage that he did this with their support. I cannot be sure of this, since they were anxious to whitewash his character after the event, but it seems plausible that he was aiming to express hostility of his lineage in general to the wed-

---

[11] Turkish *Nahiye Müdürü*. This village was the administrative centre for about sixteen villages, that is, one educated townsman was in residence, and was responsible for the affairs of the district or *nahiye*. It also contained a gendarme post, with a corporal in charge.

[12] See above, p. 172.

[13] M. S. Salim (1955:129) reports a similar custom from the Marsh Arabs of Iraq.

ding as much as his own. It appears that AX1 was unmoved, and announced his intention to persist.

I received two contradictory accounts of the actual shooting. Yusuf's kin said that he was being chivvied and threatened by Mehmet and two of his agnates, and acted in self defense. The other side, supported by several neutral witnesses, claimed that Mehmet was quietly driving home his cattle and that Yusuf, who was standing by a wall, simply brought out a gun and fired at close range. It seems quite possible that Mehmet was addressing some uncomplimentary remarks to his oxen, knowing that Yusuf was in earshot.

During the days immediately before the shooting, Yusuf is said to have been behaving a little queerly, refusing work, and coming and going at unorthodox times. On the day in question, he had been to see the clerk of the local Credit Co-operative, an educated young man from the small local town, who was resident in the village, and who happened to be his kinsman. Yusuf announced to him, with considerable agitation, his intention of taking some sort of action to prevent the wedding, and this seems to have been a part of his aim. But if so, why pick on Mehmet? Mehmet was a personal enemy, and was brother-in-law and neighbor to AY1-4. He probably thought to kill two birds with one bullet, to break up the conciliatory wedding, and at the same time settle his private quarrel.

Why was Yusuf so opposed to reconciliation? If I am right in saying that lineage solidarity depends on the existence of active quarrels, then peace might threaten the very coherence of the lineage. But more than this, I would say that a tough lineage carries a good deal more prestige than a peaceful one of equal wealth. A young man of nineteen might have very little standing in the village except what he gains from membership of an important lineage. If so, he would be most unwilling to see this group lose its prestige, even perhaps its solidarity as a unit, by making peace. From his point of view, his father's brother's negotiations for marriage with the enemy were not sensible and good, but traitorous. Moreover, although he was himself engaged to B11's daughter, the girl in question was his own preferred marriage partner, which gave a tenuous traditional right to raise objections to her marrying against his wishes. I do not of course know that he actually reasoned in these terms. Obviously, his anger about the reconciliation would be inarticulate, and complex in its origin. In general, Yusuf was probably aiming primarily to upset the peace overtures current in the village. This brings me back to my point that lineages not only protect their members from quarrels, but also tend to encourage quarrels from which they will need protecting.

The immediate reaction in the village in general was one of horror. Everyone was deeply distressed, and one heard people complaining continually, "The village is sunk." "The sweetness of the village is turned to sourness." The cold-bloodedness of the attack was much censured—high tempers and flying insults would have made the thing at least comprehensible, but this was so unexpected. I wonder if some of this moral indignation was not partly due to the influence of modernism—acquaintance with western notions, and consciousness of Turkey as one of the European nations. In deference to my presence, they even compared the British, who, according to popular belief based on the accounts of Turkish prisoners of war in British hands during the first World War, settle their arguments with fists instead of knives and revolvers. On the other hand, in a small community of intimately related kin and neighbors, such an act of violence is bound to provoke a strong sense of shock, and it may be that such a killing would always have provoked just such a reaction.

C lineage, to which the victim belonged, was and is by all accounts implacable. Both they themselves and all others in the village with whom I discussed the subject declared that sooner or later vengeance was inevitable. They have in any case a reputation for cold aloofness and determination. Twice just after the event, in my presence, ordinary every-day comings and goings were interpreted as a group attack by C lineage. But in any case, such an open attack is not necessary. There is nothing to stop one member of a village lying in wait for and shooting another member of the same village, as Yusuf shot Mehmet. AX2 spoke to me apparently seriously of a plan for leaving the village altogether, and going to Ankara. I doubt if he would in fact do so. Vague talk of leaving the villages may well be another standard reaction to the threat of vengeance.[14]

[14] He had made no move by 1955.

I have already said that acts of violence are not infrequent in these villages. If in each case, vengeance is liable to be exacted in cold blood, then a good few people must walk in fear of their lives. The price of belonging to a lineage of consequence is danger of assassination. These feuds are not between sharply separated territorial units, but in all cases I came across, they are within the village. And moreover, in spite of constant inquiries I was unable to unearth any evidence that there exists, or ever has existed, any recognized procedure for the settlement of homicide disputes by compensation or any other means. It has been said, and plausibly, that the existence of unsettled blood debts within a small community is intolerable,[15] and that this is why so often in primitive and peasant societies, some kind of settlement is not only possible, but morally required. Yet it looks as though we have here an exception, a case where people may be in permanent danger from their daily associates. Is there any explanation?

I returned to the village about eight months after this event, and found that it had led to an interesting series of consequences. Here again, the details are not certain, but the main events are fairly clear.

When I arrived back, I could not occupy the same room as formerly. After much discussion, I was given a room in the school belonging to what I was told was called the Youth Union or Youth Club (*Gençlik Birliği*). This surprised me not a little. Turks are not joiners, not even in the towns. Several commentators[16] have remarked on the remarkable scarcity of any purely spontaneous societies for recreational, social or any other purpose in Turkey. My own experience has confirmed this. Villagers had often told me cheerfully that they could never work together or trust each other, not even for economic gain.[17] Most associations, from national charities to village co-operatives, are begun by official initiative. Why then had this apparently ordinary village suddenly produced a Youth Club, all complete with the

[15] E.g., Evans-Pritchard (1940:156): "Corporate life is incompatible with a state of feud."

[16] E.g., R. D. Robinson (1949), especially No. 37, 5th Sept. 1949.

[17] In fact, quite apart from traditional mutual aid, villagers are beginning to found joint economic enterprises—so far mainly motor driven flour mills, and lorry and bus services.

blessing of the local administration, a meeting room in the school, and a small library of edifying books on such topics as child psychology and poultry keeping?

From various informants I pieced together this account of the events. The winter is the season of weddings, when the harvest is over, and work is slack. Weddings are almost the sole form of village entertainment. At a respectable wedding by a household with sufficient means, the people of the village enjoy four or five days' dancing and tomfoolery, with distributions of coffee and sweets, ending in the climax of the last day's ceremonies. To my knowledge, a considerable number of weddings were fixed for this particular winter—the figure of 25 was mentioned.

A death in the village puts a temporary stop on weddings, since singing, drumming and dancing are taboo for a time after a death—a week or two. But not only do people sing and dance at weddings, they also let off fire-arms. This is dangerous enough in the ordinary way, but with an implacable lineage supposedly thirsting for vengeance, it positively invited disaster. To have a murder done at one's wedding would be an appallingly inauspicious beginning to a new relationship, so it is not surprising that, even when the normal mourning period had elapsed, still no one dared to hold a wedding. This decision lay of course not with grooms, still less with brides, but with their fathers—the fathers of the grooms having the final say.

This stop on weddings was a serious matter. Holding up a wedding is risky—girls are never safe from the danger of scandal till properly married and aging parents need the help of a new daughter-in-law, and want to see grandchildren in the home. The young men were missing their only form of organized merrymaking. It seems that it was first and foremost a common desire to find a way to hold weddings that led to the founding of the Youth Club.

The president of the Youth Club added another motive. He talked a great deal about brotherly love. The young men, he said, were under pressure from their elders to continue the traditional enmities. He claimed that they revolted from this pressure, and sought to defeat the hatreds of the elder generation by a Youth Club dedicated to peace and goodwill. It is often and plausibly said that inter-lineage feuds are organized and encouraged by the senior members, and that young men are deputed to execute the deeds of violence because they are likely to get much lighter sentences in the courts. But I have not observed any lack of enthusiasm on the part of young men for feuds, and I doubt whether any general antipathy to quarrelling had much to do with the founding of the Youth Club.

Whatever the motive, it seems that the young men (*gençler*) —and that includes men up to about forty—organized a meeting, and, on the initiative of the man who became president, founded an association which then or later became known as the Youth Club. The main purpose of the Club was to make it possible to hold weddings in the village. They would approach 'the master of the wedding' (*dügün sahibi*), that is, normally, the father of the groom, and offer to take responsibility for good conduct at his wedding if he would hold it. The Club had about 100 members, and they divided themselves into eight groups, each under a leader, who were to take on so to speak, unofficial police duties, for one week each. I found a list giving the rota of duties from the middle of April to the middle of June, a period coinciding with the comparatively slack period from the end of the Spring ploughing to the beginning of the hay harvest; but the scheme may have got under way earlier in the year. This part of the plan apparently met with complete success—at least, weddings certainly took place, no deaths occurred, and no untoward incidents reached my ears.

The association insisted on all its members being reconciled, and they claimed that only C lineage refused to come in, or to have anything to do with the proceedings. Indeed, C lineage were not, in the summer, even attending the village mosque, but worshipping at mosques in other villages. On the other hand, B11 had paid a formal visit to AY4, thus effecting a formal reconciliation between B and AY, and AX1's daughter was still betrothed to AY8's son.

Once under way, the Youth Club attempted other things. It arranged public labor—some of the village streets were improved, and some of the irrigation ditches cleaned out. It reached official ears, and the Club was duly allotted a room in the school, acquired a collection of suitable books and became part of official village improvement. The club room really appears to have functioned as a meeting place, and expenses were met by collections from members. Unfortunately during my brief stay in the summer, everyone was working on the harvest, and the Club was completely inactive. Some of its members assumed that it would take up where it left off with the return of winter; others expressed doubt.

The Club, in spite of its ostensibly beneficial aims and works, was not approved of by the older and more traditional members of the village. One head of a large household, when asked to give reasons for his strong disapproval, said that it was taking the young men away from their homes, where they were no longer available to carry out their fathers' orders. Others also commented that it encouraged insubordination in the young, while some refused to state reasons, simply saying that it was a bad thing. Some members said they had been charged with subversive political activities, though none of the opponents of the association ever admitted to me that such a charge could possibly have any foundation—which indeed it could not. At all events, it seems that public criticism of the club effectively stopped their public works program.

It is clear that a Youth Club of this sort is not an indigenous feature of village social structure. The wording of the arrangements for the weekly rota of duty was clearly based on the experience of the army which the universal conscription in Turkey gives to every young man. But was it a completely new attempt to solve the problem of an endless chain of vengeance in a small community, or does it reflect some traditional form of social control, using new forms which fit with the new terminology and new values of officialdom? I know of no evidence which would suggest an answer to this question.

The blood feud is generally accepted to be a widespread phenomenon in modern Turkey, and the government is concerned to stamp it out. In this paper, I have sought only to illustrate some of the characteristics of feuding, and of the groups that carry it on, in the area in which I worked, by describing a particular case of homicide, and the remedy which the village improvised to deal with the situation created by it. The striking point about all the feuds of which I have knowledge is that they are conducted between members of one village, who are not territorially separate, and that therefore those who are quarrelling walk in fear of their lives, since their rivals may easily shoot them at any time. In spite of this apparently intolerable situation, no recognized or formal means of reconciling the feuding lineages seems to exist.

Information on the social organization of Turkish villages is scanty, even in the present. For the past, it seems likely that no adequate records exist at all.[18] Nothing I myself have read to date supplies any information which would solve this problem. But it seems beyond belief that this system of uncontrolled and unrestricted revenge has always existed in Turkish villages, or even in some Turkish villages. On the other hand, if some means of controlling feuds existed, and has now ceased to function and been forgotten, then it is surely probable that it was not an explicit institution of arbitration or compensation, for this would not be easily forgotten, but some indirect form of control, not recognized as such.

The power and importance of local leaders has certainly declined sharply with the modernization introduced by the Republic. For example, when a case of stealing occurred in Blackrock, and no action was taken, one of the old men remarked that in the old days the village elders would have forced a restitution of twice the value of any stolen property to the loser. People also often said that litigation in the courts had replaced the headman and elders as a means of settling disputes in the village, a statement supported by my observations.

A second piece of evidence points in the same direction. While in Blackrock, I was several times told that if a fight between lineages breaks out, then it is the immediate duty of neutral lineages to intervene, by force if necessary, in the cause of peace. This may be taken as indicating that feuding was as far as possible suppressed by the rest of the village, when the village indigenous political organization was still vigorous. Another factor which is likely to have been more serious in the less settled days, is the fighting between villages. This still sometimes occurs, but

[18] '. . . in all Moslem countries . . . the village . . . has hitherto been neglected. No Moslem writer in either mediaeval or modern times, has condescended to describe the organization of village life in his country. . . .' Gibb and Bowen (1950). There are, however, one or two recent exceptions to this.

immediately it does so, the gendarmes are brought in, and the fighting stopped. Administrative action and summonses to court follow. Village solidarity against other villages is not now therefore a motive for preserving internal harmony, though very probably it was in the past.

It is, then, plausible to suppose that feuding was kept in check by the strength of indigenous authority within semi-autonomous villages,—that elders not concerned in the quarrel often had enough power to enforce a settlement, aided by the recognized need for solidarity against other villages. If this is true, then, paradoxically, the first results of more efficient control by government of the villages has been, through a decline in the strength of the indigenous political control, an increase in deaths from feuding. The truth or falsity of this hypothesis would be extremely hard to establish beyond doubt.

But quite apart from this historical conjecture, it remains a fact that at present Turkish village feuds know no formal indigenous procedure for compensation or peace-making, as far as I can discover. Among a people who habitually go armed, who are quick to resent insult, and for some of whom at least quarrelling may serve to maintain the coherence and even enhance the prestige of their lineages, this leads to a considerable amount of violence. Up to date, the comparative light sentences given by the courts has certainly made State action against feuding ineffective.

The purpose of this article has been mainly descriptive. But it does, I think, also leave us with the large question, how so uncontrolled a system of feuding can exist at all in such small communities, and whether the commonly accepted 'functional' explanations of the control of feuding within small communities are adequate.

6. *Selections from* The Social History of an Egyptian Village in the Twentieth Century

KINSHIP SOLIDARITIES

The "families"[1] of a village such as Sirs classify themselves each under a name in groups of 500, 1,000 and even 1,500 people. They are residentially distributed symmetrically around a central area, the *Wasaṭ al-balad*. This quarter, neighboring the sanctuary of Abū' r-Rus, still shelters the oldest lineages: those of the Khulif, of the Nweyhi, and of the Khūli. The Copts flank it on all sides. A more thorough examination, when it will be practicable, will certainly reveal here a very special ethnological personality.

If, conforming to a reasonable hypothesis, the development of the village takes place by an expansion outward from the center in the four cardinal directions, then its orthogonal division into four quarters, *nawāḥī*, is quite understandable. It is a division common to all the villages of the Delta. It is the exception when

Translated by Dr. Alexander Fishler, State University of New York at Binghamton, with minor emendations by the editor. Reprinted by permission of the author and publisher from Jacques Berque, Histoire Sociale d'un Village Égyptien au XXème Siècle, Chapters 4 and 5, pp. 47–69. Mouton/Ecole Pratique des Hautes Etudes, Paris–The Hague, 1957.

[1] The term used to designate them is usually *'ā'ila*, or, more rarely, *usra*. Among the various sociological characteristics that define such groups, it is only necessary to note the most conspicuous, the *laqab*, which is defined so to speak by the kin group name. When there is fission, another *laqab* more limited in extent comes into being. This is what is called the *tafarru'*, literally, "the division into branches." I use "kinship" for convenience and in preference to "patriarchal." While I am by no means referring to concepts so complex as the Roman *gens* or the Greek *genos*, we should not forget that these terms have a conspicuous analogue in Arabic, *al-jins*. Curiously, the late P. Anastase, in *Nušu al-Luġa al-'arabiyya* (1938), p. 21, lists six Arabic terms derived, in his view, from this same Indo-European word.

a group abandons the security of its neighbors in order to establish itself in another quarter. In some cases this has happened, however, in Sirs, for example, the Šaršar and the Maʿāz (Ġarbiyya), descended from the Fūlī (Qibliyya); the ʿAbd ar-Raḥmān (Baḥriyya), descended from the Ġorāb (Šarqiyya). But in a more general light, this centrifugal pressure has only reinforced the individual characteristics of each quarter and of each agnatic group. This has definitely been reinforced by the rather stringent rules of intermarriage.

The entire traditional structure of the village proceeds from this configuration.[2] The quarters face each other two by two, or each confronts the three others. Established from ancient balances of power, the opposing groups generally form two factions: in Sirs a North and a South. The former existence of two *šaykhs al-balad* conveys this duality. In such a system, the power of the individual is subordinate to that of the family. And the family depends on many factors: its effective power, its solidarity in the home, its landed wealth, the extent of its internal and external alliances, the capacity and presence of able-bodied men to bring respect to their name. Finally, there are many unequally distributed qualifications of which sharifian descent, education, manual skill and successful farming constitute only the most obvious, the most elaborated.

Several serious disputes formerly brought the leaders of the village order into opposition to each other. The Muhanna were driven out by the Khūli from a district that still bears the name of Kom Muhanna. They emigrated into the district of Damanhour, at Ityayn Barūd, where once again they became prosperous, to such an extent that one of their members, Rašād, took part in a council during the Khedivial Regency. Good relations of mutual assistance and adoption become, in times of stress, the necessary reaction to these violent occasions. The story is still told at Sirs of how the Ġammāls, profiting from their profession as butchers and from the advantages attached to the supplying of meat in an almost vegetarian economy, were able to maintain friendly ties with all the families and thus pursue their social climb in a context of close relations. They avoided thus the stigma that is attached to innovations, and were forgiven their own rapid ad-

[2] See Figure 6-1.

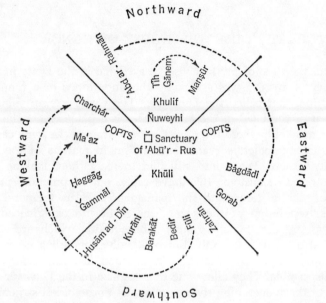

FIGURE 6-1   Concentric structure of the village. Radiation of quarters and families out from the *Wasaṭ al-balad* (Ar., "center of town").

vancement. On the other hand, the Ḥaggāg, reputed for their ostentation, immoderation, and violence, in defiance set up their scaffoldings on the backs of their camels when they built a wall. Hence there is a saying that their threshold is "blue," meaning ungrateful, *'atabathum zerqā*. In fact, each family has its own particular traits. Lively adages and taunts also emerged to express this imbalance of competing groups and further created a tension favorable to the vitality of the village.

At the center of the kinship groups, economic or ritual activities keep in play these precisely defined solidarities. Some exist intact even to this day, while others, more numerous, have died out. The following discussion will try, as far as possible, to bring out the variations and inequalities.

THE "GREAT HOUSE" OR "HOUSE OF HONOR"

From the time of my first visit to a village in the Delta in the summer of 1953, I was struck by the importance of a familiar institution, that called the Duwwār, "The Great House." This is the seat of the head of the family. This is a place where the reunions are held, where the guests are entertained. In some cases, even, among males, a real communalism in matters of food is practiced there. We would still find there, without looking too hard, traces of customs that have fallen out of practice: unity of the agnatic group and the management of its temporal interests, separation of the sexes, phases of life experienced in common by certain age groups. These traits, which are safeguarded more or less firmly, but unequally, depending upon the village or social group that is being studied, are always more or less discernible. They allow one to recognize in the Duwwār the heart of that venerable privilege attached to the oldest structures of the community. An attenuated form of it still exists: the guest house or *maḍyafa*. Here, however, is no permanent place to live, no patriarchal management. Families who are related or who are only neighbors, unite to construct a place where the men's gatherings can take place, those assemblies that play such an important role in their lives. Words derived from the Arabic root consonants, *Ḍ·Y·F*, provide the denomination of places of the same kind answering to the same function throughout the Orient. It is so, without doubt, in southern Iraq, under the name of *Muḍīf* where they [the reed guest houses.-Ed.] can be seen in the best preserved and most elaborated form.[3] But Egyptian villages also offer many instructive instances of survival. Here one can understand the importance of careful study that would be concerned with distinguishing, in the village of Sirs, a "former condition" and the changes that have been responsible for the present state of affairs.

About the time of the First World War, Sirs included the following duwwārs and maḍyafas: Duwwār ʿAlī l-Ǧammal; Duwwār al-Ḥasayma; Maḍyafa darb eš-Saykh; Maḍyafa darb

---

[3] Šakir Muṣṭafā Salīm, *Al-Tšabāiš*, pp. 173–94. Baghdad, 1956.

al-Qadayḥa; Maḍyafa darb al-Fūlī; Maḍyafa darb as-Sūq; Duwwār al-Hāgg Slīm Zahrān; Maḍyafa Šeḥḥata; Maḍyafa sidi 'Omar
al-Ğammāl; Maḍyafa darb al-Khlāyef; Maḍyafa al-Aqbāṭ (near
the church); Duwwār Manṣūr; Maḍyafa al Fišawī; Duwwār
Ğānem; Maḍyafa al-Ḥāfī. As it can be seen, during that period
there were only six duwwārs: two for the Ğarbiyya, three for the
Baḥriyya, one for the Šarqiyya. This disparity reproduces, approximately, the traditional hierarchy among the quarters, the
neighborhoods, and the families.

But a clearly perceivable evolution can be noted for one generation. The duwwār of Tih is utilized by the 'Omdè (village
mayor) as a home and as an office. This "officialized" development has prompted the family to set up another duwwār at the
Darb al-Khaṭṭāb. The Ma'āz did not keep up their usage of a
great house; they have divided their old building into individual
living units. But, on the other hand, the Ğammāls, who prospered,
are no longer content with their more modest locale of former
times. In cooperation with families in the neighborhood, they
have built the guest house of Darb el-Gazzhrim: this is a sign of
social mobility upward which came about as a result of the profitable exercise of their profession. The duwwār of the Manṣūr
and the guest house of the Fišāwī have disappeared. Meanwhile,
however, new buildings signal the economic ascent of other families: Hāgg 'Ali 'Abd ar-Raḥmān, Ṣaqr, etc., but always in the
form of guest houses [rather than great houses]. No doubt this
is the emulation by new notables of the old: but the style and
form of the maḍyafa from now on seems to outdo that of the
duwwār considerably. Of this last type, there are now only three
examples: Duwwār Tih, Duwwār Ğānem, and Duwwār Ğammāl; that is, two for the Baḥriyya and one for the Ğarbiyya
quarters. There is nothing surprising in that: the ritual assemblies, still very much in favor and honor, maintain and even
multiply the maḍyafas, whereas the decadence of patriarchal
authority and of kin group cohesion bring about also the decline
of the duwwār.

It happens in the villages of the Delta, less frequently indeed
than in those of the Ṣa'id, that the foundation and the upkeep of
the duwwār is the subject of arrangements made in a will or a

waqf.[4] Nothing illustrates better the importance and the dignity of this institution in traditional thinking. It is thus that toward the end of the nineteenth century Hāgg Slīm Zahrān had bequeathed by the *waqf* two feddans of land, one to the neighborhood mosque, the other to the duwwār. The latter was later on taken away and divided up among the heirs as a result of internal dissensions. Afterwards, Hāgg 'Abdullah Slīm Zahrān reconstituted the duwwār which included a large hall, rooms for living and for latrines, replacing the old one. He erected the whole under the form of the *waqf* endowment.

Most commonly, in any case, duwwār and madyafa are built cooperatively and under contractual arrangements. A general assembly gathers the contributors, each of whose quota is fixed in relation not to the number of individuals in a family nor of households, but in relation to their financial situations. A legal agreement is drawn up that assigns shares to each of the various participants. This will serve in the future as a basis of division of the building and the furnishings in case of a rupture: a situation that sometimes occurs, as has been seen, even among direct heirs.

The duwwār symbolizes, in the village, the old patriarchal power. From thence come the rules of traditional propriety and respect which the younger generation is beginning to neglect. Nowadays they pass in front of its monumental door without climbing off from their donkey or mule. They ignore such manifestations of respect to which the elders cling tenaciously. But such changes betray an almost revolutionary attitude. Hence, one should not be surprised to see this exhibited by a hero of the Šarqawi, who is sensitive to the reactionary symbolism of the duwwār institution. Abuses have no doubt been frequent, and the command, "Go wash the wheat in the duwwār," would mean to the women who were so told, in former times, the most humiliating of chores.[5]

But nonetheless, the evolution of custom, and sometimes the

[4] From this one can see the interest there would be in a study—which, unless I am mistaken, has not yet been undertaken—of these data in the archives, and in general, of all the documents relating to law covering land and public right, in a country in which the regime of the *miri* makes, it seems, for private property to have been rather rare in former times.
[5] See the short story "Al-Khādim" in 'Abd al-Raymān al-Šarqāwī, *Ahlām Sağīra.*

revolution, still do not quench in the hearts of the villagers nostalgia for all that which in many respects still symbolizes the past, the "good old times." Even though the patriarchal ethic is collapsing more and more, in the face of the necessities of the period, it retains its import and charm to which the poets are still faithful:

> Oh house, tell me. Where is your prince? He neglects you.
> He abandons your five-story building, Alas, your glory . . .
> He, who used to say: Hospitality and prestige will be your fortune.
> Why do I have to see the *maḍyafa,* once so famous, shutting down?
> Tell me, oh house, what men guard your closeness.
> It is enough that you have burned. Reward is in the days of your glory.

This *muwwāl,* recited in Sirs, exalts the old virtues: The munificence of the duwwār, its prestige, hospitality, and strength conveyed through the "intimate atmosphere" (*wens*) by which the gathering of the men of the family affirmed the (old) social order.

SOLIDARITY AND BURIAL

This kind of solidarity can be conceived of only within an idea of the homogeneity of time that makes of the temporary span of existence on earth the modest sister of death. From this comes the importance of burial rites in Egypt and their poetic force. We have the nearly unique good fortune to possess a careful monograph on this subject, that of the late M. Galal.[6] He knew how to underline the extent to which even in their very compactness of design, the Egyptian cemeteries proceed from a concrete idea, if I dare say so, to a monumental idea of the beyond. We have already been struck by the importance of the entire funeral service within the role of the duwwārs and maḍyafas. The patriarchal

[6] "Essai d'observations sur les rites funeraires en Egypte actuelle," *Revue des Études Islamiques,* 1937, pp. 131 seq.).

solidarity which these edifices proclaim is expressed in similar fashion in the configurations of the tombs. The same order, and almost the same pattern that cuts up the city into familial quarters, can be seen in the cemetery!

Until about the end of the nineteenth century the various quarters of Sirs, each separately, would bury their dead under the protection of a saint within cemeteries that have little by little begun to overflow, the original cemetery site. In 1905, for the northern part and for the northern and central part of the village the present *gabbāna* (cemetery) was established, the one that runs along the road of Bagūr. The '*omdè* of the period was able to execute the work by communal corvées. Then each notable family built for itself, following custom, in its own specified enclosure a partially covered *ḥawš*, with the reception room, *mendara*, constructed before it, and within this sector it grouped its tombs (*torba;* plural, *torab*). The arrangement of the cemetery reproduces thus, more or less, the same order of the large families within the topography of the village: Tih, Manṣūr, Ğānem, Šaršar, Baġdādi, Zahrān, Husām ad-Dīn, etc. . . . And further, families of more modest means built their tombs so that their location would maintain among the deceased the neighborhood settlement pattern that existed among the living. The uniformity of the construction leaves room, here and there, for more ambitious attempts. Thus the '*omdè*, whose *ḥawš* was near the street, insisted upon building into the external wall a projection with a window turned towards the city, as if he meant to continue, while dead, his position as magistrate. A rich man substituted, for the usual bank of earth that closes the tombs, a door of iron. This contempt for custom turned out badly, for the metal door is less hermetically sealing than the earthen one. The monument decayed and polluted the area: a just reminder of human misery. Another rich man, speculating on the ground of the tombs, bought out the lots of several poor men and built for himself and his family an ambitious construction. The bad relations among one branch of heirs and the rest of the family caused some of them to emigrate to another location. From that point on there was rupture of companionship in death as in life.

In brief, the structure of the village with its equilibrium, its inequalities, and even certain incidents that from time to time come to disrupt it, reappears quite precisely in the disposition of the cemetery. In all truth, the intensity of ceremony, the elaboration and rigor of funeral rites, their profoundly collective character, lead one to suppose that the passage from one state to the other only brought out the disturbances and perturbation in the order that characterizes life. And is it not one of the functions of these rites to safeguard beyond death the image of society?

ON PRODUCTION . . .

Those links which from birth until death relate and uphold man dominate, of course, his everyday activities. The most characteristic of these [in Sirs] is the one that is imposed by its irrigation economy. Beginning with the excavation of the canal, *tur'a,* the chief problem then is to raise the level of water in order to irrigate the fields which every year in former times had been covered by the floods.

The "response" of the peasant society to this new state of things consisted in the multiplication of machines for raising water, of the type that we call "noria" and that have been functioning here for a long time. These machines, called locally *sā'iya,* were originally fashioned entirely out of wood. Operated by animal power, they stood in batteries of three or four along the bank of the *Tur'a* Bāgūriyya. But, beginning in 1925, the village had to be content to get its water in the *Riyāḥ* of Sirs. Originally this complex of wooden wheels and animals to turn them required a cool and shaded place as well as the availability of wood for the repair of equipment. This is the reason for the present existence of clumps of *ṣant* or mulberry trees that are reflected in the canal. Beginning in 1920 the bucket wheel (noria) started changing in design. New models became more and more common. Thus, toward 1925, the type which is called *'ilbi,* or an ingenious disposition of leather buckets on the rim of the wheel, displaced the old pottery buckets. Later on appear buckets made out of galvanized steel; and finally, a new machine entirely made out of metal and which resembles children's water mills. This *kebbās,* imported from Alexandria, was made in Menouf itself, beginning in 1935, by an artisan whose name was Sindibisi. These modifica-

tions, however, brought about the decadence of a once flourish-
ing village carpentry industry. Nowadays, the metal type constitutes about 60% of the water wheels.

The village can make use of the *Riyāh* during six days out of
every eighteen. This period of six days is divided into *qirāṭs:*
that is, shares which last for six hours and which are further di-
visible. There are no allocations of turns in different shares of
the period. All the divisions of *qirāṭs* apply only within themselves, that is, within each *qirāṭ* taken by itself without coordination with the others. The water level tends to go down during
the dry season: consequently the users that are downstream
tend to be at a disadvantage in relation to those that are upstream, the more so because the length of the supply pipe bringing the water (called *mis'a*, plural *masā'i*) is sometimes more than
a whole kilometer. The peasant farmer suffers in general from
lack of water during the six-month period that every year pre-
cedes the rise of the water.[7] He is inclined to buy land upstream
on the bank of the *Riyāh* and to install a machine there at the
risk of lengthening the distance between it and his field. He can
look for supplementary resources also, by pumping the under-
ground water. And the ultimate in evolution is when a rich
man installs a motor pump and sets himself up for selling water
by time units. But more often the peasant will take advantage or
make use of the freely agreed-upon arrangements reached among
friends. He may thus get the share of one who decides to take
advantage of the water upstream: in this manner people continue
a village atmosphere of mutual reciprocity.

Such an arrangement, to sum it up, strikes one with its imper-
fection and with its indecision, which tends to lead to litigations.
Since the technological basis of irrigation changed only recently,
the system for division is not integrated at the same level of
depth and efficiency as other activities of the community, for the
village is a kind of organism of rather slow growth. But some
things do intervene to correct the situation. The co-users usually
come to an agreement so that one of them, recognized for his

---

[7] A period marked by psychological crises (in Cairo, for example, it is the
season of suicides); while the following season exhilarates rural society (it
is at Saʿid, for example, the time for daring banditry that gains the raider
reputation).

prudence or simply by his location near a pump, will regulate the operation of the machinery and reconcile the needs of all parties. Out of long but courteous discussions may be expected an agreement that is [to all] equally gracious and suffices in general to resolve difficult disputes among the villagers and to divide the resources in relation to agricultural needs as they are commonly felt and admitted. The system tends to go wrong only if one of the users cuts in on the others because he is a different social type (an urban proprietor) or acting through economic pressure brought against him (*iqtā'ī*, meaning "feudal"). Finally the deterioration of the communal spirit, individual animosity and fraud start conflicts which still are stopped most often at the level of local arbitration or of the *'omdè*.

In this manner the distribution of water comes to follow the same order of kin and local relations, which is true of so many other rural institutions. In correlation, the cooperative upkeep of a machine implies that the properties to be served should be contiguous or else very close to each other. Hence, there is the common localization of a patrimony of this or that family, in the larger sense, in this or that quarter. The government does not usually intervene at this functional level except for major measures taken on the occasion of fundamental changes in jurisdictional processes. The whole land and irrigation system, which is not ancient at all, for we must trace it only to the beginning of the functioning of the Barrage during the last quarter of the nineteenth century, is still dominated by family structure and the outlook of peasants who are sensitive to the agricultural uses of the land. Such a viewpoint does not belong to a juridical way of thinking but to a technical and a moral type. But whatever its merits, this outlook suffers from two evils, periodical destitution, which results from increasingly intensive cultivation, and the insecurity that tends to be connected with the arbitrariness of solidarity. This old way of thought fears all those phenomena of dispersion that threaten it and that have already been doing so for sometime.

ON CONSUMPTION

Another institution used to replicate, about a generation ago, this same type of solidarity. Sirs used to have about fifty cooperative mills (called *ṭaḥūna*, plur. *tawāḥin*) and custom made it indispensable that they be used by all the villagers.

Unlike the Moroccan city family, which grinds its own grain and kneads the dough, but gives this last to be baked in the public oven, the Egyptian housewife has her grain ground outside the house. Then, without fatigue from working the hand mill (*mankhūl*), she sifts out the flour, the bran, and the semolina, which are to be used in various ways. She kneads, shapes, and finally bakes, her bread in a household oven (*fūrn*). Only the poor get along without an oven at home. It happened thus in former times that collaterally related families, or families of friends, would unite in order to establish a cooperative mill. They would spread the expense and at the start, the right to use the mill, according to customary rule called '*orme*, which would bring out in fact the quota parts also expressed in irrigation qirāts. It is known that the *qirāt*, which can still be found among the various divisions of land in *feddan*, is the generally accepted measure. It is worth $\frac{1}{24}$ of whatever quantity is to be divided. The mill in its old form consisted of two large grinding stones, '*ā'da* and *ḥegr*, which were set in motion by animal traction. A neighbor, who kept the keys, would also oversee its functioning in the turns among the users. His work required no compensation; it was gratuitous. A jar set inside the wall, called '*ādūs*, would receive, handful by handful, the *se'iyya*, a quantity of grain whose sale would permit the oiling of the apparatus from time to time.

An important belief was that the location of the mill was considered improper for building houses. No one would have dared to live near there because it sheltered "genies". But the "genie of the grain" and its potency for trouble were in reality neutralized by the neighborhood of the mosque or the guest house; this was the kind of neighborhood commonly found for the mill, and where, in fact, the mill was normally to be found.[8] Today in Sirs,

---

[8] Thus, we note, the "double face" of the sacred.

only one, perhaps, of these buildings, remains. And the industrial mill, which appeared in the village in 1905, developed onward from 1925 at such a pace that it progressively caused the disappearance of the animal-operated mill.

WITHIN THE CULT [OF THE SAINT'S SANCTUARY]

What does affirm itself on the other hand and without discernible weakening is the particularization of cult in the large families. It is possible to consider the sanctuaries in many respects as an organ among others, of the kin group cooperatives. The state, in effect, gives it little support or does not do so at all. The interested parties collect funds among themselves in order to construct and keep up the buildings as well as to pay salaries to guardians, keepers, Qur'an reciters, etc. Sometimes the family organizes a *waqf* for the benefit of the sanctuary. But this is rather rare. It is from the daily exercise of piety and from the emulation practiced among families that the things and personnel of the cult persist.

There is in Sirs a pious man of wealth, Ğānem Bey, an old man of almost a hundred years who had participated in the Sudanese expedition. He belongs to a conservative family which originated in Ṣaʿid, and which is faithful to the rigorous rules of endogamy: from this there results considerable intra-familial aid among the "sons of the uncle." This allowed Ğānem Bey in his far distant youth to go to Officer School. Very rich (he owns sixty feddans of land), he makes all the mosques of the village the beneficiaries of his charities, without favoritism, and he has recently undertaken the provisioning of that of Abū' r-Rūs. His piety thus ignores the compartmentalization i.e., into quarters, of the town.[9] But a number of years ago he got into a dispute with the Tih family over the choice of a Qur'an reader who was in competition with another with a better voice, and who, besides, was being supported by the Tih. He gave up his support of the mosque of the latter and built a new edifice of modern type in which he had a tomb constructed for himself. In a case of this kind, the old family partisanship did overcome the solidarity of the faithful.

[9] Or transcends it, in the interest of the Saint of the central quarter.

But the Darb of Ğānem can take pride in a cement mosque that
benefits from a *waqf* of fifteen feddans of land supporting it. . . .

This is a sign of the times. There are many others. These village "corporations," examples of which are the duwwār, the guest
house, the *ḥawš* of the cemetery, the mill, the nouria, constitute
in a way the material evidences of that cooperation, which en-
compasses all the activities of life. There was no circumstance
or event that did not bring them into play in daily life or in the
major struggles that underline the history of the town. These
struggles demonstrated thus the many forms of political and agricultural mutual aid. Today they have all fallen into decadence.
An old man of Sirs recently recalled, not without regret, that
around 1910, when his father built a house, that the families of
the neighborhood, even those of the opposed neighborhood,
loaned him their camels in order to bring together enough fuel
for the baking of the bricks. But in this year, needing transportation in order to bring his wheat from the field, he met with nothing but refusals and finally had to rent animals from the Bedouins.
They were Arabs from the province of Gizeh, who customarily
came with their animals in order to rent them out for the harvest.
Help from the Nomad: what shame and perplexity for the life of
the peasant!

VILLAGE HIERARCHIES[10]

One of the first questions that raised themselves for me, from
my first introduction to Egypt, was the question of the entity of
the township. How does one define it and does the vigor of its
structure correspond to the weight of its mass? These "villages"
would elsewhere be "cities" (there are 22,000 inhabitants in
Sirs)! Marked particularism distinguishes each one of them from
its neighbors. But what is its basis? We see clearly the organization into neighborhoods and kin-based institutions actively maintaining differentiation and tension among themselves. But in
truth, the strength and almost the autonomy of this compartmentalization seems to oppose unity, that is, the persistence of a

[10] Chapter 5 of original work [ed.].

whole. But the community affirms itself and persists during long centuries. What is the source of this cohesion?

This is one of the major questions of Egyptian sociology. The facts that have been collected hitherto do not permit one to resolve it. But perhaps the inquiry will progress if it enlightens a problem that is quite closely connected to it: the manner in which the village runs itself and the internal hierarchies that are recognized. Important developments appeared at Sirs al-Layyān during the last half century. An attempt will be made here to delineate them precisely, as far as is possible. And in order to do this it will be necessary to consider successively the weight of values that are moral, economic, or that stem from historical situations.

One day in the year 1912, the *'omdè* surprised some of the village inhabitants in an infraction of the rules of managing the irrigation water. They were irrigating their lands before the time fixed by the public authorities. The chief of the village continued peaceably on his tour, however, and he only enjoined the culprits to irrigate also the field of the holy man of Sirs, Shaykh Hasanayn Abu Zāher. When he passed by the same place in the evening it had been done. Content with his pious blackmail, he went to find Shaykh Hasanayn and, by way of a joke, threatened him with a fine. As the shaykh was innocent according to his titular status, he had irrigated his field but offered as an alibi that he had fulfilled a day of service to God; then the shaykh offered the *'omdè* his riding animal. For, how happy was the shaykh and how great his gratitude to see that, going beyond the official regulations, the *'omdè* had had his field irrigated as a communal duty!

What a typical anecdote! Even at a time when the government authorities, in irrigation matters especially, were pressing heavily upon the town, its leading notables would all join and conspire in the service of these learned and holy men. This did not go on without also bringing about all sorts of "abuses." Popular credulity is often abused; but then it reacts. At least it reacts by means of proverbs and fables. So, it is told in Sirs that one day two people who were not very scrupulous buried a donkey and built on top of his body a mausoleum. They then benefited from many offerings of the folk until the day on which they fell into an argument disputing the fraudulent income, and they came to a point when they both shouted "*Aḥnā dāfnin-u b-ītnayn!*" ("We buried it together!") This was their undoing. The adage ["We buried it together"] is still used in order to denounce this kind of crookedness or hypocrisy. It betokens also an anti-clerical attitude through which popular piety seeks a counterweight for its own exaggerations.

The anecdote, drawn from the real life of Shaykh Hasanayn, like the fable of the two imposters, reveals a society in which the prestige of the holy or learned man distinguishes clearly a special category of people from the mass.

This literate group among the village people extends from the humble Qur'an reciter (*fé'i*, lit. *faqīh*), all the way to the doctor, '*ālem*, and it includes many intermediate levels. The most modest among these workers in the task of knowledge play an important role of integration in country life. If the peasant has made a vow, *nedr*, he calls them together for a collective recitation. Following a mourning ceremony he asks them to celebrate an '*itāqa*. This consists in reciting from the Qur'an as many as a hundred thousand times, one after the other, the sura *aṣ-ṣamad*. It is the word that counts, its emphatic voicing, its intonation, rather than the meaning, which no doubt has been rendered indiscernible in the confusion of many voices. The men of God, such as the *imām* and the *khatīb* of the mosque, receive seasonal contributions that associate them with the harvest of maize and wheat. From the bottom to the top of the ladder they benefit incidentally also when some, the most important and prosperous among them, render customary hospitality. For the nourishment that they provide is sanctified for all.

However, let us not look on these practices only as an archaic naturism that has been rejected by orthodox Islam. The '*ālem* or the "learned" is represented also in those more specialized persons, of the old urban culture, who are occupied with the erudite studies of the scriptures: chiefly law and the Hadīth. Around 1910 Sirs had about half a score of such doctors, two or three of whom were indeed great masters of *a'mida* (literally, "pillars"). These were like the professors teaching at al-Azhar. Thus among them were the Shaykhs Muḥammad Ḥusām ad-Dīn, Sulaymañ Ğanem, and most of all An-Neššūqi. For this last, the most learned among them, was the author of a book, was also the *imām* of Khedive 'Abbās, and memory of him remains strong. Many adults still recall how modestly he dressed: a striped robe, a cotton belt. He could be seen buying at the market a little *mlūkhiya*. Often, by way of devout exercise, he would clean from top to bottom one of the mosques in the village, including the noisome latrines. This zeal assured him, as it did others like him, a large popular following. Nothing in these times could compare with it. In the style of that time, the peasant still calls the lawyer who defends him in court, *safih al-maḥkama*, "the dupe of the tribunal." In the course of the whole century the modernizing efforts begun by Mohammad Ali drew from Sirs no more than two or three irrigation engineers and one veterinarian. The ideal type of respected men remained indeed in popular imagination that of the al-Azhar professor. He represented in a world still dominated by rural illiteracy and vulgarity, the part of man representing intellect. And also he represented the chances which a bright-eyed lad had whether he was the son of a poor man or a poor man himself, through gaining higher knowledge to rise to a position of eminent social dignity. Judicial consultations, authority in all domains of life, by preaching, by homilies: the wise man has many means to act upon the mass. Every day beginning with the *'aṣr*, especially on Friday, and more so during the month of fasting, at which time religious and social life combine and reach a climax of fervor, ties are renewed between the good villager and the *'ālam*, symbol of ageless prerogatives.

Entirely different is the function of a leader of a village religious fraternity. Towards the beginning of the century the great majority of the adults were affiliated with diverse congregations: Bayyūmiyya, Rifā'iyya, Sa'diyya, Šādiliyya. The form of these brotherhoods, at once esoteric and popular, is different from that of the followers of the wise men. Among other distinctive traits, let us note that for the most part the leaders of *tawā'if* belong to ancient families already known for having provided a Saint for the village. Among them, towards 1910, are the shaikhs Khalīl al-Baġdādi, the most considerable among them, Ġaylāmi, Kūrāni, Šeršār, etc. They assure a more direct link, a more instinctive one also, with the body of village society, its traditions and its past, whereas Islamic Orthodoxy, concentrated in the city, offers only an elaborate expression of it, more articulate, imbued with urban religion and ornate ideals: to sum it up, the sharing of tasks.

The third realm of spiritual primacy is the one that is authorized by a claim to descent from the Prophet. Less separated from the populace than in the Maghreb,[11] it has nonetheless its designated families. In the first quarter of the century, they still enjoyed substantial privileges in Sirs. The Nwayḥi who reside in the very heart of the community, claim more than all the others, an immemorial continuity in the village. But it is significant that all the other sharifian families come from elsewhere: from the Hedjaz, such as the Bedir, the Nuwwar, and the Bahnasāwi, a threefold branch of the same line; from Iraq, are Baġdādi; from Syria, are the Tih; from Minieh, are the Fūlī; from Ṣa'id, are the Zahrān. The social type of the sharifs distinguished itself, towards the beginning of the century, as devout people, wearing the green turban, marked by a pious comportment, receivers of salutary hand-kisses and entitled to customary dues, called '*āda*. But if the fertility, which seems for one reason or another to be characteristic of them, multiplies the number of their descendants, by the same token it scatters their heritage. These families have known ups and downs. They have been forced to choose an occupation and for the most part they are engaged in agriculture. Some, like the Tih, have a kind of monopoly on the weaving industry, which, in Sirs, traditionally was a balance to agriculture. Some of these families have had recourse to seeking profession of generosity. Others succeeded in attaining a proverbial ease, or else they hoard money. Others are only recognized by the beauty of their daughters. Others, finally, for at least a century, have taken upon themselves the office of '*omdè*, with all the little Machiavellisms which it can involve. Hence have come the following adages:

"You the Husāyma (sharifian family of Ḥusām al-Din), you are *kennāzin* (you seek wealth)."
"Light shines, Oh, Zahrān" (an allusion to their beauty).

[11] Compare, however, the anecdote of the marriage of Shaikh 'Ali Yūsuf, director of the *Mu'ayyad* at Cairo towards the beginning of the century, and the judicial scandal that followed. Cf. Aḥmad Baha' al-Dīn, *Ayyam la-hā Tārīkh*, pp. 47–61.

"Crooks of hospitality (*khéyynin al-'is*), Oh Tih (an allusion to the politics of feasting which is implicit in the office of *'omdè*)."

Development between the two wars has made of the sharif an ordinary citizen. Nothing distinguishes him now from the populace in his professional activity or in his economic position. Nevertheless, his self-assertion remains more vehement and whatever his comportment, the more it is resented by others. He is, they say, either devoted to edification or to scandal. He is less readily forgiven than others if he involves himself in usury or in speculation. A prestige that is almost impossible to analyze, one that cannot define itself any more except in attitudes, maintains for him through many individual events, something of his ancient magisterial position. It is thus that his daughters are particularly sought after in marriage, especially in lesser families that seek status in the municipality.

During the same period, the learned men, formerly constrained by their separate religious status in their attitude towards the government, began to seek public employment. There resulted a perceptible loss of prestige and a split between them and the populace. For no longer does the same kind of "wisdom" prevail. Next to the traditional wise men, a new kind of educated class emerges that appears, more and more, by virtue of its numbers, to supersede the former. This new class, possessors of diplomas, has risen from the multiplication of government institutions. These men affect traditional customs more and more. The conflict, which came to a climax about 1925, between the young Azhar graduate who was attracted by modernistic studies, and his father, imbued with the ancient values, has been portrayed in a most sensitive way in a famous short story by Yahya Haqqi. From 1920 to 1940, this conflict occurred several times in Sirs itself. Today it would be inconceivable. For the rush of the young people towards public service, in these days, has followed the upsurgence of liberal professions. Now commercial and industrial enterprises are their prime goals. So, three stages of development have transpired.

Although it lies beyond our chronological framework, another factor has very recently affected the role of men of religion. This is the movement of the Muslim Brotherhood, which seems, after a massive success, to have been followed by a crushing defeat (1954), and to have compromised several of the village leaders in some respects.

ECONOMIC ENTERPRISES

The standard of living of families until the beginning of the First World War showed less variation, it seems, than it shows at present. This would follow causes which were formerly, at least, tied as much to collective[12] emulation as to individual fortunes or characteristics.

It is not that the latter are lacking. The prodigal and the miser exchange, one might say, economic aptitudes, expended by the one in festivities, adventures, and gallant displays, while the other patiently gathers and invests. A simple worker, the Mu'allem 'Abd al-Hamīd Zahrān, became rich through selling wood and now he owns in the district of Ġārbiyya a domain of 100 feddans of land. Another, a modest vegetable merchant, prospered to the point where he monopolizes today the whole production of the village.

Meanwhile, the Šaršar family, when harvest time comes about, gathers together and feasts a hundred people. Hospitality and the excesses of ostentation thus ruin an ancient lineage. Others lose their fortunes in long-drawn-out litigations: for instance, the Tih and the Husām ad-Dīn, towards the end of the nineteenth century. Every time that a severe economic crisis occurs, regardless of the time, it does not spare the peasant from using up that part, no matter how meagre, which he has set aside for savings and for external exchanges; then the economy of the household

[12] Formerly in Sirs there was a very clear allocation of vocation of certain families to particular specialized services. For instance: weaving (the Qādi family); construction (the Zahrān al-Bennā, Šabrawi, and Khiri families); butchers (the Ğammāl family); carpentry (the Coptic Ammār family); trading in animals (the Ma'āz and Ašmūni families); animal husbandry (the Qādi and Dennūn families); hair dressing (Madkūr); finally, the Seyfi family provided specialists, *gessas*, who were qualified to determine the state of pregnancy of cows and water buffalos. Today very little remains of these "professional" specializations.

is endangered. The great fertility of marriages is particularly pronounced at this time. As soon as the social level of families rise, the wives are selected more carefully, their pregnancies are more peaceful, the babies are better fed. Such fertility operates like a regulator and reduces that family which raises itself by scattering the patrimony into tiny inheritances. As the folk saying goes, "The children are the worm which eats up fortunes."

To these permanent and, one might say, natural factors, the period that opened at the First World War added considerable aggravation, and at the same time it introduced new factors of trouble. At the value level the old pattern of rustic emulation was no longer fulfilled with the ceremonies of feasting. Nowadays, everyone is ambitious to build and to furnish a dwelling well. One often hears of the peasant who wished to construct a house exceeding his means, wasted an inheritance of 15 feddans, and died at work without having been able to complete the building: this is a sign of the extravagances that are characteristic of the new times. The bridal gift of daughters rises by extraordinary proportions. The Ma'az married their three sons to three sisters. Each cost them 300 pounds for the *mahr*, whereas the average cost during the period about 1922, was between 40 and 50 pounds.

While the factors that maintained the old equilibrium are going out of line in this fashion, a succession of new crises have produced, by mass promotion, one might say, the classes of the newly rich and the new poor. From 1920 to 1924, land that sold for 1000 pounds for a feddan fell back to 100 pounds. This meant ruin for some. For others it meant great wealth. The catastrophic collapse of the prices[13] of cereals—wheat (from 6 pounds to 0.8), maize (from 5 to 0.4), rice (from 40 to 0.4)—brought about ruthless devaluation. The humble village economy, which was subjected from then on by its dependence on cotton to this "form of modern destiny" that is the world market, reflects the variability of prices in the greater world of crises. Several leading and large families collapsed during that period. More than others, indeed, speculation tempted them. Their old pride made them

[13] For the collapse of the price of the cotton during the First World War and the consequent ruin of many peasants, see 'Abd al-Rahman al-Rāfi', *Tawra sana*, 1919, V. 1, p. 55.

curious about upper-class "superiorities," about new pleasures of wealth, and made them quick to engage in extravagant ventures. They were the first to expand their ambitions beyond the local village horizon. These are the families paying for their children to pursue expensive studies; this meant then a leap into the unknown. One *shaykh al-balad* ruined himself totally for the sake of his son by selling his inheritance of 12 feddans; he reduced to misery not only his own household but that of his brothers and his sisters. But, nonetheless, his venture succeeded in producing a high official in the police!

This is because, in the midst of this dramatic conflict, the prestige of an office in the administration does rise as a result of the security involved in having a salary. People with fixed incomes seem like privileged people, they seem better off than the peasant, who is pitilessly dominated by the speculator and the shopkeeper. The best profits now go to the butcher who can buy much land and which he pays for in part by the delivery of meat. The requisitions of the First World War gave tempting profits but frequently imaginary ones. Hidden savings were invested in cattle raising. As the proverb says, "Raise your calves among the poor devils" ('*aleyk be-terbiyat el-'ogūl 'ind awlād en-nodūl*). This is what happened to a wise man who one day found himself with forty coupons worth 100 pounds each. He put them in a box which he hid behind a lamp in a niche in his wall. The money "slept" there for ten years, and came out only for very wise investments.

The period between the two wars abounded in a great number of daring ventures, and painful falls—enough to shatter the old rural structure. The shattering process was translated into serious psychological mutations. The latter were accentuated after the Second World War.

Contingencies, state controls, and the commercialization of the cereal economy produced from that time on the same phenomena that had occurred between 1914–18. Dealing in animals enriched those who engaged in it. The weavers, forced for a generation to a lower economic level by the expansion of industrial weaving, found again an unexpected outlet opened by the black market. Astute craftsmen then combined up to thirty looms which were, of course, hidden from the tax officials. As everywhere else in the world, regulations profit only those who are clever. Some not too scrupulous employees, who were in charge of the governmental *shūnas* (the granaries in which cereals were stocked) cheated, it is said, on weights and prices. They gathered in the process a rather solid economic base. It is true that according to one subtle suggestion their success was eventually spoiled by their use of hashish! Fair turnabout . . .

More to be expected and more "just" is the upsurge of the liberal professions: this brought about the restoration of a family ruined in 1920. Another phenomenon accentuates this kind of reparation. The soil, whose fertility had regularly decreased for fifty years as a result of ill-advised irrigation, began to revive from expert drainage work. Thus, the government's hydraulic project began to bear fruit.

POLITICAL TOPOGRAPHY OF THE TOWN

Traditionally the village was governed by two shaykhs belonging to the two major families, Tih and Zahrān. Dependent upon the first are the quarters in the North, West, and Central sectors. Dependent upon the other are the South and East quarters. When the office of *'omdè* was instituted, which continues to the present in the midst of more and more virulent criticism, it was Mahammad al-Layti et-Tih who was selected as *'omdè*. Supporting him are eight *shaykhs al-balad,* two for each quarter, representing the main lineages. The familial character of the institution is so vivid that when, about 1908, a Manṣūr was named, he thought he must install himself in the *duwwār* of the Tih in order to receive the congratulations and, of course, the gifts of his fellow citizens. After him, one whom we shall identify by the initial N. was named *'omdè*. He fills the office at present. He is said to have been rather violent and authoritarian in his younger days. A short time before the First World War, the opposition to him, maintained chiefly by the Ğārbiyya quarter, was such that one day the young men with him in the fields knocked him off of his donkey and covered his face with dung.[14] The governmental

---

[14] This no doubt was a well-fed donkey, rather light in coloring, which is the mark and mount of an important man. It is to be noted that one rides

requisitions and exemptions of the period of 1914–18 allowed certain abuses, according to some gossiping tongues, to be made by the chief of the village. As a result of many denunciations, he was suspended from his duties. He spent more than a year in Cairo, then, in various intrigues in order to regain his position. He had vowed that he would not return to Sirs until he was re-established. When his mother died in the midst of all this he did not attend her funeral. This was a vengeful assault upon the ethics of the family. Once he was reinvested with his duties, he showed skill in the repression of theft and robbery. It is from this time on that numerous bullies were exiled from the town. With his own hand he arrested a famous thief, Al-Halīs. Today, he is neither without virtue nor without color. For his truculent past survives in him and he still sets himself against regularity and conformity.

Came the revolution of Zağlūl. Up until this point, the village had little interest in general politics. It was with Zağlūl[15] that politics entered definitely. A committee of the Wafd, set up immediately, participated in a campaign of sabotage and boycott. At the head of this committee was Sayyīd el-Bağdādi, chief of the Khelwaṭiyya: political agitation and the propaganda of brotherhood were built up in the process. From 1919 to 1924 the influence of the Wafd rose. It is told that during these times the naïve peasant would come home from his field claiming to have read the name of Sa'd written by God on the leaf of a cucumber plant or bean bush. During the elections of 1924 the Wafdist candidate, 'Abd el-Ḥamīd Fahmi, of the neighboring village of Serūhīt, was elected over the candidate of the Waṭani party, a member of the 'Id family. The town was divided from that time on between a Wafdist majority, led chiefly by the Šaršar, Ma'āz

on the animal with one leg on each side, contrary to the custom prevalent in the rural Maghreb which is to ride a donkey with both legs on one side. In Morocco only the military horse ('aūd s-snāh) is mounted with one leg on each side, in contrast to the common horse and donkey. There are many conclusions one could derive from observation of these styles of posture which were just of concern to M. Mauss.

[15] Id., *ibid.*, pp. 158 ff. and particularly pp. 160, 164 (seen at Menouf, Chebin, al-Kom, Tala, etc., all in the vicinity of Sirs). The rural revolution of 1919: there is a lively description in Ahmad Beha' al-Dīn, *Ayyām la-hā tārīkh*, pp. 90 seq. (it concerns especially Zefta, the central town of the Delta).

and Bagdādi families, and minorities that were led by the Zahrān or the Ğammāl. However, in 1928, the triumph of the Wafd was very much disputed. And, in the elections of 1942, a Zahrān was elected in opposition to the local committee of the Wafd party. The events that followed are too terrible to be related.

Political parties were important among the groupings that were multiplying in the village during this period. Among those that penetrated extensively into the rural areas, like the Wafd, it is necessary to appreciate at once the factor of their drive, the development of individuals, and the link with the purely rural institutions. Yet it would still be premature to write a sociology of political parties in Egypt.[16]

That which is always evident in Sirs, despite all electoral variations, is the confrontation of the two village divisions, the South half and the North half, each of which is structured in more tenuous subdivisions. In the final stage, political conflict penetrates into the families. The young people speak more and more loudly. The duties of the *shaykh al-balad* and the *khofara,* once so hotly disputed, are looked upon today with contempt. Only the prestige of the *'amūdiya* or the office of the *'omdè* remains. The position is still held by a representative of one old family of the North quarter. Through all the electoral competitions, he has known how to maintain an availability to all that is discreetly backed by the Copts. His influence, although more and more contested, continues to carry weight in a by no means negligible manner. But his prestige is wearing out, undermined by a growing general discredit of the office itself.

[16] Critical and historical considerations of the life of the political party in Egypt, in Ibrāhīm Madkur and Merrit Gali, *Al-Adāt al-Ḥukūmiyya* (1945), pp. 81–94. But there is scant allusion to the rural environment, no more than in the interesting historical account of Muḥammad Zaki 'Abd al-Qādir, *Miḥnat al Dustūr* (1955), above all concerned with the trajectory of the Wafd. The latter, however, is devoted to the country people. Nahhās, in his ministerial declaration of 1936, speaks of the peasant, and abolished the *Khafar* tax, which was very hard on him. Cf. *Al-Rāfi'ī, A'quab al-Tawra al-Misriyya* (1951), pp. 13, 15. The memoires of political men with rural connections should allow us one day to complete this study. There is also what is revealed by ᶜAbd al-Rahmān al-Rāfi'ī, *Mudakkirāt-ī* (1952), p. 92. See good notations by J. M. Landau, *Parliaments and Parties in Egypt* (New York, 1954), and by J. and S. Lacouture, *L'Egypte en Mouvement* (1956).

RESTORATIONS AND DECAY

Although menaced by the ascent of new powers and institutions, the families are still powerful. They have maintained the real power all along during the last half century. It has expressed itself by turns or simultaneously, under the guises of education, wealth, or political action. The relative importance among the three modes of expression itself varied. Religious prestige, more and more rivaled by that of a university diploma, is weakening in its importance today. Yet the society is still saturated with piety. Its religious equipment, its ritual behavior remain, though not altogether intact. However, the strictly spiritual offices have declined. Perhaps they have only aroused in the form of excitement that which they have actually lost in power. Would it be an exaggeration, in their case, to see their forms descending into folklore? Without doubt, but there is more. Economic life, grown more difficult, more hazardous, but thereby more fascinating, has taken a more and more leading role. However, the breach with traditional values that it has established is still counterbalanced by other factors, where the ancient ethic can find compensation and justification.

For some changes that have been set in motion—the expansion of education, the increasing variety of employment offered by the city to the enterprising literate man or the strong-willed artisan—coincide with post-war euphoria, with independence, and now with the hopes sprung from the Republic, to relieve other graver realities and to make the present period appear more firmly established and in any case more exciting than that which preceded it.

Several families, reduced for many years, have recovered their former prosperity. A patient widow, ruined by the wasteful spending of her husband, has educated her three sons. They are now a bank inspector, an industrial director, and an expert working for the Shell Oil Company. The last mentioned has profited from two missions abroad. He has married a European. In his case the transposition of the old social values is typical. In Sirs there are still other kinds of success stories. One is the story of a "son of its works" or *'iṣāmī:* for instance, 'Abd al-Ḥamīd Šiḥḥāta. He emigrated from the village in 1916 as a laborer in the flour mills of Remadi, opened a small shop to sell bread, rented, then bought an oven. He returned in 1943, like many city people of village origin, when the fears of bombardment caused an exodus from Cairo. He installed ovens and a factory. Muhammad 'Abd al-Salīm Ḥamza, who left Sirs around 1935, has even become wealthy. Other examples could be cited.

The village is thus oriented toward new types of success, the most notable of which is the success promised to the enterprising spirit of the itinerant knife-grinder or to the ingenuity of the intellectual. Yet an old regime seeks to survive under these unforeseen new forms. It can even be said that the recent years, all in all, have been more contributive to this regime than the period between the two wars. The Ğammāl family was able to continue its rise for two generations. The *nouveaux riches* do not yet have a decisive influence on the old village hierarchies. The individual success is, in effect, weakened by a still powerful patriarchal structure that allies the poor cousin and the rich, the prodigal son and the avaricious uncle under the same names, still full of village spirit.

However, something has changed. Even if they were persistent, the collective actors of the rural order would have to adapt themselves to the new conditions, to take the new roads: A race towards well-provided properties, economic ingenuity, and competition in the election. These successes, be they re-establishments or continuations, have a unique quality. They are made at the expense of change, of adventures, and at times revolts. In many cases, they run counter to the ideals of former times. Thus the popular poets denounce, like Hesiod long before them, the decline of the old-fashioned values. They lament the fall of the obligation of mutual aid and patriachal emulation.[17] Let us listen to two poems.

The insult of the time has made the lions sleep.
Thirsty, hungry they sleep under the rogue's wall.

[17] Cf. for a very different milieu, the Sa'id, the paradoxical regrets of Muhammad Gallāb, *Khayatu al-Itjimā 'iyya,* pp. 59 seq. It is a very "old-fashioned" testimony.

The dew wets them under the rogue's wall.
Formerly their *maḍyafas* were open to everyone.
They protected their client from all that could humiliate him.
The time has changed. They now solicit the most humble.
It is hard for the noble to see himself humiliated by the rogue,
Who insults honor, who knows neither good deed nor nobility.
Unhappy the time which looks pleasantly upon the man with
    little,
Leaves the generous on the sidelines, to hide in solitude or in the
    past,
And places men of no means on the highest stand!

O you, so weary of days, what is happening to you?
Why do you shed tears from your eyes?
You used to spend in all munificence,
You used to descend on the battlefield and then dart forth,
Dragging with you friends, running *en masse.*
You appeared among them like the moon, when you darted
    forth,
They whose *maḍyafas* gathered people in crowds.
You mounted on horseback at midnight and darted forth,
You spread your riches everywhere, freely.
You gave mercy at midnight, you darted forth.
At the rise of the day, every veil fell from you.
The times are against you. The people have left you.
All friends gather far from you.
The world and the times . . . They have forsaken you.
Your fortune has fallen, luck has deserted you.
You have now for friends base men, O! what is left to you!
Where have your friends left forever, what is left to you!
A passer-by says to you: What has happened? What is happen-
    ing to you?

Yes, what has happened to the village? The industrial revolution surrounds it from all sides. Yet it opposes to the changes a
fidelity that is dictated by its old peasantry. The permanence of
this world is evident to whomever observes this sort of heaviness

with which the peasantry still walks on its soil, but also the self-willed patience which it puts into its renewal, while asking, generation after generation, of its young women, of its poets, and of its adventurers, for that which makes life worthy of being lived.

PART II

Life in Middle Eastern Towns and Cities

7. The Mzab [Algeria]

About 560 kilometres South of Algiers, and extending for about 250 kilometres further south, there lies a region of limestone in the Sahara which is known as the Shebka. The word signifies a net in Arabic, and the reason for this is that the ground of bare stone has been eroded into a criss-cross network or maze of short ravines and clefts. Roughly in the centre of this barren wilderness, the bed of the river Mzab forms a valley between low, yellowish hills, and in the lower part of this valley lie five cities, perched on the slopes, or on higher ground in the river-bed. They are built fairly close together so that from each it is easy to see one or two of the others. They were all founded in the 11th century A.D., they are all surrounded by stout walls, and each is crowned by the minaret of its mosque, shaped like an obelisk and lacking any kind of decoration.

Their total population is about 30,000, of whom Ghardaya, the capital, contains half. Next in importance comes the city of Beni Isguen, with 5000 inhabitants, while the smaller cities of Melika, Bou Noura, and El Ateuf share about 10,000 between them. Ghardaya is also the centre of one of the four large military and administrative territories into which southern Algeria is divided, and the only one of the five cities that has admitted Europeans, Arabs, Jews, and other foreign elements—not within

This is a paper read at a meeting of the Institute on February 5, 1953. It had previously formed the substance of a lecture, illustrated by slides, to the Oxford University Anthropological Society on November 19, 1952. It is reprinted here by permission of the author and of the Council from the *Journal of the Royal Anthropological Institute*, Vol. 84, pp. 34–44 (1954). Four plates, with accompanying descriptive captions, have been omitted with regret.

it walls, but within its precincts;[1] the others remain completely homogeneous and, with one small exception at Melika, untouched by alien habitations.

The river Mzab, from which the district takes its name, flows very rarely, rising only about once in twelve or thirteen years. Rainfalls or showers are not quite so rare, but there are years without any precipitation from the atmosphere, and one or two heavy showers in a year are regarded as a blessing. Water is found at depths varying between 8 and 55 metres and has to be drawn from wells. One is therefore almost astonished to find palm-gardens at a short distance from each city, maintained by constant labour, and to discover whole towns of summer-houses among the date-palms and fruit trees, not lightly built as bungalows, but constructed with stone in the same way as the townhouses (Brunhes 1952, p. 181).

Besides the five cities in the valley, the confederation of the Mzab, as it is sometimes called, comprises three other places: the oasis of Berriane, 47 kilometres to the north; the city of Guerrara, 99 kilometres to the north-east; and, nearer to the Mzab valley, the oasis of Metlili, partly owned by Mozabites, but inhabited by sedentary Sha'amba from the large Arab nomad tribe of that name.

The Mozabites are peculiar in several respects. They represent a small Berber island in a vast Arab sea; they are the only city-dwellers in the Sahara; they practise a fierce and exclusive form of Islamic puritanism, not unlike that of the Wahabi of Arabia, but in an *urban* and not a *tribal* frame of society; and they have kept their institutions intact, only giving up their political status as independent republics and becoming part of the territory of Algerian France.

Why do they live in such a remote and barren place? How can they afford to keep gardens and summer-houses at great expense? How were they able to withstand, for a thousand years, the vicissitudes of sedentary life in the Sahara, and, even more surprisingly, the impact of 20th-century competitive civilization?

To find the answer to these questions one must begin by tracing the history of the Beni Mzab back to the period of the Arab

---

[1] The foreign elements number about 10,000; the original population is Berber by descent and language (Doutté & Gautier 1913, p. 139).

conquest of North Africa in the 7th and 8th centuries, as it is recorded, for example, by Ibn Khaldūn (de Slane tr. 1852) and others (Masqueray tr. 1879; Lewis 1950; Julien 1952). At that time bitter quarrels and feuds were being fought out in Arabia among the Prophet Muhammad's successors, and a sect of non-conformists, the Kharijites, gained considerable influence for a short period. Their political and religious teaching was republican, democratic, puritan, and fundamentalist, and in all these respects they were radically opposed to the orthodox and absolutist Caliphate at whose hands they suffered a series of defeats which led to their practical disappearance in Arabia by the beginning of the 8th century.

The Kharijites disappeared, but they were not extinguished. 'Ali, the Prophet's son-in-law, crushed their first revolt under 'Abd el-Wahb, but they found another leader in 'Abdalla ibn 'Ibād, who gave their passionately held beliefs the form of doctrine and the rules of conduct.

The original and immediate cause for their disaffection was that 'Ali had been prepared to accept arbitration between himself and the other pretender to the succession, Mu'āwiya. To the fundamentalists among his followers, compromise or arbitration in this case was inadmissible. There was one law and one law only: the Koran. According to a fundamentalist interpretation of the Koran, arbitration is applicable in two cases only: in the case of conflict between husband and wife (Koran iv. 39) and in the case of killing of game while on pilgrimage, when certain compensation becomes due (Koran v. 96). No other differences can be resolved by arbitration. Any action is either right or wrong. If wrong, it must be resisted, 'with the hand, with the tongue, or with the heart' (a rule based on Koran iii. 106).

Secondly, and of like importance, was the fundamentalist belief that all Muslims were equal, and that the office of Shaikh el-Islām, or Caliph, or Imam should be an elected and not an hereditary one.

Based upon these two propositions, that all Muslims are equal, and that any action is either right or wrong, the principle tenets of 'Ibādi doctrine are (Masqueray 1879, preface):

(1) That the law is laid down once and for all time in the Koran, that therefore it is essential not only to know the Koran,

but to understand it; also that prayers must not merely be repeated but understood.

(2) That there is only one way of being righteous, any other ways being sinful and leading to certain damnation.

(3) That sin can never be expiated or forgiven; and that punishment by the law can only have secular and not spiritual or redeeming effect.

(4) That Works are as important as Faith; that sinners are damned whether they are true believers or not; and that a man's conduct in this world determines precisely his position in the next.

(5) And, finally, that since all Muslims are equal, luxurious living and ostentation by some is sinful; that no man can command who is not expressly elected to do so; that a man should live soberly and modestly, shunning all stimulants and intoxicants including music and dancing; and that he should practise charity and strict honesty in his personal and business dealings.

'Abdalla ibn 'Ibād, during whose lifetime the Kharijites or Dissenters were persecuted, cut down in battle, oppressed, and killed, taught that there were four states or ways in which true believers could achieve Grace: (i) the State of Defence in protecting their faith; (ii) the State of Devotion in its practice; (iii) the State of Glory in its victory; and (iv) the State of Secrecy when its concealment became a duty.

A story or two may illustrate the stoic faith of these Puritans: Rahan, one of those who revolted against 'Ali, was captured, his hands and feet were cut off and his enemy, Ibn Ziyād, asked him 'What do you think now?' 'I think,' he replied, 'that you have spoiled my life in this world, and that I have spoiled yours in the next.' Another, Arūa, when asked by the same Ibn Ziyād to choose his own torture, replied 'Choose the form of your eternal damnation yourself!'

The State of Secrecy had been reached. The dissenters could meet only in small conventicles, where they comforted and helped one another and made converts when possible. One such conventicle, or *ḥalqa*, from Bosra, decided to emigrate in order to escape persecution, to preach the pure doctrine, and to seek the State of Glory in North Africa.

There, the 'Ibādi doctrine fell on fertile ground. The Arab conquest of the Maghreb (the West) had been slow and difficult. After fifty years of campaigns and of expeditions organized from Egypt and Damascus, Byzantine power was at last broken, and by A.D. 698 all the Greek fortresses of the coastal belt from Carthage to Ceuta as well as those of the interior were in the hands of Arab governors. But the Berber population of the plains, the high plateaux and the mountains, from Tripolitania and the Jebel Nefūs in the east to the Sūs and the Anti-Atlas in the west, remained largely unsubdued. Great tales and legends are told of heroic Berber resistance under chieftains like Kossila and the Kahina, the Jewish queen of the Aures mountains. However, from their firm bases on the coast, the Arab governors, who frequently took advantage of inter-tribal feuds between Berber leaders, succeeded in obtaining the submission and also the conversion of ever-increasing numbers of Berber tribes.

In matters of religion the Berbers had never been too difficult. The tribes in the interior remained largely pagan and idolatrous, but many in the mountains had adopted Judaism, and in the coastal plains Christianity had found entry under the Romans. But already under Roman and later under Byzantine rule, the christianized Berbers were given to sectarianism. Byzantine governors in particular had great trouble with the Donatists and the Circoncellions, sects that professed an equalitarian and primitive creed, revolted against their bishops, and refused to pay taxes.

In their efforts at converting the Berber tribes to Islam, the Arabs were aided, on the one hand, by the successful invasion of Spain (A.D. 709), which almost immediately brought to their side large numbers of Berbers eager to take part in battle, conquest, and loot—this, of course, they could do only as soldiers of the Prophet—and, on the other hand, by the rule, based on Koranic law, that Muslims were exempted from certain land and poll taxes that non-Muslims had to pay. Conversions under those circumstances were largely a matter of form and were mostly regarded as such by Arab governors, who continued or resumed the exaction of these taxes from their fresh co-religionists. Revolts and apostasies naturally followed, and so did repressions. The situation was complicated by quarrels and fights between the Arab governors themselves, who had not failed to import their old tribal feuds and hostilities from Arabia, and repeatedly

called to their aid native forces in order to gain a local advantage.

It was in the midst of this state of affairs that the 'Ibādi *ḥalqa*
from Bosra arrived, led by a young Persian nobleman, Ibn
Rustem. They quickly collected a following of Berbers who at
last found in these Arabs other Muslims by whom they were
treated and regarded as equals. The Berbers, who had been
Christian sectarians and rebels under Byzantine rule, became
Muslim sectarians and rebels under the Caliphs. As Bernard
(1932, p. 89) put it, Islamic Calvinism found in North Africa its
Scotland.

Soon Ibn Rustem was strong enough to be considered worth
an alliance, and he was called in to put down a palace revolution
that had upset the city of Kairouan. He proceeded to occupy
Kairouan himself and held it for four years until an army sent
from Egypt obliged him and his followers to give way. They left
Kairouan and trekked for 700 miles, going west all the time, until
they reached a place in the mountains of western Algeria, situated at 3000 feet, by a pass leading from the highlands of the
Tell Atlas down to the fertile coastal plain. There was an ancient
Berber settlement in this place, based upon a Roman camp,
and near it in A.D. 761 Ibn Rustem founded the city of Tahert, or
Tiaret, which became the capital of the so-called kingdom of
Tiaret, comprising a good deal of present-day Algeria, and which,
according to Ibn Khaldūn (de Slane tr. 1852, pp. 242–43), lasted
for a century and a half.

It was a kingdom without a king—it was a theocracy. Ibn
Rustem and his successors took the title of Imam, leader of
prayer; and the people, unlike the Children of Israel, did not
demand a king. No ass was lost, no Saul anointed! Merchants
and artisans of different persuasions brought wealth and affluence, and they and their trade were protected; but the Imam
and his band of elect continued to live an austere and simple life,
devoted to the study of the law and the sciences, especially
astronomy. No family or tribe arrogated to itself the spoils of
power or office, which was the rule practically everywhere else
in the Muslim world. All Muslims were equal. The Imam was
surrounded by his theologians, and his acts of government were
performed with their advice and moral support (Motylinski

1908). It is not possible here to study this theocracy beyond mentioning these few of its principal features. In A.D. 909 Tiaret, and with it the State of Glory, was suddenly destroyed by an army of orthodox Muslim fanatics, believers in the hereditary succession of the Prophet, who later were to lift the Fatimid dynasty on to the throne of Egypt.

The 'Ibādites of Tiaret that were not killed or dispersed began under their Imam another long trek, this time south-east, into the Sahara. They crossed 400 miles of steppe and desert and finally reached Ouargla, a large oasis south of Touggourt, where an 'Ibādi community had settled earlier and where the refugees from Tiaret started to build the new city of Sedrata (van Berchem 1953). The Imam who had led them renounced his leadership and returned to private life; and from that moment the religious as well as the secular authority of this 'Ibādi community rested in the hands of its clergy. As his final act the last Imam proclaimed the State of Secrecy by which the 'Ibādites separated themselves from the heterodox world and decided to live entirely on their own, instead of in mixed communities.

Sedrata was not a very safe place. It lay in the open desert, only a few days' march away from other centres of population, and it was within striking distance of powerful Negro kingdoms in the south. It grew and prospered, thanks to the industry and application of its citizens and its position on a main caravan route from the south-west to the north-east; it also attracted 'Ibādi communities from other parts of North Africa; but the sectarians looked for a safer place and soon found it, only some 120 miles to the north-west, in the region of the Shebka that was avoided, even by nomads, because it was lifeless and afforded no grazing (Bernard 1939, p. 338). In the year A.D. 1011 men from Sedrata founded El Ateuf, the first city of the Mzab; thirty years later Bou Noura and Melika were built, then Beni Isguen further up the valley; and finally Ghardaya in A.D. 1053. The precaution proved to be wise, for in A.D. 1075 Sedrata was destroyed by a hostile Berber tribe.

These, then, are the five cities of the Mzab valley. It can now be understood how they came to be founded in this particular location. But it will be necessary to examine whether they really are cities in the accepted sense, and not just fortified places.

After all, there are numberless fortified places, or *ksour,* all over
North Africa.[2] In what way do those of the Mzab differ from the
others? Nearly all the Berber *ksour* have two features in common: every *ksar* is inhabited by people standing in some kind of
blood-relationship to one another as members of the same tribe,
or clan, or family—always excepting Jews or slaves attached to
many of the *ksour*; and they are nearly all dependent upon a
higher authority, be it a local chieftain, a territorial ruler, or a
nomad tribe. There are indeed some places in Kabylia and the
Aures where Berber families or clans not necessarily related have
moved together constituting townships with a form of local self-
government; the cities of the Mzab, however, were each founded
not by several families, but by several *groups* of families who
continue to this day their separate identities but who gave up
their juridical and executive tribal powers to the higher political
entity of the city. These family-groups, or *qabā'il,* correspond
closely to the ancient Roman *curiae* which were each composed
of several *gentes*; and the city, called *'arsh,* corresponds to the
Roman *urbs* in its political sense, or to the Greek *polis* (Masqueray 1886, p. 221).

Not all the families or clans that founded the cities have survived; but the *qabā'il* or family-groups have.[3] For instance, the
'arsh of Ghardaya is based upon two *qabā'il,* the Ouled Ammi
Aïssa and the Ouled Ba Sliman, each occupying a ward in the
city. The Ouled Ammi Aïssa are composed of three *ḥashā'ir* or
clans, two of which came from the west and one from Sedrata.
The two from the west have their own burial ground near the
tomb of a western marabout, or saint. The other *qabīla,* the Ouled
Ba Sliman, consists of two clans, each of a different origin. Beni
Isguen has three *qabā'il,* one of which is from Sedrata, the second
composed of *ḥashā'ir* from the Atlas, and the third of later migrants grouped in five *ḥashā'ir* of different origins and integrated into the city under the name of Ouled Anan. Bou Noura
has two *qabā'il,* but one of them consists now of a single *ḥashīra,*

---

[2] It should be noted that *ksar,* plural *ksour,* is the French transcription of
the word as it is spoken in the Maghreb instead of the correct *qasr* (plural
qusur).

[3] 'Le mot *qebila* signifie au Mzab toujours un groupe politique dépendant
d'un autre plus considérable, une fraction en un mot' (Masqueray 1886,
p. 175).

which occupies half the city, while the other is composed of
seven *hashā'ir*. A comparatively recent document, the chronicle
of a new city, dating from A.D. 1613, when, for reasons of overpopulation and civil strife, a number of families left Ghardaya
and went to found Guerrara, opens with the declaration: 'The
Ouled Betamer composed of six *hashā'ir*, and the Ouled Ben
Brahim and the Ouled Debbat, each consisting of one *hashīra*,
found this city and make certain laws.'[4]

The social structure of the Mzab city has been compared with
the Roman *urbs* or the Greek *polis* in their early stages. Another
comparison can be made with Italian city-states of the Renais-
sance. The *qabā'il* not only jealously guard their separate identities, they frequently used to assert them by force of arms, and
the *sofs*[5] or bloody quarrels between the wards or between
leading families in different *qabā'il* or factions in different cities
were as notorious in the Mzab as were the fights between the
Pazzi and the Medici in Florence, or between the *contrade* of
Siena.

Although the *qabā'il* are strong vestiges of tribal organization, they retain no political or administrative rights within the
city.[6] Each *qabīla* elects a magistrate, or *kebir*, and one or two
sheriffs, or *muqaddemīn*. The magistrates collectively pass sentences and impose fines, and the sheriffs execute judgements,
keep the city's accounts, and receive strangers. Each individual,
no matter from which ward, enjoys the protection of, and is subject to, city law, and the authorities are responsible for the peace
of the city as a whole. Besides the officers of the law, every *qabīla*
elects a number of elders, each from a different *hashīra* who,
together with the magistrates and the sheriffs, form the *jum'a*,
or assembly. This assembly is summoned by the magistrates only
in exceptional circumstances or for special reasons like important

---

[4] The Chronicle of Shaikh Sliman ibn 'Abdalla (Masqueray 1886, p. 176).
Motylinski (1885*a*) gives a translation of another and later chronicle. Here
the names differ from those quoted above, but the account of the city's foundation is very similar.

[5] The word means 'party' and, by extension, 'party quarrels' (Huguet
1903, p. 94). See also Bernard (1932, p. 219).

[6] Nevertheless, their local cohesion is strictly safeguarded. Property may
be sold only to members of the same *sof* which, in this context, means the
qabīla and its assimilated families inhabiting the same ward (Capot-Rey
1953, p. 244).

litigation, public security or the making or revision of laws. It is a legislating body and a high court at the same time, and an immemorial institution among all Berber tribes. However, in the Mzab it is powerless by itself; it may meet only in the mosque and in the presence of the *ḥalqa* or conventicle of the learned clerks whose chief, the shaikh of the mosque, presides. Of the lay members, only the magistrates have the right to speak. The elders' part is to listen and to give assent. The mosque is, in fact, the government of the city; the authority of the clergy is supreme. The higher clergy, or clerks of the first degree, setting an example of the State of Secrecy, hold themselves aloof from the day-to-day management of affairs; but nothing of any importance can take place without their consent. The laity are associated with acts of government through their elected representatives in the assembly which must be consulted; but in a conflict of opinion it is always the clergy who have the last word, for they have at their disposal two powerful weapons—excommunication against the individual, and, against the community, the sit-down strike: in grave cases the clerks lock themselves up in their mosque; there are no prayers, no funerals can be held, no benedictions, purifications, circumcisions, marriages, no teaching—in fact, the whole life of the community comes to a standstill.

So the theocracy of Tiaret and Sedrata continues in the Mzab, and through it the Puritan doctrine of the sect is upheld in all its severity. The *qawānīn*, or laws of the cities, abound in proscriptions of vanity, ostentation, levity, and pleasure.[7] Here, for example, is the *qānūn* of the city of Melika regulating the expenses for a wedding (Masqueray 1886, pp. 62–63):

> For the preparation of a wedding-feast no more than two slaves in the house of the bridegroom and two slaves in the house of the bride shall be employed. In neither of the two houses shall musical instruments be played. The Negress who is sent with the dish of *ghedara* shall have one measure of corn: the *ghedara* must not contain eggs, neither must it contain saffron, and it must not be made with *ajid*-flour. All these things are forbidden. Also forbidden is the use of a

[7] A *qānūn* of Beni Isguen punishes him who boasts of his descent from an ancient family (Morand 1910, p. 440).

mule or a horse for conveying the bride: she shall walk on foot. No flute-player shall enter the house of the bridegroom and no one shall smoke in his house, for tobacco is hateful. The Negress who carries the bread to the house of the bride shall be given two small measures of corn. The bread of the seventh day must not exceed one small measure of corn: the bridegroom shall give in exchange half a real, no more.[8] The servant who fetches the dish of *refis* [a sweet made of dates and semolina] shall receive from the hand of her mistress one mouthful of it, no more. The woman who remains with the bride shall be given one-eighth of a real. Flute-players and slaves shall not make music in the city, and within the city-walls it is forbidden to let off firearms. After the bride has entered the house of the bridegroom, it is forbidden to send her food, be it dates, or corn, or any other victuals, and the *ghedara* made by the mother-in-law on the first day must not exceed the measure of eight dishes. The mother-in-law shall not offer any food to the friends of her son-in-law, nor shall she make nor send him any *refis* on the day she receives his presents.

Whosoever does any of these things shall be subjected to the censure of the Faithful.

Given by the Assembly of the people of Melika, clerics and laymen, the first day of *rejeb* of the year 1108 after the *Hijra* of the Prophet [A.D. 1697].

It has been mentioned that the cities of the Mzab form what is sometimes called a confederation. This must not be understood in the sense of a political union. There are no federal organs of government, no constitution, and no federal council. The union of the cities is founded in their common history and their common dangers, and both these are the consequences of their common faith. This sectarian faith, the state of secrecy in which it is practised and the self-denial which its puritan doctrine demands, produce an inordinate pride in its adepts. They call themselves 'God's Family', in other words the Chosen People.

[8] A Spanish real was worth approximately one florin. See Morand (1910, pp. 427–28) on the real, its history in North Africa, its various coinages, its value, etc.

Nothing will normally induce a Mozabite to part from his community and mix with others whom he deems so much beneath
himself—not the hard and barren ground where his ancestors
took refuge, not the fact that he has to spend half his life away
from home to earn his living (as will presently be explained),
not his neighbour's jealousy and hatred, nor even the banishment
he may suffer for a murder he may have committed in pursuit of
a *sof*. There may be disunity among the cities through their
autonomy and conflicting interests; there may be violence and
hostility among citizens; but stronger than all dissociating influences are the unity created by the pressure of the control the
community exercises over all its members for the sake of the doctrine, and the social cohesion produced by the energy, one might
say the high temperature, of this religious sect. Indeed, any
lowering of the temperature, any concession or relaxation of the
religious and moral doctrine, must, in this artificially created
society—existing in an artificially created living space—entail
gradual disintegration and loss of identity. This, in fact, is happening in the island of Jerba where the old and important Mozabite community, under the influence of easy living conditions
and the relaxation of rules, is slowly dwindling (Mercier 1927,
p. 11). In other words, if doctrine no longer separated the Mozabite from other people, there would be no particular reason why
he should go on living in the Mzab rather than elsewhere—on the
coast, for instance, or in some other practical and less costly surroundings.[9]

Since the soil of the Oued Mzab had to be created, because
there was practically none to begin with, it was clear from the
start that the only salvation of the Mozabite communities lay in
trade. Of this they had centuries of experience, first in Tiaret
where they were placed between the stock-breeding plateaux and
the agricultural plains of the coastal Tell; and then in Sedrata
which lay on the route connecting the western Sudan and the
Niger valley with the Mediterranean, through the oases of the
Rhir and the Jerid. The Mzab was less favourably placed, in fact
that is why it was chosen as a retreat; so—although a north-south
route through their valley was gradually established by the Beni

[9] Mercier (1922, p. 51), in this context, points out the effect of 'une logi-
que collective et emotionelle', as opposed to practical, individual reasoning.

Mzab—it became necessary to trade elsewhere and send the proceeds home. Puritans make good business men: a high standard of literacy, necessary in order to study the holy scriptures; a high standard of honesty as part of the doctrine; a disciplined will, which is the essence of Puritanism, and the avoidance of dissipation make successful trading almost inevitable (Weber 1922, p. 352; Tawney 1926, p. 201). From the earliest times of their settlement in the valley, Mozabites went to the north trading in slaves, hides, wool, and livestock from the Sahara, and in produce, commodities, and imported groceries from the coast and the ports. Nowadays, they dominate the trade in textiles and groceries in Algeria and Tunisia and they are very large property owners in the cities and the countryside of the Tell as well as in the oases of southern Algeria (Vigourus 1945).

In the normal course of events, a small boy would be sent or taken by his father to his own or a friend's business in the north to learn to trade.[10] He is brought home to the Mzab at the age of between fourteen and sixteen to marry, then returns to the north and pays periodical visits to his home until he has made enough capital to take things easier, look after his family and his property, and concern himself earnestly with his salvation. Since he cannot spend money on luxuries, he makes investments, he marries frequently but never more than one wife at a time (which, of course, means a fresh payment for every wife), he endows his mosque so that the clergy is kept and every child can be taught, and—last but not least—he improves his garden and his summer-house, which is costly, because it needs constant care and the employment of servants and animals to draw water, keep the water-channels in repair, add fresh soil and fertilizers, and look after the plants and trees. "The Mozabite," said Gautier (1923, p. 153), "is a shrewd business man from the Tell who—at ruinous expense—keeps a country-house in the Sahara" (see also Charlet-Cozon 1905, p. 68; Capot-Rey 1953, p. 320).

Judging by appearances, this would seem true. But nothing is quite what it seems in the Mzab. The State of Secrecy still obtains, and although there may not be very much more to hide now, it was not so long ago that little was known about the Beni

[10] It is estimated that about 5000 Mozabites, or about one-sixth, are absent from their homes every year (Capot-Rey 1953, p. 164).

Mzab except that one met them everywhere. In 1878 Émile Masqueray visited the Mzab and, as the first outsider of any race or creed, was allowed to see and then to copy one of the important Mozabite books, the *Chronicle* of Abu Zakaria (Masqueray tr. 1879). Some years later he was given insight into the *qawānin,* or written laws of the Mzab,[11] and thus opened up the Mzab as a field of study. In 1882 France annexed the Mzab and made Ghardaya the military headquarters of a territory stretching from Jelfa in the north to El Golea in the south. The Beni Mzab cooperated willlingly with the French administration, and accepted nominated caids, French law-courts, mission-schools, and hospitals, while the French, of course, respected their religious practices and customs, including that of locking the gates of their cities every night when the strangers had left (Robin 1884).

It was not until 1925, when Mlle Goichon came to live in the Mzab, gained the confidence of some women, and was able to study family life, that any particulars concerning the life of women and small children became known at all. And incidentally, stories of massacres, assassinations, and religious upheavals came to light that had happened during the preceding thirty or forty years without ever so much as a murmur reaching the world outside.

The role of the women is determined by one fundamental law: no Mozabite woman is ever allowed to leave the Mzab (Goichon 1927, p. 1).[12] Apart from the hived-off colonies, no Mozabite woman is found in any other place. William Marçais, in his preface to Mlle Goichon's important work, calls the women the armature of Mozabite society; they do, indeed, hold it together, since a man cannot take his family when he goes away and would lose it altogether if he did not return. The women of the Mzab are, therefore, in a very special sense the guardians of the hearth not only of the family but of the whole city; and since young wives of the age of twelve or thirteen can hardly be expected to run a family and a household in a fully responsible manner, the

[11] In the Mzab, these laws, although not codified, are written down and registered, while in the Berber townships of the Aures and in Kabylia, where religious government is absent, they are preserved by oral tradition only (Masqueray 1886, p. 50).

[12] This law is discussed by Zey's (1886), Morand (1910, ch. 11), and other authorities.

city-fathers set up an authority whose duty it is to supervise the conduct of the women and to see that they observe the laws strictly and that the children are brought up in the correct way. This authority is vested in the guild or order of women who wash and lay out the bodies of the dead—in French, *les laveuses des morts* (Goichon 1927, pp. 220 ff.).

The women who fill this office, which is unpaid and highly respectable, are chosen by the clerks from among the most virtuous, capable, and intelligent matrons of the town. Their influence on family life is all-pervading, and they are feared and respected, because they have access to every house, they must be consulted on all occasions, and they have the disciplinary power of excommunication, delegated to them by the *ḥalqa*. It may be believed that they do their duty conscientiously, methodically, and strictly.

Their principal function is to teach. The dogma that all Muslims are equal includes women, who have therefore to be taught to understand the Koran and to understand their prayers, for prayers merely recited do not go to heaven (Masqueray 1886, p. 57). They have also to be taught something of the laws and the history of their city and sect. Women do not go to the mosque, so the *laveuses* lead their prayers and occasionally preach to them. They are really female clergy, dons, and provost-marshals, all in one.

There are five *laveuses* in Ghardaya. There are also five men in this city who perform the same pious office on the bodies of men. The *laveuses* deal only with women, dead and alive. Once a year, the *laveuses* from the five cities of the Mzab meet in conference to exchange information, learn from one another's experiences, revise old regulations, and define any modern transgressions or deviations from proper behaviour.

Every detail in the conduct of a woman is regulated: her dress, her ornaments, her hair style, her use of cosmetics (which is allowed in certain ways, forbidden in others), and her deportment in the street (provided she is allowed to leave the house). She must not show her hand to a man when paying in a shop; it must be covered by a corner of her garment. She may not dance, nor sing at a feast, although singing at work is allowed if the text is approved. She is forbidden to weep over the body of a dead

person (be it her own child or mother)—Arab weeping-women
are engaged to do that, Mozabite women remain silent. She must
not raise her voice in laughter, in conversation, or when calling
someone—one calls by clapping one's hands. She is forbidden to
speak from roof-terrace to roof-terrace, and so on.

Children are reared in equally precise and strict ways. For example, a baby is made to stand upright in its second month; it is
exercised by being held up by the feet, head downwards, and
having its back and sides slapped; it is rocked on the left knee,
the mother's left foot resting on the right knee. The baby is
carried on the arms while it is in swaddling-clothes, and later
astride on the left hip—never on the mother's back.

A Mozabite woman may not marry a stranger, but men are
allowed to marry women of other races and creeds, including
Christians and Jewesses.[13] She retains her father's surname, but
in all other respects passes into the family of her husband. In the
husband's absence it is his mother who supervises the household,
lives in the house if possible, and exercises authority.

Shortly after the annexation of the Mzab by France, European
observers began to speculate how long the medieval and reactionary society of the pentapolis could survive close contact with
the progressive, scientific, and rational forces of the modern age.
E. Zeys, a lawyer and humanist, advocated annulment of the law
prohibiting the emigration of women and looked forward to the
emigration of whole families from the inhospitable valley and to
the 'victory of civilization' (Zeys 1886, p. 54). Dr. Amat, army
physician and scientist, who gave the first accurate account of
the valley and its people, predicted the rapid decadence of the
Mzab for economic and social reasons. He argued that the loss of
the slave trade, improved transport, and above all the newly-
found security would tempt the people from their walled cities
in the desert and draw them to the easier and more comfortable
life in the fertile regions of North Africa (Amat 1888).

It has already been suggested that the determination of the
Beni Mzab not to mingle with the population of the country, but
to maintain their homes and families in the desert and to wish to
die and be buried in their native valley, is founded on pride in

---

[13] Except in Beni Isguen, the 'holy city', where marriage with a non-
Mozabite woman entails banishment (Morand 1910, p. 442).

their exceptional faith, in the sacrifices which this demands, and on the superior attitude towards the world which it engenders. However, a traditional social group on the defence could not resist the pressure of 20th-century Western civilization by will-power alone; it would have to dispose of considerable material, spiritual, and intellectual resources, to make good that defence. Does Mozabite society possess these resources?

If it is true to say that tribal and traditional societies succumb to Western influence principally through poverty, ignorance, and inferior organization, it follows that the Beni Mzab are protected by their wealth, education, and privileged urban government. They are sufficiently in command of modern commercial practice and capitalist procedure to hold their own in highly competitive markets, they have long been familiar with European ways and languages, and their domestic authorities, who admit no strangers, have to contend only with traditional problems. But these meritorious or fortunate circumstances would be of little avail without the spiritual strength of this community. As in the case of Calvinism and its insistence on personal responsibility, discipline, and asceticism, the acquisition of wealth is not allowed to become merely an instrument of individual advantage, but remains a moral duty with the aim of glorifying God and sustaining the community. So the Mzab is still a theocracy and a society of equals.

WOLFRAM EBERHARD

8. *Change in Leading Families in Southern Turkey*

Contents:

1. Introductory
2. Antakya
3. Hassa
4. Conclusion

1. INTRODUCTORY

Rural as well as urban settlements in Turkey show differences in social structure to such a degree that almost each settlement is a type in itself. This is a direct consequence of the historical developments that went on in this area. Some cities have a history of several thousand years, and as centers of commerce and trade their population has always had a fairly high mobility and a considerable influx of foreigners or minorities. Other places, mainly centers of agrarian production, show a high stability and little change.

To date very little has been done to study the structure of Turkish villages or towns. Here, a purely socio-economic approach[1] does not, in my opinion, sufficiently explain the prominence of certain families within the settlement. A historical and genealogical approach is often quite helpful. In many cases, the

The research on which this article is based was done in 1951/2 with the help of a grant from the J. S. Guggenheim Foundation to which I wish to express my gratitude. [The article is reprinted here with the permission of the author and the publisher from *Anthropos*, 49:992–1003 (1954). *Ed.*]

[1] Such as the village studies by Fei Hsiao-T'ung in China, or J. F. Embree in Japan. B. Boran (Toplumsal yapı araştırmaları, Ankara 1945, p. 24) believes that the way in which a village was created does not mean much at the present time and need not be studied sociologically. — In general cf. A. Tanôglu, The Geography of Settlement, in: Review of the Geogr. Inst., Univ. of Istanbul, Internat. ed., no. 1, 1954, pp. 3–27.

importance of certain families within a settlement is due not so much to their economic power but to the fact that these families were the founders of the settlement or that they were socially prominent even before they became members of the community. There is a strong aristocratic tendency even in a place where the leading family is not of aristocratic origin. Interviewing in a settlement immediately brings forth the names of the leading families (in small places usually two to four, in larger cities six to eight families); further questioning reveals that data on the history of the settlement and genealogical data are known only to members of these prominent families, while "commoners" very often have only vague knowledge even about their grandparents. Questioning on rules of intermarriage, too, shows that only these prominent families have definite knowledge of all marriages concluded in the last three to five generations and know the rules that were applied, while "commoners" cannot say whether a certain pattern was used, and their knowledge about the families with which they have intermarried is too limited and vague to be used.

It is surprising to find out that very many Turkish settlements, especially villages and small towns, in spite of the long history of the country are recent creations, often not older than a hundred years. The reasons for this fact are still not quite clear, and no definite answer can be given before the official taxation and population lists ("defter") of the Ottoman Government are made available and studied.[2] The foundation of the present settlement is very often connected with the settlement of formerly nomadic tribes.[3] This has already been pointed out by S. Aran,[4]

[2] This extremely large and valuable material, an ideal source for statistical research, is now studied by Halasi T. Kun, Halil Inalcik and others.

[3] See remarks in my articles: a) Types of Settlement in Southeast Turkey, in: Oriens (Leiden), Vol. 6, 1953, pp. 32–49; b) Nomads and Farmers in Southeastern Turkey, in: Sociologus (Berlin), Vol. 3, 1953, pp. 49–64. The field work on which these articles are based was done in 1951–52 with the help of a grant by the J. S. Guggenheim Foundation, New York.

[4] Sadri Aran (Evedik Köyü: Bir köy monografisi, Yüksck Ziraat Enst. Calış malarından, No. 66, Ankara 1938, p. 33) in his study of a village near Ankara shows that the village had been founded by one family. After this family died out, three families that had married daughters of the founder's family were regarded as the leading families of the place. One of them is descended from a religious teacher, the other from a former shepherd, the third from a successful farmer.

P. Stirling,[5] M. Tuğrul,[6] B. Boran[7] and others.[8] In cases where the settlement was enforced by the government, the history of the settlement usually goes back to the 1860's; in other cases the settlement may be older. If this process took place when the social organization of the former nomads was still intact, i.e. when they still lived under their tribal chiefs, or if only one or two extended families settled down, the descendants of the former chiefs or first settlers are still regarded as the prominent families of the place; they have more authority and prestige than the others, and they are the natural functionaries of the place. At the present time, from these families still come the party leaders of the political parties or the administrators, such as city mayor, village headman. This pattern has now begun to change with the emergence of a new group of leaders coming either from the "intelligentsia", i.e., the Western-trained city-youth, or from the successful merchants. But for an understanding of the present

[5] P. Stirling (The Social Structure of Turkish Peasant Communities [Ph. D. Thesis, Oxford 1951], I quote from a mimeographed edition published in Ankara in 1952 with the author's consent) in his study of a village near Kayseri does not pay much attention to this question but points out that the village seems to have been originally the summer camp of nomadic tribes which later settled here voluntarily (p. 13). This process, by the way, is still going on according to interviews I had with nomadic groups in Southeastern Turkey. While most tribes prefer to settle in their winter camps, some now prefer the summer camps, because they can get more land there in spite of a colder climate and less fertile soil.

[6] Mehmet Tuğrul (Ankara Örencik ve Ahi köylerinin türküleri, Ankara 1945, p. 5) in his study of two villages near Ankara says that one of these villages was founded by a few nomadic settlers who made a clearing in the forest. Later settlers were refugees from neighboring villages who fled banditry.

[7] In spite of her general attitude (see note 1) Mrs. Boran mentions that several of the villages near Manisa, which she has studied, were founded by nomads in the place of their former winter camps (l. c., p. 31 f.).

[8] Niyazi Berkes (Bazı Ankara Köyleri üzerinde bir araştırma, Ankara 1942, p. 135) mentions in one case three "founding families," but does not give much more detail. Ibrahim Yasa, in his still unpublished work, Hasanoğlan köyü: toplumsalekonomik yapısı, a village near Ankara, does not enter into this discussion, nor does John A. Morrison, in his Alişar, a Unit of Land Occupance in the Kanak Su Basin of Central Anatolia (Ph. D. Thesis, Chicago 1939). The short village studies published by the "People's Houses," such as Bergama'da Köyler (four studies; available to me were No. 2: Pınarköy, Narlıca, Tepeköy, Yalnızev, Bergama Halkevi yayınlarından, No. 14, 1944, 63 pp.; No. 3: Timarlar, No. 16, 1945, 52 pp.; and No. 4: Bölcek köy, No. 18, 1945, 80 pp.) also do not touch upon this problem.

social structure of the country and its power relations this older "elite" is still of greatest importance.

2. ANTAKYA

The famous old city of Antakya near the Syrian border lost most of its importance as a center of trade when the port of Iskenderun was enlarged and connected with Anatolia by railway. Moreover, when Antakya was taken over by Turkey (1938), all Armenians and many important middle and upper class Syrian families left for Syria or Lebanon. Only the old Turkish and some Syrian families with large landed property and old local ties remained. Today, most government officials in the city are recent immigrants from other parts of Turkey, while a large sector of the poorer population is still linguistically Syrian. The factual leadership is still in the hands of five old families who view with a certain jealousy the growing importance of the immigrants who keep control of key positions and who by their connections with the capital are in a position to fortify their status. The old families, after some twenty years of Syrian protectorate, have practically no connections with Ankara, and their connections with Damascus and Aleppo have lost their importance or even work against them.[9] At least two of the five leading families are descendants of former Turkish feudal lords.[10] Later on we shall give some typical examples of the development of this type of family.

The family of greatest prestige in Antakya is the Halefoğlu family; it represents a good example of another type of "aristocratic" family. The Halefoğlus are ultimately an Albanian

[9] In this case the families are mainly of Syrian origin. The important families of Antakya were, according to Mr. Hüsnü Halefoğlu: 1) Halefoğlu, 2) Bereketoğlu, originally Syrians from the Ben-i-Halit group, 3) Karaman, 4) Karabey, 5) Civelek; according to Mr. Karaoğlan, Director of Education: 1) Halefoğlu, 2) Bereketoğlu, 3) Civelek, 4) Kuseyri, 5) Adalı, originally called Yahyaoğlu (interviews on November 14 and 15, 1951). The difference in the names and the sequence of importance indicates the struggle for prestige among the leading families.

[10] Civelek and Karabey. On the Karabey, see below.

family;[11] it is known that a branch of the family is still living in Albania.[12] The family had close ties with the family of Mehmet Ali, the reformer of Egypt after Napoleon and ancestor of the last Egyptian kings, and also an Albanian family. At the same time that Mehmet Ali was appointed by the Turkish Sultan as administrator of Egypt, the ancestor of the Halefoğlu, Hüseyin, became administrator of Aleppo. Hüseyin soon moved to Antakya, because he preferred the climate; thus, the family became an Antakya family in the early years of the last century. Hüseyin's son Halef ağa built the military barracks of Antakya (still existing) and a big mosque near the residence of the family. He became first *Kaymakam,* later Vice-Governor of Damascus, and died 1278 H (= 1861) in Arabia. A brother of Halef was a colonel of the army in Istanbul. Hüseyin had already acquired much land in and around Antakya and the district under his administration. In clear distinction to feudal landed property, property of this type is scattered and not contiguous; its administration, too, is not uniform. At the present time, the property is used in three ways: a) according to the *murabe* system: the landlord gives land, seed, implements and animal power, and the tenant has the right to keep one-fourth of the produce; b) according to the *ortalık* system:[13] the landlord gives land and seed, and the tenant keeps one-half of the produce; c) on some land, mulberry trees are grown; land, trees and the implements for silk-

[11] The following data were kindly given by Mr. Hüsnü Halefoğlu (November 15, 1951).

[12] The Müftü Numan family.

[13] This system is quite common in other parts of Turkey. In the case of modernization a change has been observed (in 1951 and 1952): when landlords introduce machines, they adopt the *murabe* system and leave only one-fourth of the product for the tenant. The machine, thus, replaces implements and animal power; higher cost of investment is mentioned to justify the change in the relation to the tenant. As the tenant usually does not get more land, he has less work to do but, getting less, is impoverished. The next step, already taken by some landlords, is to cultivate their land with hired "operators" (usually U. S. trained) and to terminate the relation with the tenants. These can now only get temporary work as agricultural workers in peak times and rely upon the government for resettlement. Mr. Halefoğlu indicated that he, too, would like to set up an oil press, but would not change the contracts with his tenants.

production belong to the landlord; the tenant keeps one-third of the production.[14]

Thus, when the family had definitely settled in the area and become the local landlord-family, in addition to functioning as a representative of the government, it started a conscious marriage policy by intermarrying with the most important local landlord-family, the Bereketoğlus. This policy began with Halef who married a daughter of the Bereketoğlus. His son, too, married a Bereketoğlu, and his daughter married a son of the same family. At least one of his grandsons continued this policy. Thus, the two families became close allies to the present day. The Halefoğlus remained administrators: Halef's son Abdulrami ağa played an important role as local administrator in the Crimean war, drafting soldiers for the army. His son Hüsnü became Member of Parliament (1327 H = 1910), almost at the same time as Rıfat Bereketoğlu, the husband of his father's sister. Thus, the landlord-family of the Bereket had gained political influence by its alliance with the Halefoğlu, as the Halefoğlu had become the leading local landlord-family by the help of the Bereketoğlu. Hüsnü had many important official positions, among which was office as mayor of Antakya for many years. A cousin of his is a high official in the Foreign Office in Ankara whose son has studied in Paris and probably will also go into government service. With Hüsnü, the family reveals the traditional marriage pattern of the area: Hüsnü married his paternal cousin; his son his maternal cousin. Ortho-cousin marriage is the preferred type of marriage, if political reasons, such as mentioned above, do not make political intermarriages (always more than one; if possible in both ways) preferable. The history of this family shows another trait in which it differs from a feudal family: the family came as government official and remained for one hundred fifty years to function in this capacity; while the typical feudal family has passed through a period of landlordism and entered public office only in the last generation or two.

The history of the Cankat family in Reyhanlı is quite similar in many respects, but the development is already one step further

[14] Here the rate is higher than the one-fourth that should be expected, because special skill is needed. In the whole Near East the situation in tree plantations always differs from that of ordinary land.

advanced. This family traces its history back to the first rulers of the Circassians.[15] In the late eighteenth century, the connections with the Ottoman Empire began; at the same time, the family split into two branches, as shown in the following simplified genealogy (Figure 8-1).

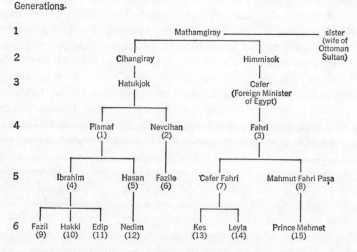

FIGURE 8-1   Simplified genealogy.

Explanations:

(1)   had to leave Circassia in 1284 H (1867), emigrated first to Bulgaria, then to Turkey (1293 H = 1876). He soon left for Syria and became leader of Circassians there. Half independent.

(2)   wife of ruler of Egypt, Ismail Paşa (since 1863).

(3)   professor in Egypt.

(4)   Turkish administrator in Syria.

(5)   ?

(6)   married to a Yakup paşa of the Yediç family; she died without children and the property went to the wife of (4), a daughter of the mother's brother of Yakup Paşa, of the Yediç family.

(7)   lawyer in Alexandria, with French wife.

[15] The following data were kindly supplied by Mr. Fazil Cankat (No. 9 in generation 6 of the simplified genealogy). Mr. Cankat knew the mythical ancestor of the family, *Atik*, and the three following generations, but a gap existed from then on to Mathamgiray.

(8)   Egyptian embassador in France; married sister of former King Farouk of Egypt.

(9)   chief of the Circassians in Reyhanlı and local chairman of the Democratic Party.

(10)   teacher in Gaziantep.

(11)   official in the railway administration in Istanbul.

(12)   doctor in Iskenderun.

(13-15)   live in Paris.

The Egyptian branch was able to retain the social status of the family by intermarriage with the rulers of Egypt. Here, a change can be expected since the 1952 events in Egypt. The Turkish branch, which also has some high connections with Egypt, changed definitely in the sixth generation; today, the family has almost completely lost its landed property; it has also lost its political influence. The position of a leader of the Circassians in Reyhanlı is contested and of no practical importance; the position as leader of the local Democratic Party will probably not be kept for any time.[16] On the other hand, the family is paying great attention to education and is moving into the professions, thus becoming an upper middle-class family. Developments in other countries seem to indicate that this line of change, still atypical for Turkey, might become typical soon.

3. HASSA

The small district-town Hassa is on the new road from Antakya-Iskenderun to Gaziantep, a road that is quickly gaining importance and that will soon exercise a great influence upon the development of all cities it touches. Hassa has some 2000 to 2500 inhabitants plus almost 500 government officials.[17] The city is located in the exit of a narrow valley; its fields are all in the adjacent plain along the Syrian border. It is a new city; the old center is Teyek, now a village two to three miles further up in the

16 Local information gathered in Reylanlı and Kırıkhan.
17 Information given by the *Kaymakam* of Hassa, November 20, 1951.

valley. Teyek, too, is less than one hundred years old and was the place where the rest of the Karabey family (see Figure 8-2) had to settle.

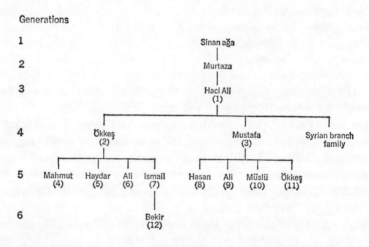

FIGURE 8-2

Explanations:

(1)   married daughter of Yussuf ağa in Teyek (Karabey family).

(2)   married daughter of Seyhan Nebizade from the Kurdish Mountain in Syria, the Syrian branch of our family, thus reenforcing the connection between both branches.

(3)   married daughter of Çamzade family, a noble family; still living.

(4)   married a daughter of (3).

(5)   married a daughter of (3); was appointed chairman of the local People's Party organization because he was one of the influential leaders of the city.

(6)   now city mayor; administers family property together with (5).

(7)   married daughter of the Karabey of Akbez.

(8)   married a girl from a village near Reyhanlı; now chairman of the People's Party in Hassa.

(9)   married daughter of the Karabey of Akbez.

(10)   married a daughter of (2).

(11)   married a daughter of the Çamzade family.

(12)   married a daughter of (8).

Hassa has two important families, the Ergüneş and the Sarıbey. The Ergüneş[18] were leaders of a branch of the Seyhan tribe which lived in Adaman (now Adıyaman) near Malatya. Four generations back[19] the tribe moved into this area and settled in two villages, Adamanlı, now in Turkey, and Adamanlı, now across the border in Syria. Both villages still "belong" to the Ergüneş family. The Turkish branch still has some ten thousand *dönüm* of land, seven to eight hundred goats and as many sheep, two hundred cattle, twenty water-buffaloes and some horses. This indicates that the family is fairly conservative, as most similar landlord-families in the area already have completely given up animal husbandry and have specialized in agriculture or even monoculture. Another aspect of the conservatism of the family is that all property is under the administration of two brothers. At the same time one of these brothers controls the family village, and the other as city mayor controls Hassa and conducts all business with the central government, traits that may be called "feudal". The fact that no family member so far has gone into any profession or obtained a position in the political hierarchy of the country is another aspect of their conservatism. The marriage pattern follows these lines: soon after settlement in the area the family concluded a marriage alliance with the powerful local feudal family of the Karabey in Teyek and later with the other branch of the Karabey in Akbez (both places near the home of the Ergüneş family and other noble families), while continuing the Arab system of cousin-marriage as far as possible.

While this family can be regarded as an excellent example of a small feudal family that became a local landlord family, the other family of Hassa has changed much more.

According to family tradition,[20] the Sarıbeys ("Yellow Bey") believe they are a branch of the Çobanoğullar of Kozan. In spite of attempts to settle the family and the tribesmen belonging to it, they remained nomads until 1865, when they were defeated by Derviş Paşa in the general drive against nomads. Karabey ("Black Bey"), the brother of Sarıbey, was forced to live in

---

[18] This is a new family name, not the original one, as its form shows.

[19] Counting from Mr. Ali Ergüneş, our informant; the time of his fourth ancestor seems to have been the period of forced settlement, around 1865.

[20] According to Mr. Süleyman Sarıbey in Hassa, November 20, 1951.

Aleppo. He became the ancestor of the Karabey family that now consists of ten "houses". The main branch settled in Akbez near Hassa.[21] Sarıbey's son Mehmet was exiled to Adrianopolis and his son Halil to Nish in Yugoslavia. The rest of their families settled in Teyek, together with the rest of the tribe. A branch of the family accepted the name Sarıbey, others are still called Karabey.[22] Without reproducing the whole genealogy the marriage pattern of the family, in terms of generations, is as follows:[23]

Second generation: Mehmet married (a) a daughter of Çirkin ağa, a branch of the famous Mursaloğlu family of Reyhaniye, the most powerful noble family of the area, (b) a daughter of the Karabey branch, (c) a daughter of a local small feudal family (Turan ağa). Mehmet's brother Halil married (a) a daughter of the famous feudal family of the Fettahoğlu in Bahçe,[24] (b) a daughter of the feudal family Uşakzade in Akbez, the place where the Karabey were forced to settle.

Third generation: Five women from different branches of the Karabey; one ortho-cousin; one daughter of the Çirkin ağa.

Fourth generation: Seven women from different branches of the Karabey; three ortho-cousins; two maternal cousins, two cousins; one daughter of the Ulaş tribe (settled mainly in Osmaniye); two marriages with tribal girls of the original tribe and two with non-tribal girls.

Fifth generation: Two women from different branches of the Karabey; seven ortho-cousins; three cousins; one non-tribal girl. Some members of this generation are still unmarried.

As in other cases, this shows that the generation living around 1850 to 1890 made many "political" marriages with families of neighboring lords. The reason for this, as was pointed out to me, was to enable the family to live in peace in the assigned place of settlement; in the period before settlement, to be able to pass

[21] Misak Kelesian (Sis madian [History of Kozan], Beyrut 1949, p. 91) says they were the Ali Bekir oğullar of Akbez.

[22] M. Kelesian (l. c., p. 91) mentions the Haci Omar oğullar of Teyek as a famous feudal family. According to our information, the Karabey of Teyek are descendants of one of Halil's sons.

[23] Sarıbey and Karabey are counted as first generation, although earlier generations are remembered.

[24] A famous feudal family; cf. M. Kelesian, l. c., p. 91.

through an area belonging to another tribal leader on the way to or from their summer camps. With increasing pacification of the area marriages within the family, especially ortho-cousin-marriage, increased. This type of marriage holds the property within the extended family, holds the family together, enables the marriage partners to know each other before marriage, and enables other male members of the husband's family to enter his house in his absence and to talk to his wife, because she is their sister or cousin. It also enables the wife to be present at family meetings because she sees only her own blood-relatives.[25]

Similarly interesting is the change in profession which this family made in the course of generations:

First generation: Feudal lords and tribal leaders.

Second generation: Id.

Third generation: Two members were appointed by the government as governor or district-commander; one member moved away to live with his in-laws as farmer; the others all lived in Teyek as landlords.

Fourth generation: Two members were colonels in the army; one later became a teacher of arithmetic, in a military school; one high school teacher; one official in an office of land survey; one chairman of the local branch of the People's Party; one mailman; one foreman in a blacksmith factory; one employee in a cotton factory (the last three in cities at some distance from Hassa). The others still live in Teyek.

Fifth generation: No details; most of them are still less than twenty years of age.

The loss of status in the fourth generation is very obvious in contrast to other families which specialize in certain fields of activity, such as the law and medical professions, which are quite profitable at the moment, or government service which gives high security; the family had grown too large in size to be fed by its property and had thus felt it must accept any occupational

[25] Daughters of the Sarıbey family married men from the Mursaloğlu, the Paşabey family, the Çirkinoğlu and the Kiliçoğlu families, all noble families.— On the ortho-cousin marriage pattern see now Fr. Barth, Principles of Social Organization in South Kurdistan, in: Univ. Ethnogr. Museum Oslo, Bull., No. 7, 1953 and his article in: Southwestern Journ. of Anthrop., Vol. 10, 1954, pp. 164–71.

opportunity even one having no real prospect for the future. As the property in Teyek is not ideal for modernization,[26] further loss of status for the rest of the family seems possible.

Investigation of genealogies of other prominent families of the area reveal the same picture as far as the marriage pattern is concerned. In the process of social transformation the families are on different levels of development. The city of Reyhanlı (approximately six thousand inhabitants)[27] has four important families: the Cankats (see above) play a special role. The others are: a) the Çirkinoğlu, a branch of the Mursaloğlu. One member of this family is mayor of Iskenderun, another was defeated as candidate for the Democratic Party. All other members of the family are still landlords or landowners. b) The Bahadırlı, most important in Reyhanlı, descendants of former tribal leaders, have one member as mayor of the city and chief of the People's Party; before him, his cousin was mayor, and before him, two of his uncles. The candidate for the job is another cousin. One cousin is founder of the local Democratic Party and local lawyer and judge; another cousin is also a judge; one cousin and a nephew are agricultural economists, another nephew a chemist and one cousin is a doctor. The chief of the family expressed a clear family policy: professions like lawyer, judge, doctor are necessary if the family is to keep its prestige in a changing city; for the landowning members of the family, more and modern knowledge, such as agricultural economy and chemistry, is necessary. All other members of the family are still farmers or landlords. c) The Altunlu, a branch-family of the Bahadirli: one member is now chief of the Democratic Party; another, the owner of the hotel in the city (a cousin of his is a tenant in this hotel).

It seems, thus, that the leading families of Reyhanlı have changed little; only one family has a clear development that shows the intention to keep its position in the city by modernizing and by controlling the party apparatus, the importance of which they have clearly recognized is necessary for keeping in power. When the balance of power changed in 1950 from the People's Party to the Democratic Party, the family tried immediately to

[26] The valley is too narrow to be suitable for extensive mechanization of agriculture; torrents recently caused heavy property losses (1950).

[27] Information given by the mayor.

assume leadership in the new party as they had had in the old one. The same was done by the Kılıçoğlu family in Kırıkhan.[28] All members of this family, too, are still landlords or farmers, but one man was former People's Party chief, whose nephews are now city mayor and chief of the Democratic Party. This situation clearly shows that in this part of Turkey the party system and the ideologies of the parties are not yet fully understood; as in Syria powerful individuals of influential parties control the local (and often the central) organization of the party. But it should be added that this situation has already changed in other parts of Turkey and is quickly changing here.

4. CONCLUSION

It has been shown that in the Hatay province of Turkey[29] each city has a small number of prominent families;[30] these families have been the leaders of the city for about a hundred years, i.e. since the forceful settlement of tribes in the area. The origin of these families is either from former tribal chieftains or from military officials of the government who remained in the area because the government was not strong enough to transfer them to other places at the end of their terms of office. These families, as far as they are of nomadic origin, had the custom of intermar-

[28] The leading families of Kırıkhan are the Kılıçoğlu, the Karaman (see above), and the Fatay.

[29] Similarly in the Çukurova.

[30] The situation in villages is similar. For example, the village Acemli near Kırıkhan has sixty households (i.e., approximately three hundred inhabitants). The village headman is a commoner from the Ulaş tribe (of Osmaniye), and knows that he still has relatives in other parts of the province. Around 1865 his family was forced to come to Iskenderun; his father and his uncle then bought land from villagers in the mountains who did not like the fields far away in the plain. Today his family and its five sub-families are the landowners in the village; all others are landless agricultural workers. It is interesting to note that the next village, Reşadiye, is absolutely different in structure: it was created by government order for settlers from European Turkey. Therefore, all inhabitants own some land. A third village nearby, Karadurmuş (built around a big *höyük*, mound) consists of hereditary tenants only; the soil, on which their houses are built, belongs to their landlord.—Changes in a large city, Antep, will be discussed in a forthcoming dissertation by E. Landauer, Culture Change in South Central Asia Minor (Univ. of Calif.).

riage with other powerful nomadic families according to their concepts of nobility and in order to keep peaceful relations with them. This custom was continued until the end of the last century, when the tribe had become sedentary. It is disappearing now and gives way to an originally Arabian system of ortho-cousin-marriage or more general cousin-marriage. Free marriages are still the great exception. New families secured their position in the area by similar intermarriages.

After settlement the tribes were given large tracts of land. The families of tribal chiefs got much land for themselves and acquired more by taking over land belonging to the tribe, as the tribe in the first period of settlement did not show much interest in land and anyway regarded the chieftain as legal owner of all tribal land. The tribal chiefs (often with the help of Syrian fellahin as tenants) accepted agriculture, but at first still kept many animals. By now most of them have given up their herds and specialize in farming, mainly as absentee landlords. In order to keep their social status they have tried to secure administrative rights in their home, such as governor, district-administrator or city mayor. Since the creation of parties they have also tried to secure the control of the parties. Although the general change in the country has not yet adversely affected most of them, they try to keep in line with the changes by going into certain professions, such as lawyer, judge or doctor (which will change them more and more into real city families) or to learn techniques by which they can earn enough money from their land. Cases in which a part of the family works as employees in factories in large cities and thus loses status are still rare.

SAMIH K. FARSOUN

9. Family Structure and Society in Modern Lebanon

The evolution of the contemporary kinship structure in Lebanon is part and parcel of the general structure and the process of change of a complex agrarian society in the direction of modernization: industrialization, urbanization and a highly interdependent, internally and externally, market economy. Any society or nation-state can be viewed sociologically as a social ecological system having certain characteristics that are common to any system, social biological or otherwise. These include such attributes as boundaries, boundary maintenance, and interdependence of parts. In social systems, logically interdependent parts include the kinship, economic, political, religious ecological and stratification substructures. The interrelationships are not one-way effects; on the contrary, the structures are highly intertwined, richly cross-connected to form more complex "circuits" of influence than a simple "dominant" or "feedback" system.[1] Thus a change in one substructure or in the relations (connections) between a given two (or more) substructures sets off or causes transformations in others or in the relations between others. Hence the structure and function of the contemporary kinship system of Lebanon is intimately connected with other structures of the society. This essay will analyze the continued existence, the conditions that promote the perpetuation in modern Lebanon of a particular form of kinship structure: the functionally extended family. The functionally extended family, *unlike the classical residentially extended family, is not residentially nucleated*

This paper by Dr. Farsoun was prepared especially for this *Reader* at the request of the editor.

[1] W. R. Ashby, *An Introduction to Cybernetics,* New York: John Wiley & Sons, 1966.

but nevertheless continues to perform most all the same functions and with the same basic structure. It will show that in contemporary Lebanon the complex pattern of interdependence of the economic, political, religious, and stratification substructures virtually prescribes this form of kinship organization. The essay is based on data already published in the social scientific literature on Lebanon and the Middle East and on interviews conducted with a sample of professional families in Beirut in the summer of 1966 for a study on contemporary urban middle-class kinship structure. The following analysis delineates the interrelationships and linkages between kinship and the other societal structures: economic, political, religious and stratification. Emphasis will be on the urban areas. However, before we begin, a brief analytic review of the socio-historical context out of which modern Lebanon emerged is necessary.

ORGANIZATION OF ISLAMIC OTTOMAN SOCIETY AND ITS CHANGES

Much of the character of the extended family structure in the Middle East, but especially in Lebanon, is derived from its structural position in a highly ethnically fragmented, ecologically varied, but religio-politically united, complex agrarian society. This (Sunni Muslim Ottoman) complex agrarian society has remained fundamentally the same since the fifteenth century. Serious winds of change blew on this orientally despotic empire, however, with the Napoleonic invasion of Egypt, a clear and successful challenge from the West which shook the Ottoman Empire out of its torpor. The political and military reforms known collectively as the Tanzimat were soon instituted. These were the first measures of serious modernization, or more accurately, Westernization, for they were in frank imitation of the Western European nations.

Islamic theology itself describes the ethnic fragmentation of Near Eastern populations: the people compose religio-political communities or collectivities, each living wherever it can, but by its own religious law, and yet all united under the political hegemony of the Muslim ruler. Under the Ottomans, this theocratic principle was elaborated into the *millet* system in which religio-political communities were each independently represented *vis-à-vis* the Sultan by their highest clerical official, but all "united" under the rule and control of the Sunni Muslim Ottoman Sultan in Istanbul. What mediated structurally between the larger collectivity, i.e., the religio-political community, and the individual, were the extended or lineage kinship networks and, in the urban areas, the guilds as well. The extended kinship or family lineage groups had important functions for the survival and maintenance of the individual and the group—so important, in fact, that an individual as such had little significance except through his membership in an extended family or lineage. And the religious collectivity was important directly in proportion to its size and influence. Family and religious collectivity constituted the major structures within which an individual lived out his life. To a large extent political, economic, educational, welfare and religious functions were performed through the structure of the extended kinship units or lineages. Relations between kin members were institutionalized with the obligations and rights fairly well delineated. These seemed to cut across even stratification lines. However, this organizational structure varied, to a greater or lesser degree, as a function of the intrusion of local ecologic, demographic, economic, political (including taxation) and technological factors. The interrelations within and between the differing ecological "niches" (i.e., desert people, plains people, mountain people and city people), the varied ethnic groupings (sectarian, religious, and linguistic), the quasi-feudal stratification structure, and economic and political links to the West, made for a very complex social system that is quite unlike the systems pictured in the folk/urban or *Gemeinschaft/Gesellschaft* dichotomies.

The Ottoman Empire differed from the industrial West by the degree of societal and economic differentiation. If the process of social differentiation means the development of relatively autonomous and formal institutions other than kinship to perform necessary and numerous societal functions, and where each such institution is specialized and limited, then the Ottoman Empire and pre–World War II Middle East were only slightly "differentiated." Whatever differentiation in these terms existed, it only existed within the major lines of social organization identified above. Those few differentiated social institutions other than kinship and religion that did exist functioned not in opposition to, but rather in reinforcement of, the major structures. For example, welfare agencies were in existence, but were either familial or religious, that is, composed of members of and serving a certain family or a certain sect. Almost all local welfare agencies in Lebanon until this day continue to be so.[2] Social change including societal differentiation and a class-like stratification system began earnestly in the Ottoman Empire and the Lebanon only after the First World War, with the disintegration or dismemberment of the Ottoman Empire and the institution of the Mandate System by the Allies through the League of Nations. The French mandate in Lebanon, similar to the other mandates in other eastern Arab states, began, after World War I, the systematic building of some of the technological and organizational prerequisites for a modern, territorially based nation-state. The already established European, primarily French, influences in Lebanon were intensified and new ones were instituted, and the social transformations were many.

Nevertheless, from all indications, the kinship organization throughout the Middle East, including Lebanon, remained fundamentally the same and continued to be strong during the Mandate era. Industrialization hardly made serious inroads; the economic base remained largely just above self-sufficiency in rural agrarian villages, and mercantilistic in the urban centers—types for which cohesive extended family relations are very well suited. Given the paucity of resources and of work, the extended family both in the rural and urban areas remained the major institution for guaranteeing the survival and happiness of the individual human being. Political, religious, educational and welfare structures all contributed to and reinforced this kinship organization. Furthermore, the numerous emigrants or refugees moving from one part of the empire to another or from one nation-state to another, such as the Armenians, Palestinians, Egyptian Christians, came with a similar kinship system and adjusted quickly to their new nations.

---

[2] See Al-Jumhuriyyah Al-Lubnaniyyah, *Al-Kidmah Al-Ijtimaʿiyya Al-Ahliyya fi Lubnan,* Beirut, 1965. (Social Welfare in Lebanon.)

But since the First World War, and especially since the Second World War, more and more people in Lebanon have been drawn into a national and international market economy with cash remuneration. Emigration from Lebanon and return to it was and continues to be strong. Scientific farming is increasing and more industrialization has taken place; a few large-scale economic enterprises have developed. In particular, highly skilled educated and professional groups have appeared in numbers—engineers, doctors, lawyers. Urbanization has gained momentum. A political system and government that is increasingly "public minded," a modern army, and some semblance of a modern class structure have all developed. All of these contribute to the cracks in the "cake of custom" or the traditional social organization. Evidence of this may be seen in the development of ethnically heterogeneous and architecturally modern city quarters, like Ras Beirut in Beirut, where the outlines of the new social order are spelled out in embryonic form.

The most important factors in the evolution of the contemporary kinship organization in Lebanon have been: (1) the ecological structure of the region, (2) the traditional Islamic culture and "theocracy," (3) political, military and economic modernization, (4) the emergent class stratification system, and (5) social and physical mobility. Let us now turn to the interrelationships between kinship and other structures of Lebanese society.

KINSHIP AND THE ECONOMIC STRUCTURES

Kinship and economic structures in any society are to some degree or other interdependent. The degree of interdependence varies in terms of the local conditions and, perhaps, the level on an evolutionary societal scale. An index of this interrelationship may be the extent of institutional differentiation. Presumably, in industrial-urban societies, separation of kin structures from economic and other structures is almost complete and necessary, while in the most primitive autonomous folk communities kin and economic structures are one and the same. In between these extremes fall a great number of social systems where the relationship between the two is complex and is not necessarily separated. The complex agrarian-based Ottoman Empire was a case in point. Modern Lebanon is another. The analysis here will review the functionally extended family and its (1) ownership and control of economic enterprises, (2) employment function, and (3) emigration and mobility functions.

In much of rural Lebanon, the extended family remains the economic productive unit.[3] In urban Lebanon where there is little food production, small manufacturing establishments (furniture, footwear, etc.), retail stores, and commercial enterprises are to a large extent family owned and run.[4] Data from Sayigh's study, for example, show that of a total of 1861 manufacturing and mining establishments surveyed in the 1955 Industrial Census of Lebanon, 1129 were vested in single ownerships, 694 were partnerships and only 38 were classed as corporations.[5] Percentagewise we see 60% singly owned establishments, 37.3% partnerships, and only 2% corporations. The majority are, in fact, family firms and frequently the partnerships are also of kin. These two forms clearly predominate in Lebanese economic structure. Such economic enterprises use and usually need the help of extended kin. Extended family structure is excellently suited for operation and control of these types of economic structures (i.e., family firms). Further, such economic structures are inheritable. Inheritance of property and/or business establishments and influence obviously preserves extended familial control over economic structures; in turn such economic structures reinforce extended family organization and continuity. Familial ownership and control of economic structures do not by any means stop at the small enterprises, however. The study of entrepreneurial activity in Lebanon by Sayigh includes a most reveal-

[3] See the many village studies made in Lebanon: e.g. T. Touma, *Un Village de montagne au Liban: Hadeth el Jobbe,* Paris: Mouton, 1958; A. Fuller, *Buarij, Portrait of a Lebanese Muslim Village,* Cambridge, Mass.: Harvard University Press, 1961.

[4] A. J. Meyer, *Middle Eastern Capitalism: Nine Essays,* Cambridge, Mass.: Harvard University Press, 1959; Y. A. Sayigh, *Entrepreneurs of Lebanon,* Cambridge, Mass.: Harvard University Press, 1962; and S. Khalaf and Emile Shwayri, "Family Firms and Industrial Development: The Lebanese Case," *Economic Development and Cultural Change,* 15 (October, 1966), pp. 59–69.

[5] Sayigh, *op. cit.,* p. 54.

ing table[6] on the form of ownership in relation to the type of activity of establishments registered at the Beirut Chamber of Commerce (which in Lebanon covers over three-quarters of the establishments in the categories listed). Of the categories listed (trade; trade in combination with some other activity; advertising, publishing and printing; insurance; transport; engineering works and contracting; finance; banking and money exchange) only banking and money exchange enterprises had more corporations listed than single ownerships and partnerships: 20 out of 35. On the other hand, of a grand total of 3492 establishments, 2160 were single ownership, 1230 were partnerships, and 102 were corporations. Even engineering and contracting establishments were overwhelmingly "single ownerships" or family firms. While further details on these establishments are not available, my own sources maintain that most of the partnerships and corporations of urban Lebanon are partnerships of siblings, cousins, or other extended kin, and that even the corporations are most often nothing more than legal protection for wholly family-owned or extended kin-owned establishments.[7] Recently more and more new establishments have been incorporated. Most of these are in industry and have been established since 1944. According to Sayigh these are in manufacturing activities new to Lebanon and the entrepreneurs "import" the shell along with the substance, the form of organization as well as the new type of activity.[8] There are no studies of the distribution or concentration of ownership of shares and stocks of these "corporations," but judging from the fact that many of them fall or stand on the good faith and credit of its president, and from other evidence to be presented below, there is reason to believe that these also are establishments owned by a single man, an extended family, or a very small group. They are in essence, patrimonial enterprises, but cast in corporate form for the above quoted reasons.

In America large-scale economic establishments have become the rule. In the trend of growth towards corporate bigness, sepa-

[6] *Ibid.*, p. 52.
[7] Interview with the director-general of the Beirut Chamber of Commerce and Industry, April, 1966.
[8] Sayigh, *op. cit.*, p. 58.

ration of ownership and control has taken place as well as decrease in influence of originating families and their descendents.[9]
In Lebanon a very limited number of establishments have
reached such bigness. Yet even those that have, such as a well-
known bank or a major regional airline,[10] two of the largest
companies in the number of workers and assets, have by no
means become too big for family ownership, influence or control,
or for that matter, "ethnic" influence and control.[11] Though no
published studies of the organizational kin and ethnic structures
of these two or other large Lebanese companies have been made,
it is a well-publicized fact told by most of the executives that
the above-mentioned bank and others like it are staffed, at least
at the senior and middle executive positions, by direct relatives
(kin) of the chief executive (and the other most important shareholders). His brother, nephew, brother-in-law, the partners and
their relatives hold the highest positions and are managers of the
bank branches. In fact the bank employees and employees of
other such large companies, represent at different levels of the
organizational structures separate networks of extended kin. In
addition, according to the executive interviewed, most all (no
figures were given) employees are Lebanese citizens of a particular ethnic origin. This ethnic and/or religious[12] concentration is very typical.

An engineer who works for a major airline stated that "about
forty of my relatives work for the airline."[13] If one argues that in

[9] R. Williams, *American Society,* New York: A. A. Knopf, 1965, pp. 150–
209.
[10] The major regional airline has a total of over three thousand employees
according to the Personnel Manager, an interview, August, 1966.
[11] See for example, R. Crow, "Confessionalism, Public Administration
and Efficiency," in L. Binder, ed., *Politics in Lebanon,* New York: John
Wiley & Sons, 1966.
[12] One doctor interviewed in his office at a very large private hospital in a
predominantly *Moslem* quarter stated that *"all* the doctors attached to the
hospital or with clinics in the hospital compound were *Moslem."* A check on
the list of the doctor's names in the hospital's main lobby proved him largely
correct. Over 90% of the list were easily identifiable as Moslem names.
[13] It was impossible to check on this figure. However, considering that he
was a second cousin of a very senior executive, the figure is likely to be correct. Moreover, for the Western reader, it is worth stating explicitly that a
Middle Easterner knows precisely the number of his kinsmen; and under
conditions of confidence, such statements can be taken as indeed accurate.

a highly technical establishment such as an airline one cannot just employ relatives without regard for skill and technical know-how, he is right. However, Lebanese extended kin and lineages get so large[14] and so varied that a kinsman with the proper technical skill will be easily found. For, in fact, the young kinsmen are advised to go into technical and educational areas which are needed in such large and growing companies. Such "nepotism" may be construed as economically dysfunctional from a Western vantage point. However, for Lebanon the reverse is true. In all developing countries including Lebanon, as Khalaf and Shwayri point out, critical shortages of professional and managerial talent exist both at the higher and middle management levels. Thus patrimonial owner-managers draw upon their own family resources. Further, kinship loyalty makes for greater trust and involvement in the affairs of the patrimonial business establishment. A basic value-belief that is still current in Lebanon is that of "amoral familism," to use Banfield's[15] phrase; thus, suspicion of the outsider and trust of the family in-group are strong social-cultural patterns that have consequences on the economic structure. Patrimonial establishments, even those cast in corporate form, are quite uneasy about placing strangers (non-kin) in pivotal positions, especially when a trusted kin has the necessary skills.[16]

Industrial manufacturing enterprises are very similar in their ownership and control patterns to the airline and bank discussed above—patrimonial and nepotistic, although again, no exact numerical data exist for Lebanon. In fact, at this stage of industrialization the extended family can be the most important source of investment capital[17] and of the necessary talent. One respondent

[14] One respondent was very proud to tell me that his clan, both in the cities and rural areas, "comprised four thousand *men*, not counting women!"

[15] E. Banfield, *The Moral Basis of a Backward Society*, Glencoe, Ill.: The Free Press, 1958.

[16] Khalaf and Shwayri, *op. cit.*

[17] E. E. Hagen corroborates this when he states: "Where one can neither trust a stranger or an acquaintance as a business associate, nor persuade him to lend one money, then the extended family may be a necessary source of capital and a necessary bond between business associates. Its abolition would not modernize the society; in the circumstances it would merely paralyze large-scale relationships."

who was the manager of a textile factory, one of the largest in Lebanon, was the son of the founder and one of several major shareholders along with several kinsmen. There were several relatives working in top positions in the different phases of the manufacturing, distribution and marketing operations. On the other hand, the wage workers in the factory came from a nearby village and many of them were kin of each other. Mothers in fact brought along to the factory their infants and children who played and/or worked near close and/or distant kin or village members. This of course is reminiscent of Smelser's family workers in his study of industrializing England.[18]

A most intriguing comment by a respondent has to do with the role of the new concept, for Lebanon, of the corporation. In many an old family enterprise, when the founder or owner passes on the inheritance to his children and they to theirs, the heirs become so numerous that often the enterprise is broken up or one kinsman buys out another in a process conducive to extended kinship fission. However, with the new concept of corporate shareholding, there is no more need for breaking up the enterprise or for one kin buying out another; the numerous heirs of large families become "shareholders" of an extended family corporation that is run by the most competent and, lately, most educated. In fact, this is precisely what happened to the textile manufacturing company.

Competence and achievement come to be critieria for control and reward. In other words, industrial and other establishments continue to be kin-owned, and family members still occupy controlling, pivotal positions, but they are, more and more, judged by their other owning extended kin in universalistic terms; control thus is more rationalistic. This pattern of incorporation has begun to appear also among heirs to real-estate land in high-priced areas in Beirut. One respondent, highly educated, complained that this was his unheeded advice to his extended family, similar to other families, in its quarrels over real-estate inherit-

---

See E. E. Hagen, "The Process of Economic Development," *Economic Development and Cultural Change,* V (April, 1957), p. 198, and as quoted in Khalaf and Shwayri, *op. cit.,* pp. 62–63.

[18] N. Smelser, *Social Change in the Industrial Revolution,* Chicago: University of Chicago Press, 1959.

ance. Hence the new legal concept of the corporation which is conducive to the emergence and maintenance of large-scale economic enterprises in America and Lebanon has in Lebanon the latent function of enhancing the solidarity of the extended family organization. Put differently and in reverse order, those extended families that are most cohesive or solidary are the ones that pool their resources for greater economic and commercial power and success. In rural Lebanon this relationship was clearly demonstrated by Williams and Williams[19] in their discussion of extended family cohesion and economic development. The corporate idea is thus introducing into Lebanon also the necessary conditions for the emergence of the pattern of the separation of ownership and control so typical of large industrial societies. Nevertheless, in Lebanon corporate organizations represent only 2.6% of the total number of businesses. It still is a very minor pattern. Of importance here, concerning the above discussion, is to keep in mind the fact of *cooperation* among relatives (kin groups) in economic endeavors in the urban areas. If this is naturally expected among the upper classes with property, power, and influence to protect, as Goode[20] argues, we have also shown it to be important among Lebanese middle or lower classes. We began this part with that discussion. Let us continue it here briefly. The small entrepreneurial establishments—manufacturing, trading and financing—that are the most numerous in Lebanon tend to be family firms. Different kin members pitch in to help, including the younger ones (as errand boys) who work there or in other kin-owned or kin-operated enterprises. In Lebanon as in all developing societies labor is in great supply, and kin get first chance at an available job; they are trusted and are loyal—values often repeated as desirable in Lebanon. Petty bourgeois are famous for this sentiment and practice all around the world.

Lebanon is the location for a large number of international commercial, philanthropic and political organizations operating in the region of the Middle East. These organizations are West-

[19] H. H. Williams and J. R. Williams, "The Extended Family as a Vehicle of Culture Change," *Human Organization*, 24 (Spring, 1965), pp. 59–64.

[20] W. J. Goode, *World Revolution and Family Patterns*, New York: The Free Press of Glencoe, 1963.

ern or Western controlled. In Lebanon they hire personnel strictly on universalistic criteria, although occasionally they are known to bow to tradition and make a "political" appointment. It is these Western commercial establishments and other organizations that are paying the highest salaries and are setting the pace in Beirut. Skill, competence, and talent "finally" is paying in the new universalistically oriented Western-owned sectors. Despite this there are many indications,[21] though no studies, that the local Lebanese personnel are relatively successful in subverting the universalistic criteria in favor of ascriptive (nepotistic) traditionalistic measures, still, in most cases, within the criteria of the required skill and talent.

This then brings us to the second major locus of linkage between the kinship and economic structures: employment. Insofar as we have seen the importance of family enterprises, employment of kin wherever possible or feasible is generally admitted as a good practice in Lebanon. Small shop owners, as in the West, employ their immediate as well as extended kin. Extended family help is sought in high season and in the summer. Indirect evidence is also available. Members of several kin groups worked together in the textile factory, noted above. Other evidence is gleaned from newspaper accounts. A construction accident reported in the Beirut daily newspaper *An-Nahar*[22] and others tells of the story of seven kinsmen workers dying when a sandy earth siding collapsed on top of them, burying them alive. The seven kinsmen were: a father, two sons, two nephews and two other "relatives." In fact they all died because they were working side-by-side near the wall as a team.

There is really little numerical data showing the percentage incidence of relatives employed in different types of establishments. On the other hand, frequent incidence follows logically from the fact of the high incidence of family-owned enterprises and the givens of the culture where a relative is considered the only reliable and trustworthy employee. When the size of the enterprise grows and it necessitates a larger number of employees, then other than kin are hired. Here again, who is hired

[21] Stories told proudly by respondents and others presumably for "outwitting" their foreign bosses.

[22] *An-Nahar*, Sept. 5, 1966, Beirut, Lebanon, p. 1 (daily newspaper).

is largely determined by other ascriptive criteria: religio-ethnic and/or other-ethnic (nationally, linguistic) membership as well as by locality (i.e., from the same village, city, or region). In small or large companies, the more influential officers are nevertheless able to ensure jobs for their extended kin. Again, the multifaced and complex companies such as airlines, manufacturing and banking are good illustrations. They have been cited above.

Concerning a large company one respondent stated that "many employees have several relatives working in different departments of the company." And yet, in an engineering (design) consulting firm where all employees were highly educated and skilled, no high incidence of kin as co-workers was observed. Only the major shareholder had a brother-in-law in the company. For highly specialized firms of this sort, it is difficult to employ kin unless they are trained and in just that specialty. Structurally, such firms are, employment-wise, antithetical to kin. Their increase in the modernizing society works against the reinforcement of the kinship system. However, this employment limitation should not give a false impression of the significance of kin and ethnic ties for such specialized and highly skilled firms. Their own survival (i.e., securing contracts, etc.) may still depend strongly on extended family contacts.

Thus we see that larger or smaller networks of relatives can be and are employed in a single company. This fact leads us to the discussion of the third major connecting link between the kinship and economic structures. This is the "job-finding" function or the extended family as an "employment agency." To appreciate this function fully, one aspect of the Lebanese and perhaps Middle Eastern social structure must be explained: the *wastah* system. The term *wastah* is colloquial Arabic for an "intermediary," a go-between, or the process of employing an intermediary or go-between, "a procedure of mediation"[23] in almost any and all types of activity. The *wastah* system is generalized in the

[23] V. Ayoub, "Conflict Resolution and Social Reorganization in a Lebanese Village," *Human Organization,* 24 (Spring, 1965), p. 13. See also, L. Nader, "Communication between Village and City in the Modern Middle East," *Human Organization,* 24 (Spring, 1965), pp. 21–24.

society and performs important functions within the family and clan as well as outside it. One needs a *wastah* in order not to be cheated in the market place, in locating and acquiring a job, in resolving conflict and legal litigation, in winning a court decision, in speeding governmental action, and in establishing and maintaining political influence, bureaucratic procedures, in finding a bride, and, in fact, for the social scientist to locate and convince respondents to give an interview. The *wastah* procedure is complex, its rules varied depending on the sphere and nature of activity, whether it is legal, familial, economic, etc.

Kin groups, men and women, function in urban areas as an informal group for the collection, storing, and transmission of information on available jobs in or *out* of kin-owned and kin-operated enterprises. In this function, kin, and to a certain extent the friendship clique, are the major channels of communication concerning job placement. In addition, kin act by recommending, sponsoring and guiding relatives into jobs. In short, kin act as *wastah* in job finding and the extended family is an employment agency. This particular function will be of especial relevance in the discussion of the relationship between the political and kinship structures. In an industrializing society like Lebanon, the *wastah* system with regard to "job finding" varies inversely in frequency of application with the degree of occupational "skills." In other words, the higher the degree of training and education the lesser the use of the *wastah* procedure, except in the form of recommending and sponsoring. That is, the greater relevance of the universalistic criteria, the lesser the relevance of the *wastah*.

Finally, the interdependence of kinship and economic spheres is best evidenced by the pattern of emigration both for urban and rural Lebanese. For example, the villages studied by Ayoub, Gulick, Fuller, Nader, Touma, Sweet, Williams and Williams all show the importance of émigrés' remittances from abroad to their kin in Lebanon. Economic well-being and development of the villages is strongly dependent upon the inflow of capital from the émigrés. Ayoub states that village "wealth has been generated by the capital input of villagers who have emigrated to West Africa and South America, principally, *while retaining close bonds with kinsmen within the village.* They have accumulated capital to enhance their status in Lebanon, not elsewhere."[24]

The usual pattern of emigration is for the parents to finance the son. It is a nuclear family affair not possible, as the Williamses argue, without extended family help both in Lebanon and the country of emigration. Emigrants rarely leave without assurances from emigrant kin of support and of a job usually in an ongoing extended family concern in the new country or something like it. On the other hand, the emigrant, especially if he is a head of a household, depends on his kin (usually father, brothers, etc.) to look after his nuclear family, his affairs, etc. Money sent back for investment usually goes into an extended family enterprise. For Haouch, the Williamses' village, economic betterment was brought about by the most solidary kin groups. The same can be said for sending a family member to study abroad for a professional degree. Economically, a professional degree will bring about similar capital to that from trade or any work in the new country. For the "investing" extended family, emigration for work or for higher professional education is functionally equivalent in consequences. This in the society represents an extra-societal channel of social mobility that could have serious consequences on the power and stratification structure of the local community and perhaps nationally as well.

Although evidence on the question of emigration has been presented only in the rural context the same essentially holds for the urban centers. First of all, many of more successful émigrés not only buy village lands, etc., but they also start urban enterprises of all sorts including industrial ones. The Arida family are a case in point. The nearest to statistical evidence on urban Lebanese extended families and their involvement in emigration is found in Churchill's Beirut survey. Sources of income for the family from other than employment included 18.53% from relatives and 11.16% from remittances from overseas.[25] It is likely that the figure on overseas remittances is really higher since the category "relatives" is inclusive of those overseas. Further-

[24] Ayoub, *op. cit.*, p. 12. Emphasis added.
[25] C. W. Churchill, *The City of Beirut, A Socio-economic Survey,* Beirut: Dar Al-Kitab, 1954, p. 57.

more, these figures do not include overseas capital input strictly for business activity or enterprise. Hence the real figure could be much more than 11.16%. The post–World War II heavy influx to America and Europe for higher education of students from the developing countries represented mostly middle-class people. These in fact are city people or urbanites sent by their families for professional training—a "profitable" investment for the whole family, especially if the young man returns to be placed in strategic governmental and/or business position. In addition, the son's increased earning power is good security for the old age of the parents particularly, and other close kin. Thus, though the data are sparse there are many clues pointing to the importance of urban emigration relating the kinship and economic spheres.

With the opening of the desert and Persian Gulf oil areas, Lebanon has become an exporter of highly trained professionals to those areas. Doctors, surgeons, dentists, engineers, technicians, lawyers, teachers, even skilled workers, all urban people, emigrate temporarily to the desert areas to work a few years there at very high salaries and collect good sums of money. With the saved money the professionals return to Lebanon to open their own clinics, their engineering and consulting firms, their own schools, etc., usually in cooperation with interested kin. These were urban enterprises by urbanites who capitalized on an institutionalized but extra-societal channel for social mobility or, in many cases, "social stability" (i.e., in order not to become downwardly mobile).

Finally, the extended family, both in the rural and urban areas, performs a "banking function" of money-lending, especially for those in need of small sums or other members without any assets. Churchill reports for the city of Beirut a high incidence of indebtedness—44.7% of household heads are reported as being in debt. The amounts of debts reported ranged anywhere from £25 ($8) to over £3000 ($1000). Of these 92.31% were private debts owed to persons rather than "institutions" (i.e., banks!).[26] Although Churchill does not state that these debts were owed to kinsmen, given the cultural phenomena of distrust of the stranger and of the trust of kin, and given the economic cooperation be-

---

[26] Churchill, *op. cit.*, 1954, p. 65.

tween kin shown above, it is reasonable to argue that most of these debts were in fact owed to near and/or distant kin.

In summary, interdependence of kinship with economic structure continues to be complex and strong, even in the most "modern" sectors of Lebanon's economy. The foci of articulation include ownership and control of economic enterprises, employment practices and attitudes, placement (job-finding) functions as well as promotion, economic betterment and economic development, money lending, emigration and even education. These relationships probably will not wane in the near future. The overall economic structure in its local, regional, and international settings, in which these kin-economic relations are found, has been unchanged since the War and has little immediate prospect of changing radically. Any major socio-political upheaval or catastrophe is likely to band the extended families together and increase their solidarities. For example, during the Palestine War (1948), Palestinian Arab families found refuge with their Lebanese kinsmen and with each other in Lebanon. Palestinian extended families lived together in the same rented house for varying lengths of time. Also, during the 1958 upheavals or civil war in Lebanon, Beirut nuclear families who happened to be near the fighting lines moved to kinsmen's houses in safer parts of the city or in the villages. Again, economic considerations were of relevance here too, since work activity was disrupted.

KINSHIP AND POLITICAL STRUCTURES

As in the earlier section, some complex relationships obtain between the kinship and political structures. If one keeps in mind a general socio-cultural evolutionary perspective, one can point to a greater or lesser degree of differentiation or separation between these two subsystems. Anthropologists have documented the existence in less technologically advanced societies of political structures formed on the basis of kin relations.[27] In

[27] M. Swartz, V. Turner, A. Tuden, *Political Anthropology*, Chicago: Aldine, 1966; M. Fortes and E. E. Evans-Pritchard, eds., *African Political Systems*, Oxford University Press, 1940; M. Gluckman, "Political Institutions," *Institutions of Primitive Society*, Oxford: Basil Blackwell, 1954, pp. 66–81; E. Leach, *Political Systems of Highland Burma*, London: Bell, 1954.

these societies, kinship organization is the structure in terms of which political functions are performed—a clan or tribe, for example. In contrast to this, in advanced industrial-urban societies political structures have a high degree of separation from the kinship structures. Nevertheless, this does not mean that there are no links at all. Voting behavior, for example, and party membership are highly influenced by kinship ties in the United States as Lipset[28] and others show. Furthermore, legal statutes, governmental (on the local, state, and federal level) rules and regulations on nepotism, and tax policy all influence the behavior of the nuclear and extended family in the United States. Thus, social systems such as the Lebanese fall between the two poles of the continuum and may have varied and complex kinship-political interrelationships.

The analysis of kin and political structures in Lebanon will be with regard to three aspects: (1) the political organization in general, including any rural urban variances, (2) the legal structure directly concerned with the family, and (3) the welfare function.

The general political structure of Lebanon is to be discussed in terms of the concept of *za'im* (pl. *zu'ama*) in the context of confessional or sectarian loyalties,[29] and within that, in the context of familial loyalties. The Ottoman Empire, we have seen, was an agrarian feudal hierarchical system. The feudal lord was a warrior and tax farmer appointed politically or perhaps only confirmed by the Central Ottoman authorities.[30] Thus, the feudal lord "spoke" for his "community" (*millet*) and fief, mediating between it and the higher feudal lords or the Central Government. Higher and stronger lords "spoke" or mediated for larger *iqta'* (feudal estates) and "communities." Even the highest religious

[28] S. M. Lipset, *Political Man,* New York: Anchor Books, 1963.

[29] Arnold Hottinger, "*Zu'ama* and Parties in the Lebanese Crisis of 1958," *Middle East Journal,* 15 (Spring, 1961); see also A. Hottinger, "*Zu'ama* in Historical Perspective," in L. Binder, *op. cit.,* 1966; also, L. Binder, *op. cit.,* 1966; Ralph Crow, "Religious Sectarianism in the Lebanese Political System," *Journal of Politics,* 24 (1962), pp. 489–520; and especially, Clyde Hess and Herbert Bodman, "Confessionalism and Feudality in Lebanese Politics," *Middle East Journal,* 8 (Winter, 1954).

[30] I. Harik, "The Iqta' System in Lebanon: A Comparative Political View," *Middle East Journal,* 19 (Autumn, 1965), pp. 405–22.

clerics of the Christian and of other minorities and who were the sects' leaders were themselves feudal lords, but in these cases, of church estates. The functions of the feudal lord included military obligations to the feudal hierarchy, tax farming, mediation between his *millet* and the alien outside world, and many social functions some of which can be described as economic, welfare, aid, and many others. However, the Ottoman reform movement to modernize the empire, known as the Tanzimat, put an end to this feudal fief-holding system. As the feudal system declined gradually, the Tanzimat established a rudimentary civil service system wherein the military and tax-farming functions of the lords declined. Yet, many of their social functions remained, especially where their feudal (*iqta'*) mandates were turned into estate possessions. In Lebanon for example, old *iqta'* families like Arslan, Jumblatt, Frangieh, Khazin, Himadeh, Zain, and As'ad continue today to own vast estates. Hence, today a *za'im* is the descendent of the old feudal lords (and others who have achieved the status) whose power is now based on vast land holdings or extensive businesses and a strategic government position, mediating for a "community" (*millet*, confessional group), and performing some of the traditional social functions of the feudal lord. The modern *za'im* is a leader who "looks out" for the interests of his client group by political, economic and social (including welfare) means for political loyalty and support.[31] In the contemporary context political support means, among other things, electioneering and voting for the *za'im* in the deputy elections to the Parliament of republican Lebanon.

The followers expect favors and benefits from the *za'im*; they give him support because of these expectations. Hence, the *za'im* must be rich. But property and money can be exhausted quickly with all the favors to give. Thus, an indispensable necessity for the *za'im* is high public office, especially in the executive and legislative branches; from these offices he is able to grant favors to his clinetele as well as to amass or protect his own wealth. In Lebanon, favors and benefits include: (1) employment, (2) job finding, (3) *wastah* making, (4) information communication, etc., and (5) channeling all available government favors. Politi-

[31] Hottinger, *op. cit.*, 1966.

cal office also is an institutionalized channel of social mobility for the highest levels of social status.

For the government, the *za'im* and especially the *za'im*-deputy is a most important intermediary. His "community" or his clientele, i.e., his people, trust him. This makes it possible for the government to reach the people through him in order to influence their behavior, get support and/or commitment for action. And, reciprocally, the *za'im* is important for the people since he is their means of communication with the government and the channel of services and favors from it. Structurally, the *za'im* is at the focal point of relations between the established government and the confessional, territorial and ethnic groupings, as well as *between* the different religio-political communities (*millets*). This kind of political phenomena is perhaps also the pattern in the pluralistic ethnically heterogeneous nation-states of Africa and Asia. Communal, ethnic, tribal and such loyalties are not conducive to the development of a state-oriented citizenry, of consensus, and of a sense of national loyalty. The political and sociological dynamics of such states have been documented in the flood of literature on Africa. Using Hottinger's phrase, for Lebanon, then, the structure of political dynamics is the relationship of "state-*za'im*-client community," and *not* "state-citizen," or "state-party-citizen."

In Lebanon, except for one legal and one illegal one, there are no genuine functioning political parties, i.e., ones that have a hierarchy, a political bureau, a secretariat, local chapters, a platform or program and the aim of influencing the society by political means. Nor are there parties in the sense of organizations with programs that mobilize total strata of the populace throughout the nation.[32] The self-styled political parties of Lebanon are no more than factions or coalitions of different *zu'ama* alliances,[33] alliances that quickly emerge and as quickly dissolve themselves after elections, on issues and policies. Hence, in essence the higher politics of Lebanon is to a large extent the interplay of *zu'ama*, their alliances clustered around a dominant

[32] See L. Zuwiyya-Yamak, "Party Politics in the Lebanese Political System," in L. Binder, ed., *op. cit.*, and Hottinger, *op. cit.*, for a more detailed analysis of parties.

[33] P. Rondot, "The Political Institutions of Lebanese Democracy," in L. Binder, ed., *op. cit.*; see also Hess and Bodman, *op. cit.*

za'im, and coalitions, particularly as they ebb and eddy around the president, the office with the strongest power in the nation.

The "state-*za'im*-client group" relationship is thus a major structural feature in Lebanon. But *za'im*-ship is effective only in the context of the religious (i.e., confessional or sectarian) and familial structures. Confessionalism (religio-political group autonomy), as we have seen, had its origin in the Ottoman Empire *millet* system. But with the intervention of the European Powers in the nineteenth century, and the French mandate in the twentieth, the confessional basis was given legal status and became the organizing principle of Lebanese political, administrative and judicial life. Confessionalism thus was the organizing principle to ensure that the needs and interests of rival "religio-political communities" would be considered in the allocations of influence, of rewards and services of the new state. Furthermore, confessional or sectarian divisions generally but inexactly correspond to regional and/or city-quarter boundaries. And the *za'im* of a certain territorially based confessional group (clientele) would be of the *same* sect and a native of that territory. In sect-sensitive Lebanon, this obviously is a major reason for the "trust" given the *za'im* in his role as spokesman-intermediary in the important "state-*za'im*-client group" relationship. An alliance between the *za'im* and the religious structure in Lebanon is a superbly effective coalition reinforcing the traditional power structure and pattern of influence. It is through the informal organization that the religious establishments actively cooperate with the *zu'ama* to influence policy on the national and on the local level. This "informal organization" is primarily the extended family networks.

Za'im-ship is not strictly an individual quality; it is an extended family affair that is inheritable! A clear illustration of this are the happenings after the untimely death of a *za'im*, Emile Bustani, in an accident: "The family council, consisting of both Bustanis and Khazins, since Myrna Bustani had married a Khazin, decided that she [the *za'im*'s daughter] should stand for deputy, and it possessed enough weight in the region that no opponent appeared and the young lady was elected without opposition."[34]

[34] Hottinger, *op. cit.*, 1966, p. 97.

She, in fact, was the first woman to be elected a deputy in the history of the country. Further evidence of inheritance necessitates no more than a comparison of the parliamentary membership of the thirties and earlier with that of today. The sons, nephews, etc., of the earlier *zu'ama* are today's *zu'ama*: for example, Karami (the present prime minister), Salaam, Solh, Himadeh, As'ad, Al-Khalil, Zain, Khuri, Edde, Frangieh, Khazin, Bulos, Arslan, Jumblatt, Skaff, Taqla, Abu-Lama', Usayran, etc.

These are primary *zu'ama* families. In large parliaments many secondary *zu'ama* families ally themselves with the primary ones on the election lists[35] and ride to success on their coattails, as it were. They form parliamentary blocs. Most parliamentary blocs are formed on this principle, such as and around a Maronite *za'im* who is a potential president, since Lebanon's president is required by custom to be a Maronite. A great deal of leadership thus depends on remnant, feudal, kinship, and confessional ties, and relations of self-interest and nepotism. It was the competition with and between the feudal lords during the 1920's that necessitated the organization of Lebanese "parties" as loose associations or blocs surrounding a particular personality, *za'im* or clan, rather than as programmatic and disciplined organizations. The absence of long-range platforms or programs and stable memberships contributes to the opportunism and fluidity so characteristic of Lebanese politics.[36]

Again, the only real party is the Kata'ib Party, despite the titles of the others. The "Progressive Socialist Party" is nothing more than a bloc: secondary Druze *zu'ama* allied to a primary *za'im* Kamal Jumblatt. The "Najjada Party" is the Moslem (Sunni) answer to the Christian (Maronite) Kata'ib. It is a bloc of urban Moslem *zu'ama* who are riding the crest of the pan-Arab (and strongly Moslem) sentiments among the poorer sections of Beirut. However, even the Kata'ib, most genuinely a party, depends on a social base and loyalty structure similar to that of the *zu'ama*: confessional and kinship but only grossly regional. The Kata'ib Party has chapters in numerous Christian (particu-

[35] See N. Ziadeh, "The Lebanese Elections, 1960," *Middle East Journal,* 14 (Autumn, 1960), pp. 367–81.

[36] J. Landall, "Elections in Lebanon," *Western Political Quarterly,* 14 (1961), pp. 120–47.

larly Maronite) villages, towns and city quarters all over Lebanon.

Thus, political leadership for the most part in Lebanon remains largely an affair of aristocratic and feudal extended-families, is inheritable, and along with economic patronage and influence structures; it operates effectively within the context of the confessional group or *millet* in alliance with the formal religious organization.

So far, we have concentrated on the "state-*za'im*" and "*za'im*-*za'im*" relationships of the "state-*za'im*-client group" structure. Let us look in some detail at the "*za'im*-client group" relationship. The *za'im* does not come in contact directly with every individual; on the contrary, the *za'im* uses the established informal familial systems of communication and loyalty. The direct contact is with heads of extended families, heads of influential families and clans. Thus the most important structure mediating (1) between the *za'im* and the individual "client" and (2) between the *za'im* and the client group as a collectivity is the extended family and clan.[37]

The informal mechanisms of socialization, pressure and control of the extended family build up and direct the loyalties of family members (individual clients) to a particular *za'im* . Thus, the real effective structure is "*za'im*-extended family-individual" and *not* "*za'im*-individual," reflecting exactly the larger state organization. Hence, the mediating structure, the extended kinship networks, are the fundamental bases of political power. In the mountain regions of Lebanon these kinship structures have grown into large clan structures and continue until this day to operate in their political capacities. In fact, these clans can grow so strong as to challenge the authority of the state in their regions. Different extended families and clans line themselves up as opposing factions. From time to time conflict and feuding erupts. The government in Lebanon is unable for long time spans

[37] ". . . if the sect is the domain of the religious institution, the clan is the domain of the notable [*za'im*]. We can even say that the clan, which is the most elementary political organization outside the family, exists not so much for its own sake as for the sake of the notable. Politically, it exists not in its own right, but in order to be manipulated by the *za'im*. . . ." Zuwiyya-Yamak, *op. cit.*, 1966, p. 153.

to quell the local clan feuds. The last such outbreak required the
Lebanese government to send its army with an armored corps
into the village of Zghorta in northern Lebanon[38] in order to
contain the fight.

Again, generally, the extended kin network is the informal
structure within which political loyalty is built up. Furthermore,
the so-called "informal organization" of the religious institution
that helps perpetuate traditional patterns of influence (*za'im*-
ship) are these same extended family networks and such other
structures as church (generic sense) youth clubs, men's welfare
and aid societies, and auxiliary ones for women.

Loyalty to a *za'im* is built up on the grass-roots level. Moral,
political and even commercial allegiance can be said to be owed
a *za'im* and his family on the part of the follower families. Of
course, the bonds of commitment to a *za'im* vary in strength.
The *za'im*'s control is most decisive over those in his immediate
household, kin, and servants and those economically dependent
on him and his extended kin. Thus, in most rural areas, the
"*za'im*-follower family" relationship is often a landlord-tenant
one. An informal hierarchy of feudal landlord, his agents, overseers, administrators, and "controlled" government agents (usually his own clients) and tenants exists in terms of which
allegiance and loyalty to the *za'im* is reinforced and guaranteed.
Beyond this circle political allegiance, both rural and urban, is a
function of a service performed or the promise of one on the part
of the *za'im* to a member of a distant or unrelated family—a
service-reciprocity system. Thus a *za'im* is a landlord, an employer, a provider, and a protector to client families or members
of such families within the context of the same sect. In short, the
relationship is a system of traditional patronage to families. By
election into important political positions (i.e., parliamentary
deputy) a *za'im* can enhance his wealth and strengthen the
bonds of loyalty of his client-families by protecting their interests
(including the ideological), and providing for their greater material well-being.

[38] See the nearly two month running account of the feud in Beirut daily
newspapers such as *An-Nahar* and *Al-Hayat*, August–September, 1966.

Let us now look more closely at the particular conditions of urban *za'im*-ship. The primary circle of followers or political clients beyond the *za'im*'s extended family are the families of those employed in his businesses and enterprises owned or controlled by him, his extended family, and the families of other allied notables supporting him and electioneering for him; and there are, of course, the families of those who received a service or who hope to receive such services. "In the cities it is common practice for the notable families, particularly those who actively participate in politics, to have 'men' (*zilm* or *'abada'iyyat*) who constitute the elementary political organization for political activity. These notables and their 'men' operate within well-marked quarters of the city in the same manner as a rural notable exercises his authority within the region dominated by the clan."[39]

Furthermore, according to Hottinger, the urban *za'im*, who is less of an economic lord than in the rural areas, has to be, by necessity, more of a politician. The economic interrelationships with client families are less stable, less permanent, and more delicate. Urbanites in developing countries in general are politically aware, thus urban *zu'ama* need popular slogans in order to help cement their following among those who are not directly economically dependent upon them. On the other hand, in the smaller cities such as Tripoli, a *za'im* such as Rashid Karami preserves and reinforces his position by means of traditional patronage. "The planned 'Foire de Trablous' is a modern form of such patronage come to the city thanks to the fact that her *za'im* is Lebanon's Prime Minister."[40] In building, operating and maintaining this fair, including all the tourist money expected, Karami created a government-sponsored economic enterprise which gives employment to many of *his* client-families and supporters in Tripoli. Extended families in the urban centers may have much the same functions in Lebanon as clans and extended families in rural regions; they are mediating structures for the mobilization of political support in return for traditional patronage and some more modern benefits. Similarly, Morton

[39] Zuwiyya-Yamak, *op. cit.*, p. 153.
[40] Hottinger, *op. cit.*, 1966, p. 97.

Fried reports important political functions for clans in modern
urban Taiwan.[41]

Thus, in urban Lebanon, also, the "state-*za'im*-client families"
is an important relationship. The *za'im* and his family serves as
an informal channel of communication from the government to
the client families and hence the individual. As in rural areas,
the urban *za'im,* along with influential family elders, may become
mediators between individuals and/or subfactions, usually families, of his own following, who are conflicting. They keep disputes out of government courts. The family is a mechanism also
of social control that keeps the individual within the political
fold, so to speak.

Finally, extended client families in the urban context, along
with the *za'im's* "men" (henchmen, bodyguards, etc.), are the
most elementary organization for electioneering, both legitimate
and illegal. Since the reciprocal relations between *za'im* and
client families in the urban context is relatively tenuous, urban
za'im turnovers in the Lebanese Parliament are more frequent
than rural feudal ones.

The above description of the interrelationships between state,
za'im, client families, and individual has been deliberately simplified for the sake of clarity. The interrelationships are much
more lively, dynamic, and complex in reality. Factions and subfactions with competing *zu'ama* exist in Lebanon, a feature con-
sonant with the segmented structure of the nation-state but more
importantly with the segmented structure of the kinship organization.[42] Confessional, territorial, and ethnic "communities" are
invariably factioned into two segments competing with each
other, especially for power. Factions are of long standing and
have deep historical roots in the "communal," village and territorial structure of Lebanon and the Asiatic Arab Middle East.[43]
In Lebanon, lineages, villages, city quarters, and sometimes ex-

[41] M. Fried, "Some Political Aspects of Clanship in a Modern Chinese
City," in Swartz, Turner and Tuden, *op. cit.,* pp. 285–300.
[42] Ayoub, *op. cit.,* p. 114.
[43] Philip Hitti, *History of the Arabs,* London: Macmillan, 1960; K. Salibi,
The Modern History of Lebanon, London: Weidenfeld and Nicolson, 1965;
W. R. Polk, *The Opening of South Lebanon,* Cambridge, Mass.: Harvard
University Press, 1963.

tended families are factioned, and divide to one side or the other. Their factional loyalties are carried with them wherever they go, to the city in Beirut or to the towns to which they emigrate. In the political tug of war, alliances of the kin segments and/or families may shift. This shifting will, in many a local rivalry, mean success or defeat for a *za'im* in deputy elections. Political office, as pointed out above, is sought for its strategic locus in building a *za'im's* fortune, influence, and clientele, and in channeling government benefits.

Dual factioning[44] of ethnic, confessional and territorial groups is functional for guaranteeing the survival of the whole group. The whole group or sect is never on the wrong side of an issue, or a conflict. Furthermore, structurally, "communities," lineages and perhaps urban extended families grow large enough in size so that segmentation or fission is necessary for social organization, social control, and efficient functioning. Thus Lebanese higher politics become a bewildering interplay of *zu'ama* and alliances of *zu'ama*, opposition of *zu'ama* of confessional groups, opposition and/or alliance of *zu'ama* of factions of confessional groups, and personal rivalries, as they swirl around political, economic, and ideological issues and personalities. On the local level the interplay is just as lively since it takes the form of clan or lineage politics, or extended families in the urban context, of one confessional group as they swirl around the rival *zu'ama*, who espouse, as well, the differing issues. For example, the 1958 "civil war" in Lebanon had at least one faction of each confessional group on the side of the government and another on the side of the rebel *zu'ama*.[45] On the local urban level the same cleavage appeared so that quarters or parts of quarters barricaded the streets and "fought" on their side; and in the provinces, whole

[44] Dual segmentation is a most visible and widespread characteristic of Middle East social structure. See above-mentioned village studies and others on Syria, Jordan, etc. Dual factioning of kin and political organization has been suggested by L. E. Sweet as due partly to the system of land ownership traditional in the Middle East, use of other resources such as forests for wood, and the ecological structure and limitations of the land. (Personal communication.)

[45] See accounts of the 1958 civil strife in Lebanon. For example, Fahim I. Qubain, *Crisis in Lebanon,* Washington: Middle East Institute, 1961. C. Chamoun, *Crise au Moyen Orient,* Paris: Gallimard, 1963.

villages or parts thereof sided with the government or the rebels. Skirmishes between the opposing sides were frequent. Within the context of such a conflict, many a feuding clan tried to settle long-standing "scores" or carry out long-planned revenge—a purely local affair that became colored by national rivalries.

When the American Marines landed in Lebanon, on the asking of the Lebanese President, in 1958, they did not find an "enemy." The soldiers did not know whom to fight and whom to protect. The conflict, a local Lebanese one between pro-government and anti-government *zu'ama,* took on international significance and involvement largely because of the typical international links of the different confessional groupings. The presence of the Marines seemed to have dampened the conflict while the American ambassador, along with the Lebanese Army Commander (the Army was not involved for fear of internal fission), acted independently and at times in concert as a third party of mediators (*wastahs*) in speeding the solution. There was, in fact, no "Communist threat" or threat of a takeover by Syria, as American newspapers would have had their readers believe.

In conclusion, the interrelationships of "state-*za'im*-client families-individual" has been shown to be multiply reciprocal in nature, functionally interdependent, and contributing to the maintenance of a fairly "traditional" family organization. Unless a radical change in one of the interdependent structures takes place, the functional necessity of each for the others is guaranteed. But the continuance of this contemporary political structure is probably contingent upon several factors, most important of which are: deep-rooted social traditions, and values, wherein an individual in a politically unstable and resource-poor environment finds security and meaning only within the narrow group of kin and sect. This kind of solidarity is much more acceptable *and understandable* to its membership than an association of wider solidarity based upon occupational class, or ideological lines, that might cut across the whole society horizontally. Furthermore, the *de facto* preponderance among the populace of low skill and income compared to industrial nations reinforces the *za'im* pattern even in the cities, since here the *za'im's* rudimentary political organization like the old political "boss" machine in New York City[46] provides for these people some means of livelihood. As Hottinger argues, these low-skill people must trade political loyalty for economic support, services, and other survival advantages.

Finally, the legal structure, the constitution, and the electoral system of the republic, clearly provide for and reinforce this political structure. People now living in Beirut or even born in Beirut, still vote in their villages of family origin. Only its abolition or radical change in the formal legal structure could set up new conditions for the emergence of new political institutions and leadership.

However, Zuwiyya-Yamak and Hottinger both point out that since 1958 the government of Lebanon, under the leadership of the two presidents (Shihab and Helou), has been engaged in modernization of state machinery. More agencies, a greater number of officials, and some administrative reform and decentralization have increased the number of loci of direct contact between the state bureaucracy and the individual. The traditional intermediary function of the *za'im* and in turn the dependent extended families is slowly being by-passed. In the large city of Beirut the residential overlapping of sects and of other ethnic groups (Egyptian, Palestinian, etc.), in some quarters had also done away with the urban *za'im* "spokesman." In short, the citizen-individual, and not the extended family, is gradually being involved directly by the state machinery. This slow process has hardly made itself felt outside limited metropolitan areas. But until such time when extended familial, clan, and sectarian loyalties disappear, displaced by loyalty to the nation-state, Lebanon will remain a "traditional" society organized primarily in vertical rather than horizontal terms, despite the appearance currently of some of these "modern" attributes.

The second part of the discussion of the interdependence of kinship and political structures refers to the legal institutions. Ever since the legalization of the old Ottoman *millet* system under the French mandate, the Lebanese constitution and legal

[46] Robert K. Merton, *Social Theory and Social Structure*, Glencoe, Ill.: The Free Press, 1949, pp. 71–81.

code have left family law (known as "Personal Status" law) to
the traditional ecclesiastical law courts, while the state established a criminal and civil code modeled after the French. Marriage, divorce, inheritance, adoption, etc., are all the domain of
the church courts. The rules governing family behavior in such
courts follow, of course, traditional religious prescriptions. For
example, Moslem Shari'a (church) Law is the Law of the Quran
and the Sunna.[47] These are the chief sources of Islamic doctrine. Theoretically the Holy Law (Shari'a) deals with constitutional, civil and criminal matters; in strictest Moslem theology,
it is the only valid code. In reality, however, the Shari'a law has
competed with customary and state-made law, and today, except
in a few areas, it is largely replaced by secular codes modeled
after the European[48] codes. Islamic law is different from Western
codes insofar as the former is divine and the latter secular, "man-
made." Islamic law is broad; it deals with all areas of human
conduct, including the performance of religious duties and the
giving of alms as well as with domestic, civil, economic, and political institutions. To illustrate the relevance of this traditional
religious law for the extended family, let us look at the law of
inheritance. The Shi'a Moslem law prescribes that inheritance is
distributed according to the statuses of heirs; in the primary status are the parents and the children of the deceased; in the
secondary status are brothers, sisters and grandparents of the deceased, for they are "once removed"; in the tertiary status are
paternal uncles and aunts and maternal uncles and aunts, for
they are "twice removed." The claim on the inheritance takes
precedence in terms of these statuses. For example, if no one of
the primary status lives, then the whole inheritance goes to those
in the secondary status. Among the Sunni Moslems, the Shari'a
law of inheritance is much more complex, and again for a differently defined set of heirs who include paternal and maternal
aunts and uncles and grandparents and grandchildren. The Sunni

[47] See treatise on "Personal Status" (Family) Law among the five major
"schools" of Moslem Shari'a. For example, Mohammad Jawad Maghniyah,
Al-Ahwab Ash-Shakhsiya, Beirut: Dar Al-'Ilm Lilmalayin, 1964.
[48] See J. N. D. Anderson, *Islamic Law in the Modern World,* New York:
New York University Press, 1959. See also, M. Khadduri, "From Religious to
National Law," in R. N. Anshen, ed., *Mid East: World Center,* pp. 220–34.

laws of inheritance involve varying fractions of the estate (with lower and upper limits) and dependent on (1) the degree (status) of the relationship of the survivors to the dead person and to each other; and (2) the sex of the surviving relatives. For example, a daughter inherits half as much as a son's inheritance. A concrete example taken from Maghniyah illustrates this complexity. A man who died was survived by a wife, a mother and a paternal grandfather; the estate is by law distributed in the following way:[49]

Wife	*Mother*	*Paternal Grandfather*
3/12	4/12	5/12

According to Islamic law there is no need to write a will to ensure the inheritance of one's estate by one's heirs. In fact, if a Moslem wishes to will his estate to other than his prescribed legal heirs, he can do so to the maximum of one-third of his estate only.[50] If more than the third is to be willed, then the permission of the legal heirs is required.

Another illustration of the direct influence of Islamic religious law on the family deals with the question of economic support. The different "schools" of Moslem law prescribe support for different relatives ranging from strictly parental and child support to the support of *all* relatives who are potential heirs, but only if they are needy. Islamic religious law of "Personal Status," moreover, covers also rules of marriage, specifying who can marry whom, the terms and requirements of the marriage contract, the conditions and process of divorce, etc.[51] Obviously, such traditional religious law is eufunctional for nuclear and extended family solidarity, for it guarantees a "fair," religiously sanctioned distribution of inheritance among kinship-defined heirs and avoids the need to write a will that could be biased or show favoritism, and hence conducive to jealousy, conflict, and fission. Despite this, conflict between relatives including siblings over inheritance has, in fact, been traditionally a major factor in the fission of kinship units in the Middle East. The religious family

[49] Maghniyah, *op. cit.*, p. 291.
[50] *Ibid.*, p. 186.
[51] See Zuhdi Yakun, *Az-Zawaj*, Beirut & Saida, Lebanon: Al-Maktaba Al-'Asriyah, second ed., n.d. (*Marriage*).

law prescribes for the different heirs the ratio of the inheritance only. If the estate is composed of land, businesses, orchards, etc., the law does not prescribe what of one is equivalent to how much of the other kinds of property in the estate. The source of conflict is essentially over what part of the estate constitutes the proper ratio.

As for the Moslem sects, the Lebanese government, constitution, and legal code guarantee for the Christian sects *their* church courts and the currency of their traditional religious law in the area of family relations. Furthermore, as in the U.S. and most nation-states, the Lebanese tax system is graduated both in terms of income level and in terms of the number of dependents an earner has. This of course is a fair "subsidy" for the economics of the extended family.

Major reforms in Islamic law were begun during the 1800's. In Egypt, Muhammad Ali encouraged Europeans and European enterprises to settle. Such was also the case for the Ottoman Sultan. As the capitulation agreements with foreign trading colonies increased, legislation for the protection of foreigners resulted in mixed courts (local and consular) around 1875, patterned after the French. And by the early twentieth century a separation in most Middle Eastern Islamic countries between civil courts and Shari'a courts had taken place. In 1958, the Egyptian government decreed all Shari'a courts under the jurisdiction of the Egyptian civil court system.

Unlike Egypt, Lebanon has not put the religious law courts under the civil court system. Attempts to do so reached a climax in 1951, when the syndicate of lawyers went on strike in order to force such a government change of policy. The lawyers were not successful and the pressure from the clerics and the confessional "communities" was strong enough to defeat the lawyers' strategy. Until today such "family" affairs remain as the domain of the religious law courts presided over by clerics.

Unquestionably a traditional legal system of this sort not only is conducive but in fact reinforces the continuity of a traditional kinship organization and in particular the extended family structure. Reforms concerned with "Personal Status" law have been instituted in Egypt, Syria, and Tunisia, primarily, but not in Lebanon.

Finally, the welfare functions were and are still the domain of the large or extended kin group. Before the demise of such an important part of the whole societal structure can take place, alternative structures must emerge to provide for these functions. In the West, strong central state authority has in part played that role—one which perhaps aided the emergence and maintenance of nuclear families.[52] In the Middle East, central state or imperial authority has historically been weak. The twentieth century, however, witnessed the rise of nation-states and governments that for the first time have the technological and organizational means for the development of strong central authority. The effects of such a relatively strong central authority in the framework of the modern nation-state have already been felt; for example, in family life in the United Arab Republic. New legal statutes regulating age at marriage, divorce, etc.[53] have slowly been introduced and implemented. Yet one must not be overly impressed by the power and means of the states, for government authority is not easily instituted if the families are part of a "lineage capable of providing aid and protection and able to muster much support for active resistance to this authority."[54] This is the case in much of the rest of the Middle East—the desert areas and the more hilly regions of Lebanon, Syria, Iraq, Yemen, and Saudi Arabia. Furthermore, Middle Eastern Muslim states cannot easily contradict or set aside Muslim Shari'a family law. Radical changes in family law cannot be expected until much more extensive secularization takes place. As we have seen above, the Muslim Shari'a law prescribes that one support his near and extended kin if the kin is in need. The only security in old age, in retirement, in sickness, and in social and natural catastrophe remains predominantly the kin group. And the closer the degree of relationship, the more assured is this security.

Only a few years ago Lebanon established a social security plan on a national scale. The government, however, had instituted earlier an occupational indemnity system by which the individual received from his employer a month's worth of income

---

[52] J. Pitts, "The Structural-Functional Approach," in H. Christensen, ed., *Handbook of Marriage and Family*, Chicago: Rand McNally, 1964, pp. 109 ff.

[53] Yakun, *op. cit.*, pp. 220–21.

[54] J. Pitts, *op. cit.*

for every year of service. There were no studies showing the effectiveness and consequences of the indemnity system, but one can point to the fact that it benefited mostly the salaried "middle class." The transient and seasonal semi-skilled and unskilled wage-earners in the cities suffered most in that they had little chance for steady, permanent, and secure work and hence could not partake of the indemnity system. Petty entrepreneurs still possessed their little enterprises to sell or to pass on to grateful children or other kin.

The establishment of the state social security program in Lebanon reportedly received much opposition from almost all classes and sects in the country. Employees and workers still resent the state collecting their "indemnities" as part of the state social security plan, for they have no guarantee of reimbursement from an inefficient state bureaucracy or confidence that the state itself will continue to exist in the future when they retire. Employees and workers have much more confidence in their employer, usually known face to face and so often a kinsmen, than in an impersonal agency or an unstable state. The history of Middle Eastern states and life experiences of the populace certainly justifies their attitudes both in Lebanon and elsewhere in the Middle East. On the other hand, employers also mistrust the state and resent its interference in relationships with their employees. The effects of the new state-operated social security system on the national economy and on family economics cannot be gauged yet, for it has not yet been instituted in full force and it is still very recent.

The "indemnity" system, on the other hand, for certain classes of people was quite important. For the salaried middle and lower middle class the lump-sum indemnity at the end of a lifetime career or of long years of work was the only real capital accumulation that could build a house, launch a son or relative into business, or be loaned for an interest or share in an enterprise. This kind of function, which includes the pooling of other such capital resources, is conducive for extended family economic cooperation among the humble classes in the cities. But there still are no statistical data on this point. However, repeated cases of siblings, cousins, father-son(s), uncle-nephew(s) combinations for pooling capital resources for economic endeavors can be pointed out in the descriptive ethnology and other literature of the area.

The retired, the old person, or the unproductive single person still lives with the nearest of kin, usually a son or a nephew. Churchill, in his sample survey of Beirut, cites the following figures: about 15% of the households had a father or mother living in, and 15% other "miscellaneous family members," 55% of whom were unmarried; of those in the household who were not children, grandchildren, and spouses, 67% were female.[55] It is to be expected that many of these are relatives who for one reason or another are economically unproductive and hence are partaking of the "welfare functions" of the kinship group. Such people, if they had no income, would be "out in the streets" had it not been for their kin. Furthermore, because of the housing situation, small size of many apartments, and the changing husband-wife relationships, many a retired couple live in their own apartment near their children's apartments, but are fully supported by their children. Fifteen percent as reported by Churchill may seem a low figure for the number of parents living in the children's household. The smallness of such a percentage can be partially explained in terms of two factors: (1) the high mortality rates in Lebanon especially among the lower classes; it is also much higher for men than women; and (2) parents generally live with their eldest male child[56] if ever they are likely to reside with children; hence the sample size of the eldest male children may be partly responsible for the smallness of the figures.

Of course, in the rural villages of Lebanon, common residence with close kin is frequent enough to suffice it to say here that the welfare aspect of the family is inseparable from the familial structure of village life.

The welfare function should not be construed to apply only to parents. The 15% "miscellaneous family members" were not parents and can be anyone from a sibling to aunts and uncles, and in some cases more distant kin. Usually unmarried kin

[55] Churchill, *op. cit.*, pp. 5–9, and relevant tables referred to by Churchill.
[56] *Ibid.*, p. 7.

members, such as sisters and aunts who have little chance for personal economic autonomy, live with kin, helping in the housework. These are important members of the household, contributing, among other things, a "baby-sitting" function and also to child rearing. With regard to children, incidentally, they tend to perform almost purely expressive functions rather than disciplinarian functions.

If female, this unmarried relative helps in the daily chores, sewing, etc., and is in many respects a second mother to the children. Such unmarried individuals tend to be good storytellers to children, gossipers, and companions to the wife. If male, the unmarried relative helps by his financial or work contributions to the family support. Much of the rest of his money tends to be spent on the family children in the form of allowances, gifts, toys, etc. He is like a second father, sometimes more liked because he is all "good" and rarely, if ever, negatively sanctions. Such spinsters or bachelors live generally with the nuclear families that are closest consanguinally and who themselves are greatest in need of such help, financial or otherwise.

In conclusion, the family as a "welfare agency" continues to be important in Lebanon, especially in the face of the fact that an effective social security system administered by a trustworthy state authority is absent, or more accurately, only recently has been established and is as yet untested. Furthermore, values and proverbs asserting the "goodness" and the "necessity" of taking care of the old and unable (the welfare functions), are constantly articulated while shame, gossip, and even familial ostracism are heaped upon those who do not contribute. In a politically and economically unstable society "the children and relatives are the only security."[57]

Other than the family welfare, social welfare in the form of voluntary and "church" related institutions are, as mentioned above, primarily sectarian in nature, and help is dispensed to its needy on a very informal basis. The information, contact, and recommendation is channeled through the informal extended-family channels and at other times through the *wastah* of a *za'im* or his extended family. The content and nature of these

[57] An Arab saying.

welfare services range from occasional cash grants to medical and educational services, including orphanages.[58]

THE KINSHIP AND RELIGIOUS STRUCTURES

Unlike the United States and other Western industrial nations where a separation of church and state has taken place, Lebanon, because of its ecology and its history, incorporated the religious aspect as a legitimate and *legal* structure of the political organization of the nation-state. The articulation of religious and political organization in the parliamentary democratic system formed under the French mandate has been called confessionalism or sectarianism, a system through which a fairly high degree of religious-ethnic "communal" autonomy was guaranteed. The most explicit area of autonomy, as has been pointed out above in tho section on politics, is "Personal Status" laws and we have seen how these laws have direct relevance to reinforcing the continuity of the traditional kinship organization. Reciprocally, by helping to sustain the kinship organization, they help to perpetuate the very autonomy of the religious communities themselves. This autonomy, in addition, is sustained politically by the factional organization of the communities, by the confessionally based but secular *za'im*-ship system, and the confessional basis of the civil service or public administration. In Lebanon appointments into the state bureaucracy, especially at the highest levels, are primarily on the basis of confessional membership and only secondarily on the basis of qualifications. A "confessional balance" in the number of appointees is always maintained.[59] This is a mechanism that indirectly contributes to the traditional kinship organization. Thus a functional, reciprocal, mutually reinforcing dependence of the kinship and confessional organization exists in Lebanon.

Religions are organized formally as "churches" ("church" is used here in the generic sense and includes those of the Islamic sects). "Church" organization in Lebanon has a long history and

[58] See Al-Jumhuriyya Al-Lubnaniyyah, *op. cit.*
[59] See Crow, *op. cit.*, and Hess and Bodman, *op. cit.*

an intimate influence on the social and political life of the society.[60] In contemporary Lebanon each sect has a "church" and clergy that speak in the name of that confessional group. Hence, until this day, because of the confessional organization, religious leaders play a very important role in the life of Lebanon.[61] Many points of contact between the "church" and the family are formalized in Lebanon in the well-known, ancient life cycle ceremonies of birth, baptism or confirmation, education (including religious education), courtship, marriage, divorce, death, and inheritance. These functions, in the context of the confessional organization, reach virtually everyone in the population and follow them and their family through generations. There is still no acceptance of civil marriage, only church marriage. In Lebanon, in fact, there is no such thing as a person without a religion. Religion is not a "preference" but is a most necessary social identity, regardless of the individual's "beliefs."

There is no accurate data on inter-religion or inter-sect marriage, but religious endogamy is at least a universal dogma.[62] Some confessional groups may so totally excommunicate a member, especially a woman, who marries out of the group that contact with the family is cut off. On the other hand inter-marriage between sects of a major religion such as Christianity does take place. Again statistical data is unavailable. In that case the marriage takes place in the sectarian church of the husband.

The influence of "church" teachings on family life can be illustrated with regard to the use of contraception. The Catholic churches in Lebanon (Maronite, Greek Catholic, and others), which constitute the majority of the Christian churches, have followed Rome in their antithetical stand against the use of mechanical and chemical instruments of contraception. The Moslem *"ulema,"* the religious scholars who are the interpreters of the Shari'a law to the Moslem population, have also considered this problem and have recently concluded that the use of contraception in Islam is permitted.[63] Yet tradition and other socio-

[60] Harik, *op. cit.*
[61] See the role of religious leaders in the 1958 crisis in Lebanon: Qubain, *op. cit.,* and Chamoun, *op. cit.*
[62] Ayoub, *op. cit.,* p. 121.
[63] Yakun, *op. cit.,* pp. 217–19.

economic and ecologic factors seem to be more significant on this issue, for fertility is as high among Moslems as among Christians; city Christians alone, unlike city Moslems, do have significantly lower fertility rates.[64] Religious values, including those directly concerned with the family in general among the Moslems and Catholic as well as Orthodox Christians, tend to uphold and reinforce the sentiments towards the traditional kinship system.

Perhaps the most significant point of contact between church and family is in education. Education in Lebanon has traditionally been, though less so today, primarily an endeavor of the religious communities and a private effort. An educational system in Lebanon, as such, began almost two centuries ago as part of the activity of the Maronite church. Since that time other sects have opened their own schools for their own people and this plurality of educational systems has become more complicated as a result of the development of Catholic and Protestant missionary education. Catholic missionary schools, which generally catered to Christian Catholic communities, such as the Maronites, Greek and other Catholics, and even Greek Orthodox, if anything reasserted the legitimacy and values of the kinship organization. Even in the West, Catholic parochial education stresses traditional familistic values;[65] one need only add that such Catholic familistic values are much more appropriate for the Near East than the West. Protestant missionary education and activity was barely successful in converting people to Protestantism (the number of Protestants in Lebanon is still very small). In any case, Protestant values that can be construed as antithetical to familism hardly seem to have had any impact on large numbers of people, in spite of the success of some of the Protestant mission schools. In the face of strong familistic values and structures current in the society over the last hundred and fifty years, Protestant education has not accomplished more than introducing certain "subversive" (to familism) values such as "individualism," "romantic love," etc. Furthermore, Lebanese of all religious

[64] David Yawkey, *Fertility Differences in a Modernizing Country*, Princeton: Princeton University Press, 1961.
[65] W. Seward Salisbury, *Religion in American Culture*, Homewood, Ill.: The Dorsey Press, 1964, pp. 398–406.

backgrounds—Christian, Moslem, and Druze—studied in the Protestant schools. Those families who became Protestant were predominantly Greek Orthodox. Conversion seems to be more a function of economic factors than of ideological or belief change: the Greek Orthodox converts found better-paying jobs with the mission, and could get free education for their children, so providing for them the means to be socially mobile upwards in a slowly economically expanding society.

Moslems have also developed their parochial schools—the extensive Makāsed schools—where Moslem values, including those of familism, are reinforced. Except for some Maronite, Druze, and Greek Catholic schools, most Lebanese sectarian schools have been and presently are situated in the larger towns and cities of Lebanon. Over 84% of the primary students in Beirut are in private, non-governmental schools,[66] which include the religious ones. Ironically, the most traditional provinces of Lebanon have the most secular educational system: the government schools. Even in these village schools one must not belittle the importance of the religious influence, for the teachers are usually correligionists of the students. But the secular, private, and government schools are not known at all to follow a policy or an ideology antithetical to familism or familistic values.

Education in religious schools where religious education and traditional including familistic values are propounded, as well as education in secular schools, does lead some to higher education. Here, however, higher education, even in religiously affiliated centers, seems to be conducive to secularization. The most "modern" Lebanese are regarded as the most highly educated Lebanese, but educated in the fields and disciplines of industrial society, not in religious clerical training. Higher education, we shall see in the section on stratification, is a most significant factor in the creation of a new and important class in the society.

Other formal points of contact between the "churches" and the family system also contribute to solidarity of extended family organization. Birth, baptism or confirmation, religious holidays, etc., are all significant occasions for which the extended family

[66] Al-Jumhuriyyah Al-Lubnaniyyah, Wizarat At-Tasmin Al-'Am, Muslahat An-Nashatat Al-Iqlimiyah, *At-Ta'lim fi Lubnan*, Beirut, 1965, p. 13.

and other kin gather. These gatherings reinforce the commitments, sentiments, and bonds of members to each other. Considering that nuclear and extended families are large, such occasions, along with the religious holidays, are relatively frequent in a given year for all those in the whole unit.

"Church" organizations in Lebanon also provide recreational facilities, especially for youth, in the form of sports clubs, social and religious clubs, etc. These facilities contribute to stronger feelings of identification with the "church" (religion or sect), to the perpetuation of the autonomy of the religious communities, and in so doing, sustain the kinship organization. Recreational facilities other than the "church" facilities and those of the "church"-run schools, were provided chiefly within the extended family and neighborhood, and only recently have commercial establishments (i.e., cinema, etc.) opened to the "whole" society.

Thus, functional interdependence between confessionalism and extended familism in the form presented above and in the section on political institutions is of prime importance in and is greatly responsible for the perpetuation of both structures in Lebanon.

THE KINSHIP AND STRATIFICATION STRUCTURES

Until this section the analysis of the organization of Lebanese society has been cast primarily in ethnic terms; more correctly, in religious or confessional terms and in familial, lineage, or clan terms. The social basis of the political order as well as much of the economic structure has been shown to be organized in these same terms. Thus the lines of cleavage are vertical ones creating several co-existing, interacting socio-religious or ethnic groups. Ethnic plurality, ethnic countervailing balance, the formal and informal checks, and the international links of the ethnic groups are primary factors in guaranteeing stability (despite the 1958 troubles) and perhaps the democracy of the republic of Lebanon.

This, however, is an incomplete picture of Lebanese society. While there are social groups organized in terms of sectarian lines, there are also lines that cut across these cleavages. For example, there are people of all sects in the upper, middle, and lower classes of Lebanon. Occupationally, most all sects have members in all categories: landlords, businessmen (merchants), professionals, white-collar workers, petty bourgeoisie, farmers and peasants, and proletarian laborers. Numerous modern associations or organizations of merchants, doctors, engineers, lawyers, teachers, students, as well as labor unions include members of all sects from among Christians, Moslems, and Druzes. All these organizations ostensibly bring different ethnic and familial or clan members together to plan and act in concert for their own benefit. Members of the different ethnic groups live both in the cities and in rural areas. These organizations, along with the class structure and the rural/urban gradient, are the major lines of cleavage that are *horizontal* in character. Thus the flow of social life is quite rich and complex in nature. To comprehend it adequately, one must understand the stratification structure, especially, for our purposes, as it interrelates with the kinship structure.

In the nineteenth century Mount Lebanon was a relatively autonomous part of the feudal agrarian-based Ottoman Empire. The stratification structure was pyramidal; at the base was a mass of poor peasants. The Christian villages in the north were perhaps slightly better off because of their silk cocoon cottage industry. At the top of the pyramid were feudal families supported by a feudal clergy. In the towns that are presently a part of the Republic of Lebanon, groups of artisans, some of whom were organized in guilds, were the core of the old middle strata of the society. The towns were also provincial and subprovincial administrative and garrison centers for the Ottomans. Scribes, inspectors, and even teachers lived there, and along with the artisans bought much of their living needs in the small market places (*suqs*) found in the centers of towns and managed by a "class" of small traders and peddlers. Again, these were distinct groups who led somewhat different lives from the feudal families and peasants and from each other, and were fairly endogamous. Along with these there were Europeans, mostly French, who owned and operated commercial export houses and some mills for spinning natural cocoon silk. These houses employed some local people (usually Christians).[67] The small towns, including the coastal ones, were essentially small market, administrative, and perhaps garrison towns that differed from the villages both in size and function. The coastal towns with their European commercial enterprises and consular legations provided a locus of culture contact.

Population pressure, the decline of the sericulture industry, and civil wars started the Lebanese (especially Christians) on serious emigration to the West, particularly to the Americas. Originally, with the coming of the Allied military forces during World War I and after, Western-like administrative "governmental" systems that employed myriads of urbanites and also some ruralites were implanted. For the first time, the native population began to work in bureaucratic settings on an extensive scale, drawing salaries as employees. The transportation and public works projects that had barely begun with the last Ottoman years were speeded up and increased in volume, drawing thousands of people into modern unskilled, semi-skilled, and skilled work. Peasants became laborers, especially construction laborers. The presence of extensive foreign armies sparked economic development in general. Trading families and suppliers to the armies grew wealthier and became more influential; they began to compete, in this new order, with old established feudal families. Their sons became lawyers, engineers, doctors who studied both locally and in Europe. Thus, the trading and services sectors grew quite rapidly and soon became the two most important sectors of the economy. Some emigrants returned to retire or to start businesses or industries. Small industrial, locally oriented enterprises sprang up,

[67] For an account of these times see: J. L. Burckhardt, *Travels in Syria and the Holy Land;* Polk, *op. cit.,* 1963; C. H. Churchill, *Mount Lebanon, A Ten Years' Residence, from 1842 to 1852,* London, 1853; H. H. Jessup, *Fifty Three Years in Syria,* New York: Revell Press, 1910; M. H. Kerr, *Lebanon in the Last Years of Feudalism, 1840–1868,* Beirut (a translation of part of Al-Aqiqi, Antun Dahir, *Thawra was Fitnah fi Lubnan*); A. Martineau, *Le Commerce Français du le Levant,* Paris, 1902; Ismail Haqqi Bey, *et al., Lubnan,* Ottoman Gov. Com. Survey, Beirut, 1906; Ali az-Zain 'Arif, *Tarikh Saida,* Saida, 1913 (History of Saida); Salih ibn Yahya, *Kitab Tarikh Bairut,* Beirut, 1927 (The Book of the History of Beirut); A. Latron, "En Syrie et au Liban. Villages communeutaries et structure sociale," *Annales d'Histoire, économique et sociale,* 1934; B. Lewis, "The Islamic Guilds," *The Economic History Review,* VII (Nov., 1937), pp. 20–37.

creating a small managerial class and an expanding proletarian class. Oil exploration and discovery in the Middle East led to extensive engineering works in all the phases of the oil industry and affected not only the oil-producing countries, but countries that had pipelines passing through their territories and terminals of export as well. This expanding economic activity required not only trained personnel, but construction firms and financial institutions, which were originally opened as branches of larger ones in Europe or as European-owned enterprises. However, the oil, banking, the railroads, and all the rest required masses of literate low- and middle-range bureaucrats (clerks and middle managers), as well as skilled and semi-skilled workers. Middle Easterners, including Lebanese, rushed to fill the jobs. In general, the Christians, with their higher rates of literacy, occupied these clerical positions while the Moslems in general became laborers.

In short, political and economic changes in Lebanon that were sparked by international dislocations and the local military conquest shortly after the turn of the century set up the conditions whereby totally new classes of people were created. A new middle class of bureaucrats, of middle managers, of professionals, and of officers in the new Western-styled army emerged. Also a new lower class of urban proletariat, generally unskilled and illiterate, developed. At the top, new men of power, wealthy urban merchants and educated, literate "liaisons" (lawyers) between the mandate officials and the native populace and bureaucracies, emerged to compete with and to lead, alongside the traditional feudal or quasi-feudal lords, the modernizing of Lebanon.

Perhaps because of the cultural affinity to the Christian West and because of the educational and literacy tradition (i.e., missionary schools), native Christians tended to fill the new occupational opportunities, bureaucratic and otherwise, that can be termed middle strata. A word of warning is in order here. Despite the rapid emergence of the new middle class, the number of people that can be termed as such is fairly small in absolute as well as percentage terms. The masses of the people remained poor and rural. The lower class of urban proletariat also was fairly small and predominantly Moslem ethnically. Not until after the Second World War do we see a rapid and uncontrolled increase in the urban lower classes, which created a large mass and the problems of over-urbanization. The new urban men of power, primarily the upper class, remained largely the old feudal and quasi-feudal leaders organized in religio-ethnic terms. In addition, the new families of large and wealthy merchants in the cities were primarily Christian (and these primarily Greek Orthodox). The new French-educated lawyers who spoke equally the idiom of the mandate authorities and that of the natives were mostly Christian Maronite. By being nearest to the source of power, the mandate government, these men became the new men of power who finally ruled independent Lebanon, once the French troops were evacuated in 1946.

The Second World War was the major turning point. It speeded up the previously generated economic expansion and increased its volume again with extensive troops, construction activity, oil industry, etc., but especially as the Allies encouraged local industry and local agricultural self-sufficiency in order to free greater shipping space for military purposes. The larger and more modern troop concentrations provided innumerable jobs for native civilians who were drawn not only from the urban centers but also from the small towns and more remote villages. After the war, further oil discoveries, especially in the Persian Gulf area, created new impetus as new money and wealth came to Lebanon, which benefited the economy insofar as it created new jobs in industries to supply and transport to these oil desert areas food products and some manufactured things, in addition to the tourist, summer estivage, and banking services. Further, Lebanese of all classes went to these desert areas, where salaries and income were double and sometimes triple those in Lebanon.

The Palestine War further contributed as Palestinian Arab refugees fled to Lebanon. Almost all those refugees who did not live in camps were middle- and upper-class Palestinians, most of whom became naturalized Lebanese, managed to find jobs, sometimes started businesses or industries of their own, and added themselves to a growing Lebanese middle class. In the late 1950's and early 1960's, Egyptian Christians also moved to Lebanon in great numbers, bringing with them their money (usually smuggled) and skills and increasing the middle class in Lebanon. The same, but to a much lesser degree, can be said of wealthy Syrian

and Iraqi Christians and some Moslems who came to Lebanon
also in the late 1950's. The Egyptians, the Iraqi, and the Syrians
fled from the socialist regimes of their own countries. Beirut with
its medical schools, its pleasant climate, its entertainment possibilities, became the medical center of the Asiatic Arab world for
the wealthier oil and other people. Hence medicine, dentistry,
and pharmacy became profitable professions and ones which increased rapidly in number and specialization. Again, Beirut also
became the center for almost all consulting, design, and advisory
technical activity for the more underdeveloped, unskilled, but
rich Gulf states. Hence technical professionals of all kinds quickly
increased in number, adding to the ranks of the new middle class.
In short, the internal and external economic and political changes
all contributed to a great increase in the absolute number and
the percentage of the old and new middle class in Lebanon. In
percentage terms Lebanon may very well have the largest middle
class (old and new) in the Middle East.

Statistics and data on the size and composition of the different
classes in Lebanon are not fully available, neither historically nor
currently. The IRFED Mission study of the late 1950's gives some
important estimates of income distribution which can be used to
give us some clues into the stratification system[68] in Lebanon.
The IRFED data show the following results: 9% destitute or
miserable (L.£1200 per annum), 40% poor (L.£2500 per annum), 30% near average (L.£5000 per annum), 14% better off
(L.£15,000 per annum), and 4% wealthy (above L.£15,000 per
annum). Note that most people who can be classified as middle
class live generally in the urban centers and the suburbs around
the urban centers. This is most assuredly the case when one refers
to the new middle class of bureaucrats, sales, managerial, and
professional people. A pioneering study conducted by two sociologists[69] in five rural villages in the southern Biqa' valley
distinguishes five socio-economic levels showing economic differentials and lack of homogeneity in the villages. On the local

[68] République Libanaise, Ministère du Plan, *Besoins et Possibilités de
Développement du Liban*, Tome I, 1960–61 (Mission IRFED Study).
[69] L. Armstrong and G. Hirabayashi, "Social Differentiation in Selected
Lebanese Villages," *American Sociological Review*, 21 (August, 1956),
pp. 425–34.

or village levels these differentials may be meaningful in the lives of individuals. But on a larger national level these small differentials have perhaps much less significance in contrast to the larger differentials between absentee landlords and peasants. The rural "middle strata" are probably marginal in that region. But a rural middle strata may very well exist in the more developed land-owning farmer communities of highland Lebanon, both south and north. Their structure and role is yet to be investigated.

The (30%) "moderate" income category of the IRFED classification seems misleading. Given the average family sizes in Beirut and Lebanon of six persons per family, an income of L.£5000 per annum ($1600) is much less than necessary to live on adequately, even though the standard of living is presumably low. In other words, if one is to argue that such a "near average" income group is a middle class, one would be correct only in the sense of an arbitrarily designated middle *category*. Nevertheless, considering starting salaries of office clerks (starting salary with the equivalent of a high school diploma), L.£150–250 per month; of secretaries, L.£125–200 per month; and of sales clerks, L.£150–200, one is bound to conclude that most of the 30% of the "near average" income category are lower clerks in a services-heavy economy, and some skilled workers. Furthermore, the 14% "well to do" income category is the upper middle class of professionals, managers, large businessmen, etc. Following the argument of Goode[70] and others, the upper class in any society, in order to maintain familial economic and political power and supremacy, has the proper sociological conditions and mechanisms to sustain and reinforce a fairly strong extended family organization. Lebanon has been shown to have strong leading extended families, *zu'ama* families were extensive and inheritable political and economic influence. According to Daghestani,[71] Sunni Moslem families in Damascus also exhibit strong solidarity. The connections and similarities of Muslim Damascene and Beirut families are very strong. Hence we would expect the same strength of upper-class families in Beirut. No doubt then, upper-

---

[70] W. J. Goode, *op. cit.*

[71] K. Daghestani, *Etude Sociologique sur la famille musulmane contemporaine en Syrie,* Paris: Leroux, 1938.

class families both in Lebanon and Syria maintain a lively degree of contact, interaction, and interdependence with their extended kin.

Looking at the lower class, again little data is available on urban Lebanon. However, a study of infant care and health in Beirut led Harfouche, a public health researcher, to write a short volume describing the "social structure" of low-income families.[72] Harfouche supplies some data describing the pattern of relationships. For example, 26.7% of the families in her (non-random) sample were "residentially extended"—that is, close relatives or in-laws lived in. Furthermore, 21.1% (30.8% Maronite, 23.7% Sunni, and 9.9% Armenian) were married to kin, described as "consanguineous marriages." Harfouche also writes that "the elders in an extended family, especially among the low-income group, are well accepted by Muslims and Christians alike."[73] In addition, she stresses the fact that mothers and grandmothers are very important in transmitting the technique and love of infant health care. They are the major source of advice and arrange most of the marriages. Hence in urban Beirut we do see good indication of the continued functioning of an extended family system among the lower classes also. In rural Lebanon one need not reiterate the importance of village peasant kinship networks. Suffice it to say that the social structure of the peasant communities both in the mountain and plain is in kinship terms.

Finally, the conditions pivotal in sustaining strong kinship ties in the upper and lower classes in Lebanon are not so forceful in the expanding middle classes. The new upper middle class of professionals, managers, and kindred is the most universalistically oriented and most modern component of the society; its membership requires highly trained and skilled individuals in the modern occupations. Nevertheless, it can be easily shown that at least in economic terms this upper middle class, too, continues to depend on extended family structure. In Beirut, for example, young medical doctors and dentists obtain the capital necessary for opening a clinic from relatives, not from banks. Without such help they would have great difficulty in starting out. In the cases

[72] J. K. Harfouche, *Social Structure of Low-Income Families in Lebanon*, Beirut: Khayats, 1965.
[73] *Ibid.*, p. 34.

where such help from kinsmen was not possible, it was extended family contacts, *wastah,* with its support and guarantees, that enabled the young professional to obtain the necessary funds for his clinic. Many such a professional found it possible to study and to specialize abroad precisely because of extended family financial and other help. Similarly, engineers who maintained their consulting, design, and contracting companies had extended family financial support and involvement. And, of course, pharmacists who wished to buy a license for a pharmacy or drug-importing house need capital obtained frequently from extended kin or through the contacts of extended kin. Thus for this upper middle class, kinsmen or the extended family are a major source of capital. Often the new, modern, rationally organized business and services firms are partnerships of extended kin who pooled their capital and technical know-how. More systematic data on this is difficult to come by. The above is intended to be illustrative of the desire and preference for extended kin cooperation in economic endeavors. Its incidence is difficult to estimate. However, from Sayigh's data used in the second section of this essay, one would expect a higher than chance frequency. It is not intended to argue that *only* relatives cooperate in economic endeavors. In Lebanon, especially since the 1950's, corporations for financing large projects have sold stocks openly in an attempt to gather the necessary capital. Furthermore, with extensive capital accumulations in Lebanese banks from the oil sheikhdoms, capital loans for large business projects are now possible. Thus kin have become increasingly less important as a source of capital, especially of large amounts of capital.

On the other hand, of those managers in the sample I studied who were working for local Lebanese companies, the majority got their jobs through some kind of extended family action: *wastah,* recommendation, sponsorship, information exchange, etc. Some of those working in the European and American companies in Lebanon did so as well. Perhaps only with complete industrialization and secularization of Lebanon will the influence of kinship in the economic sphere be drastically cut.

Family organization is also intimately related to social mobility. According to Schumpeter, strong family bonds are antithetical to social mobility in a class stratification system. Presumably, the

individual, if he is to move upward socially, must free himself
from the "dead weight of family ties and demands. Thus a small
nuclear family system with weak solidarity is most adaptive for
social mobility." Perhaps he should have said, most conducive
for *high* rates of social mobility. Cross-culturally the Schumpeter
hypothesis does not hold true. In traditional China the strong
kinship group in fact made it possible, upon pooling resources,
to educate a son for the imperial civil service examinations. Upon
success and mobility, the whole kin group benefited. Similarly,
in rural Lebanon, the most cohesive kin group is the most successful in bettering its own economic standing. This, however, may
be possible only at a certain stage of economic development. In
the urban areas in Lebanon, similar to most modernizing societies, social mobility is primarily changing from traditional to modern occupations, as well as moving upward within the modern
economic sector. Major channels of mobility, as in the already
industrialized societies, are education and emigration. Families
in Lebanon pool resources in order to send a child to school and
higher education or work either in the country or, if necessary,
abroad. Thus higher education for Lebanese has come to be the
major medium of socialization, of acculturation, and of transmission of Western values and style of life as well as of social
mobility. Again, it is strongly linked to kinship ties.

Finally, illustrations of the pattern of the style of life of the
upper middle class, the most universalistically oriented class in
Lebanon, cannot but add emphasis to the argument of the continued existence of the functionally extended family. In the sample interviewed, of the extended family kinsmen living in
Lebanon, 40% resided within a fifteen-minute-walk radius of
each other. The residence is primarily in rented apartments—the
preference of middle-class urban families. The rate of face-to-
face contact is incredible by Western standards; it amounts to
daily contact with significant kin such as parents, grandparents,
as well as *married* children, *married* siblings, and to a lesser extent, with nephews, uncles, etc. In-laws residing nearby, at least
among the urban Christians, share in this intense rate. Beyond
this grouping the rate of contact, as expected, steadily decreases.
If a second-degree kin is not a close friend, then contact is on a
weekly and monthly basis.

However, the social context of the contact is often reinforcing for the extended-family structure. Contact takes place between kinsmen individually but also often collectively and usually at the home of an informal leader of the overlapping kin networks. These gatherings are superb sociological mechanisms for reinforcing the solidarity and the bonds of the kin group. This of course points to the expressive or emotional functions of the extended kin. In the above essay we did not consider these social-psychological aspects, although they are important factors in the continuing pivotal societal locus of the extended-family structure.

In conclusion, modernization including economic development has not had in Lebanon its universally presumed consequences, especially with regard to family structure. That extended residence of kin group has broken down particularly in the cities is perhaps true. However, even in the urban context the pivotal structural position and function of the functionally extended family, in interdependence with the economic, political, religious, welfare, and stratification spheres, remain exceedingly important in contemporary Lebanon. Hence, the kinship dimension continues to be a major principle of social organization in this most apparently Western-like of Arab countries. Perhaps only with full industrialization and extensive secularization, especially of the political structure, will we ever witness the drastic demise of the extended-kinship structure.

10. *Selections from* City and Village in Iran

TERRITORIAL SOCIOECONOMIC STRUCTURE[1]

REGIONAL PATTERNS

People in the Kirman Basin live in four types of settlements, which differ in size, complexity, economic structure, and function: the city, regional subcenters, agricultural-weaving villages, and small villages and hamlets. The economic and social bonds among these various settlements are strong. Topography and the density of settlement in the region have assured easy and continuous communication among them, except in the mountains. Economic interdependence therefore is a dominant characteristic of the regional economy; it is found in agriculture, weaving, and herding. Self-sufficient, independent, internally organized rural settlements, seldom visited and little changed since the time of Christ—a settlement type many writers on the Middle East are fond of—do not exist in the Kirman Basin.

Kirman City is the major administrative and political center of the Kirman Basin and southeastern Iran. Political leaders in rural settlements such as district governors (*bakhshdar*), mayors (*shahrdar*), and village headmen (*kadkhuda*) are appointed to and can be removed from office by the governor-general of the province, who resides in Kirman City. These local leaders settle minor disputes and officiate at local ceremonies; all serious legal

Reprinted with permission of the author and the copyright owners, the Regents of the University of Wisconsin, from Paul Ward English, *City and Village in Iran: Settlement and Economy in the Kirman Basin* (Chapters 4 and 5). Madison: University of Wisconsin Press, 1966.

[1] Chapter 4. [Ed.]

disputes are referred directly to Kirman City. Government gendarmerie posts in Mahan and Jupar maintain continuous control over the area. The few professional people in smaller settlements are also government representatives. In Mahan these include six teachers, a doctor, a male nurse, a forestry department official (despite the lack of forests), and several tax collectors.

Kirman City is also the major social and religious center of the basin. Peasants look to it for entertainment and religious leadership. Many attend movies in the city; still more visit its mosques and shrines. On religious holidays and on Fridays (the Muslim sabbath) the bazaar swells with people from Mahan, Jupar, and places much farther away. Tribesmen from Baluchistan with white turbans and flowing robes, weavers from Ravar to the north, villagers from all parts of the province, and traveling mendicants are common sights in the city. Some bring fruit, grain, brush, or charcoal to barter or sell in the bazaar during the early morning hours. Many refuse to sell their goods quickly, for the pleasure of haggling and hearing the week's gossip is not to be missed. The remainder of the day is spent visiting relatives, wandering about the city, and attending religious services. Ancient taxis and buses ply the routes in the basin and beyond to cater to this demand. On every religious holiday, at least one of these vehicles travels from Kirman to Mahan, passes through Langar, Qanaghistan, and Muhiabad to Jupar, and then returns to the city by the same route, a round trip of some seventy miles. Still others go up and down the Yazd-Kirman—Bam highway to collect villagers from surrounding areas. Before cars and buses, peasants walked or rode donkeys to Kirman, and many still do. Wheeled vehicles intensified and expanded an existing pattern; they did not create a new one. The city, then, has always been an important part of peasant life.

Perhaps this interdependence between city and village is most striking in the economic sphere. Kirman City is the financial and administrative center, the economic nucleus, for every major activity in the region. The power elite of the city control the key institutions and basic resources of the province. Landed aristocrats of Kirman finance agriculture. New villages are built and old ones repaired on their command. Every qanat in the Kirman Basin (for which records exist) was built by a member of the urban elite, whether merchant or landlord. Nor has this group relinquished control of the basic elements of production; they own much of the cultivated land and the water which irrigates it. Peasant proprietors are found in the basin, but they do not initiate new economic development except in marginal areas.

By retaining control of the elements of production and then leasing them to villagers, the power elite retain decision-making power. Urbanites decide if fertilizer is to be used, whether tractors are a wise investment, and in many cases which crops are grown. This is not to imply absolute power; landlords are bound by tradition quite as much as peasants. But the fundamental decisions of maintenance and change are theirs, for it is they who finance agriculture. Though social contacts between landlord and peasant may be few (this has been grossly overstated in the literature), the economic bond is firm; their interdependence and respective privileges and duties are at the heart of the agricultural system.

Similar control is maintained in the carpet-weaving industry and in herding. Weavers in villages and towns work for the power elite under a contract system. The carpet merchant supplies the materials, the weaver his labor. The largest herds of sheep and goats in the province are owned by carpet factories in the city and by entrepreneurs who specialize in the wool trade. In essence, the entire economy of the basin is keyed on Kirman City. There is no major segment of the population independent of its influence.

Kirman on its part requires economic support from a wide area of production. The peasantry contribute time and energy, produce and labor, toward the maintenance of the city. Recently these relationships have intensified because Kirman has sought wider and wider relationships with its hinterland to fill the lag in investment opportunities which followed its decline as a military and international trading center. The city is supplied with grain, fruit, and vegetables grown in the gardens and fields of Mahan, Jupar, Langar, Qanaghistan, and many smaller settlements. The hinterland also contributes tax revenues to the city. Tax offices on every major road in Kirman until very recently collected duties on goods flowing in and out of its marketplace. Finally, the raw materials of the carpet-weaving industry are supplied locally. Without these goods and services, the city would certainly decline.

But this very general level of interdependence masks hundreds of minor daily interactions between urbanites and their rural counterparts. The city is the major marketplace for everything the villagers produce. On a given morning, peasants travel to the city to sell a small rug, a mat, a woven cap, stockings, a goat, or any other item in order to buy fundamental necessities such as salt, sugar, tea, or cloth. If his daughter is to be wed or his social position demands that a celebration be held, the peasant asks his landlord or weaving contractor for an advance, and failing that will have recourse to the moneylenders of the bazaar. And debt is a binding tie; many debtors live in villages, most creditors in the city. If a villager has broken the law or the army threatens to induct him, his last appeal will always be to the most powerful urbanite he or his family knows. If he wishes to buy a cup, a plate, a religious photograph or icon, a samovar, or a rug, he will travel to Kirman, where the choice is great and he can hope to find a bargain. The majority of specialized artisans, craftsmen, service workers, and professional people live in Kirman.

Finally there are the small agricultural, weaving, herding, charcoal-burning villages and hamlets on the alluvial fans and in the mountains. Even these show some variety, since any of the above occupations may be the dominant economic activity depending on the location, local resources, and origin of the particular settlement. They are united in being primary producers, and the vast majority of their populations are either farmers, weavers, or herders. Many villages and hamlets are simply offshoots from a parent settlement, particularly those in the mountains. In the past these offspring were called *mazra'eh*, which translates as "hamlet" but indicates that the smaller place is to be treated as an integral part of the larger settlement for tax purposes. Usually settlements located on the water supply lines of a larger settlement have this type of relationship. Thus, the villages and hamlets in the valley south of Langar (Ahmadabad Dogu, Rahimabad, and Zarkuh) are populated by people from Langar who still consider themselves Langari and receive a fixed percentage of Langar's water supply. This same relationship obtains in Kazimabad, Toujigun, and Qudratabad in the Tigiran valley and

in the settlements near Mah Char. Peddlers from the parent settlement and sometimes barbers as well travel into the mountains
once or twice a month.

This should not suggest that villagers spend the bulk of their
time on the road to Kirman or that all villagers live in similar
settlements. The cultivator is tied to his field, the shepherd to his
flock, and the weaver to his loom. Thus, regional subcenters are
necessary to distribute vital goods and services to the rural population. On the northern slopes of the Kuhi Jupar these functions
are performed by the towns of Mahan and Jupar. Villagers travel
to these centers far oftener than to Kirman City for medicines,
for vital elements of the diet (e.g. sugar, tea), on religious holidays, to exchange goods, and in the end for burial. Mahan performs these services for an area including Qanaghistan, Langar,
and the mountain setttlements of the Kuhi Jupar. The town of
Jupar supplies alluvial fan villages as far eastward as Amirabad,
including villages such as Isma'ilabad, Shahabad, Kousar Riz, and
Muhiabad. In these two towns artisans such as carpenters, well
diggers, blacksmiths, coppersmiths, tanners, and brickmakers,
and service people such as shopkeepers, barbers, bathkeepers,
bakers, druggists, and midwives are found. Local administrators
also live here and decide minor disputes concerning ownership,
water rights, and other village problems. To a certain extent these
occupations are represented in the large villages of Qanaghistan,
Langar, and Muhiabad, but their number and importance decline
as the settlement grows smaller.

One would expect an organized chain of command in this
settlement hierarchy from the decision-making elite of Kirman
City through middlemen in the regional subcenter to primary
producers in the villages and hamlets, but such is not the case.
Arrangements, contracts, and decisions in agriculture, weaving,
and herding generally flow directly from the city to the pro-
ducer. Some landlords deal through intermediaries (*mubashirs*)
who represent their interests in local affairs, others do not. In
most cases the terms of sharecropping contracts are fixed by
tradition. The landlord visits the village in August to reaffirm
the contract and again at harvest time to collect his share of the
produce. There are no intermediary grain dealers, storers, or

processors in Mahan and Jupar. Wheat and barley are harvested from the fields and delivered directly to the city; only the peasant's share (20 to 30%) remains in the hinterland. In weaving, the contract between factory and weaver is also direct. Supplies are sent from the city to the weaver's loom, intermediaries perform regular inspection tours as the carpet progresses, and final payment is made upon delivery in Kirman. There are no carpet shops in the regional subcenters, though there are managers and entrepreneurs who control upward of a hundred looms. Similar arrangements apply to the large herds of sheep and goats.

To be sure, some secondary economic activity is created in the regional subcenters. Local landlords and peasant proprietors sell grain to the weavers of neighboring villages. Independent weavers produce mats or rugs ordered by local residents. Shepherds care for flocks owned by weavers and farmers in the alluvial fan settlements. But these are variations on the major theme in economic activity: urban dominance. The origin and mechanisms of urban control are detailed in Chapter 5.[2]

ECONOMIC STRUCTURE OF KIRMAN CITY

The occupational structure of Kirman City reflects its diverse functions as an administrative, political, commercial, social, and religious center. Its streets are clogged with a variety of specialists: landlords, merchants, booksellers, beggars, hawkers, artisans, civil servants, chauffeurs, weavers, *mullas,* entertainers, millers, bakers, poets, clerks, bankers, goldsmiths, and a host of other men who serve the city and its hinterland. The professional class composed of teachers (classical and modern), religious leaders, lawyers, doctors, bureaucrats, and clerks makes up a tenth of the male population over ten years old; most of these men (77%) are employed by the government. Service workers form 14% of the labor force, among them barbers, bathkeepers, domestic servants, policemen, and others. The traders of the city (another tenth of the labor force) are divided into two groups, the export-import merchants (wholesalers) and the retail shopkeepers. Many of the former migrated to Tehran when trade declined; but

[2] Beginning on page 332. [Ed.]

TABLE I

Generalized Occupational Structure of Kirman City

Occupation	Number	% of total
Professional and administrative	1,943	9.9
Service	2,791	14.1
Commercial	2,089	10.6
Artisans and craftsmen	6,885	34.9
Agriculture	2,586	13.0
Unemployed	1,571	8.0
Not reported	1,891	9.5
TOTAL	19,756	100.0

Source: Government of Iran, *Census District Statistics of the First National Census of Iran, Aban 1335 (November 1956)*, Vol. 17, Part 1 (Tehran: Department of Public Statistics, Ministry of Interior, Government of Iran, 1960), pp. 26, 34–36. These figures represent the total number of males aged 10 years or older, excepting students. The population of Kirman City was too large and diversified to assure complete reliability, although efforts were made to check data in the field.

the latter are more numerous than ever, particularly the retailers of cloth, food, and household goods.

Artisans and craftsmen form the largest occupational group in Kirman City, representing nearly 35% of the labor force. Carpet weaving is the major craft (24% of all artisans and craftsmen); it employs designers, dyers, cleaners, carders, and clippers as well as weavers. Unskilled construction workers (including brickmakers) are the largest artisan group (35% of all artisans and craftsmen). Recently, both of these activities have increased in Kirman. Carpet factories have enticed village weavers to the city with offers of better facilities and higher rates of pay. The construction group increased when landless peasants and ambitious sharecroppers migrated to the city in search of work. Having no other skill or training, they carry bricks, clay, dust, and straw for the professional builders. Other large craft groups in Kirman include tailors, blacksmiths, bakers, and carpenters.

Although one does not usually think of farming as a major urban occupation, agriculturalists are numerous in provincial Persian cities. In Kirman they form 13% of the labor force. Among their number are landed aristocrats who own land and water in settlements as distant as the coast of the Persian Gulf, gardeners and sharecroppers who work in the newly constructed orchards and fields (irrigated by deep wells) on the outskirts of the city, and professional gardeners who tend the formal household gardens of the urban elite. In the past, agriculturalists were more numerous; they fed the city when it was under attack and grew fruit and vegetables for the marketplace. The smaller percentage of them in modern Kirman reflects its growing dependence on produce from its hinterland.

The low percentage of unemployed people in Kirman City (8% of the labor force) is deceptive. Many seasonal laborers work in agriculture at harvest time and in construction during spring and early summer. Others work sporadically when there is need for their services—among them donkeymen, domestic servants, and street cleaners. Most of these men probably reported themselves as employed in one or another occupational group. The unemployment rate in Kirman City, therefore, is higher than the figures show

Most of the people in Kirman City are occupied in secondary and tertiary activities. This in itself does not distinguish Kirman City from other settlements in the region which perform similar functions and have similar occupational structures but operate on a smaller scale in a more restricted area. The principal characteristics which do distinguish Kirman City from smaller places such as Rafsinjan, Bam, Mahan, and Jupar are its full range of social strata and high degree of occupational differentiation.

In Kirman City the social stratification characteristic of many preindustrial cities is well developed. At the top of the social structure is an urban elite, a small (probably a twentieth of society) group of powerful families who control the elements of production in the city and its hinterland. Beneath this elite group there is a small but growing middle class of intellectuals, second-rank civil servants and bureaucrats, progressive merchants, and professionals, making possibly a tenth of society. Next is the large commoner class composed of petty bazaar merchants, service workers, artisans and craftsmen, and agriculturalists—the bulk of the urban population. At the base of the social order are people isolated by occupation or background from those higher in the socioeconomic scale. In the past, members of the Jewish and

Zoroastrian communities of Kirman were included in this class, but today the main ethnic group still viewed with distaste by society is the Gypsies.

The Urban Elite

Kirman City's upper class is a small, heterogeneous group of leaders drawn from all segments of society but unified in wealth, power, and influence in local affairs. Membership is restricted to individuals with wealth and/or power; entrance cannot be accomplished by family name or contacts alone. To be sure, established families command greater respect than *nouveaux riches,* and a family with a record of past achievement has higher prestige than an equivalent family with an undistinguished past. But these are social shadings. The key to inclusion is ownership—of land, water, animals, or carpets. Accumulation of wealth is usually derived from positions in the governmental, military, or religious hierarchy.

Two traditional groups in the urban elite of Kirman City are the regional political and religious leaders. The political leaders of Kirman, the governor-general and his assistants, are appointed by the central government in Tehran to run both city and province. They have no fixed term of tenure and are frequently removed from office. In the past, political appointments to such provincial governorships were sure roads to fortune (if not fame), and these men acquired large personal fortunes from gifts, bribes, and through manipulation and connivance with members of the local elite. Landlords and merchants favored by one ruler or another would amass riches rapidly; others less fortunate would lose land, water, and carpets. But corruption has declined in recent times. Political appointees are rarely in Kirman long enough to develop intimate contact with one member of the local elite or distaste for another. Hence their impact on the composition of the urban aristocracy, local governmental decisions, and the economy of Kirman is less.

The influence of religious leaders has declined, because secular institutions now perform many of their previous functions. The courts, once the province of *imams* and *mullas,* are now filled with civil judges and lawyers. Religious elementary schools (*maktabs*), supported by private contributions and religious foundations, formerly trained the children of the upper class and shaped their thoughts along traditional lines. Now, government teachers in secular schools train the young, and religion is a minor part of the curriculum. Clerical control of law, education, and mass media has been broken, and thus the wellsprings of religious power are severely limited. That mullas are still treated with great respect by landlords and merchants is probably a tribute to the pervasiveness of their past influence. Young "modern" members of the aristocracy often mock tradition, yet they flatter, subsidize, and defer to religious leaders.

Since the real basis of social and economic power in Kirman is ownership, few religious or resident political leaders in the city fail to root their power firmly in land or carpets. Many landowners of modern Kirman are descendants of powerful government officials, religious leaders, and merchants of the nineteenth century; others belong to the nouveau riche group, men who have accumulated wealth in the bazaar or in civil service and have invested it in land. Nouveaux riches do not view land ownership exclusively as an economic venture, though a substantial amount of their income may derive from it. Land is a tool in their climb to and maintenance of prestige and social power. Any purchase of land is a gain in power, any sale of land symbolizes a (real or imagined) decline in fortunes. Extensive low quality holdings are preferred to fewer high quality properties of equal value, and in some cases landlords retain uneconomic holdings rather than lose prestige by disposing of the land.

The traditional members of the landowning class disdain contact with the masses and surround themselves with managers, clerks, and servants to represent them in dealings with the common people of the city and region. Maids shop for them in the bazaar, clerks handle commercial dealings with retail shopkeepers, and managers negotiate contracts with sharecroppers. Such men conform closely to the stereotype of the Middle Eastern landlord—but they are few in Kirman. Many have migrated to Tehran and others have been replaced by their educated sons, who have a markedly different attitude and approach than their tradition-bound fathers.

The younger members of the landed aristocracy have been educated in Tehran or at Western universities and return to Kirman with progressive technical and (to a lesser extent) social ideas. These men spread knowledge of tractor plowing, fertilization, improved seed, and insecticides throughout their holdings. Most of them are not content simply to be landlords. They are proud of their knowledge and use it as civil servants in government bureaus. They associate informally with middle class contemporaries who share their viewpoint on "modernization"; they do not respect the moralistic attitudes of the commoners toward women, alcoholic beverages, or illegal foods, and they adopt the characteristics of Westernized elements in Tehran society.

In addition to landowners, the elite includes some wholesale import-export merchants (*tajir*) who export carpets, wool, dried fruit, and nuts from Kirman and import sugar, rice, tea, cloth, hardware, and machinery. These men live in large houses in the suburbs of Kirman but work in small, sparsely furnished rooms around the caravanserais. These surroundings are deceptive, for the tajir's money and influence are spread throughout the city at all levels. Most of his capital is in real estate: slum dwellings, orchards, booths in the bazaar, and land and water in surrounding villages. Some is in merchandise, however, and the wealthiest of these merchants are creditors for hundreds of retailers, hawkers, and vendors.

Despite their enormous influence, merchants find entrance into the elite class difficult. Their extensive dealings with lower classes and manipulations for profit have always made them suspect. But a few merchants have achieved upper class status in Kirman, as is to be expected in such a commercial center. And if the merchant who desires inclusion is as socially clever as he is commercially adept, he follows a standard pattern. First, he segregates himself from dealings with the lower classes by hiring the trappings of the landed aristocrat—a host of servants, middlemen, and brokers—and abstains from manual labor of any type. He invests in land, realizing that it is less profitable than trade, to build his image as a member of the upper class. Other less status-conscious merchants are content to manipulate power without position.

The Middle Class

Between the elite and the masses is a growing middle class in Kirman. This group includes representatives of a wide variety of occupations: lesser landlords, lower echelon bureaucrats, young religious leaders, small merchants, shopkeepers of the bazaar, clerks, and professionals, all of whom have less power and wealth than the elite but are above the mass of commoners. The bulk of the middle class is traditional in viewpoint, but a vocal minority is progressive. On the basis of this difference in attitude two groups can be identified: the young and vigorous, Western-trained intelligentsia, who favor modern education, technology, and social progress; and the traditional bazaar retailers, artisans, and craftsmen, who are organized in a complex guild system.

The young intelligentsia are the "modernizers" (or to use Lerner's term, the "transitionals") of Kirman City. Drawn from aristocratic, religious, and commercial backgrounds, they are united in their contempt for traditionalism, emphasizing its worst aspects, and in their desire for change. All are literate and some have a high school education; most have aspirations which they believe can be realized only through revolutionary social change. Thus they form a frustrated, unhappy group, but they have played a positive role in Kirman. Many recent changes in the city such as the paving of major avenues, provision of new bathing facilities (shower baths versus pool baths were a critical issue), the building of an ice factory, and the introduction of numerous paperback bookstores have been initiated and supported by members of the middle class and financed by sympathetic members of the elite.

The bulk of the middle class is composed of retail merchants of the bazaar and master artisans and craftsmen. In Kirman this class includes cloth sellers, small grocers, carpet sellers and weavers, silversmiths, blacksmiths, carpenters, leather workers, coppersmiths, master tailors, moneylenders, dyers, designers, bathkeepers, shoemakers, potters, booksellers, and other tradesmen. These lower middle class shopkeepers and craftsmen form the heart of the city's economic and social life; they pray regularly at the mosque and attend all religious ceremonies, they converse for hours each day with all classes in their stalls in the bazaar, they belong to a guild and probably a *zurkhana* as well. The artisans and merchants produce luxury goods for the elite and sell lesser products to commoners, villagers, and visiting tribes-men.

Perhaps most important, tradesmen and artisans train the youth of Kirman through a guild system, first as apprentices and later as journeymen. The young men pattern themselves after their guild masters. While performing menial chores as errand boys, they learn that manual labor is the proper function of the lower class, not of the master artisan. They are trained in guild loyalty, regular prayer, and attendance at the mosque. The length of the apprenticeship varies with the ability of the boy, the tenacity of the master, and the difficulty of the craft, but in all cases it is long enough to ensure that the apprentice turned journeyman has absorbed the proper values of the bazaar.

Members of each trade and craft or specialized segment of a trade or craft belong to a guild; membership is a prerequisite for practice of every trade. The guild maintains a monopoly over its given economic activity through informal social pressures rooted in tradition. Some crafts have guild courts which regulate internal disputes and represent members in dealings with other guilds and the government. A guild council formed of elders (*rish safid*) is presided over by the head of the guild. The strong-est guilds in Kirman City are the cloth sellers, carpet weavers, shawl makers, rug sellers, and wool sellers. After these come the tailors, potters, blacksmiths, carpenters, coppersmiths and finally noncraft groups such as the bathkeepers, barbers, midwives, storytellers, and darvishes. In some cases, guilds cut across re-ligious boundaries, as with the cloth sellers' guild of Kirman City, which includes Zoroastrians and Jews as well as Muslims. But the members of these religions sell their wares in different parts of the Vakil Bazaar, so that Kirman has three cloth-selling bazaars though only one cloth sellers' guild.

Forces of modernization have nullified many of the economic and social powers of the guilds in Kirman. Guilds are no longer treated as corporate units for taxation purposes, whereas in the past guild members paid government taxes in seven installments to guild leaders. Guild control of the training of middle class youths has been affected by compulsory primary education and military conscription. Guild social and religious activities have been curtailed by government control of assemblies, and identification with the religious class has led to a corresponding loss in prestige. Monopolistic guild control of economic activity has been weakened by the introduction of new techniques and crafts such as automobile repair, mechanized carding and weaving, and truck driving. Finally, government bureaus have assumed regulatory control of economic activity (previously the province of the guild): laws regulating working conditions, minimum health and sanitation standards, and minimum wage laws, though rarely enforced, now place the power of regulation in the hands of bureaucrats rather than of artisans. Continuing changes in industry and commerce seem likely to prevent any return of guilds to their former role in the economic structure of the city.

The Lower Class

The lower class of Kirman City is a large and varied group, comprising well over half its population. The lowest echelons of religious and government service, poor journeymen and unskilled laborers, sharecroppers and gardeners, servants, carriers, lesser shopkeepers, hawkers, and vendors fill the ranks of this commoner group. As a class, it is unified only in the sense that it forms a composite group of similar status in the eyes of the elite. Its three most numerous elements are the vendors, the agriculturalists, and the unskilled laborers.

Hawkers and vendors form one of the most colorful groups in any Persian city, and Kirman is no exception. They travel about the city calling their wares: water, bread, vegetables, fruit, brooms, cloth, rugs, and hundreds of other things. Each specializes in a particular item, dresses in a particular fashion, and has a unique way of advertising his product. Some work seasonally, such as the sellers of Shahdad oranges, but most travel their routes daily throughout the year. Among the noisiest are the kettle sellers and water sellers, who beat their tins while chanting their wares. The latter are divided into sellers of water from Husaynabad, a spring three miles from the city, and sellers of Kirman City water. The spring water sellers look down on their competitors as handlers of an inferior product. Both drive donkey-powered vehicles with large tanks mounted on the rear axles of World War II jeeps. As these are pulled through the lanes of the city their drivers vie for the attention of the citizens. One of the major reasons for the number and variety of hawkers in Kirman is the restriction of upper class women to the home. It is only when peddlers come to their door that many of these women have the pleasure of examining and purchasing goods.

Most of the agriculturalists in Kirman City are part-time culti-vators who combine farming with construction work and other unskilled labor. But even in this group there is some diversity and specialization. A few cultivators have attached themselves to up-per class landlords and run errands throughout the city when not working in the fields. These men aspire to positions as watchmen, gatekeepers, or overseers in the household. If successful, they acquire power over several lesser jobs and considerable status among their peers. Another group of agriculturalists specializes in cultivating cash summer crops. Often, by a sharecropping con-tract, the landlord's household is supplied with fresh vegetables in return for use of an uncultivated plot of land. The remainder of the crop is sold on the outskirts of the bazaar by the cultivator or a member of his family. Several of these gardeners have be-come famous for the quality of their crops and have developed a faithful clientele among the elite. Such farmers dress in West-ern clothing and take part in urban social and religious functions; their wives weave carpets or are domestic servants. Finally, there are those cultivators, newly arrived in the city, who have been driven by drought or flood from their villages. These men retain their rural dress, speech, and behavior patterns but assimilate urban characteristics rapidly.

Probably the largest group in the lower class is formed of un-skilled laborers. Kirman teems with these: servants, ditchdiggers, haulers, burden bearers, construction workers, donkeymen, and car washers. They are humble in their poverty. Many of these men gather at the western end of the Vakil Bazaar each morning, some with shovels and others without, in hopes that an employer will appear. Carpenters, builders, blacksmiths, and other artisans hire laborers daily from this group. They are paid anywhere from

30 to 40 *rials* ($.40 to $.53) per day after a small gift is given to the employer for providing work, enough money for bread and a bowl of yoghurt.

But there is a group beneath these unskilled laborers, whose status is not only humble but defiling because of occupation or birth. Butchers, barbers, washers in public baths, leather tanners, privy cleaners, night soil collectors, and street scavengers are members of this lowest class. The Gypsies, for instance, are not allowed to touch food or water before use by other members of town society, despite the fact that they are Muslims, nor are they encouraged to settle in Kirman. Intermarriage with Gypsies or others of the defiled class is considered repugnant by elite and commoners alike. In some cases it is expressly forbidden. Forces of change are steadily eliminating people from the group of the unclean, and their numbers are decreasing. Entertainers, for instance, have achieved a type of prominence through their association with the elite. Refrigerated butcher shops and modern barbershops are utilized by upper class Kirmanis, and their proprietors gain respect through this patronage. The craft of leather work is declining and its members are migrating to Tehran in search of other jobs with higher status.

The most striking feature of society in Kirman, then, is the distance between the elite and the lower classes. The social gradient is steep, and differentiation is clear. The prevailing immobility in Kirmani society is ameliorated (at least in the eyes of the residents) by striking cases of vertical mobility. One of the very prominent families in modern Kirman, for example, is of peasant background and achieved wealth and power through speculation in the carpet trade. This case is widely quoted by middle and lower class Kirmanis to establish the possibility of miraculous rise to riches and power through cleverness, luck, and the aid of Allah. The social system in Kirman generally discourages mobility of this type, however, and clear crystallization into distinct classes is the rule. It is the existence of this full range of social strata within Kirman City that distinguishes it from all other settlements in the basin. In the towns and villages there is no comparable elite group and few men of very low status, the social gradient is gentler, and variations in wealth and power are fewer.

THE REGIONAL SUBCENTERS: MAHAN AND JUPAR

Mahan and Jupar, as we have mentioned, are secondary administrative, economic, and religious centers for the people living on the northern slopes of the Kuhi Jupar. These functions date from the Middle Ages, when Mahan and Jupar grew into towns because of favorable location on major trade routes. After the construction of the Shah Ni'matullah Vali Shrine in the fifteenth century, Mahan outstripped its rival and became the county (*bakhsh*) administrative center governing the two townships (*dihistans*) of Mahan and Jupar.

TABLE II

Generalized Occupational Structures of Mahan and Jupar

Occupation	No. of heads of households	% of total
Mahan		
Professional	76	4.4
Service	101	6.8
Weaving industry	452	30.3
Artisans and craftsmen	184	12.3
Agriculturalists and herders	509	34.1
Unemployed	182	12.1
TOTAL	1,504	100.0
Jupar		
Professional	29	3.3
Service	49	5.6
Weaving industry	353	40.5
Artisans and craftsmen	108	12.4
Agriculturalists and herders	236	27.1
Unemployed	96	11.1
TOTAL	871	100.0

Data based on original village questionnaires and IBM cards from the 1956 Census of Iran. The cards were checked thoroughly in the field. See Note to Table I.

The occupational structure of Mahan and Jupar exhibits many urban characteristics. Full-time agriculturalists and herders compose only one-third or fewer of the heads of households; the bulk of the population are artisans, craftsmen, weavers, shopkeepers, traders, and service workers. In Mahan particularly the occupational diversification of the market town is found. This characteristic differentiates Mahan and Jupar from Langar, Qanaghistan, Muhiabad, and other smaller settlements on the slopes of the Kuhi Jupar.

The Upper and Middle Classes

The upper and middle classes of Mahan and Jupar are not as distinctively different as in Kirman City. Their members are neither as powerful nor as exclusive as the urban elite. The leaders of the resident upper and middle classes are the county governor, mayor, and village headman (all appointed by the governor-general of Kirman), members of the town council, wealthy shopkeepers, local landlords, doctors, bank managers, some teachers, a priest, and several carpet factory managers. These men exercise power over the town and surrounding villages but are careful not to interfere with direct commands from the urban elite. Thus, a local carpet factory manager may hire or fire a weaver or punish individuals through local officials for theft or poor weaving, but has no voice in the pattern, design, size, or number of carpets woven. Locally, he is a highly respected member of the community, but in Kirman he is simply a hired representative. The village headman selects military conscripts to fill the local quota, but if a landlord needs a particular sharecropper, the headman will not interfere. The county governor settles land and water disputes when local residents are involved, but if the assets of a landowner are at stake, he will withdraw completely from the dispute. Even the few professionals—the doctors, teachers, and mullas—are completely subservient to the powers that be in Kirman. They all do everything in their power to maintain smooth, frictionless relations with that powerful group.

Membership in the resident elite is based on a variety of factors which span occupational boundaries. One of the government teachers, for example, is the grandson of a famous religious leader and has inherited shares in the Mahan water supply. Shopkeepers in this group own land in town and have servants who run their retail shops. Because the degree of wealth and power attainable in Mahan and Jupar is limited by the size of the population and resource base, great variations in wealth are not found; secondary factors such as level of education, piety, and family background play a greater role in determining an individual's position than they do in Kirman City.

Many members of the resident upper and middle classes mimic the trappings, manners, and attitudes of the urban elite of Kirman City. They use urban furnishings (notably chairs and tables) in their homes, disdain working with their hands, practice the exaggerated politeness of the urban upper class, and emphasize their privileged position in town society through displays of conspicuous consumption and studied leisure. In some cases this imitation is carried to an extreme. A banker in Mahan, for instance, believed it inconsistent with his position to drive an automobile, and hired a chauffeur. As he owned a Volkswagen, this caused great discomfort to his family and friends by overcrowding the rear seat. Despite this cultivated urban orientation, the resident elite have far greater contact with the commoner class in the towns than do the elite of Kirman City. It is impossible for them to be completely divorced from manual labor.

The Commoner Class: Agriculturalists and Craftsmen

Most of the people in Mahan and Jupar are either agriculturalists (peasant proprietors, sharecroppers, tenant renters, and agricultural laborers) or craftsmen who weave carpets and rugs and make mats, felts, donkeybags, shoes, and clothing. The agriculturalists are the traditional core of the population, the transmitters of rural culture in these urbanized town settings. They wear distinctive peasant garb—blue cotton trousers, long shirts, and felt caps—in contrast with the Western clothing of the artisans and craftsmen. They are conscious of their long residence in the area and refer to the weavers as *khushnishin* or "new settlers." Because the water supply is relatively stable in Mahan and Jupar, these farmers are closely tied to the land. Tenancy and sharecropping rights are handed down from father to son for generations. Variations in speech and manner further emphasize their apartness.

The artisans and craftsmen are members of the largest single occupational group in Mahan and Jupar. Most are carpet weavers, but carpenters, blacksmiths, tinsmiths, mechanics, tailors, shoemakers, bakers, tanners, and qanat builders also live in these towns. Most weavers inherit their craft, but recently second and third sons of peasant owners and sharecroppers have been forced off the land by population growth and have become weaving apprentices. The weavers are more closely linked with urban life than the agriculturalists. Market prices of wool and dyes, current wages for carding, spinning, and dyeing wool, and the international export trade in Kirmani carpets are of far greater concern to them than the advent of the spring rains or the condition of this year's crops.

But peasants and weavers alike balance their time and energy to produce as many of the basic necessities of life as possible. Farmers till part of the communal grainfield, part of the double-cropped garden area, and if possible some walled garden or orchard land. By working three different types of land, they can supply their household needs for food and fodder. In the winter villagers scour the uplands in search of brush and wood for the potter's kiln, the village bath, or for household fuel. Farmers also work as day laborers hauling mud and straw for a builder or turning a windlass to lift dirt from a qanat. Weavers cultivate gardens and keep animals to reduce the number of items they must purchase in the city.

Rural households typically own several chickens, a few goats or sheep, a donkey or a cow. If a weaver or farmer does not own a donkey or cow, he must rent them from donkeymen and cattle owners. Animals therefore are often shared by several households of an extended family to lessen this expense. Donkeys are the major beasts of burden in Mahan and Jupar. They are used for short-distance hauling of carpets, wool, dirt, dung, wood, and produce. Cattle are rarely used for transport; their major task is plowing the fields. Sheep and goats supply meat, milk, wool, hair, and down for domestic use and sale. These animals often represent the accumulated capital of each household and are bought from other villagers or from transient herders in good years and sold in the city in famine years. The small gardens within the household compounds are largely devoted to alfalfa, fruit trees, and herbs.

Women and children also contribute to the family economy.

They weave carpets, short-napped coarse rugs (*gilim*), and loosely woven woolen mats (*jajim*). Carpet weavers earn a high wage (by local standards), so a woman skilled in carpet weaving has no difficulty in finding a husband. Less talented women work at lesser crafts, spinning wool into yarn, cleaning hair from the down of Kashmir goats, and making woolen hats, stockings, and felts. In the poorest households women work as day laborers in the fields, sowing grain, weeding, and harvesting the crops, or else they collect wild rue seeds to sell for protection against the evil eye.

The bottom of society in Mahan and Jupar is rounded out by the poorest elements of the commoner class: beggars, scavengers, and the many unemployed. As a group, these people are poverty-stricken, live in ruined dwellings at the base of the town, and have little chance of improving their position. More than a tenth of the population is unemployed most of the year. Only in the harvest season, the bottleneck in the agricultural system, is work available. Many have migrated from satellite villages to these towns with the same aspirations as their counterparts who emigrated to Kirman. Both groups lead a marginal existence.

In the regional subcenters of Mahan and Jupar, then, there is less occupational diversity than in Kirman City, and the distance between the top and bottom of the social structure is smaller. The social gradient is compressed because the elite class is less clearly separated from the masses and the lowest elements (e.g. defiling occupations) are poorly represented. But Mahan and Jupar do have more complex social and economic structures than smaller settlements on the slopes of the Kuhi Jupar. Through their mixture of urban and rural people important regional functions are served: food production and provision of labor for the city, and transfer of goods and raw materials between Kirman City and the villages and hamlets of the Kuhi Jupar.

LARGE AGRICULTURAL-WEAVING VILLAGES

Qanaghistan, Langar, and Muhiabad are intermediate in size and complexity between the regional subcenters of Mahan and Jupar and the small villages and hamlets of the alluvial fans and mountain valleys. Each of these large villages has more than a thousand residents, and a few professionals, service workers, and artisans who satisfy local needs. These centers have few facilities —a bath, a small shrine, a mill, and several shops—but these are enough to attract villagers from nearby smaller settlements when a plow needs mending, a funeral is to be held, grain must be milled, or a guest arrives and there is no tea in the house. In these settlements, all members of society fall within the bounds of the commoner class. The few shopkeepers, millers, and bath-keepers work part-time in agriculture or weaving. There is some diversification of labor, but less specialization of laborers. Except for minor service activities, the population has a single regional function: it supplies the urban market with carpets and crops.

Most of the wage earners in Qanaghistan, Langar, and Muhiabad are either agriculturalists or weavers. Muhiabad and Qanaghistan are primarily weaving centers, but in Langar agriculturalists and herders are a majority. Langar is located where the Tigiran valley opens onto the alluvial fan, and has pasture and water rights in this valley; thus few of its people (2.8%) are unemployed. In Qanaghistan the landlords have failed to repair the water supply system, and their stern religious beliefs (Shaykhi sect) are not attractive to weavers; hence unemployment is extremely high (15.3%).

In all three of these large villages the occupation division between weavers and cultivators is the most significant social division. There is little cooperation or exchange between the two groups. The agriculturalists cannot supply weavers with food-stuffs, since most are sharecroppers and have no surplus. Weavers do not buy wool directly from herders; both groups work under contracts with carpet factories in Kirman City. Nor do weavers sell carpets or mats to the peasants. Their best market for non-contract merchandise is in the bazaar in Kirman City. Most transactions therefore pass through Kirman City, Mahan, or Jupar. But there is one minor area of cooperation between weavers and agriculturalists: the payment of dues to the priests, barbers, carpenters, and blacksmiths. A standard sum is collected from each household in the village to support these facilities. The amount of the levy varies from place to place depending on the number of facilities and the total population. Agriculturalists pay directly from the harvest either before or after the division of

TABLE III

Generalized Occupational Structures
of the Large Agricultural-Weaving Villages

Occupation	No. of heads of households	% of total
Qanaghistan		
Professional	4	0.9
Service	27	6.1
Weaving industry	218	49.2
Artisans and craftsmen	50	11.3
Agriculturalists and herders	76	17.2
Unemployed	68	15.3
TOTAL	443	100.0
Langar		
Professional	6	1.4
Service	16	3.8
Weaving industry	147	34.4
Artisans and craftsmen	23	5.4
Agriculturalists and herders	223	52.2
Unemployed	12	2.8
TOTAL	427	100.0
Muhiabad		
Professional	3	1.2
Service	5	2.0
Weaving industry	133	52.6
Artisans and craftsmen	15	5.9
Agriculturalists and herders	79	31.2
Unemployed	18	7.1
TOTAL	253	100.0

Source: See notes to Tables I and II.

crop between the landlord and the peasant. Weavers pay in cash throughout the year.

SMALL VILLAGES AND HAMLETS

Only in the small villages and hamlets on the alluvial fans and in the mountain valleys of the Kuhi Jupar can one find a rural peasantry similar to that described in the Middle Eastern literature. These settlements have fewer than four hundred residents and are occupied by peasant proprietors, sharecroppers, herders, and fuel collectors who are closely tied to the land. Differences among individuals are slight; all are equally lacking in power and wealth. Over a period of time most residents become interrelated by blood or marriage, which gives the settlement a cohesiveness that is lacking in town and city.

Agriculture is the major economic activity in small villages and hamlets. Almost three out of every four households (73.9%) derive their principal income from agriculture. Weaving is practiced in less than a tenth of the households, because craftsmen migrate to larger settlements where wages are higher and facilities are better. The few nonagriculturalists in these places are unskilled laborers and charcoal burners, who remain in the villages by preference or because there is no work for them in the towns. The only members of the professional class found in small villages and hamlets are teachers assigned there by the Education Office in Kirman City.

But even here one must speak guardedly about an isolated traditional peasantry unaffected by the economic and social changes occurring in the larger centers of the basin. The settlers are still serviced by traveling peddlers and barbers from alluvial fan towns. Their land and water (except in the Hanak valley)

TABLE IV

Generalized Occupational Structures of the Small Villages and Hamlets

Occupation	No. of heads of households	% of total
Professional	3	0.7
Service	6	1.3
Weaving industry	42	9.2
Artisans and craftsmen	54	11.8
Agriculturalists and herders	333	73.9
Unemployed	19	3.1
TOTAL	457	100.0

Source: See notes to Tables I and II. This table includes data for 18 small villages and hamlets in the region which were covered in the 1956 Census.

are owned by urban or town residents. Their products, whether charcoal, wheat, or wool, are destined for an urban market. On the other hand, barter is more common in these small villages and hamlets, their inhabitants dress uniformly in rural costumes, and their speech and manners differ from those of urban dwellers.

To a considerable extent, the location of the village or hamlet determines its degree of isolation and ruralness. Mountain hamlets are the most isolated settlements in the basin. From some of these a trip to the alluvial fans may take as long as a day. Life is difficult and primitive in such places, but land hunger, grazing resources, and available fuel supplies are attracting new settlers from the plain each year. The possibility of bringing water to the surface without a large capital investment attracts some. Others simply come to work as sharecroppers or herders because there is no work on the plain. As this process intensifies, the small villages and hamlets will undoubtedly be drawn more completely into the urban-dominated regional economy of the basin.

URBAN DOMINANCE AND THE REGIONAL ECONOMY[3]

The preceding descriptions of city, town, village, and hamlet reveal one major fact: settlement, economy, and society in Kirman are urban-dominated. Why in a land purportedly filled with self-sufficient villages should such a rational, fully developed, regional pattern of settlement and economic organization exist? Its genesis probably lies in the settlement history and physical environment of Kirman. That settlement was initiated here by the advanced urban society of Sassanian Iran is not surprising. The basin is a marginal environment at best. Its winters are cold, its summers hot; above all, it is so dry that all crops must be irrigated. Development of this land by technologically primitive tribal groups was unlikely, though not impossible. Substantial capital had to be invested in irrigation devices (qanats), without which organized permanent settlement would be difficult. Nor was the motive for establishing settlement in Kirman unusual; defensive outposts are frequently birthplaces of cities in marginal areas. So Kirman City was founded for political reasons; and later, when population increased, settlement expanded onto nearby alluvial fans and into the mountain valleys to utilize their various environmental assets.

But if the genesis of urban dominance in Kirman is not perplexing, its continued existence—some sixteen hundred years

[3] Chapter 5. [Ed.]

later—certainly is. Established mechanisms to maintain urban dominance are surely necessary to explain such continuity. It is the modern forms of these mechanisms and the ways in which they function to concentrate wealth and power in the city that form the heart of this chapter. In the view taken here, the social and economic structure of modern Iran is seen as fundamentally similar to the feudal structures of Parthian and Sassasian Iran. The peasantry is an integral, functioning part of a larger society, not a divorced element. After all, agriculture has always been the fundamental source of governmental income in Iran, and it is unreasonable to suppose that the powerful and shrewd men who led Iran to fame in the past did so with three-quarters of its population existing in isolation beyond the influence of urban centers. Some have suggested (in opposition to modern land distribution laws) that Iran's peasantry survived precisely because it had few relationships with the great cities and societies that periodically rose and fell. Further, according to this reasoning, modern efforts to bring villages within the scope of governmental administration endanger this survival. The evidence from Kirman suggests the reverse: the villager of Iran, whether sharecropper, weaver, or herder, is inextricably involved in an urban-dominated, regional economic organization and probably was so in the past.

MAINTENANCE OF URBAN DOMINANCE

Traditional systems ensure the maintenance of urban dominance in the three major economic realms of Kirman. In agriculture, the mechanism is the land tenure system; in animal husbandry, herding contracts; and in craft activities, weaving contracts. In each sphere, the upper class of Kirman City retains ownership of the production factors. Thus, in agriculture, land and water are principally owned by large landowners (*arbabi*); in animal husbandry the sheep and goats are owned by urban residents; and in weaving the large flocks, dye-houses, and looms are owned by carpet merchants. These elements are rented by members of the elite to lesser individuals—farmers, weavers, and shepherds—who, in return for their labor receive a subsistence wage.

Land Tenure

The majority of the agriculturalists in Kirman are landless sharecroppers, who cultivate the land on the basis of annual written or verbal contracts with landowners. This contract guarantees the sharecroppers a percentage of the harvest in return for their labor and any other element that they contribute, such as fertilizer, draft animals, or seed. Theoretically, the division of crop is based on five factors—land, water, draft animals, seed, and labor—and one-fifth of the harvest is allotted to the supplier of each factor. In practice, sharecropping contracts vary from settlement to settlement. Usually the peasant supplies the labor and the landlord provides water, land, seed, and draft animals. The sharecropper receives 30% of the harvest and the landlord 70%. There is no distinction between winter cereal crops and summer crops, but the division of tree crops depends on the size of the orchard. If few tree crops are grown, the peasant's share is 30%, if orchards are extensive it will be only 20%.

The distribution of sharecropping agreements throughout the basin provides a clue to the criteria most critical in the division of crops. At lower elevations in stable alluvial fan villages the peasant receives 30% of ground crops and 20% of tree crops in return for his labor. In the mountain valleys the peasant's share of ground crops is still 30%, but his share in the tree crops increases from 20% to 30%. In high mountain hamlets sharecroppers receive 50% of the total harvest. In all areas the peasant supplies the same element, labor, and the landlord supplies all other factors in the production of the crop. These differences in the terms of crop-sharing agreements appear to vary according to the needs of the peasant household relative to crop yields. Because yields are lower in the mountain valleys and high mountain hamlets, the peasant's share is correspondingly higher.

The actual division of the crop takes place on the threshing floor. Before the crop is divided into the landlord's share (*minal*) and the peasant's share (*insaba*), deductions are levied for the carpenter, blacksmith, bathkeeper, crop-watcher, water distributor, and village headman. In most cases these dues amount to 10 or 15% of the total harvest. In Mahan, for example, the water distributor theoretically receives no share in the harvest, but a token offer of five *mann* of wheat (15 kg.) is an investment in the future. The village headman receives one kilogram of wheat for every share in the water supply. Further deductions for personal services are paid individually, since a choice of baths, carpenters, and blacksmiths is available.

A number of secondary factors are also considered in cropsharing agreements in Kirman. Usually the peasant has the right to the same proportion of straw as of grain. In some cases, however, the landlord takes all the wheat straw and the peasant all the barley straw. In the mountains the peasants keep both wheat and barley straw. In large settlements the sharecroppers receive one-third of the grain and straw left in the fields and on the threshing floor after the harvest. In smaller places this debris is not collected; the peasants graze their sheep and goats on the stubble.

Because the landlord provides every essential for cultivation except labor, the sharecropper is little more than a landless laborer and thus has no security of tenure. This lack of security is particularly critical in the Kirman region because unemployment is so high. Sharecroppers can be evicted from the land at any time during the year, though it is rarely done until after the harvest. The peasant plows the land with no guarantee that he will sow it. The landlord has full powers of ownership and use of the land. To some extent this is modified by local custom in the more stable villages on the alluvial fans. Here, peasants transmit sharecropping rights from father to son. This does not mean that the peasant cultivates the same land at all times, for the landlord may redistribute tenure rights at will. But customarily land is left in the hands of the same peasant for many years unless some disagreement occurs. In these stable settlements the peasants own their houses and even some agricultural implements.

Insecurity is a greater problem in the mountain valleys of the Kuhi Jupar. Here, sharecroppers do not work the same village or field from year to year; they work a valley or a region. Within one valley, as the fortunes of each village rise or fall depending on winter rains and the condition of the qanat, peasants migrate from place to place to maintain an equilibrium between population and water supply.

Given these conditions of insecurity of tenure, arbitrary redistribution of land, and unstable water supply, it is clear that the sharecropper's status and standard of living are extremely low. He cultivates cereals in a marginal environment, receives 30% of the harvest, from which dues must be subtracted, and has no cooperative marketing facilities. He must survive periods of want and depend on the landlord or a moneylender in the bazaar to tide him over these bad years. All loans are raised on the security of next year's harvest. Usually the landlord is willing (and expected) to supply the needed grain, because if the sharecropper is indebted to a moneylender, he may steal from the harvest to meet his commitments. Surprisingly, debt is not viewed as a totally negative condition by the sharecropper in Kirman. Some measure of security is derived from the fact that the landlord will lend him grain, and it is clearly understood that the landlord will not take so much of the next harvest that the sharecropper cannot feed his family. But debt keeps the sharecropper at the subsistence level; he works his way from harvest to harvest with little prospect of bettering his condition.

Herding Contracts

The urban elite also retain control of production factors in herding. Most of the sheep and goats grazed in nearby mountain pastures are owned by carpet merchants, wool dealers, and landowners of Kirman City. Through ownership of land and water in alluvial fan settlements, these men have maintained control of pasture resources. But their dominance is less complete in herding than in agriculture or weaving. There are independent sheep owners—residents of Mahan and Jupar and traveling shepherds from Baluchistan, southern Kirman, and Yazd—who own animals and rent graze. There are also shepherds who work for a village, caring for the flocks of its residents, in return for wages. But whether the flock is owned by an urban resident, a traveling sheepherder, or a group of villagers, the shepherds work under a contract system.

Herding contracts have striking similarities to sharecropping contracts. Both are initiated in autumn when the winter grains are sown; both are binding for one year. Some shepherds are paid a fixed annual wage (like tenant renters), others receive a percentage of the milk and lamb or kid crops (like sharecroppers). The criterion for determining shepherds' wages is also similar to that used in the tenure system. Shepherds must be paid a subsistence wage; thus, a man with many children is paid more than one with few. Only where this minimum standard is satisfied is the shepherd paid on the basis of the other factors such as the number of animals herded, the condition of local graze, or available village facilities.

Sheep and goats owned by landlords and carpet merchants in Kirman City are farmed out to shepherds under a variety of contracts. In every case the owner supplies animals, graze, and housing for the shepherd. Shepherds who work for a fixed annual wage (ranging from 3,000 to 4,500 rials [$40 to $60]) are paid in cash or kind in monthly installments; they receive no wool, milk products, or lambs. Other shepherds graze a flock for one year and return the initial number of animals of each age group to the owner, keeping the lambs but delivering all milk products and wool to the owner. Under a third type of contract, the shepherd is paid a small cash sum and receives a percentage of the flock's milk products and all lambs and kids above a minimum number. In all of these contracts wool, the principal commercial product from a carpet merchant's viewpoint, is the property of the owners.

Herding contracts between shepherds and villagers are more variable. At Hujatabad the shepherd is paid 3,500 rials ($46.66) per year plus clothing and shelter in the village. The shepherd of Kupang receives 4,000 rials ($53.33) per year, the other terms being the same. In some hamlets in the Hanak valley the shepherds are paid on a per animal basis. In Hanak Bala and Hanak Pa'yin shepherds receive 3 kg. of wheat and .75 kg. of barley per animal per year; the wheat is eaten by their families, the barley by their dogs. At Daristan, however, the shepherd receives half the milk, half the progeny, but none of the wool or down produced by the flock. In Mahan shepherds are paid 10 rials ($.13) per animal per month, 3 kg. of wheat when each lamb or kid is born, and one-seventh of the flock's milk production.

Weaving Contracts

Capital from Kirman City subsidizes and standardizes weaving. The agents of large Iranian and Western carpet firms live in the city, which is the principal collecting point for wool and dyes produced throughout the province. The primary role of the city in this industry is indicated by the fact that the designs of village-woven carpets are identical to those of Kirman City and that nearly three-quarters of the village weavers are under contract with carpet factories located in Kirman City. The organization of the industry is strikingly similar to the systems in agriculture and herding described above. The elements of production—wool, dyes, designs, and looms—are owned by carpet factories, wool merchants, and entrepreneurs in Kirman City. Each carpet is subsidized through several processes—washing, sorting, dyeing, carding, spinning, weaving, and clipping—by these urbanites. Craftsmen are paid a subsistence wage for their labor; the profits are accumulated by the entrepreneurs and merchants. The production process may be organized in several different ways depending on the size of the carpet firm.

The largest carpet firms in Kirman City keep a stable of designers, draftsmen, and weavers, and own dye-houses and weaving factories, some with as many as forty or fifty looms. These firms hire the best weavers from villages and towns throughout the province and bring them to Kirman. When the demand for carpets is great, there is a lively competition for master weavers. Wages are high, the weavers are given houses rent-free, and a subsidy is granted to the weaver conditional upon his continued work. But master weavers are few and the demand for Kirmani carpets is declining, so that this system of operation is confined to a few large, well-established weaving houses in Kirman, the only firms capable of controlling the entire production process.

More commonly, the large carpet firms in Kirman City (particularly those owned by Europeans) sign contracts for the production of a certain number of carpets of specified design, color, and size, with weaving entrepreneurs, middlemen, and brokers who are active members in the weaving guilds. Such a man controls anywhere from ten to one hundred weavers in Kirman City and surrounding weaving centers through debt and/or influence. The carpet firm supplies all materials to this subcontractor except for the loom; he in turn negotiates contracts with individual weavers, handles the distribution of materials to them, and oversees the production of the carpets. The entrepreneur's success depends on careful administration of contracts and the production of high-quality, well-woven carpets. His value is measured by his ability to detect faulty weaving and synthetic dyes and his vigor in urging the weavers to work quickly and well. Individual contracts are negotiated for each carpet by the carpet firm and the entrepreneur. The price varies with the design, color, and density of the carpet. Complicated designs such as the famous teardrop pattern are expensive. Those with many colors or great density are also expensive.

The entrepreneur negotiates a contract with the weaver for the desired carpet. In a typical contract, the entrepreneur supplies the weaver with dyed wool already spun into yarn and warp threads. If the entrepreneur supplies the loom, the weaver must rent it. The weaver is paid in six or seven installments. The initial payment is given before he begins, when an agreement has been reached. It usually amounts to about 10% of the total contract. Other payments are made as the work progresses, and the final payment when the carpet is completed. This last payment is adjusted to account for any defects in weaving which lessen the value of the carpet. The unit of payment in Kirman is 16,000 knots (*sad nishan*), 100 rows each 160 knots in length. A skillful weaver can produce 16,000 knots a day, for which he is paid from 50 to 60 rials ($.66 to $.80). The monthly income of a trained weaver therefore is less than $20, a small fraction of the carpet's market value.

The alternatives to these contracts for a weaver are few; thus non-contract weavers are a minority in Kirman. Carpets woven by private weavers are usually of inferior (70/35) quality and may contain numerous defects. Private weavers cannot afford to purchase the wool for an entire carpet from one lot; hence variations in color and density lessen its value. Also because the *jufti* knot (tying four warp threads together instead of two) is nearly impossible to detect once the carpet is woven, carpet firms and customers are reluctant to buy carpets of questionable origin.

IMPACT OF URBAN DOMINANCE ON RURAL SETTLEMENTS

The major influence of urban dominance on rural settlements in the Kirman Basin is to retard independent town and village economic growth and specialization. Carpet designs are uniform in all settlements and cropping patterns vary little from place to place, because economic activity is standardized by the urban elite. What specialization does exist, such as concentration of herding in mountain hamlets, Langar, and Jupar, is directly related to differences in local environments. In every economic sphere, rural settlements are drained of vitality by contracts which concentrate profits in the city. But local economic organization does exist in the larger towns and villages. For the most part this activity is administrative rather than wealth-producing. It regulates resource use, but does not represent the interests of peasants vis-à-vis urban landlords or merchants. Its minor importance as compared with city-town or city-village economic activity needs to be emphasized, because the importance of internal village organization has been overstated in the Middle Eastern literature.

Village Farming Organization

In large rural settlements, formal village-level decisions regulate the rotation and distribution of water, the dates of sowing and rotation of cropland, the levying of dues and taxes to support local officials and service personnel, and the appointment of village officials such as the water distributor and crop-watcher. In smaller settlements cooperation on these matters is handled informally.

The most critical community decisions involve the water supply. Some of these, such as the rotation of water, are determined by tradition. Others such as the maintenance of qanats are recurring problems which vary with winter rains, summer dust storms, and the local water table. In Mahan, formal meetings of the owners (both resident and nonresident) of each qanat are held to decide maintenance questions when the flow of the qanat is decreasing; each owner has a vote proportionate to his share in the total flow of the qanat.

Water distribution is another constant problem in the larger settlements, where water must be guided through a maze of channels to the right field at the right time. This is the task of that locally appointed official, the water distributor. He is a respected and trusted man, locally called "the bailiff of water" (*mubashiri ab*), who is appointed by vote of water owners. His duties involve not only supervision of water distribution but administration of the reserve fund for qanat repair and regulation of disputes rising out of conflicting water rights. Where variations in crop combinations exist, the water distributor administers all borrowing and trading of water within the rotation system. He knows when each owner needs water, where it can be acquired, and what terms will effect an exchange. His salary is derived from these water arrangements; hence he is often called "the water dealer."

Local regulation is also necessary in decisions relating to land use within each village. The dates of plowing and sowing and cropping patterns must be coordinated with water distribution so that needs and supply are in balance. Winter grains are rotated in large blocks to take advantage of existing irrigation networks. The number of large blocks is determined by local topography, soils, and ownership conditions. Such coordination requires conformity on the part of the individual owner to village-level decisions and contributes to the homogeneity of cropping patterns from place to place. The specific choice of crop is still decided by the owner, but the food needs of most peasant families, soil and water conditions, and other factors make it essential that the principal effort be expended on producing winter grains. There is greater individual choice in the selection of summer crops.

In settlements where cultivated fields are extensive, another local official, the crop-watcher, is found. This office represents a local community solution to the problem of insecurity; thus, the crop-watcher is elected locally by the peasantry with the concurrence of the village owners. He is charged with protecting village crops against damage and theft, and sleeps in a small, round, adobe hut in the middle of the fields. The crop-watcher is paid by deductions from the harvest or a fixed wage in cash or kind, amounting to about 5,000 rials ($67) per year.

The regulatory nature of village-level cooperation is apparent. It is probable that constant demands of maintaining qanats, protecting crops, and regulating water distribution and cropping patterns encouraged such coordination and proved its necessity. Without it, the potential size of settlements would be severely limited. In the one settlement in the region where administration failed, chaos resulted. At Sehkunj shortage of irrigation water led to a duplication of water deeds by the owners, so that water claims exceeded water supply. No decision was reached concerning water regulation, and distribution is now decided by lots cast daily by the farmers. The farmer with the last hour's water is responsible for distribution, and his day is spent attempting to prevent others from taking water; if he fails, he gets no water and so tries to steal it from another man the next day. The situation is so confused that no local official will become involved. As a result, farmers have begun to leave Sehkunj to work as sharecroppers in nearby villages. The importance of village-level organization is emphasized by this example, but such organization should not be confused with creative economic activity.

Other Village-Level Organization

In weaving, guilds regulate some economic activity in the regional subcenters and large alluvial fan villages (see pp. 319–21). As in agriculture, guilds do not represent members in dealings with the carpet firms of Kirman City, except when a guild leader is also a weaving contractor. The guilds do not press weaving factories to pay higher wages or provide better working conditions. They function as cooperative societies, and their powers are limited by the contract system through which weavers deal individually and directly with the carpet factory or one of its agents.

As in Kirman City, rural guilds limit knowledge of the weaving craft to guild members and control entrance into the profession by the apprenticeship system. They also arbitrate disputes among guild members and between guildsmen and outsiders. But guild control is less restrictive in these rural areas than it is in the city. Some farmers work part-time at low rates (on a piecework basis) for professional weavers during the winter. In many households women and children weave carpets and spin yarn while the men work in the fields. Full-time professional weavers will accept a farmer's son or daughter as an apprentice if paid for their trouble. In theory the guild exercises restrictive control, but in practice it is lenient, particularly since the use of spinning machines in Kirman City has caused greater competition for apprentice positions in Mahan and Jupar.

The principal functions of rural weaving guilds are social. If a weaver dies, guild members are present at the grave and efforts are made to find work for his widow and children. If a weaver is ill, other weavers devote hours to his loom so that the family will still receive income. Guild members attend religious ceremonies and social events together and march as a group in religious processions during the month of Muharram. In one settlement, Mahan, there is a specific shrine dedicated to weavers which is rarely used by farmers or herders. Essentially, rural guilds protect the welfare of their members without economic restrictions; they provide some measure of security to a weaver where the larger economic system provides none.

There is no local organization in herding comparable to those in agriculture or weaving. The very nature of this activity, its dependence on migration to and from grazing areas, disperses shepherds and their flocks over wide areas and precludes such a development.

11. *Aq Kupruk: A Town in North Afghanistan*

PART I: THE PEOPLE AND THEIR CULTURAL PATTERNS

"People have lived here since the world began," said the Tajik *rish-i-safid* (literally "White Beard," or, figuratively, a respected old man), when asked about the first appearance of man in Aq Kupruk. The old Tajik's pride of region would not let him think that Allah neglected Aq Kupruk in the original act of creation; and man did in fact come to the area quite some time ago. During three separate archaeological-ethnographical research periods in Aq Kupruk (in fall 1959, summer 1962, and summer 1965), I found evidence of continuous occupation going back at least to the Upper Paleolithic (probably fifteen to twenty thousand years ago), and the area may indeed have been one of the very early centers for the development of agriculture (wheat and barley) and the domestication of animals (sheep, goats, and cattle).[1] Also, for centuries, until a decade or two ago, a main north-south, commercial-nomadic route went through Aq Kupruk. Then, three years ago, further changes occurred which forced Aq Kupruk into a process of deurbanization: a town becoming a village, rather than the more usual, other-way-round pattern.

Reprinted by permission of the author and publisher, with minor textual revisions and omissions, and omission of photographs, from American Universities Field Staff, Reports Service, *South Asia Series*, Vol. 10, nos. 9 and 10, 1966.

[1] Louis Dupree, "An Archaeological Survey of North Afghanistan," *Afghanistan*, 15 (3): 13–15 (Kabul: 1960); Louis Dupree and Bruce Howe, "Results of an Archaeological Survey for Stone Age Sites in North Afghanistan," *Afghanistan*, 18 (2): 1–15 (Kabul: 1963); Louis Dupree, "Prehistoric Surveys and Excavations in Afghanistan, 1959–60 and 1961–63," *Science* 146 (3644): 638–40 (Washington: 1964).

The processes of urbanization, especially that accompanying the rapid shift from the agrarian Middle Ages to the Industrial Revolution, have fascinated generations of European scholars.[2] American social scientists (sociologists, anthropologists, psychologists) have, for at least sixty-five years, explored the cause and effect of the great burst of energy which led to the complexities and contradictions of American urbanization, and the recent trends toward deurbanization brought about by shifts in commercial activity and changes in routes of communication. What happened at Aq Kupruk relates to some universal processes of urban change—yet is different in several distinct ways.

THE DEVELOPMENT OF URBAN CENTERS

Before man learned to control his food supply through agriculture and the domestication of animals, he was merely one more animal chasing others or grubbing for roots and berries. The game he hunted and the wild plants he gathered dictated his roaming patterns. He lived in caves in winter, often moving to open-air camp sites in summer; but whether in caves or in the open, Stone Age man lived near water, which both the hunters and the hunted needed for survival. Major ecological changes between eleven to nine thousand years ago probably established climatic patterns as we know them today and forced prehistoric man to make drastic adjustments. Man at last began to control his food supply.

The first agriculturists and herdsmen probably developed in the hills in an altitudinal (500 to 1,500 meters above sea level), latitudinal (34° to 40° N), ecological zone stretching from the northern Hindu Kush mountains of Afghanistan to Anatolia, and possibly to Greece. Food surpluses enabled man to settle down, and overpopulation forced him to move to the riverine valleys where towns developed based on the development of full-time

[2] Marc Bloch, *Feudal Society, Part I: The Growth of Ties of Independence; Part II: Social Classes and Political Organization* (London: Routledge and Kegan Paul, 1965); Fustel de Coulanges, *The Ancient City* (Garden City: Anchor Books, first published 1873); Henri Pirenne, *Medieval Cities* (Garden City: Anchor Books, first published 1925). Also see, John H. Mundy and Peter Riesenberg, *The Medieval Town* (Princeton: Van Nostrand, 1958).

specialists (potters, weavers, dyers, metallurgists, masons, priests, etc.) and supported by the surrounding village farmers and nomadic herdsmen. The larger towns developed into administrative, commercial, and communication centers, and the mutual interdependence of city-town-village-nomad still exists in Afghanistan and most of the modern Middle East. These terms require definition:

Village: A self-sufficient subsistence unit, but one which must obtain many necessities (e.g., iron, cloth, tea, sugar) from either a town bazaar or itinerant peddlers. Almost no full-time specialists are found in a village, although there are many part-time specialists, such as carpenters, brickmakers, and *mullahs.* These men practice their specialties after finishing their farm work.

Town: The lowest commercial, administrative, and communication center. Usually, raw materials from the village are brought to a town and then shipped to the cities by truck, camel, or donkey. Here the lower-grade civil servants and quasi-military police have headquarters. Often, landlords owning land in the surrounding villages also live in the towns. Finished products are brought from the cities to the town, which always has a bazaar street, frequently the main—and sometimes only—street. Full-time specialists (ironmongers, potters, weavers, dyers) generally live above their shops in the bazaar.

City: The major commercial, administrative, and communication center, which also serves as the link with the outside world. Large numbers of guildlike specialists live in separate sections of extensive bazaar areas in the "old city." Individual artisans and, more recently, factories produce items for export and for sale in town bazaars. A provincial governor, his staff, and a major army garrison are normally stationed in the "new city." Courts administer justice under the Constitution and Islamic laws. The city grows rapidly; the town, more slowly; while the village continues as always, sending both surplus crops and population to the towns and cities.

The above refers to completely sedentary folk. Three other categories have developed:

Semi-sedentary farmers: Agriculturists who own a few head of livestock which are moved in the summer to highland pastures and returned to the permanent villages in the winter.

Nomads: Herdsmen who seasonally move in a group from summer to winter pasturages and back again.

Semi-nomads: Herdsmen who practice agriculture. A sizable portion of the group move with their livestock to summer pasturage, while the remainder tend some crops in the winter headquarters.

THE CULTURAL PATTERNS OF AQ KUPRUK

Like most of northern Afghanistan, Aq Kupruk lies in a mixed ethnic zone, and several different groups live in and around the town. The *rish-i-safidan* claimed 300 households for Aq Kupruk in 1965, the same number as in 1959 (the year when I first visited the town), but I find this hard to believe, for many houses and compounds have emptied and slowly crumbled since then, becoming sites for future archaeologists. The town elders claim the following: about 200 Tajik houses; 50 Uzbek, 50 Sayyid (*Sa'adat*) and Khoja; and one extended family of Afghans (Safi Pushtuns). In the hills surrounding the valley of Aq Kupruk live Hazara (mainly Dai Zangi) and a few Moghul groups (some of the old men south of Aq Kupruk speak Mongolian).[3]

All groups agree that the Turkic-speaking Uzbeks were in the area first, but the lingua franca is a Tajiki-Persian and Uzbeki mixture, with the Tajiki element dominant. Although Uzbeks do speak Uzbeki Turkish in their homes, they are all bilingual. The inhabitants in and around Aq Kupruk exhibit varying degrees of Mongoloid physical traits, indicating intensive miscegenation, but the separate ethnic groups still prefer in-group marriages.

The Tajiks, who live in the southern watershed of the Hindu Kush (i.e., the Andarab and Panjshir valleys), seldom have Mongoloid features, and speak Persian dialects void of Uzbeki influences.

The Sayyid (*Sa'adat*) and Khoja groups present interesting

---

[3] André Mariq and Gaston Wiet, "Le minaret de Djam, La découverte de la capitale des sultans Ghorides (XIIe–XIIIe siècles)," *Mémoires de la Délégation Archéologique Française en Afghanistan,* Volume XVI (Paris: 1959); H. F. Schurmann, *The Mongols of Afghanistan,* Central Asian Studies IV ('s-Gravenhage: Meuten and Company, 1962). Also see review of Schurmann by Klaus Ferdinand in *Acta Orientalia* XXVIII, 1–2 (1964), pp. 175–203.

problems. Sayyids are traditionally supposed to be descendants of the Prophet Mohammed through his daughter, Fatima, and his nephew and son-in-law, Ali. The Khojas, according to Aq Kuprukis, are the descendants of the first Caliph, Abu Bakr.[4] Four separate units of Khojas exist, but only one, the Shahniya, is found in Aq Kupruk. Probably none of the Sayyids in Aq Kupruk are truly Sayyid. None speak Arabic, and most are Mongoloid-looking. They are probably simply Tajiks whose forefathers adopted the Sayyid title to enhance their prestige; but, more importantly, the Sayyids of Aq Kupruk and the other Aq Kuprukis believe the local Sayyids to be descendants of the Prophet.

The origins of the Khojas in Aq Kupruk present a more complex problem. Like the Sayyids, the Khojas are found throughout the Islamic world. In India and Pakistan they are the followers of the Aga Khan and are Shi'ites, whereas all the Aq Kupruki Khojas declare themselves to be Sunni. Incidentally, all the people in Aq Kupruk now claim to be Sunni, although in 1962 one family told me that they were Ismai'ili Shi'ites (another name for Khoja). Either the Khojas of Aq Kupruk are Tajiks passing as descendants of the Caliph Abu Bakr or they are Ismai'ili Shi'ites practicing *taqiya* (i.e., denying that one is a Shi'ite under duress or for advantage, but remaining pure in belief). I believe the Aq Kupruki Khojas to be Tajiks, whose ancestors, like those of the Aq Kupruki Sayyids, have adopted titles without knowing the true meaning in order to improve their prestige. Some of the Sayyids and Khojas, however, claim that their ancestors came first from Arabia to Bokhara in Russian Turkistan and then to Aq Kupruk. Originally, the Afghan Tajiks and Uzbeks probably did come from the Central Asian area.

The single family of Safi Pushtuns were moved forcibly to Aq Kupruk in 1949 after the unsuccessful Safi revolt against the government, which split up the dissident Safis and sent them to many parts of north Afghanistan. The Aq Kuprukis refer to all Pushtuns as "Afghans," in spite of the government's campaign to convince all ethnic groups to consider themselves Afghans first. Uzbeks, Tajiks, and Hazara still refer to themselves as Uzbek, Tajik, and Hazara—but they always call Pushtuns "Afghans." If

---

[4] Abu Bakr served as the first Caliph of Mecca (A.D. 632–34) after the death of Mohammed.

non-Pushtuns are reminded that they are Afghans, too, they deny it, preferring their old tribal names. The Safi Pushtuns have intermarried with the Tajiks and often refer to themselves as Tajiks in Aq Kupruk, but always as Afghans outside the town—for example, when they travel to the provincial capital, Mazar-i-Sharif.

In 1962, seven mosques, including two large ones, served the religious needs of the Aq Kuprukis. With the one exception previously mentioned, all the inhabitants claim to be Sunni, and the Shi'ite family of 1962 subsequently departed and moved to the Buina Qara area (a fact which in itself contradicts the claim of the town elders that no one moved during the shift of administrative capitals).

By 1965 the number of mosques increased to eleven: Id Gah (the major mosque, from which the principle Friday sermons are delivered); Madrasah (which also functions as the mosque school); Alakadari (situated near the local administrative center); Bazaar (situated in the commercial center of town); Turighar; Donai Julgah; Lahmi; Sorkhtan; and two small *masjids* (mosques) with no local names. Most of these mosques have *mullahs* (religious leaders) who are also farmers. Only the five largest have full-time *mullahs*.

Although technically forbidden in Islam, saints continue to proliferate, and five *ziarats* (shrines) exist in Aq Kupruk. At many shrines Afghans hold annual festivals in honor of the saint, who is usually famous for one miracle or another. For example, the saint buried at a shrine near Charikar, forty kilometers north of Kabul, specializes in curing mad dog bites, and anyone visiting the site after being bitten by a rabid animal is guaranteed a cure. Of course, the trip often involves several weeks, so the individual will either be dead from rabies before he reaches the shrine or will prove to have been bitten by a non-rabid animal. In the latter case, the saint gets the credit for another cure. Near Jalalabad in eastern Afghanistan there is a shrine for curing madness; and north of Kabul's airport in the valley of Paiminar, about forty shrines devoted to fertility exist. On certain days buses ply back and forth between Kabul and Paiminar, laden with women who desire children, particularly sons.

The people of Aq Kupruk know surprisingly little about their shrines, none of which has special festival days. The first, called *Ziarat-i-Chopan Khoja*, sits on a hill northeast of Aq Kupruk. According to several *rish-i-safidan*, an inscribed marble tombstone existed there in the days of their fathers, but it disappeared decades ago. No one knows anything about the saint. Another shrine, the *Ziarat-i-Shaheed Baba*, near the home of one of the local carpenters, houses a saint presumably killed (for *shaheed* refers to someone who has been killed), but again the people know nothing of his life and accomplishments. Two more shrines are located near the bazaar: the *Ziarat-i-Khosh Awleah* and the *Ziarat-i-Bazaar;* but the only shrine with any definite stories connected with it is the *Ziarat-i-Khoja Boland*, near the *Ziarat-i-Shaheed Baba* mentioned above.

The Khoja Boland, who it seems was a saintly soldier, always warns the Aq Kuprukis by firing a rifle when danger threatens. A recent example can be cited: A cholera epidemic occurred in north Afghanistan during the summer of 1965, and the Aq Kuprukis held a *kheyrat* to ward off the evil spirits causing the disease. (A *kheyrat* is a ritual feast to which all the local population contributes. The best cooks [always men] prepare a large meal, including a sweet *halwa*, and all men attend and eat the food, always sending some to the women and children.) On this occasion, the local religious leaders asked Allah to look down at His people being brotherly and loving, and to please keep cholera away from the town. The Aq Kuprukis hoped that this magic would work—but four people still died of cholera when the epidemic reached the town. According to many, Khoja Boland fired his rifle in the early afternoon before the first death to announce the coming of the plague. Ear-witnesses swore on the Koran that they heard the shot. A few local skeptics scoffed, but most of the people believed.

Each of the shrines in and around Aq Kupruk sports a *panjah* (a band of brass). These occur throughout much of the Muslim world, always associated with the tomb of some saint or other honored personage. Although the function is always the same (to honor the saint), explanations of the origin of the *panjah* vary. In some parts of Afghanistan and Iran, village *mullahs* have told me that the *panjah* represents the hand of Fatima, the daughter of the Prophet Mohammed and the wife of Ali, son-in-law of Mohammed and the fourth Caliph. Once Fatima had touched the earth with her hand, leaving its imprint as she said, "From dust thou art, to dust returneth." In Aq Kupruk, however, the town elders and religious leaders told me that the *panjah* represented the hand of Ali, who visited the area before his death. (Ali, incidentally, is supposed to be buried at Mazar-i-Sharif, which means the "shrine of the Sharif Ali," and he supposedly performed great feats of valor in Afghanistan, especially as a dragon-killer. Almost every locale in Afghanistan contains aberrant rocks, which are dragons killed by Ali and then turned into stone. This Saint George of the Muslim world is also buried in Iraq—probably a more likely tomb site.)

One old Uzbeki *rish-i-safid* of Aq Kupruk told me the following story about Ali: "Many, many years ago—more than I can count —the Hazrat [another honorific title] Ali stood up in north Afghanistan and stretched out his hand. By the will of Allah, he placed his hand on the ground and drew five lines. These five lines became the five major valleys of north Afghanistan, with mountains to separate them. Water flowed down the five valleys, and one, the Ab-i-Band-i-Amir, came past Aq Kupruk. From these five valleys the water flowed onto other areas until all 366 valleys in north Afghanistan were watered. The *panjah* we place on a *ziarat* gives thanks to Allah for his bountiful mercy, praises Hazrat Ali for his good works, and does honor to the *pir* [saint] in the *ziarat.*"

Bits of gaily colored cloth flutter from the *ziarats*, for when a petitioner visits a shrine, he or she asks the saint to intercede with Allah to grant a favor, and then ties a bit of cloth to the shrine as a reminder to the saint. In some areas (though not at Aq Kupruk), shrines are equipped with notches for candles or pottery lamps, which are burned in much the same manner as candles in Roman Catholic churches, after a blessing or favor has been requested or granted.

I was surprised not to see the horns of wild goats or sheep on the *ziarats* at Aq Kupruk. Over most of the Iranian Plateau's subcultural areas (Iran, Afghanistan, Soviet Central Asia, northern West Pakistan), the faithful decorate shrines and mosques with goat and sheep horns, but no one really knows why. When asked, the people variously reply: "It is custom"; "It is to honor the saint"; or "It is for decoration." One old man in Aq Kupruk told me that he had put horns over his father's grave to identify it from among all the identical graves which lie on three separate hillsides outside Aq Kupruk.

However, the cult of the mountain goat goes back at least to Mousterian times in Central Asia,[5] and has had a wide distribution ever since.[6] Probably the origins of the cult were related to the prehistoric belief in the totemic efficacy of the vigorous mountain goat—admired for his strength and stamina in a harsh terrain. Presumably, the early practitioners of the cult believed that the strength of the animal could be passed on to honored men for use in the afterlife.

In other areas of Afghanistan wild sheep and goats still abound, and hunters say that they put the horns of their better kills on graves in order to ask a saint for the same luck in future hunting —thus combining magic with religion.

Today, only pigeons, doves, quail, and the Chuker partridge are hunted near Aq Kupruk. In the mountains, local hunters near Tring hunt mountain gazelle and ibex.

The oldest Aq Kuprukis informed me, however, that in the days of their fathers many mountain goat horns decorated the local *ziarats,* but that the hill villagers (i.e., the Hazara) stole the horns and placed them on the shrines of their saints—a clear case of stealing supernatural power from one place and moving it to another. The horns, as described, were probably chiefly those of ibex and markhor.

A belief in witches and witchcraft also exists, but it is little talked about. Old women past menopause would often turn into witches and place curses on individuals through the medium of straw dolls; but, said the *rish-i-safidan,* the last witch was stoned to death "long ago in the days of our fathers." Still, all men wiggled uncomfortably when they spoke of witches or witchcraft,

[5] Hallam L. Movius, Jr., *The Mousterian Cave of Teshik-Tash, Southeastern Uzbekistan, Central Asia,* American School of Prehistoric Research, Bulletin 17 (Cambridge: 1953).

[6] Karl Jettmar, "Ethnological Research in Dardistan, 1958, Preliminary Report," *Proceedings of the American Philosophical Society,* Vol. 105, No. 1, pp. 79–97 (1961).

and several of the illiterate, part-time *mullahs* admitted that, if necessary, they knew rituals to counter the evil spells of witches.

From the foregoing discussion, it is obvious that much animism still exists along with Islam, and has indeed been integrated into local Islamic beliefs.

Another surprising feature of Islam in Aq Kupruk is the number of the men over twenty who have made the *hajj* (pilgrimage) to the paramount holy city of Mecca. In the Alakadari (District) of Kishindi (Aq Kupruk is actually the capital of the Alakadari of Kishindi), over 1,000 men (out of the officially estimated male population of 19,005) had made the *hajj*, an indication of the relative wealth of this area when compared with the rest of Afghanistan and the Middle East in general.

LAND TENURE AND AGRICULTURAL PRACTICES

Seventy per cent of the 1,500 Aq Kupruk males own land, the average holding being about 10 *jiribs* (one *jirib* equals a half-acre). The remaining 30 per cent work as tenant farmers. With some modifications, the classic "fiver" system operates here. Under this system, the landlord and tenant supposedly get one-fifth of the crop for each of the five elements furnished: land, water, seed, animals, labor. However, even if the landlord furnishes four of the five elements in Aq Kupruk (land, water, seed, and animals), the tenant still gets one-half of any crop for his labor. If the tenant furnishes water, seed, and animals, as well as labor, he gets five-sixths or four-fifths, depending on the annual contract he can extract from his landlord. If the typical landlord in Aq Kupruk furnishes more than land, he usually also furnishes seed, animals, and water. Conversely, a tenant seldom furnishes labor plus only one other element; he will usually also furnish animals, seed, and water. There are few instances of two-fifths or three-fifths of a crop being shared. Almost always the tenant's share is one-half or four-fifths—again a sign of relative affluence in the valley.

Both *abi* (irrigated) and *lalmi* (mountainside) crops are grown. A thick cover of loess blankets the hillsides of northern and central Afghanistan, and annually more of this rich aeolian deposit pours down from Russian Central Asia. Nature has been

giving Afghanistan tons of Russian topsoil for eons in an involun-
tary assistance program, and the Russians can do nothing about
it. The loess is blown down during the summer months, and
sometimes hangs in the air for days—blocking out the sun, creep-
ing into clothing, settling on the skin, and making the teeth gritty.
But it helps account for the farming wealth of Aq Kupruk and
its neighboring villages.

The major crops grown are *lalmi* wheat (at times on the tops
of mud huts), corn, *gasnitch* (coriander), *zera* (cuminseed),
some *abi* cotton (on about 15 *jiribs*, all owned by one man), and
lalmi melons of various types. Farmers harvest crops during the
summer, with the exception of *abi* vegetables (turnips, onions,
carrots, and eggplants), which are harvested in early fall.

The diet of the people reflects the local resources. The round,
unleavened Uzbek-type bread forms the staple. Aq Kuprukis seldom bake daily, so the bread hardens rapidly and must be dunked
in water or tea to make it edible. Goat and mutton vie for the
meat honors, along with chicken; and occasionally beef is also
eaten by the Aq Kuprukis. (The transient nomads, however, kill
lambs and kids for meat, saving the adult herds for breeding
and dairy products.) For breakfast, the typical farmer will have
bread dunked in green or black tea, imported from Pakistan,
India, or China. Sugar is a luxury that few can afford, but *mast*
(yoghurt) and other dairy products such as *krut* (dried curds)
and *kruti* (curds boiled in *rogon-i-dumbah*—lard from fat-tailed
sheep) are also popular. Cooks prepare food in either *rogon-i-
dumbah* or, rarely, *rogon-i-zard*, a clarified butter called *ghee* in
India and Pakistan and often referred to by that name in Afghanistan.

The Aq Kuprukis eat all foods with their right hands; the left
hand being reserved for the excretory and other "less sanitary"
functions. People eat from a communal dish, while sitting cross-
legged on the floor or on a *takht* (a high wooden bench which
supports several people). *Shurwa* (a thick meat and tomato
soup, with the meat eaten as a side dish) is a popular luncheon
or dinner dish. Chunks of unleavened bread float in the soup,
soaking up the liquid, and the diners pick out the soaked bread
with their fingers. The Aq Kuprukis eat locally grown and imported melons in season, and grapes are brought in from the out-

side, primarily from Sangcharak to the west and Mazar-i-Sharif to the north. Rice is also brought in from the outside, and rice dishes—such as *pilau* (with mutton and sometimes raisins) and *chilau* (without meat)—are popular, although few can afford them daily. Another popular dish consists of a scrambled mixture of eggs, tomatoes, and onions, floating in *rogon-i-dumbah*. (Several merchants, using stone mortars and pestles, pound local rock salt, an important item in the diet, into palatable size.)

The cuisine of Aq Kupruk represents a mixture of the Iranian Plateau and Central Asian types. Noodle dishes have wide distribution, and scholars still argue over the origin of the spaghetti-noodle complex: i.e., whether it originated in China or Italy. In any event, noodle dishes spread in a belt running from China to Italy, probably during the heyday of the Silk Route trade, which reached its peak in the early Christian centuries. In Aq Kupruk, Uzbeks in particular eat *arsh* (a noodle dish cooked with *mast*) and *arshak* (a ravioli filled with meat, cheese, or leeks).

The Aq Kuprukis literally "eat crow." Large Central Asian ravens inhabit the limestone cliffs near the town and periodically make massive forays into the fields of corn and other seed crops. The Aq Kuprukis, in turn, hunt these rapacious creatures and eat them. I must admit that fat, corn-fed crow is delicious. We hunted them for our workmen and often downed more than ten with one shot, so thick did they cluster along the trail. Our workmen, knives open, would rush to slit the throats of the wounded birds, thereby making them *halal* (or ritually clean). Those killed by the shotgun blast were left for us, because they were *haram* (unclean). Muslims cannot eat meat unless the animal has been killed by cutting its throat.

The hygienic habits of the Aq Kuprukis would horrify most sanitarians, for the whole world constitutes an outhouse; but in spite of what Westerners would call unsanitary conditions, the Aq Kuprukis lead relatively healthy lives, because of the adequate diet and high and dry ecological situation. Of course, infant mortality and death from childbed fever are high. No one knows exactly how high, but I know one workman who had had five wives and twenty-seven children, out of which one wife and seven children now survive.

One local custom helped the spread of the 1965 cholera epidemic. The townsmen placed anyone with a high fever in a *jui* (an irrigation canal, which also provides drinking water), so the germs rapidly transmitted the disease to downstream villages. Malaria, until recently, caused about a 50-per-cent work loss, but the efforts of the United Nations and of Afghans trained by World Health Organization teams have made great improvements in the Aq Kupruk area. Whereas malaria constituted a major health hazard in 1962, it had practically disappeared by 1965.

Gastrointestinal diseases abound and flourish, and continue to debilitate sizable segments of the population. We spent much of our time in Aq Kupruk practicing medicine without licenses and giving advice and drugs for dysentery and diarrhea.

SHELTER AND CLOTHING

House types in Aq Kupruk also reflect a mixture of Iranian Plateau and Central Asian origins. The rectangular houses are constructed of sun-dried mud bricks or *pisé* (pressed mud), and they usually have several rooms leading off a long veranda-like porch. Pressed-mud walls surround the compounds to ensure privacy. The better-off Aq Kuprukis have special guest rooms where they entertain, and where guests may spend the night. Storerooms are often dug into hillsides in order to keep perishables cool; and in the house itself scrubby bushes from the mountains are placed over the open windows and then wet down, so that the evaporation process will cool the rooms.

No potters live in Aq Kupruk and the earthenware jars, jugs, and bowls come from Buina Qara and Mazar-i-Sharif. The semi-porousware allows some of the water to seep through the jugs and evaporate, keeping the water cool.

A second major house type, the *khedgah*, a variety of portable *yurt* (a circular tent covered with felt or skins) reminds one of the Central Asian nomadic past of the Uzbeks. None of the Uzbeks of Aq Kupruk follow nomadic lives today, but the *khedgah* still functions as a comfortable summer house. Many Uzbeks and Tajiks in Aq Kupruk put up *khedgahs* inside their compounds, and live in them during the hot summer months. In addition, farmers move to their highland (*lalmi*) fields in the summer, taking their families on donkeys and camels. There they set up the *khedgahs* on hilltops, and live in them while they reap, thresh, and winnow wheat.

Usually farmers complete their harvesting in less than a month, and have moved back down the mountain to their compounds in Aq Kupruk by September. The *khedgahs* are easier to keep clean than mud huts, and on the inside personal belongings hang from wooden hooks supported by the frame, or are stored in intricately carved and painted wooden chests, another specialty of the Sangcharak Hazara.

The mixed ethnic picture in Aq Kupruk is again reflected in clothing, which can no longer be used to identify a specific group. Uzbeks wear the Tajik turban cap (*kola*) and Tajiks wear Uzbeki headgear, while anyone who can afford a gold-embroidered turban from Qandahar wears one. The men wear locally made, long-bottomed cotton shirts which slip over the head and button at the right shoulder. When working, they tuck these shirts into their wide-waisted, pajama-like trousers. They wear either local sandals (often made from old automobile tires) or embroidered shoes from Sangcharak. Shoemakers in Mazar-i-Sharif produce Western-style shoes, especially the pointed Italian variety which are popular among the younger men. Wearers of Russian-made rubber overshoes and boots increase year by year, and many prefer to wear these all the time. Uzbek horsemen wear ankle-high (and sometimes higher) riding boots, distinctive to the Central Asian Steppes. Most men sport either a waistcoat, embroidered in the local style, or a secondhand Western vest. Others purchase secondhand Western sports coats or suit jackets. In fact, much of the secondhand clothing of the Western world seems to end up in the bazaars of Afghanistan. Surplus uniform jackets are especially popular, and I have seen men wearing, among many others, World War I high-necked tunics of the U.S. First and Second Divisions; World War II Eighth Air Force officers' blouses complete with silver wings, the ubiquitous DFC, the Air Medal (with three oak-leaf clusters), and the ETO ribbon with battle stars; patches of the U.S. Marine Corps First, Fifth, and Sixth Divisions; officers' coats of the Merchant Marine and U.S. Navy; and RAF and West Point greatcoats. Afghan regulations prohibit the import of uniforms, so merchants arrange for shipments to be sent to Pakistan, and smugglers bring the goods across the border. A wristwatch, whether it works or not, serves as a major prestige item, and so does a fountain pen, or simply the top of a fountain pen clipped to a coat. (Literacy in Aq Kupruk probably does not exceed 2 per cent.)

Women wear traditional clothing without any sign of Westernization, flowered cloth being the most popular material. Only a few well-to-do Uzbek ladies wear a *chadri* or *burqa,* the sacklike garment which covers the body from head to toe. The *burqa,* while rapidly disappearing in the larger urban areas of Afghanistan since 1959, has been making a comeback in the smaller provincial towns—quite a reversal of social values. Until recently no women in the villages and nomadic camps—and few in the towns—wore the *burqa.* They did wear head shawls, which could be coyly drawn down over the face if a stranger approached. (Women still turn away from strangers in most towns and villages, but their "brazenness" in the cities alarms not only traditionalists but also liberal-minded, middle-class parents.)

The wearing of the *burqa,* once an exclusively citified custom, reaches down to some towns, especially in north Afghanistan, as a prestige item, which in itself contradicts one of the original reasons for the *burqa*: that is, that rich and poor women could look alike, for the garment hid both wealth and poverty. Even in the past, however, those who could afford them purchased fancy embroidered, silk *burqas* instead of plain cotton ones. The original function of modesty and egalitarianism before Allah has been lost, and the wealthier Uzbeks (who are stricter than the Tajiks) clothe their women in fancy *burqas* when they come to town. This is an interesting example of an apparently worldwide tendency of certain provincial townspeople to adopt obsolete or dying city customs in order to appear sophisticated and citified in their own eyes.

WORK AND THE LIFE CYCLE

Women's work in Aq Kupruk mainly consists of cooking (although the husbands consider themselves the better cooks and prepare meals for guests) and of mending and washing clothing.

The washing is done in iron vats full of boiling water near the riverside, where the clothes are strongly beaten to clean them and soap is seldom used. Women also work in the fields at the peak harvest time, moving with their families to the hilltop *khedgahs*.

The responsibility for rearing the children also rests largely with the women, including disciplining them. Fathers, on the other hand, pamper both sons and daughters. Sons receive the bulk of the attention, for they personify the future, whereas the older men represent the past. Grandparents also have a large role in training children, for they have usually ended their active economic functions in the family, and the father-mother generation is constantly at work in the fields or around the home, with little leisure time for the children. The young Aq Kupruki begins to learn his role in society from the time he or she can toddle. The older children take care of the younger ones, and by the time a boy or girl reaches the age of eight or nine, he or she helps to watch over the family livestock as well. By their early teens, boys are working with their fathers and girls with their mothers as full-fledged producing units of the family.

In addition to several *madrasahs* (mosque schools, where the boys learn by rote), two secular schools exist. These secular schools have existed since 1963, one for boys, the other for girls. Classes go only through the third grade, and parents desiring further schooling for their children must send them to Buina Qara, where there are schools for both sexes through the sixth grade. For a high-school education, Mazar-i-Sharif offers the nearest school.

Marriage comes relatively early and usually within the family. The preferred marriage is to the daughter of a father's brother, but often a more distant relative must be accepted. The Aq Kuprukis will admit to no cross-ethnic marriages: Uzbeks, they say, always marry Uzbeks, Tajiks always marry Tajiks, and so on. But miscegenation must take place or the people could not look so homogeneous. The Aq Kupruki Tajiks, for example, would not look so unlike the Panjshiri or Badakhshan Tajiks, who are fundamentally more Caucasoid than the often Mongoloid-looking Tajiks of Aq Kupruk.

Marriage, like birth and death, gives the Aq Kuprukis a chance for close group interaction. Each man and woman is associated with these life crises, and the individual association tends further to unite the group. Although the acts are done one by one, the fact that the group participates makes the crisis more palatable. The *kheyrat* (ritual slaying of livestock and sharing of food) during the cholera epidemic is an illustration of this type of group activity.

At marriage, a boy's family gives his bride's family a specified number of sheep and goats, sometimes cattle, as a "bride price." The girl brings a complete set of clothing as a dowry. Perhaps "bride price" is the wrong term, for actually the two families make an economic exchange—the groom's family gets another good worker and the bride's family loses one, so the livestock compensates for the labor lost. In addition, as cousin usually marries cousin, the goods naturally remain in the same family.

One significant and negative cultural feature characteristic of Afghan villages in general is the lack of the wheel. Some towns and a few villages with potters naturally have the potters' wheel, while others have water-powered or horse-powered millstones. But the oxcart and the horse-drawn *tongas* of the rest of the Middle East and South Asia are absent, except in the larger towns and cities. Recently, however, bicycles and motor vehicles have come to these wheelless towns and villages. In 1959, one lorry a week came to Aq Kupruk carrying mail, government documents, passengers, and commercial items for the bazaar. By 1963, however, the major local administrative center had shifted to Buina Qara, and a Russian jeep made casual trips to Aq Kupruk from Mazar-i-Sharif and Buina Qara—coming whenever enough passengers or cargo could be found. The same jeep still carries the passenger trade, and its owner recently purchased a Russian lorry to ply between Buina Qara and Aq Kupruk. The lorry leaves for Buina Qara only when it makes up a load, and sometimes several days pass before it returns to Aq Kupruk.

Even so, in spite of its relative isolation, Aq Kupruk can now be reached from Kabul in about sixteen hours of hard driving in a jeep or lorry (as compared with three days a few years ago), and from Mazar-i-Sharif in four to five hours (rather than the former eight hours). Improved roads and the new Salang Tunnel through the Hindu Kush (opened in 1964) account for these improved schedules.

SPORT AND PLAY

Entertainment remains scarce in Aq Kupruk. Most men spend at least a part of each day and night in *chai khanehs* (teahouses), drinking tea and passing gossip, or perhaps listening to one of the many transistor radios now to be found in Aq Kupruk. Bazaar shops also provide open forums; customers and shopkeepers spend as much time in socializing as in buying and selling. The two *ruz-i-bazaar* (bazaar days) afford great entertainment as the hillsmen and townsmen meet and interact.

Music plays an important role in the lives of the people, and there are many songs. Love songs (including songs of homosexual love), folk-hero songs, and songs ridiculing other parts of Afghanistan constitute the more important varieties. As in most societies, Aq Kuprukis seem to talk more about sex than actually devote much time to it, but an undetermined amount of homosexuality does exist and extramarital affairs occur with alarming frequency. All this forms a large part of the folk singers' repertoire. In Aq Kupruk there are two famous men who sing and play the *dhamboura*, a plucked, two-stringed instrument. (Dancing plays little or no role in festival fun—unlike the Pushtun areas of eastern and southern Afghanistan, where men and women dance individually and separately.)

There are two other games which have great popularity—with both participants and spectators—in north Afghanistan: *buzkashi* (goat-grabbing) and *palawani* (wrestling). *Buzkashi*, a game of horsemanship which involves two teams, emphasizes individual performance. A goat or, more often, a calf is killed and placed inside a circle drawn upon the ground. Horsemen gather from two teams, which may vary in size from five or ten to a thousand, depending on the size of the field, the event being celebrated, and the amount of prize money to be distributed. In the early fall after harvesting, many Uzbek villages all over north Afghanistan play sand-lot *buzkashi* over ploughed fields. At a given signal, often a rifle shot, the game begins. The horsemen try to pick up the goat or calf and ride with it to a boundary point, then return to drop the carcass in the circle, which is usually outlined with straw and about five feet in diameter. The rules are quite flexible, and the players ride with the élan of their Central Asian ancestors. The ground almost seems to move as they thunder by. Watching the game, one is impressed with the man-horse teamwork and can see how this game provided excellent training for the mobile shock cavalry which developed in Central Asia and which even Alexander the Great could not defeat. (The cavalry Alexander met operated in the manner of the American Plains Indians and rode in circles around his less mobile forces, firing arrows from all angles and positions.) *Buzkashi* can probably best be described as a combination of polo, mounted football, and unorganized mayhem. Cracked skulls are common and quirt-type riding whips draw blood freely from both horses and men. The general tendency seems to be to hit an opponent or an opponent's horse if one gets in a tight squeeze.

Usually, Afghans play *buzkashi* on the wide, open fields, up the hillsides, and even across graveyards. But there is a special style, *buzkashi-i-darya,* played in rivers, which is particularly dangerous and slippery. During *Jeshyn* (the national Afghan holidays in late August) in 1965, the best *chapandaz* (*buzkashi* players) of the Alakadari (District) came in for two days of play in both the *maidan* (field) and *darya* (river). The *chapandaz* rode into Aq Kupruk the day before the games, each riding one horse and leading another. About a hundred horsemen arrived, so there were about fifty players for each side, usually Aq Kupruk versus another area or combination of areas. On the first day, the *chapandaz* played one game on the *maidan* and one in the *darya;* the second day, they played only one game on the *maidan,* where we witnessed the finest displays of horsemanship I have ever seen. Throughout the two days of play, no one was seriously injured, and the *Alakadur* (governor) and the wealthier shopkeepers singled out six excellent riders for special awards.

Although technically a team sport, *buzkashi* honors the individual for scoring goals. After each goal, the crowd showers the scorer with money; and anyone may offer money and a large kerchief as special inducements for each goal before the play begins. The large red kerchiefs are important items of clothing, and a winner often ties the kerchief over his shoulder to publicize his winning efforts. The highest honor is the turban cloth (*lungi*), which is usually given for the final goal.

Wrestling took place in front of the boys' school each day after the *buzkashi*. Both times men from Aq Kupruk wrestled against men from Zari, a nearby village, and both times Aq Kupruk won. Winning wrestlers, like goal-scoring *chapandaz*, receive gifts and prizes. Wrestlers are not chosen before the event; instead the communities to fight form a circle, and the coaches from each area pick out men on the spot. The coaches—retired *palawani* (strong men)—know the relative fighting qualities of the men in their respective villages. But being chosen is an honor which few men accept calmly, for to lose a match means losing face before one's peers, and the entire village also loses face. Thus, a man picked to wrestle often exhibits signs of panic: his eyes roll, his lips tremble, his skin sags, tears come to his eyes, his body slackens, and he prays or moans. The two coaches drag their victims to the center of the ring and stand them side by side to see if they are about the same height and weight. Either coach or either contestant may protest at an overmatch, but usually the glassy-eyed contestants leave the decision to the coaches. If both sides agree, the contestants return to their respective circles of friends who prepare them for the match. Clothing must be arranged in a certain way. A man must wear two turban caps to protect his head if he falls. A *chapon* (many-colored coat) must be worn, with a cummerbund or kerchief tied around the waist, and another cummerbund tucked into the long-tailed shirt underneath the *chapon*. Pajama-like pantaloons complete the costume. The men wrestle barefooted.

Before the action begins, several Aq Kuprukis sprinkle water on the ground to hold down the dust. The two coaches serve as referees and search the contestants for hidden weapons. They constantly watch the wrestlers and each calls the other's attention to fouls committed against his man. The two wrestlers stand apart and pray for Allah's support, touching their chins as a sign of respect and submission to God. Then they advance on each other, formally shake hands (both hands), and bow low to one another. After this, they walk in circles around the edge of the ring of people, loosening up, tucking in their long shirts, stalling for time. The impatient crowd urges them on and they approach one an-

other, rocking from side to side and flailing their arms out-
stretched above their heads—looking, in fact, rather like a pair of
mating scorpions. The whole object is to throw the opponent and
pin his shoulders to the ground. When it seems apparent that one
man has another pinned, the coach of the winner lifts up his man
by the waist and runs around the circle. The victor clasps his
hands over his head and the crowd applauds. The coach then
deposits his man in front of the *Alakadur* and the *rish-i-safidan*
to collect his prize. The opposing coach, however, may enter a
protest, claiming either a foul or a non-pin. The cheers or jests
of the crowd determine whether or not the match continues.
Some matches end quickly, within a few seconds, while others
last for fifteen minutes or more—in which case the contestants
rest during other matches. One bout between an Aq Kupruki and
a Zari proved so evenly matched it took a half hour and three
separate intervals to complete, but most matches end within five
minutes.

The rules are simple: the wrestler may grab arms or clothing,
but not legs. Much clothing is ripped and occasionally must be
replaced before the match can continue. Spectators gladly loan
chapons to be torn to shreds, for, after all, the honor of the village
rests on the outcome. Balance is all important. Usually, the wrestlers grab one another's forearms in overlapping grips, and move
sideways in a crablike, rocking motion, testing each other's
strength and trying to catch each other off balance. Often, a man
will leap high into the air, trying to toss his opponent with a judo
hip throw. To counter this, the other wrestler will twist in mid-air
and end up behind his opponent with a headlock. Sometimes only
one such move as this ends the match.

The atmosphere reminds one of an American high-school football or basketball game with everyone very serious and rah-rah.
Often, the loser will cry openly. His fellow villagers shun him.
One man chickened out on a match, saying he couldn't go on because of fear, and his kinsmen roundly thrashed him. When the
Zari villagers lost in the first day's matches (five to two), they
sent home for reinforcements for the second day's contests. The
Alakadur, however, called these off after two matches, for he
sensed that the crowd was getting into an ugly mood. With Af-
gans, it matters not how the game is played—as long as it is won.

Another great indoor and outdoor sport, throughout the rest of Afghanistan as well as in Aq Kupruk, is gambling. I am beginning to suspect (without having adequate data at hand, however) that non-literate societies which exist just above the subsistence level have a greater percentage of gamblers than more affluent societies. The American Plains Indians of the eighteenth and nineteenth centuries come to mind. Most modern nations with lotteries fall into the category of "just above subsistence," and national lotteries exist in almost all underdeveloped countries. One reason may be that gambling is a way of investing the small available surplus. In technologically more advanced societies, men and companies gamble money on new industries, new commercial enterprises, and the stock market. In Aq Kupruk, a winner at gambling can buy a few more luxuries in the bazaar, such as a transistor radio, the ultimate prestige item which must be ordered from Mazar-i-Sharif, or a watch, which would usually be bought from a wandering nomad.

Gambling games include pinochle-type games (*fa-lush* or flush) and *guice* (dice) games played with the knucklebones of sheep or with dice imported from Pakistan. Women and children also gamble for eggs, astraguli, and nuts, but seldom for money.

The entertainment aspects of folk-singing, folk-story telling, *buzkashi,* and wrestling go far beyond the "fun" syndrome. Good folk singers, folk-tale tellers, *chapandaz,* and *palawani* gain prestige in a society where there is little chance to acquire individual prestige. Each ethnic group, each village, and each region feels proud of its extracurricular specialists. For example, the best known retired *palawani* in Aq Kupruk had never been defeated, and claimed the title of "Champion of North Afghanistan." He won many matches in Mazar-i-Sharif, Maimana, and Shibargan, and although only a small landholder, he was the idol of Aq Kupruk.

THE NOMADS

The cultural picture at Aq Kupruk is further complicated by about 3,000 families of Pushtun nomads (mainly Mandozai of the Ghilzai tribe, but also Kandahari, Alozai, Barakzai, Mohmand

Khel, and Khalki) who pass through Aq Kupruk from mid-May to mid-September. The nomads flow down from the north, following the old trail along the Balkh River, and they usually arrive between midnight and dawn, with their camel bells bouncing. In the early morning light, the caravans move to the traditional camping areas, both north and south of the town. The camels groan under loads of household effects: tents and poles, pots and pans, buckets made from sixteen-gallon Russian gasoline cans, drums, pets, lambs, chickens, and children. Also on top of the swaying camels ride the unveiled women in gold- and silver-embroidered dresses, laden with jewelry and coins. The townswomen often look with envy on these nomadic women, but few realize that the women do the bulk of the work in the camps. They make the tents and repair them, put them up and take them down, pack and unpack the animals, cook, make cheese and other milk products, and bear and raise the children.

The nomadic men take care of the livestock, which travel on separate, higher tracks along the rich loess highlands. Most of the groups passing through Aq Kupruk are *maldar* (owners of large herds of sheep and goats), and the wealthier nomads have excellent horses. Both camels and horses wear fancily woven gear. The farmers speak of the *kuchis* (a generic term referring to all nomads in Afghanistan and including the *maldar*) in hushed, embarrassed tones. They fear the nomads, but have a symbiotic relationship with them. The nomads have the traditional right to graze their flocks on the same fields each year after the harvest. The sheep and goats eat the wheat stubble on the loess hillsides and deposit manure, which is later plowed under by the farmers to enrich the soil. While in their camps near the villages and towns, the nomads often hire villagers to watch over their flocks while they loll about in their tents—singing songs, drinking tea, and puffing on their *chillums* (water pipes)—or perhaps bestir themselves to hunt.

Nomad camps range from five to twenty tents, with large groups more common in the Aq Kupruk area. Each group represents a kinship unit, usually a father and his sons or a grandfather-father-grandson lineage. Closely related groups come together on the Turkistan Plains in the winter.

The nomads have little to do with the townsfolk socially. They sell specific items in the bazaar and purchase their cereal needs from various shopkeepers. Often, they have traditional annual relationships with the same shopkeepers.

Throughout the summer months, thousands of nomads swing south from the dry Turkistan Plains into the mountains, moving along predetermined routes in a predetermined order. Many go at least as far south as Pul-i-Khumri and then turn north along the Balkh River, passing through Aq Kupruk and arriving at their winter quarters near Mazar-i-Sharif, Balkh, Shibargan, and Maimana in September and October.[7] Most groups remain in the northern watershed of the Hindu Kush mountains.

Other than the *maldar,* groups of *jat* (gypsy tribes) pass through Aq Kupruk, selling charms and hiring themselves out as seasonal labor. "Arab" groups (possibly *jat* trying to pass as respectable Arabs), living in dirty white tents, also pass through to work as seasonal labor.

A special group of nomadic traders called *Shaikh Muhammadi* (or *Qawwal*) pass nearby but do not come through Aq Kupruk. They stop over at Sangcharak, a large bazaar center west of Aq Kupruk in the Hazarajat, occupied by the Mongoloid-looking, Persian-speaking Hazara people, in the central portion of the Hindu Kush mountains. Many goods, such as shoes, leggings, and *gelems,* in Aq Kupruk's bazaar come from Sangcharak. The *Shaikh Muhammadi* also function as holy men, selling amulets to the faithful, which are guaranteed for everything from capturing a lover to preventing lead poisoning. They live in the distinctive white tents characteristic of the traders from the Arabian Peninsula, from which they also claim to have originally come.

Each group of nomads remains in Aq Kupruk for a day or two—selling, buying, swapping gossip and news, while their flocks graze and defecate. Then the tents are folded up, the camels are loaded, and they depart northwards toward the Turkistan Plains and their winter quarters. The Aq Kuprukis heave a collective sigh of relief at their going.

[7] For studies of other groups see: Klaus Ferdinand, "Nomad Expansion and Commerce in Central Afghanistan," *Folk,* Vol. II, pp. 33–50 (Copenhagen: 1962); Louis Dupree, *The Green and the Black* (LD-5-'63), American Universities Field Staff Reports, South Asia Series, Volume VII, No. 5, April 1963.

PART II: THE POLITICAL STRUCTURE AND COMMER-
CIAL PATTERNS

Aq Kupruk, a town of about 1,500 men, is the bazaar center
for several villages, whose natural geographic cluster forms an
administrative unit of the Afghan government: the Alakadari
(District) of Kishindi (Aq Kupruk is the capital), which belongs
to the Province of Balkh, one of the twenty-eight provinces
created in 1964 (see the map, Appendix A). Previously, two types
of provinces existed in Afghanistan: the Wilayat, or major province, and the Hukumat-i-Ala, or minor province.[8] In fact, the
patterns of provincial government changed little from the satrapy
system of the ancient Achaemenian Empire (ca. 600–330 B.C.)
up to 1963.[9] The boundaries of provinces and empires constantly
shifted while governments rose and fell, but the provincial governors ruled almost independently of a central authority, feeding
taxes and conscripts to the capital. Governors sometimes revolted
against their rulers, and occasionally they succeeded in forming
independent states. Autonomy usually varied with the degree of
control exercised from the center.[10]

The new provincial system in Afghanistan attempts to decen-
tralize in order to speed up economic and political development.
At first, the concept may seem illogical, but, on closer examination, it reveals a realistic approach to development. The provinces
vary in size: the more accessible the area is to roads and telecom-
munications, the larger the province; those geographic regions
with forbidding zones of inaccessibility are the smallest. Theoretically, a man can reach his provincial capital in one day by foot
or horseback, whereas before it took several days in most provinces. However, even today, for example, the trip from remote
Hazara villages in Wardak Province to its capital, Maidan, re-

[8] Before 1964 the Major Provinces were: Kabul, Ningrahar, Pakhtia, Qandahar, Mazar-i-Sharif, Herat, and Kataghan. The Minor Provinces were:
Parwan, Ghazni, Giriskh, Farah, Maimana, Badakhshan, and Shibargan.
[9] A. T. Olmstead, *History of the Persian Empire* (3rd imp.; Chicago: University of Chicago Press, 1960).
[10] Louis Dupree, "The Changing Character of South-Central Afghanistan
Villages," *Human Organization* (Volume 14, No. 4, 1956), pp. 26–29.

quires two or more days. As old roads and trails improve and new ones penetrate the less accessible areas, it is probable that some neighboring provinces will be joined and the total number reduced.

At the present time, young, energetic, and usually Western-educated provincial, subprovincial, and district governors (see chart below) are actively trying to spread the "new democracy"

COMPARISON OF PROVINCIAL SYSTEMS: AFGHANISTAN

OLD TERMINOLOGY		NEW TERMINOLOGY (POST 1963)	
Name of Unit	*Name of Governor*	*Name of Unit*	*Name of Governor*
Wilayat (Major Province)	Naib-i-Hukumat (Called Wali in Kabul Province)	Wilayat ("Province")	Wali
Hukumat-i-Ala (Minor Province)	Hakim-i-Ala		
Hukumrani (or Hukumat-i-Kalan) (Subprovince)	Hukumran (or Hakim-i-Kalan)	Wolus Wali ("Subprovince") 4 grades	Wolus Wal
Hukumat (District) 4 grades	Hakim-i-Mahalli		
Alakadari (Subdistrict) 2 grades	Alakadur	Alakadari ("District")	Alakadur

NOTES

(1) In spite of the changes in governor's titles into Pashto terms at the Subprovincial and District levels, the people continue to refer to holders of these administrative officers as Hakim Shahib. Custom dies hard.

(2) Although theoretically all provinces are equal, three provincial governors (of the provinces of Qandahar, Herat, and Ningrahar) have civil service rank equal to cabinet members.

(3) Only one Hukumrani still exists on the border with Pakistan in Ningrahar Province because of its importance on the disputed Durand Line. The Hukumran has precedence over the other Wolus Wals and reports directly to the Wali.

(as it is called by Afghans) brought in by King Mohammad Za-
hir's accession to power in 1963 and the promulgation of the
Constitution of 1964.[11] Previously, Hakims and Alakadurs used
to govern with little check from the center, although the "eyes
and ears of the king" (the ancient Achaemenian custom of having
royal spies among civil servants) generally kept the provincial
governors in line and discouraged them from seeking too much
personal power and riches.

In the summer of 1962, for example, the people of Aq Kupruk
genuinely hated their Alakadur. A Pushtun, he had the Pushtun's
classic contempt for all non-Pushtuns, and slapped anyone
around who displeased him. He would actually sit at the windows
of his office and fire shots across the river to frighten the townsmen. Fortunately for Afghanistan, the two Ministers of the Interior since 1963 (Dr. Abdul Kayeum and Abdul Satar Shalizi)
have purged most individuals of this sort. The present Alakadur
in Aq Kupruk (a Qandahari Pushtun) is universally respected
for both his personality and his professional judgment, and he
seriously tries to implement the "new democracy." His staff—the
police commandant and six police, the tax collector, a statistician,
and a telephone operator (a battery-powered field telephone,
which will reach only Mazar-i-Sharif, Buina Qara, and Darra-i-
Suf)—assist him, even if often reluctantly, in his mission. The
Commandant of Police (a Pushtun) opposed the elaborate 1965
Jeshyn (national holiday) celebrations proposed by the Alakadur
on the grounds that he could not control such large crowds. No
trouble developed, and the Alakadur scored several merit points
with the people. The Commandant also opposed holding the
August and September national elections according to the new
election law. He thought that the Alakadur should instead decide who would be the most pro-government among the candidates and select them, as was the custom in the past. The

[11] See Louis Dupree, *The Decade of Daoud Ends* (LD-7-'63), American
Universities Field Staff Reports, South Asia Series, Volume VII, No. 7, May
1963 and *Constitutional Development and Cultural Change, Part III: The
1964 Afghan Constitution* (*Articles 1–56*) (LD-3-'65) and *Part IV: The
1964 Afghan Constitution* (*Articles 57–128*) (LD-4-'65), American Universities Field Staff Reports, South Asia Series, Volume IX, Nos. 3 and 4,
September 1965.

Alakadur, however, chose to follow the new election procedures scrupulously, and the voting went off with only a few hitches.

When I first visited Aq Kupruk in 1959, it was the capital of a Hukumat (District) governed by a Hakim (District Governor) and his staff, which consisted of a commandant of police and draftees serving as policemen, a director of education, a tax collector, a statistician, a *qazi* (judge), and a telephone operator.

Under the pre-1964 system, the chain of command usually went from a Wilayat (Major Province) or Hukumat-i-Ala (Minor Province) to a Hukumrani (Subprovince) to Hukumat (District) to a Alakadari (Subdistrict), with a few exceptions—i.e., several border Alakadurs reported directly to the provincial governors. Aq Kupruk was involved in the hierarchy as follows: orders passed from Mazar-i-Sharif (Wilayat) to Haibak (Hukumrani) to Aq Kupruk (Hukumat) and then to Buina Qara (Alakadari).

The new system, however, places many Alakadaris directly under the Wilayat, especially in the more isolated and inaccessible

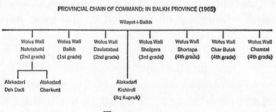

PROVINCIAL CHAIN OF COMMAND: IN BALKH PROVINCE (1965)

Wilayat-i-Balkh

Wolus Wali Nahrishahi (2nd grade)	Wolus Wali Balkh (1st grade)	Wolus Wali Daulatabad (2nd grade)	Wolus Wali Sholgera (3rd grade)	Wolus Wali Shortapa (4th grade)	Wolus Wali Char Bulak (4th grade)	Wolus Wali Chamtal (4th grade)
Alakadari Deh Dadi	Alakadari Charkunt		Alakadari Kishindi (Aq Kupruk)			

FIGURE 11-1

areas and along sensitive border areas. In such situations, the Alakadur does not need to go through a Wolus Wal (Subprovincial Governor), but goes straight to the Wali Sahib (Provincial Governor) with his problems and requests, thus eliminating one bureaucratic link which often held up decisions in the past. (See the chart above for a diagram of the new chain of authority.) In addition, the central government encourages provincial officials to make independent decisions without referring them to their superiors, a difficult scheme to implement in a land where previously a wrong decision meant immediate dismissal, arrest—or both.

The geographic location of Aq Kupruk, south of Mazar-i-Sharif

on the Balkh River, made it an important commercial and political center on the main north-south route of north Afghanistan
for centuries. A series of Buddhist paintings in a cave, dating
from about the sixth century A.D., and the discovery of six early
Kushan (ca. first century A.D.) column bases, indicate the importance of Aq Kupruk during the days of the Silk Route trade
between China and the Classical World. One of these column
bases, incidentally, now helps to support a teahouse wall, one
serves as the pedestal for a table in another teahouse, and four
have been included in the construction of a local mosque, the
Masjid-i-Alakadari. No one in Aq Kupruk, of course, knows anything about the Kushan Empire or the origin of these bases. Aq
Kuprukis merely refer to the objects as *pish-i-Islam* or *qabl-i-
Islam* (before Islam).

Many local legends relate to the times of Al-Bud ("the idol,"
or the Buddha). For example, near the caves where we excavated in 1959, we discovered one of the most spectacular natural
bridges in Asia. The Aq Kuprukis call it *Gauz-i-dokhtar-i-padishah*
("Swing of the Daughter of the King"). She must have been a
big girl. One story tells that her swing broke and she fell on the
other side of the Balkh River and was killed. Heartbroken, her
father buried her on the spot—which the local inhabitants
pointed out to me. I must confess it looked logical enough, a small
mound just opposite the natural bridge; but when I excavated a
test section, I found nothing but river gravel. The legend persists,
however, for many people in Aq Kupruk now believe that I took
the skeleton away at night. "We do not really object," said one.
"After all, she was not a Muslim."

The trail along the Balkh River leads from old Balkh—the ancient Bactra, called the "Mother of Cities," to Bamiyan, another
famous commercial and religious center of the Kushan (political)
—Buddhist (cultural) period.

Nomads still follow the old route, but the construction of a new
motorable road from Pul-i-Imam Burkri (about 20 kilometers
west of Mazar-i-Sharif, where the Balkh River runs into the Turkistan Plains and subsequently disappears before reaching the
Amu Darya, or Oxus River) to Darra-i-Suf has lessened the importance of Aq Kupruk as a commercial and administrative cen-

ter.[12] Actually, the process began earlier, for motor vehicles have used a more direct trail leading from Buina Qara to Darra-i-Suf for twenty years or more. Nomadic and commercial caravans generally follow water in Afghanistan, often over terrain quite unsuited for motor traffic; while motor traffic travels as directly as possible, at times over areas unsuited for grazing livestock.

The 1961 administrative changes (Buina Qara became capital of the Hukumat; Aq Kupruk capital of the Alakadari) simply recognized a reality long in existence. With the introduction of the new provincial system in 1963, Buina Qara (its name now changed to Sholgam) became the capital of a Subprovince (Wolus Wali), and Aq Kupruk remained downgraded as the capital of the Alakadari of Kishindi.

Aq Kupruk quickly felt the impact of this administrative shift, for thirteen small villages in the area (a total of about 9,000 men) moved to the vicinity of Sholgam, even though few people left Aq Kupruk itself. More importantly, Sholgam witnessed an immediate upsurge of economic activity. New shops sprang up, and the bazaar began to remain open every day, instead of just two days a week as in 1959. Today, the process continues and shops proliferate. With 200 shops constantly open, the town is now building a new bazaar area of 1,500 new shops and *caravanserais* (stables for animals) and motor-*serais* for lorries.

The population of Sholgam—only 1,500 men in 1959—now exceeds 3,000 men, and the total for the Wolus Wali is about 31,000 men. Tajiks represent the major ethnic group in the Wolus Wali, but there are also Uzbeks, Sarhad Baluchis, Arabs (Sayyids and Khojas), and Afghans (again, the local name for the Pushtuns forcibly brought to the area thirty-four years ago—the tribes including Momands and Afridis).

The Baluchis moved up from Afghan Baluchistan about sixty years ago and live in a separate village near Pul-i-Burak, between Sholgam and Aq Kupruk. During the summer, most of them move to the high mountain pastures of the Hazarajat, about a day's march from the village. There the Baluchis live in barrel-vaulted, black goathair tents while their flocks graze on the suc-

---

[12] See Louis Dupree, *The Green and the Black* (LD-5-'63), American Universities Field Staff Reports, South Asia Series, Volume VII, No. 5, April 1963.

culent grasses and flowering plants. They return to their mud-hut village in September, but continue to live in their tents. Only those Baluchis living permanently in the village reside in mud huts.

Pul-i-Burak, a village which is developing its own bazaar street because of its location on the new road from Sholgam to Darra-i-Suf, is mainly Hazara, many of whom are also transhumants, living in yurtlike *khedgahs* from late spring to September. The sedentary Hazara of Pul-i-Burak live in domed, beehive huts of the Iranian variety, which differ from the flat-roofed, rectangular huts of the neighboring ethnic groups.

Lorries always line the main street of Sholgam, and the entire bazaar hustles and bustles daily. A large government grain-storage building sits on the edge of town to safeguard against famine and to feed the army, the gendarmery, and the police. In addition, government officials may purchase grain for personal use at reduced rates.

Sholgam thrives, but Aq Kupruk is far from dead.

THE BAZAAR AT AQ KUPRUK

When I first visited Aq Kupruk in 1959, the 111 bazaar shops were open daily, but on my return in 1962 the bazaar was open for only two *ruz-i-bazaar* (bazaar days) a week: on *Dushambeh* (Monday, the traditional bazaar day in many Central Asian areas) and *Panjshambeh* (Thursday, the day before the weekly Muslim holiday, Friday or *Juma*). In 1965, only about seventy of the total 111 shops opened on the *ruz-i-bazaar*, a certain indication of a lack of economic activity. For example, on July 15, 1965 (a bazaar day), sixty-three of the total 111 shops opened for business, but most had closed by three in the afternoon.

(Appendices B and C provide a sketch of the 111 shops in Aq Kupruk and schematically present their activities and owners.)

Of the 111 shops, fourteen have remained permanently closed since 1961, and two are now used as residences. Only forty-six remain open every day, including five *serais*, nine teahouses, eighteen *bonjaraghi* (general stores), five agricultural produce and shoe shops, one barbershop, one ironmonger's shop, one shoe-repair shop, one metal-repair shop, three butcher shops, and two *bazazi* (cloth shops). The shopkeepers listed above work as full-time specialists; all the others are part-time specialists who are primarily farmers. (Actually, all shopkeepers, whether specialists or not, own some land.) In addition to these full- and part-time specialists of the bazaar, other part-time specialists function without shops: three carpenters, one iron worker, three mechanics, and four tailors work at home in their spare time or go where needed.

Cash-and-carry is the rule in the Aq Kupruk bazaar. Although there was much barter in 1959—when a hilltop farmer would bring grain and vegetables to town and return with a kerosene lantern (called a "hurricane"), kerosene, tea, sugar, salt, and cloth, and when passing nomads would trade milk, milk products, and citified trinkets (mirrors, knives, beads) for grain and melons —little exists there today. Today, the shopkeepers have thousands of afghanis (70–75 afghanis = US $1) tucked away in their shops, and often function as money-lenders—although few require these services. (I must confess that I did, however, for I underestimated my archaeological labor expenses.) Interest rates—usually under 50 per cent—are mild when compared to those imposed on the inhabitants of Darra-i-Suf by the nomadic money-lenders.[13]

The shopkeepers have no general association, in keeping with the lack of co-operation common to peasant societies everywhere. Similarly, the various full-time and part-time specialists have no guildlike structures, such as those found in Sholgam and other larger towns and cities. There is an informal *kalantar-i-bazaar* (head of the bazaar), however, and he presides over the infrequent meetings held by the small group of merchants who hire a *chowkidar* (night watchman) to roam the bazaar streets at night and watch for robbers. (All shopkeepers, however, contribute to his pay.) He is not a full-time specialist but a farmer with several sons, who take turns at patrolling the streets.

Another difference between the Aq Kupruk bazaar and those in larger towns and cities is that the shops here have only one story, and the shopkeepers live in town away from the shops. The traditional shopkeeper in the larger urban centers lives above his shop, so the city bazaar has a dual function, residential and economic.

Bazaar activity at Aq Kupruk reaches a peak in the months of October and November, between the end of reaping and the

[13] See Louis Dupree, *The Green and the Black, op. cit.*

beginning of snow. During the extensive winter months, the bazaar days continue, but only about a half (fifty or so) of the shops open. In the spring, with the new year, full activity returns.

The administrative shift has certainly had an impact on the Aq Kupruk bazaar, for Aq Kupruk is now definitely outside the area of primary commercial activity. The readjustment has been rapid, however, and a balance now seems to have been reached. It is true that lorries no longer come into town every day; but laden donkeys and reasonably prosperous farmers still come down from the hills on Mondays and Thursdays to buy and sell, swap gossip, listen to the transistor radios (about 150 transistor radios now exist in Kishindi Alakadari) or records of Indian movie music on hand-wound phonographs, and drink unlimited cups of black and green tea.

INFORMAL POWER STRUCTURE IN AQ KUPRUK

Outside the formal power structure in Aq Kupruk, as represented by the government hierarchy discussed previously, informal pressure groups play great roles in decision-making. An ethnic peck order, for example, must be included in any discussion of the local power structure. Here the few Pushtuns occupy the highest position, followed by the majority group, the Tajiks. Within the Tajik group, the Sa'adats (Sayyids) and Khojas feel superior to the general run of Tajiks. The Uzbeks are the "low man on the totem pole" in Aq Kupruk, except for the Hazaras, living in the hills around the town, for all Aq Kuprukis look on them with contempt. There is also a village of Moghuls (the older men speak some Mongolian) south of Aq Kupruk, and they rank with the Hazaras at the bottom of the ethnic peck order.

The Pushtuns came to Aq Kupruk in 1949, forcibly moved there by the government, after an unsuccessful revolt by the Safi Pushtuns, who attempted to seize the Jalalabad garrison. The government then scattered these dissidents over north Afghanistan. The Safi leader in Aq Kupruk controls a "gang"—and there is no better way to describe it, for although the Aq Kuprukis have no word in Farsi or Uzbeki for this type of informal grouping, several such "gangs" do exist. The "gang" chiefs usually remain outside the recognized village governing bodies, but they are consulted when important decisions must be made, such as who shall clean out the irrigation canals, who shall work on various other outside projects (such as my archaeological excavations), who shall go to the army, and so forth.

The most intensive loyalties, however, center around kinship groups: primarily the extended family. In descending order of intensity, the following list indicates the current chain of loyalties: the extended family, the informal "gang," the local ethnic group, and the town of Aq Kupruk. Still, it is now possible to observe shifts in the loyalty patterns. In recent years, particularly since World War II, the patriarchs of extended families have been rapidly losing influence as the Afghan Army has extended its long reach to draft the local young men, as new development projects have siphoned off surplus labor, and as the secular schools have set new ideals and aspirations before the younger people.

The "gang" leader, a relatively new phenomenon, has developed as the ethnic groups have become more mixed in heretofore ethnically pure localities (see Appendix A); and the "gang" itself usually includes men from several ethnic groups, thus continuing to break down ethnic and tribal loyalties. Thus, the "gang" intrudes between the ethnic or tribal group and the extended family to meet the new conditions brought about by the increased democratization in the political sphere and the new economic conditions brought about by the development programs. A "gang" usually grows out of a work group (such as coal miners, factory workers, or lorry drivers from the same routes), and here we have incipient unionism on the rise.

Naturally, loyalty to the town of Aq Kupruk is the weakest of all, because people still fear the government and prefer to have as little as possible to do with it. No longer do hereditary *maliks* (village chiefs) rule with the assistance and advice of the *rish-i-safidan* (village council of elders). Each area is divided into Kariehs, and every village or town has a number of Kariehdurs (probably "ward leader" would be the closest translation). For example, the average in the Alakadari-i-Kishindi is one Kariehdur for every five Kariehs. The village of Zari near Aq Kupruk is divided into twelve Kariehs and has four Kariehdurs. The people elect Kariehdurs every three years, but the central government must approve those elected. Just as small-town officials in the

United States make careers of small-time political jobs, so do the Aq Kuprukis. Of the three Kariehdurs I know reasonably well, two had been in office for twenty years, and the other for seven.

Although officially a local *jirgah* (village council) does not exist, both the Kariehdurs and the Alakadur seek out the *rish-i-safidan* for advice and counsel. The Kishindi District has a total of fifteen Kariehdurs for its 19,005 men, and they form an informal council for the Alakadur. Although he never consults them collectively, he often invites a few to discuss the problems in their respective areas.

The "government" for the people of Aq Kupruk primarily means law and order in the form of the police, tax collections, and conscription officers—and the town has benefited little from any one of these three. In fact, most contacts with government officials have been unpleasant, although under the enlightened policies of the new government, conditions have improved tremendously. A recent incident, however, will illustrate the incongruities of the situation:

The Afghan government, greatly concerned over the cholera epidemic which swept northern Afghanistan in the summer of 1965, dispatched health teams to combat the spread of this killer. The teams blocked roads and established checkpoints all along the main roads leading north and south. All travelers had to have proof of immunization against cholera with them or be vaccinated on the spot. The motives behind this were pure and noble, but in practice the effort probably brought more misery than relief. Several people died of cholera in Aq Kupruk before an Afghan medical man arrived by motorcycle (how he made it over the road from Pul-i-Burak still mystifies me), laden with serum (but no ice) and one syringe and needle. For three days he wandered through the bazaar shooting people as he came to them, one after the other, until he had emptied the syringe. Then he would refill—"Without even cleaning the needle in boiled water," as one shopkeeper observed—and began to vaccinate again. In a few days, over a hundred people thus treated came down with high fevers and vomiting, but, luckily, no one died. Those who had not been shot considered themselves fortunate, and I considered myself extremely lucky that none of my archaeological workmen had bothered to be vaccinated.

CONCLUSIONS

Aq Kupruk, because of its intermediate position between true town and true village, illustrates many of the changes occurring today outside Kabul, the national capital. I like to say that two Afghanistans exist: Kabul and the rest of the country; for while Kabul is rapidly becoming a modern city, the rest of Afghanistan lags far behind. The economy of Aq Kupruk can be described as a Neolithic farming self-sufficiency in an Iron Age technology. With the change from a higher to a lower government administrative center, the dominant commercial bazaar economy has slowly been reverting to an almost exclusively agricultural economy. The "new democracy" in Afghanistan and the new breed of administrators (such as the energetic Wali Sahib of Balkh Province and the Alakadur of Kishindi) have helped arrest the process of de-urbanization, however, and Aq Kupruk may grow again in importance as a commercial center. Probably, however, the new Wolus Wali of Buina Qara (Sholgam) will continue to grow faster and remain the foremost center in the region, mainly because of the new motorable road running north and south. Whereas today the Sholgam bazaar has a plethora of full-time specialists, only a few now exist in Aq Kupruk.

After World War II, land began to lose its primary role as a traditional source of power in Aq Kupruk, although it is still a first step. In the past people used their surplus cash to purchase more land. Now because most capable farmers own land, surplus cash is used to purchase additional commodity and luxury items (transistor radios, watches, clothing, furniture, glassware, gas lanterns, flashlights, etc.). Less competent farmers still serve as tenants, trapped in a system which tends to encourage their incompetence.

The mobility of ethnic groups, especially here in north Afghanistan where many people were forcibly migrated between 1880 and 1949, has been phenomenal and few areas north of the Hindu Kush can now be considered ethnically pure. Ethnic mobility, plus the "new democracy," has caused important changes in the old authority and loyalty patterns—giving rise, for instance, to the new "gangs."

The next national elections in Aq Kupruk and Afghanistan,

four years from now, should see the rise to power of these new "gangs" in association with the new urban middle-class literates.

The author lived in Aq Kupruk during three separate periods (for two weeks in 1959; two months in 1962; and three months in 1965). Many people contributed directly or indirectly to the writing of these Reports, and to name a few would be to leave out others. I would like to express my gratitude to all the many Afghans who were helpful.

APPENDIX A

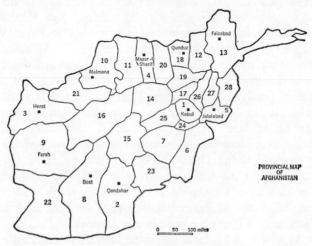

FIGURE 11-2

	Province	Capital		Province	Capital
1	Kabul	Kabul	15	Uruzgan	Uruzgan
2	Qandahar	Qandahar	16	Ghor	Chakhcharan
3	Herat	Herat	17	Parwan	Charikar
4	Balkh	Mazar-i-Sharif	18	Qunduz	Qunduz
5	Nangarhar	Jalalabad	19	Baghlan	Baghlan
6	Paktia	Gardez	20	Samangan	Haibak
7	Ghazni	Ghazni	21	Badghis	Qala-i-nau
8	Holmand	Bost	22	Chakhansur	Zaranj
9	Farah	Farah	23	Zabul	Kalat
10	Faryab	Maimana	24	Logar	Baraki-Barak
11	Jowzjan	Shiberghan	25	Wardak	Maidan
12	Takhar	Taliqan	26	Kapisa	Tagab
13	Badakhshan	Faizabad	27	Laghman	Metarlam
14	Bamian	Bamian	28	Kunar	Chighar-Sarai

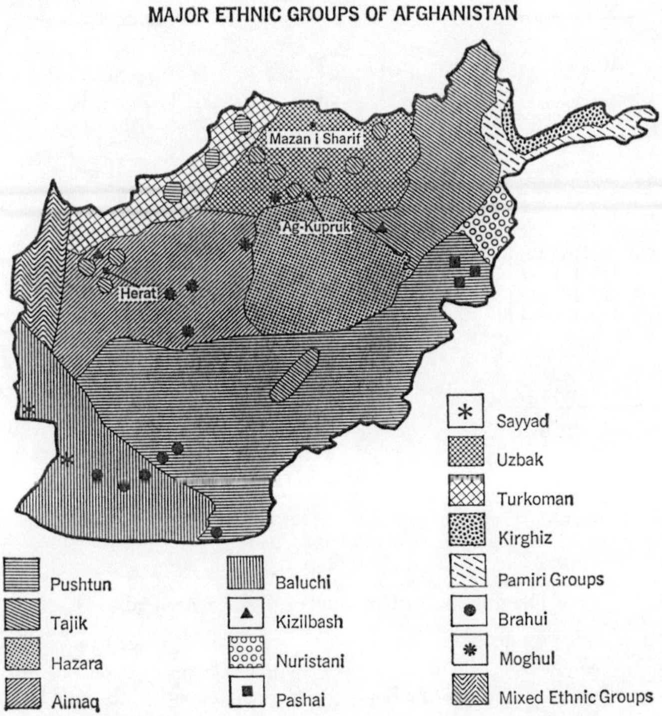

MAJOR **ETHNIC** GROUPS OF AFGHANISTAN

*	Sayyad
▨	Uzbak
▧	Turkoman
⣿	Kirghiz
▨	Pamiri Groups
●	Brahui
✳	Moghul
▨	Mixed Ethnic Groups

Pushtun		Baluchi	
Tajik		▲ Kizilbash	
Hazara		Nuristani	
Aimaq		■ Pashai	

FIGURE 11-3   Languages spoken by ethnic groups.

Sayyad – Indo-Europ.
(Baluchi specializing in
    netting birds & fishing)
Uzbek – Turkic
Turkoman – Turkic
Kirghiz – Turkic
Pamiri Groups – Turkic
Brahui – Dravidian
Moghul – Indo-Europ.
(Mainly Persian-speaking,
    some Mongolian)

Pushtun – Indo-European
(Every year more Pushtun
    move to north Afghanistan)
Tajik – Indo-Europ.
Hazara – Indo-Europ.
Aimaq – Indo-Europ.
Baluchi – Indo-Europ.
Kizilbash – Indo-Europ.
(Mainly urban)
Nuristani – Indo-Europ.
Pashai – Indo-Europ.

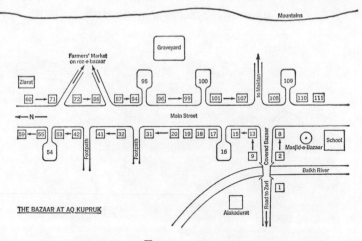

FIGURE 11-4

APPENDIX B

Bazaar Shops in Aq Kupruk (Summer 1965)
(see Diagrammatic Drawing of Bazaar Area above)

Number of Shop on Sketch	Type of Shop	Ethnic Group of Shopkeeper	Shop open every day or just Bazaar Days
1	Teahouse-*serai* (inn)	Tajik from Sang-charak	Every day
2–8	*Bonjaraghi* (general store; plus candy, sugar)	All Sa'adats (Sayyids)	Every day (2, 4, 8); Bazaar days (3, 5, 6, 7)
9	Teahouse-*serai*	Sa'adat	Every day
10–12	*Bonjaraghi*	Sa'adat	Every day (10, 12); Bazaar days (11)
13	Teahouse	Sa'adat	Every day
14	Closed shop; now a residence	Tajik resident	—
15	Rice, wheat, corn shop	Tajik	Every day
16	*Caravanserai*	Tajik	Every day
17	*Bonjaraghi*	Tajik	Bazaar days
18	Closed shop	Tajik owned	—
19	Closed shop	Tajik owned	—
20	*Chapon* (coat seller)	Tajik	Bazaar days

Number of Shop on Sketch	Type of Shop	Ethnic Group of Shopkeeper	Shop open every day or just Bazaar Days
21	*Bazazi* (cloth seller)	Tajik	Bazaar days
22–23	Shoe repair	Sa'adat	Bazaar days
24	*Bazazi*	Sa'adat	Bazaar days
25	Dried fruits, melons, corn	Sa'adat	Bazaar days
26	Dried fruits, corn, candy	Sa'adat	Bazaar days
27	Bakery	Tajik, originally from Mazar-i-Sharif	Every day
28	Closed shop	Tajik owned	—
29	*Caravanserai*	Tajik	Every day
30	*Bonjaraghi; chapon* (Best shop in town)	Sa'adat	Every day
31	Closed shop	Tajik owned	—
32	Kerosene, dried fruits	Tajik	Bazaar days
33	Closed shop	Tajik owned	—
34	*Bazazi* (good cloth)	Tajik	Bazaar days
35	Closed shop	Tajik owned	—
36	*Bazazi*	Tajik	Bazaar days
37	Small *bonjaraghi* (plus corn, dried fruits)	Sa'adat	Bazaar days
38	*Bazazi* (good cloth, plus dried and fresh fruit)	Tajik	Every day
39	Dyer	Tajik	Bazaar days
40–41	Closed shops	Tajik owned	—
42	*Ahanghar* (black-smith)	Tajik	Every day
43	Teahouse; salt shop	Tajik	Every day
44	Shoe repair	Tajik	Every day
45	Teahouse (eating place—good *pilau*)	Sa'adat	Bazaar days
46	Empty *serai*	Tajik owned	—
47	Closed shop; now a residence	Sa'adat owned	—
48–49	Closed shops	Tajik owned	—
50	Tinsmith (repairs, aluminum, pots, buckets, kettles, etc.)	Tajik	Every day
51	Small *bonjaraghi* plus some dried fruit	Khoja	Every day
52	*Bazazi*	Tajik	Bazaar days
53	*Bazazi* and tailor (*khayat*)	Tajik	Bazaar days

Number of Shop on Sketch	Type of Shop	Ethnic Group of Shopkeeper	Shop open every day or just Bazaar Days
54	*Caravanserai* (animals kept here on Bazaar days)	Tajik	Bazaar days
55	Teahouse	Tajik	Bazaar days
56–58	Closed shops	Tajik owned	—
59	Teahouse	Tajik owned	Every day
60	Corn storage depot	Tajik	Bazaar days
61	*Bazazi*	Tajik	Bazaar days
62	Good *bonjaraghi* (plus corn, tea, sugar, and fancy shoes)	Tajik	Every day
63	*Bonjaraghi* (plus corn and fancy shoes)	Tajik	Every day
64	*Bonjaraghi*	Tajik	Every day
65	Closed shop	Tajik owned	—
66	*Bonjaraghi* (plus corn, dried fruits, and locally grown tobacco)	Tajik	Every day
67	*Bonjaraghi* (plus dried fruit, shoes)	Tajik	Every day
68	*Bonjaraghi* (plus dried fruit, shoes)	Tajik	Every day
69	*Bonjaraghi* (plus dried fruit, shoes)	Tajik	Bazaar days
70	Skin seller	Tajik	Bazaar days
71	*Bonjaraghi* (plus dried fruits, onions, shoe repairs)	Tajik	Bazaar days
72	Small *bonjaraghi* (but mainly dried fruits, melons)	Tajik	Bazaar days
73	Salt shop	Uzbek	Bazaar days
74	*Bonjaraghi* (plus rice, garlic, tomatoes)	Tajik	Bazaar days
75	Shoe repair	Tajik	Bazaar days
76	Large *bonjaraghi*	Tajik	Every day
77	Kerosene, salt	Sa'adat	Bazaar days
78	Shoe repair	Tajik	Bazaar days
79	Large *bonjaraghi*	Tajik	Bazaar days
80	*Bonjaraghi* (plus shoe repair	Tajik	Bazaar days
81	Melon shop	Tajik	Every day
82	*Bonjaraghi* (plus *chapons*)	Tajik	Every day
83	*Bonjaraghi*	Tajik	Bazaar days

Number of Shop on Sketch	Type of Shop	Ethnic Group of Shopkeeper	Shop open every day or just Bazaar Days
84	*Bonjaraghi* (plus tea)	Tajik	Bazaar days
85	*Bonjaraghi*	Tajik	Every day
86	*Bonjaraghi* (plus shoes)	Tajik	Every day
87	Large *bonjaraghi*	Sa'adat	Every day
88	*Bonjaraghi*	Tajik	Bazaar days
89	*Bonjaraghi* (plus tea and shoes)	Tajik	Bazaar days
90	*Bonjaraghi* (plus tea, rice, dried fruits)	Sa'adat	Every day
91	*Bonjaraghi* (plus aluminum dishware, tea)	Sa'adat	Bazaar days
92	*Bazazi*	Khoja	Every day
93	*Bonjaraghi* (plus dried fruits, melons)	Tajik	Bazaar days
94	Eating place, teahouse, *serais*	Sa'adat	Bazaar days
95	*Caravanserai*	Sa'adat	Every day
96	Biggest teahouse in town	Sa'adat	Every day
97	*Bonjaraghi* (plus aluminum dishware, kerosene)	Tajik	Every day
98	*Bazazi*	Uzbek	Every day
99	*Bazazi*	Tajik	Bazaar days
100	*Caravanserai*	Khoja	Bazaar days
101	Large teahouse	Khoja	Every day
102	Butcher shop	Tajik	Bazaar days
103	Butcher shop	Tajik	Bazaar days
104	Butcher shop	Sa'adat	Every day
105	Butcher shop	Tajik	Every day
106	Butcher shop	Sa'adat	Every day
107	Teahouse	Tajik	Every day
108	*Bonjaraghi* (plus dried fruit, salt)	Tajik	Every day
109	*Caravanserai*	Tajik	Every day
110	Teahouse; *serais*	Tajik	Every day
111	*Caravanserai*	Tajik	Every day

NOTES

(1) *Bonjaraghi* are shops which specialize in foreign imports, basically general stores. They carry Russian matches, English flashlight batteries, Czech kerosene stoves, Italian ballpoint pens, West German hurricane lanterns, Indian mantles for gaslamps, aluminum goods from Pakistan, tea from Pakistan and India, American cigarettes, and similar goods. If a shop sells local produce as well, I have noted this.

(2) All closed shops still have owners, and the ethnic group of each has been given.

(3) Shops which sell local produce will carry other vegetables and fruits in season.

(4) No man in Aq Kupruk owns more than one shop.

(5) Teahouses (*chai khaneh*) also serve as flophouses for travellers, who sleep on the hard wooden benches on which people sit to drink tea during the day. All teahouses also serve meals.

(6) Shops tend to cluster by speciality, except for the teahouses and *serais*.

(7) Shops open every day are clustered near the bridge under a covered street.

OWNERSHIP OF SHOPS BY ETHNIC GROUP

Type of Shop	Shops Open Every Day					Shops Open Only on Bazaar Days (Mondays and Thursday)					Grand Total
	Tajik	Sayyid (Sa'adat)	Khoja	Uzbek	Totals	Tajik	Sayyid (Sa'adat)	Khoja	Uzbek	Totals	
Bonjaraghi (General Store)	11	8	1	—	20	13	7	—	—	20	40
Bazazi (cloth shop)	1	—	1	1	3	7	1	—	—	8	11
Chai khaneh	5	3	1	—	9	1	2	—	—	3	12
Caravanserai	4	1	—	—	5	1	—	—	1	2	7
Local produce	2	—	—	—	2	1	2	—	—	3	5
Butcher shop	1	2	—	—	3	2	—	—	—	2	5
Shoe Repair	1	—	—	—	1	2	2	—	—	4	5
Bakery	1	—	—	—	1	—	—	—	—	—	1
Kerosene shop	—	—	—	—	—	1	1	—	—	2	2
Dyer shop	—	—	—	—	—	1	—	—	—	1	1
Blacksmith	1	—	—	—	1	—	—	—	—	—	1
Salt	—	—	—	—	—	—	—	—	1	1	1
Tinsmith	1	—	—	—	1	—	—	—	—	—	1
Skin seller	—	—	—	—	—	1	—	—	—	1	1
Chapon (coat seller)	—	—	—	—	—	1	—	—	—	1	1
Residences	1	1	—	—	2	—	—	—	—	—	2
Permanently closed (All owned by Tajiks)											15
	44	15	3	1	63	31	15	1	1	48	111

NOTES

(1) Tajiks represent the largest percentage of shopkeepers, with the Sa'adats second. Only four Khojas and two Uzbeks own shops. One Khoja specialist, a carpenter, lives outside the bazaar and works at his home. All the bazaar artisans (blacksmith, tinsmith, dyer,) are Tajiks.

(2) Teahouses in Afghanistan almost always serve food, which they often buy from specialists who prepare the food away from the teahouses.

(3) *Caravanserais* have courtyards and stables for animals.

12. A Moroccan Jewish Community During the Middle Eastern Crisis

There have been many consequences to last summer's Middle Eastern war but not the least tragic among them is that while the lines separating the Israelis and their Arab neighbors have become still more sharply defined the fundamental relations between Moslems and Jews not as political entities but as religious and ethnic groupings have become increasingly blurred. Both sides have contributed their share to this confusion. On the one hand, many Westerners and Israelis of European origin have tended to attribute to the Arabs the same sorts of anti-Jewish attitudes so prevalent in their own recent histories, and to regard these attitudes as a predominant factor in the present antagonism. The Arabs, on the other hand, have frequently had their own distinction between Jews and Zionists vitiated by the statements and actions of extremists and their own use of their Jewish minorities as pawns in the political wars.

Admittedly there is perhaps no point in the history of the Arab nations—least of all in the highly charged emotional atmosphere of the present—when the political and social relations of Moslems and Jews have not been inextricably bound together. It is, nonetheless, vital for those who wish to come to some understanding of the basis of Moslem-Jewish relations to pry political and social relations apart just enough to attempt answers to some very fundamental questions: Are the anti-Jewish attitudes of the Moslems really the same as those expressed by Western anti-Semites? Are the Jews who continue to live in Arab nations subject to forms of discrimination similar to those associated with Western social his-

Reprinted from *The American Scholar,* Volume 37, Number 3, Summer 1968. Copyright © 1968 by the United Chapters of Phi Beta Kappa. By permission of the publishers.

tory? Or is the very nature of Moslem-Jewish relations, and the whole context in which they are played out, of a rather different type than that which is found in the non-Arab world? The answers to these questions vary significantly from one Arab nation to another and it would be foolish to think that the situation that applies, say, in the states of North Africa is identical with that in Egypt, Syria or Jordan. It is perhaps best, therefore, to begin with a careful examination of how one Jewish community in the Arab world fared during the course of the recent war and why the strain of outside events on local Moslem-Jewish relations was largely absorbed and enervated in a rather short period of time. From the basis of this example one might, then, hope to dispel some of the grosser stereotypes that Westerners have long applied to the relations between Jews and non-Jews living throughout the Arab world.

As a touchstone for the study of this problem Morocco is particularly well suited. At the time of the establishment of the State of Israel one-quarter of all the Jews in the Middle East lived in Morocco, and the Jewish population there still numbers some seventy-five thousand. Admittedly Morocco has been one of the less vociferous opponents to Israel's existence, and there is no doubt that her proclamations of brotherhood with the other Arab countries cannot hide the physical and ideological distance between them and herself. But as an integral part of the Arab world, a nation suffused with traditional Islamic values yet subjected to a full colonial experience, the attitudes expressed by the majority of her citizens toward the Jews living in their midst and the history of relations between the two groups are not greatly different from those found in most of the other Arab states. For nearly two years, including the period of last summer's war, I lived in one of the main cities of the Moroccan interior studying the lives and ideas of Jews and Moslems alike. For nearly two years I had sought to understand how this society was put together and how the members of its different parts viewed one another, and it was only against this background that I was able to understand what was happening in this city, and perhaps other parts of the Arab world as well, when war broke out between the State of Israel and her neighbors early last June.

All along the western edge of the Middle Atlas Mountains of

Morocco lie a number of cities and towns that span the predominantly Arab-inhabited lowlands of western Morocco and the pasturelands of the Berber mountaineers. Since almost all members of both groups speak Arabic and are keenly aware of their common Islamic identity, there were few people in the late spring of 1967 who could not take advantage of the fine network of communications in Morocco to follow the mounting tensions in the Middle East. The inhabitants of the city in particular knew that the United Nations peace-keeping force had been removed and that troops were being mobilized. They knew that Israeli access to the Gulf of Aqaba had been restricted and they knew too that many of the relatives of the city's remaining six hundred and fifty Jews would be among those Israelis arming for war. They felt sure that the war would be over quickly and that after a complete Arab victory the Jews would be allowed to live on under Moslem administration once the lands that had been "confiscated" had been returned to their rightful Palestinian owners. It came as no surprise to them, therefore, when, late in the afternoon of June 5th, the Moroccan radio stations carried the first reports about the outbreak of fighting between the Arabs and Israelis.

The first reports were rather sketchy. They concentrated less on what was actually happening at the front than on what was expected to happen. Military and patriotic songs were interspersed with exhortations to the people from the government, the politicians and the doctors of Islamic law. News bulletins were concerned not so much with the actual fighting as with the contributions of forces being made by the various Arab nations. It was learned, for instance, that the Moroccan King Hassan II was preparing to review a vanguard of troops who were to be sent immediately to aid their Arab brethren at the front. (Only later was it learned that it took the five planeloads of Moroccan troops four whole days to arrive in the East because of difficulties with the Algerian authorities. Indeed the war was virtually over before the Moroccans could get into the actual war zone.) Many of the city's twenty-five thousand Moslems gathered that night in cafes to listen to the local newscasts while the Jews huddled in their homes listening to Paris, London and Jerusalem.

By the following morning there was little clarification as to the situation in the Middle East. Despite Moroccan reports that Tel

Aviv had been bombed, almost all of the city's Jewish merchants went about their business as usual. They met and talked with Moslems, moved freely about the streets, and sent their children off to the Jewish school. Only the Moslem children seemed embroiled in thoughts of war and one could see groups of them marching along the streets caught up in the same sort of fantasies they display when they burst out of the theater after a James Bond film. Some children did throw stones at the Jewish school but the police were called and quickly dispersed them. The radios that are always blaring from Moroccan cafes were even at this early time beginning to carry classical music in place of the martial airs and the interruptions for news were becoming more and more infrequent.

That night an event occurred that I was later to learn had been repeated in a number of Jewish homes throughout the city. While I was seated in the home of a Jewish neighbor, a cloth dealer and head of a large family, a Berber from the mountain community in which the Jewish man and his wife had been born and where they had lived until several years ago came to call on them. He was an elegant tribesman in his long-flowing jellaba, turban and white beard. He was also a very wealthy man who had twice gone on the pilgrimage to Mecca and who was the undisputed leader of his tribal fraction. In the days before the French Protectorate began in 1912 it was this man's father who, in accordance with local custom, had received the sheep sacrificed to him by the Jew's father and had, in turn, accorded the latter his full and jealously guarded protection. With this protection the Jew was able to trade his tea, cloth and sugar for the wool and hides of the Berber tribesmen. Theirs was a bond of mutual trust and great supernatural sanction and it bound the sons and their sons as it had bound the fathers before them. At the moment war broke out the Berber chieftain had begun the long trip to the city with his young wife for the express purpose of assuring this Jewish family that no matter what happened in the Middle East they and all their family had no need to fear for their own safety or the well-being of their property. He spoke calmly and reassuringly of the fact that they were all Moroccans and that the government would continue to protect them. He offered whatever help he could and specifically suggested that during the next few weeks they jointly rent a house in the *mellah*, the old Jewish quarter, where the Jews could live upstairs and he and his family downstairs between them and the outside world. The Jews graciously refused the offer and the Berber then suggested that at least they allow him to leave his own son to sleep on the floor of their house by the door as a sign to all that any attack on this family would be an attack on his own as well. Again the Jews demurred, pointing out that the house could easily be locked and that it was only children who were causing any troubles. They parted late that night with the Berber assuring them that he would be keeping a watchful eye on events in any case.

Throughout the six days the war itself lasted, life in the city remained virtually unchanged on the surface. Those people who felt most strongly about the war, expressed most opposition to Israel's continued existence, and were most certain about a quick and complete Arab victory were the educated urban Arabs. The poorer people of the city and the Berbers of the countryside talked about making a peaceful settlement, the difficulty of keeping straight who was who in the war (Where is Syria? Does Iraq have a common border with Israel? and usually no questions at all), and they stressed that the whole business should certainly not affect the Jews of their own city. A few of the Jews themselves made a point of contributing blood for the Arab civilians being injured in the war but at no time was the Jews' loyalty challenged or their ties to the Israelis considered a threat or even a significant embarrassment to the Moslem community.

Beneath the surface, however, among Moslems and Jews alike, the dominant feeling at this point was one of uncertainty. As one Jewish man put it: "Everything would be all right if people today respected the old ways and continued to treat us as individuals. But nowadays there are so many unemployed people in town who could be turned against us at any moment." A Moslem storekeeper spoke in similar terms: "You have to understand the custom in this country," he said. "People do whatever some big man tells them to do. *What* they are told to do doesn't matter nearly so much as the fact that someone takes hold of things and tells people how they should act. If the government does nothing and someone tells us to kill the Jews that is what we will do. If the government tells us to be good to the Jews we will follow their directions." An attempt to supply some such authoritative direction was not long in coming.

On June 12th the newspapers of Istiqlal, the major political party in Morocco, called for a boycott of "all those who have close and distant ties with 'Israel' and her sinister allies." They also published a list of companies who, they said, dealt with Israel and should therefore be boycotted. The Arabs of the city now had their direction: they said they would have no business dealings with Jews since all Moslems must unite in the face of the outside enemy. Jews remained off the streets, some even afraid to try buying food. Unarmed soldiers joined the local police in casually patrolling the streets of the city as the government began to clarify its own position. On the 14th, the Moroccan representative to the United Nations Security Council spoke at length of the favorable treatment Jews had always received in Morocco, particularly when the Moroccan government refused to cooperate with the anti-Jewish legislation of the Vichy regime during the Second World War. A similar statement from the Royal Cabinet released two days later further emphasized that none of the citizenship rights of Moroccan Jews would in any way be altered by the present situation. Then, on June 15th, the government seized the Istiqlal party newspapers and when the papers reappeared two days later the call for a boycott was only slightly toned down but no specific nations or companies were mentioned by name.

The Jews of the city, meanwhile, played for time. With the boycott in partial effect and some of the Moslems actually being intimidated into not patronizing Jewish-owned stores, individual Jews reasoned that they could close their stores Wednesday and Thursday for the Jewish holiday of Shevuoth, open briefly on Friday the 16th, stay at home over the weekend, and go back to work on Monday—the day before the Moslem holiday celebrating the Prophet's birthday. The Jews felt that in the interim many even normally unemployed Moslems would become busy harvesting the area's first grain crop in two years, and, unless the fighting in the Middle East resumed and the local Moslems were forced to remain united against an enemy whose presence they could be made to feel personally, internal Moslem differences would reassert themselves and the Jews would once again be able to work

within the context of their personal and social relationships with
the Moslems. Realizing, however, their complete political impo-
tence, the Jews only feared that in the days following the war
they might find themselves used as pawns in the struggle between
the various Moroccan political factions.

For the most part this fear proved groundless. Intent on preserving public order and not allowing the politicians to seize the
initiative, the King took a strong stand in favor of protecting all
Moroccan citizens—Jews and Moslems alike—from violent action.
As the United Nations debated on into deadlock, Istiqlal continued to call for a boycott of Jews and the nationalization of
some Western-owned firms. Dubbing the boycott an act against
the order of the state, the government struck back on July 5th
charging that "the boycott is not an Islamic principle. . . . Those
who incite people to participate in it commit an act that is criminal in thought, in law, and in spirit." And on July 8th, in a most
remarkable televised speech, the King himself argued that it was
not surprising that the world should regard the Arabs as the ag-
gressors in the recent war since it was they who called for a general mobilization a week before the fighting began and it was
they who closed the Gulf of Aqaba. He said that one should never
enter into a war until one's own country is at least the economic
equal of the opponent, and he stressed the point that internal
chaos is far worse than an undesirable international political situation. The King's verbal determination was expressed in action
a few days later when the head of the largest labor union in
Morocco was imprisoned for charging that the Moroccan government itself had fallen into the hands of pro-Zionist forces. And
the papers of the Istiqlal party, threatened with another seizure,
turned to a direct attack on those whom they regarded the King
as coddling and initiated a series of articles on the Protocols of
the Elders of Zion, the notorious forgery about the Jewish world
conspiracy of which the Nazis had made such effective use. Yet
even here it is important to note that the Moroccans, like President Nasser himself, had to borrow their anti-Jewish text from
another cultural tradition simply because the Arabs lack a well-
developed anti-Jewish literature of their own.

Significantly, however, within the city itself the impact of this
struggle for power and influence on the national level was very

minimal. The King's strong stand against any sort of illegal action against the Jews was not without its impact, but the local situation had already begun to ease well before the King's determination was fully clarified. Most Jews reopened their shops right after the holiday of the Prophet's birthday and Moslems and Jews joked and conversed in near normal fashion. With the passage of time and the continued bickering among the various political factions, the people of the city reasserted their suspicions about all national party leaders and their abiding faith in personal judgments based on face-to-face relations. Those Jews who practiced trades or sold goods without competition from Moslems were fully patronized. Some Arabs and fewer Berbers, perhaps hedging against any later claim that they had supported Israel's friends, avoided Jewish shops that were in direct competition with Moslems but they were cordial in their relationships with the Jewish businessmen themselves. The Berbers practiced this avoidance even less on market day, when there were enough of them in town so they could not easily be intimidated by the urban Arabs.

In short, then, despite both a few isolated instances elsewhere in the country in which Jews had indeed been molested and notwithstanding the firm action taken by the Moroccan government to forestall any sort of civil disorder, the primary strain placed on local Moslem-Jewish relations by the course of outside events was largely nullified in a rather short period of time. A partial boycott was indeed put into effect, one which might ultimately put a great strain on a part of the Moroccan Jewish community. But the very fact that the Moslems of the city continued to treat the Jews as individuals rather than as members of a stereotyped group, the very fact that even in the face of a defeat they too felt to be rather humiliating, their relations to the local Jewish community were not significantly altered indicates that the very nature of Moslem-Jewish relations were of a rather different sort than one might generally imagine. The contrast to the West is not only one of overt acts but of an entire sociological context in which geography, history, and the structure of social group relations each contribute to a system that must be analyzed and evaluated in its own terms.

The city with which we are dealing is in almost every sense of the term a marginal one. Situated in an oasis of gardens between the grain-producing plains of western Morocco and the pasture-lands of the Middle Atlas Mountains, she effectively bridges the predominantly Arab population of the former zone and the almost entirely Berber population of the latter. In the days before the establishment of the French Protectorate in 1912 the city also stood on the border between the lands over which the King was generally able to exercise his authority and those that were frequently in a state of dissidence vis-à-vis the central government. There is at present in the city a man whom people have nicknamed "the King" because, they say, he is blind in one eye and can only see half of what is going on around him. Aside from being a lovely comment on Moroccan politics this would also seem to be an appropriate characterization of the city itself. For she has always stood with her blind eye turned toward the plains and the central government while her good eye has been directed toward the mountains south of the city. She was almost always at least nominally a government city but her inhabitants and administrators alike knew full well that their real economic and political support lay in the areas that were usually in dissidence. No mere stopping place on the Saharan caravan routes, she had a market of her own for products of her own and a position as entrepôt between mountain and plain, dissident and loyalist, Berber and Arab. It was an economic situation in which Jews had the opportunity to thrive, and it was the overall social situation that brought this possibility to fruition.

Unlike many other nations of the world that combine within a small area several distinct ethnic groups and sharply different urban and rural populations, in Morocco these distinctions are very subtle indeed, constituting not a polarity but a series of variations on a common theme. Only the fact that a man speaks the Berber language (as well, usually, as Arabic) sets him apart from the Arab: physically the two are indistinguishable. Nor is the social structure of Berbers and Arabs, townsmen and countrymen, sharply different. The Berber belongs to a tribal fraction composed mainly of close relatives linked to other fractions of the tribe not by immutable genealogical principles but by the interplay and outright manipulation of ties of proximity, marriage and political expediency as well as any real or imagined kinship bonds. For the urban Arab, not associated in a tribe or fraction, the main solidary unit is the group that partakes of a common nurture, the individual family. In both cases, however, the locus of every level of organization is the single individual, whose status is based not on some innate position in a fixed set of social categories but on his ability to maneuver within the rules of the game to consolidate and extend his personal power within and beyond his own kinsmen. Through the arrangement of his alliances and the sheer force of his own personality each man can, according to his abilities, mold the pliable social fabric into a pattern as distinctive and ephemeral as himself. Such a man knows that his personal identity—his very existence—derives from the properties and power he has accumulated, and he knows, too, that on the third day after his death, his properties divided, his power diffused, people will cease to mourn him and will say that he simply no longer exists. Throughout their lives, Berbers and Arabs alike will have judged others and themselves been judged according to the principle T. E. Lawrence once referred to when he said: "Arabs believe in persons, not in institutions."

Despite such similarities of social organization there remains, nonetheless, a distinct coolness if not tension within and between groups of Arabs and Berbers. Between the two groups there are, of course, significant differences of language, interpretation of Islamic principles, and modes of political expression. But overriding these distinctions is the fact that, for all parties concerned, kinship, politics and social relations are thoroughly intertwined and inseparable. In the competition for the material and immaterial symbols of personal prestige, an act in any one of these categories will affect and be affected by—indeed, will be defined in terms of—most or all of the other categories: an economic relation may be worked out through kinship ties strengthened by marriage and implying a later political dependency, and so on. A picture of the entire Moslem social structure might look like a single pool separated into two main sections and a number of finer divisions by a series of differentially permeable membranes. For some kinds of interaction each unit would be closed off from the others, while for some other types of relations they would all constitute a single interacting unit. The barrier between two groups might, for example, be impermeable to certain cultural features thus effectively blocking intermarriage, while the same barrier in no way impedes some kinds of political relationships. Most important, for our purposes, is the fact that, in a system of this sort, the competition for commonly shared symbols of personal prestige is carried on uninhibited throughout the entire pool of social interaction, a pool whose resources are sufficiently limited that each participant is aware that a gain for one party generally implies a loss for another. The disruptive aspects of this quest for the power and property on which a man's status depends may be mollified within any one Berber fraction or Arab family by ties of kinship, alliance, and economic interdependence: between such groups outright competition may be less constrained.

It has been to the Jew's distinct advantage that he stands outside this sociological pool. Not sharing in the same relatively limited sphere of prestige resources, the Jew has been able to have an economic dealing with a Moslem that carries with it none of the social and political implications involved in such transactions between two Moslems. A Moslem can hardly compete socially with a person who simply is not a member of the social grouping within which this competition is taking place. An economic agreement between members of two such social groups is also less a contractual relationship than a symbiotic one: each party recognizes that he will profit best by adhering to the terms of the bargain and that his interests are more closely safeguarded by the controls inherent in their relation of interdependence than they would be by having recourse solely to external legal sanctions. A sense of mutual reliability has grown out of this social situation and however much Jews are regarded as shrewd businessmen by the city's Moslems they are almost never characterized as dishonest or avaricious. The cultural life of the Jews is, then, sufficiently similar to that of the Moslems that the two communities can share many beliefs, values and even saints in common, yet their social lives are sufficiently separate that neither is in direct social competition with the other.

The articulation between the way this society is put together and the way in which members of its different parts view one another is clearly indicated in the kinds of conceptions Moslems express about the Jews. When one discusses the Jews with Arabs and Berbers of all economic and educational levels, one never hears remarks that derogate the Jews for their real or imagined economic position: there is no notion among the people of the city that the Jews have tried to gain financial control of the marketplace to the detriment of the Moslems. Nor does one hear politically oriented anti-Jewish comments, that is, that the Jews are individually or collectively conspiring to take over the government. Rather, all of the anti-Jewish remarks one hears fit into the sociological category, the gist of such remarks being that the Jews are socially separate if not outcast from the Moslem community. To the Moslem the legitimacy of the Koran lies in the fact that it is believed to be the all-inclusive, precise and unaltered word of God as transmitted through His last prophet. The Jews, say the Moslems, are, however, constantly rewriting their Torah and have thus destroyed whatever truth there was in that document. Moreover, by manipulating their sacred heritage, "the Jews no longer know who their grandfathers are"—a sin of significant proportions to a genealogically concerned Moslem. Moslems also cite as incest the fact that Jews marry their nieces, and one man even claimed that Jews do not circumcise their sons, thus turning the noncircumcised Christian's argument on its head but applying it for precisely the same purpose. Examples of this sort could be multiplied almost without end, but the common point in all of them remains that the Jews are believed to be socially inferior but hardly a threat to the "superior" tradition of the Prophet. The history of the city's Jewish community is the story of how they have been given and developed their own place in this whole socio-cultural context.

The Jews of the city are derived almost entirely not from the Spanish immigrants of the fifteenth century but from those Jews who fled Roman Palestine, Egypt and Cyrenaica in the first centuries A.D., settled out of government reach among the dissident Berber tribes of North Africa, and are said to have converted many of those Berbers to Judaism well before the arrival of Islam. Indeed, one legend has it that the first inhabitants of the city were just such a tribe of Judeo-Berbers. Little is known of the city's Jewry under the early Islamic dynasties of Morocco, but it is doubtful that their overall situation was greatly different from that of the last two centuries before the establishment of the

French Protectorate. Then, as earlier, the state was coextensive with the community of Islam, and those who rejected the duties of the latter were also denied the privileges of the former. His status as protégé legitimized by Koranic inscription, the Jew was, however, allowed to live in his own separate community and practice his own law, but he was required to indicate his inferior social and religious position by wearing distinctive clothing, removing his shoes when passing a mosque, and so on. Since "protection" often meant reserving the skills of the Jew for the protector himself, the extent to which the Jew was fairly treated or exploited varied as greatly as the power and personalities of the Kings and their largely autonomous local administrators. The death of a king, or even his local representative, generally threw whole regions into a state of dissidence, and it was at these moments in particular that Jewish communities were attacked. Yet it is important to note that almost without exception in modern times these attacks were aimed squarely at depriving the Jews of their properties and not at eliminating the Jewish population itself. In fact, when the Sultan Moulay el Hassan died in 1894 and a nearby Arab village came to the walls of the city and demanded to be allowed to "eat the Jews," the people of the city not only gave the Jews their own protection but, when the Arab villagers then broke into a neighboring garden and killed a young Moslem boy, Berber tribesmen joined the townsmen in waging a successful war against the Arab villagers.

For those Jews who lived or peddled their goods in the neighboring mountains conditions were probably even better. Here the Jew, who almost always spoke the Berber language fluently, again depended on the personal protection of a local big man. Following Berber custom, the Jewish merchant would sacrifice a sheep at the home of a particular Berber and the latter would then make it known that this Jew was under his protection and any attack on the Jew would be construed as an attack on himself as well. When the Jew led his pack train through tribal lands his protector would send along an armed guard or place his own son on the lead animal as a sign to all of the Jew's status. Should anyone, even a member of the Berber's own family, dare to violate this sanctuary, he would pay heavily in blood or money for his foolishness.

In short, then, it is no doubt true that the Jews were at times rather heavily taxed for the protection they were accorded and that they were at the mercy of King and local administrator alike. But it is a fact that European writers rarely appreciate that in the pre-Protectorate period such taxation was seldom much greater, the mistreatment seldom much harsher, and the living standards of the Jews not much lower than those of the Moslems among whom they lived. The Jews of the city tended their crafts and businesses, owned property and formed partnerships with Moslems in an atmosphere that was quite different and quite a bit less rigorous than that with which their European coreligionists had to cope.

With the beginning of the French Protectorate in 1912, Jews all over Morocco were able to move outside of their ghettos and take advantage of Western cultural and living standards. They established schools, learned the French language and prospered somewhat from French economic investment. From a population of three thousand at the beginning of the Protectorate the Jewish community of the city grew to nearly six thousand in the late 1940's, although the actual proportion of Jews in the city dropped from one-half to almost one-third. Most Jews welcomed the creation of the State of Israel in 1948 as the fulfillment of biblical prophecy, but few of them actually emigrated before the end of French domination over Morocco.

Independence in 1956 brought with it a depressed and uncertain economic situation. Although on the national level a Jew was appointed minister of the postal-telegraph-telephone system, locally the Jews were caught in the general economic decline. The Jews of the city had always kept their capital relatively liquid and mobile. The wealthier Jews now began to consolidate their holdings and look for opportunities in France and the large cities of the Moroccan coast, while the poorer Jews were attracted to Israel by offers of work and free passage. As the Jews withdrew their funds from the marketplace the economy became yet more depressed, for the Moslems had long been drawn out into investing by the Jews and in the latter's absence many of the Moslems preferred to hoard their money and avoid economic (and also prestige) competition with other Moslems. Political uncertainty was added in 1961 by the sudden death of the Sultan Mohammed V, who was justifiably regarded as a good friend of the Jews.

But whatever their reasons for departing the city it appears certain that none of the Jews left because of any real breakdown in local Moslem-Jewish relations. Rather than being happy about the situation, the Moslems—Arabs as well as Berbers—were hurt and bewildered by the Jews' departure. Some of them explain that a Jewish big man named Ben Gurion called them and they had to leave, while others say that it was written in the Jews' holy books that they should return to the east. Berbers continued to feel uncomfortable doing business with Arabs, and the shops, but not the exact role, of many Jews have since been taken over by Berber veterans of the French army. The city itself has been subjected to a significant influx of rural people seeking work, welfare payments, and schooling for their children, but the overall social environment remained reasonably close to its traditional pattern right up to the time when war broke out in the Middle East.

This, then, is clearly a very different sort of society from what one is used to dealing with in discussions of Jewish–non-Jewish relations. Fluid yet structured, expandable yet finite, human and yet somehow divine, it is a society composed of a number of individuals who forge ties of kinship and alliance in an attempt to secure themselves as best as possible within a social environment whose variability and malleability in no way discount the minimally defined and far from immutable position in which each man is born. It is a society in which people tend to group one another only on the basis of a very few characteristics concerning one another's social origins and present situation. The stereotype (if one can use that word) that they maintain about one another begins with several minimal features but quickly gives way to an evaluation and relationship based primarily on individual personalities. The stereotype of a particular grouping, then, is compiled of a number of specific cases and remains sufficiently minimal and partial rather than complete and comprehensive, so that an individual may be judged far more by his personal attributes than by a fixed model that compartmentalizes one's view of and relationship to another person automatically. Within one's own group of fellow Moslems the ties of social, political and economic life are so intertwined that whoever stands outside of this context has the opportunity to enjoy a distinctly advantageous intermediate position. But because it will be his personal characteristics that define the content of this inherent position and because no member of the society will abrogate the criteria of personal judgment that his law, his religion and his common sense tell him are applicable to all men, even this outsider will be judged by factors that acknowledge his membership in the community of men, however much they may deny his membership in the community of believers. Socially distinct but not abhorred, politically subservient but not deprived of his own group autonomy, economically envied but not severely discriminated against, the Jew in Moroccan society has long held a position among his Moslem neighbors that is neither unbearable nor ideal. He could survive the old dictum that the friend of my enemy is my enemy simply by being a closer friend to his supposed enemy than to those with whom he shares bonds of religion and blood. He may find himself vulnerable to economic pressures that are nowadays not without their political overtones and therefore more closely approximate the position of his fellow Jews in the Near East, but he will be as aware as his Moslem neighbors that this is a recent occurrence and one that very much rubs against the grain of Moslem and Jew alike.

The Moroccan Jew could, then, feel reasonably calm living among Moslems during the Middle Eastern war because he knew that notwithstanding the extreme provocation of the war itself there was no hard-core hatred of the Jews as a group and that if the Middle Eastern situation did not involve the Moroccans directly the relation of Jew and Moslem would not be altered radically from its former pattern. The Jews of the interior cities were keenly aware of the mild antipathy between Arabs and Berbers, and the social and economic advantage they held by virtue of this fact. Implicitly, they also seemed to know that, as Charles Gallagher has put it, "compared to the Middle Eastern heartland, North Africa is a much more cautious, almost furtive society of compromise, a quality which has been forced upon it by history." For the Jews of this one Moroccan city, then, the whole episode was a heartening reaffirmation of their own conception of their relations with the Moslems living around them. For the Moslem it was a brief but not all-absorbing encounter with supralocal issues. And for the social scientist it was an opportunity to see a set of social and cultural principles put to the test of scope and relevancy.

Jewish communities throughout Morocco will, no doubt, continue to shrink in size for the same economic reasons that have caused their present diminution. Jewish children will continue to move to the large cities of Morocco and France to seek an education and a livelihood, and some of their parents will continue to prepare them for this by speaking only French at home and teaching them only an hour a day of Arabic at school. The younger generation of Jews is already far less aware of and involved in the life of Morocco as a whole than are their parents, and they are consequently more eager to be physically removed from it as well. Just what the long-range effects of the partial boycott in the larger cities of Morocco will be is hard to say, but if it does prove true that the boycott is further weakened by the passage of time or the end to the state of belligerency in the Middle East, the lives of those Jews who leave the interior for Rabat and Casablanca should be no more difficult than they have been in the past. But their departure will not be for want of peaceful relations with their Moslem neighbors, relations that have proved reasonably workable even while the brothers of each have been at war with one another. Perhaps, too, their experience may offer some small hope that a political accord may yet be reached in the Middle East that will reestablish the finest features of earlier Moslem-Jewish relations, while eliminating those aspects that both sides have allowed to compound their present estrangement.

Selected Bibliography

In its original publication, each of the selections in this reader was accompanied by a bibliography often composed of more citations than we can include in the space available here. Moreover, many of the citations are to Arabic, Persian, Hebrew, etc., sources, languages not usually available except to advanced scholars. Since the advanced scholar will go to the original sources of these selections for the complete resources of the authors, a necessary if not satisfactory compromise has been made here. A list has been compiled of the more easily available and important references in these selections, omitting the ephemeral, obscure, and highly specialized citations and also omitting references to general anthropological and sociological works. It is most important to emphasize that this bibliography is derived from the selections in the reader and does not constitute an adequate guide to the Middle East. For this the editor recommends Louise E. Sweet, 1968, THE CENTRAL MIDDLE EAST, 2 vols., New Haven: Human Relations Area Files, and Louise E. Sweet, "A Survey of Recent Anthropological Literature," MIDDLE EAST JOURNAL (in press, 1969), and the bibliographic resources of any substantial library.

Abramovitch, Z., and J. Gelphat.
    1944 *The Arab Economy*. Tel-Aviv: Hakibutz Hameuchad (in Hebrew).
Alport, E. A.
    1954 "The Mzab." *Journal of the Royal Anthropological Institute*, 84:34–44.
Amat, Charles.
    1888 *Le M'zab et les M'zabites*. Paris: Challamel.
Anderson, J. N. D.
    1959 *Islamic Law in the Modern World*. New York: New York University Press.

Arensberg, C. M.
   1968 *The Irish Countryman.* New York: Natural History Press.
Armstrong, L., and G. Hirabayashi.
   1956 "Social Differentiation in Selected Lebanese Villages." *American Sociological Review*, 21:425–34.
Asad, Talal.
   1964 "Seasonal Movements of the Kababish Arabs of Northern Kordofan." *Sudan Notes and Records*, 45:48–58.
Aswad, Barbara C.
   1963 "Social and Ecological Aspects in the Formation of Islam." *Papers of the Michigan Academy of Science, Arts, and Letters*, 48:419–42.
Ayoub, Victor F.
   1965 "Conflict Resolution and Social Reorganization in a Lebanese Village." *Human Organization*, 24:11–17.
Baldensperger, Phillip G.
   1906 "The Immovable East." *Palestine Exploration Fund, Quarterly Statement.* Published at the Fund's Office, London.
Barth, Fredrik.
   1953 "Principles of Social Organization in South Kurdistan." *Univ. Ethnogr. Museum Oslo*, Bull. no. 7.
   1954 "Father's Brother's Daughter Marriage in Kurdistan." *Southwestern Journal of Anthropology*, 10:164–71.
Benet, Francisco.
   1957 "Explosive Markets: The Berber Highlands" in *Trade and Markets in the Early Empires*, Karl Polanyi *et al.*, eds. Glencoe, Ill.: Free Press.
Berchem, Marguerite van.
   1953 "Deux campagnes de fouilles à Sedrata (1951–52)." *Trav. Inst. Rech. sahar.*, 3:123–38.
Bergheim, Samuel.
   1894 "Land Tenure in Palestine." *Palestine Exploration Fund, Quarterly Statement.* Published at the Fund's Office, London.
Bernard, Augustin.
   1932 *Le Maroc.* Paris: Alcan.
   1939 *Afrique septentrionale et occidentale*, 2 vols. (1937–39), II. Géographie Universelle, XI. Paris: Colin.
Berque, Jacques.
   1955 *Structures Sociales de Haut Atlas.* Paris: Presses Universitaires de France.
   1957 *Histoire Sociale d'un Village Egyptien au XXeme Siècle.* Paris: Mouton.

1953 "Qu'est-ce c'est une tribu nordafricaine?," *Hommage à Lucien Fèbvre*, I, Paris: Colin.

Binder, L., ed.

1966 *Politics in Lebanon.* New York: John Wiley.

Brunhes, Jean.

1952 *Human Geography.* (Translation by E. F. Row of *La géographie humaine,* abr. ed., Paris, 1942.) Edited by Mme. Jean-Brunhes Delamarre & P. Deffontaines. London: Harrap.

Burckhardt, J. L.

1822 *Travels in Syria and the Holy Land.* London: John Murray.

Capot-Rey, Robert.

1953 *Le Sahara français.* Paris: Presses Universitaires de France.

Chamoun, C.

1963 *Crise au Moyen Orient.* Paris: Gallimard.

Charlet-Cozon, le lieutenant.

1905 "Les palmiers du M'zab." *Bull. Soc. Géogr. Alger (Afr. N.)*, 9:11–87.

Chevrillon, André.

1927 *Les puritains du désert.* Paris: Plon.

Churchill, C. H.

1853 *Mount Lebanon, A Ten Years' Residence, from 1842 to 1852.* London: Saunders and Oatley.

Churchill, C. W.

1954 *The City of Beirut, A Socio-economic Survey.* Beirut: Dar Al-Kitab.

Coon, C. S.

1931 *Tribes of the Rif.* Harvard African Studies, IX. Cambridge, Mass.: Peabody Museum.

Cunnison, Ian.

1966 *Baggara Arabs: Power and the Lineage in a Sudanese Nomad Tribe.* Oxford: Clarendon Press.

Daghestani, K.

1938 *Etude sociologique sur la famille musulmane contemporaine en Syrie.* Paris: Leroux.

Davies, E., and A. Rees.

1960 *Welsh Rural Communities.* Cardiff: University of Wales.

Dayan, S.

1947 *Moshav Ovdim.* Tel Aviv: Palestine Pioneer Press Library No. 6.

Donaldson, D. M.

1933 *The Shi'ite Religion.* London: Luzac.

Doughty, Charles M.
   1930 *Travels in Arabia Deserta*. London: Jonathan Cape.
Doutté, E., and E. F. Gautier.
   1913 *Enquête sur la dispersion de la langue berbère en Algérie*. Alger: Jourdan.
Dupree, Louis.
   1956 "The Changing Character of South-Central Afghanistan Villages." *Human Organization*, Vol. 14, no. 4.
   1960 "An Archaeological Survey of North Afghanistan." *Afghanistan*, 15(3):13–15.
   1963 *The Green and the Black*. American Universities Field Staff Reports, South Asia Series, Volume VII, No. 5.
   1964 "Prehistoric Surveys and Excavations in Afghanistan, 1959–60 and 1961–63." *Science*, 146:638–40.
Dupree, Louis, and Bruce Howe.
   1963 "Results of an Archaeological Survey for Stone Age Sites in North Afghanistan." *Afghanistan*, 18(2):1–15.
Durkheim, Emile.
   1893 *De la Division du Travail Social* (1960 edition). Paris: Presses Universitaires de France.
Eberhard, Wolfram.
   1954 "Change in Leading Families in Southern Turkey." *Anthropos*, 49:992–1003.
English, Paul Ward.
   1966 *City and Village in Iran: Settlement and Economy in the Kirman Basin*. Madison: University of Wisconsin Press.
Evans-Pritchard, E. E.
   1940 *The Nuer*. London: Oxford University Press.
Ferdinand, Klaus.
   1962 "Nomad Expansion and Commerce in Central Afghanistan." *Folk*, II:33–50. Copenhagen.
Flannery, Kent V.
   1965 "The Ecology of Early Food Production in Mesopotamia." *Science*, 147:1247–56.
Flapan, Simha.
   1962 "Integrating the Arab Village." *New Outlook*, 5:22–29.
Fortes, Meyer.
   1953 "The Structure of Unilineal Descent Groups." *American Anthropologist*, 55:17–41.
Fortes, Meyer, and E. E. Evans-Pritchard, eds.
   1940 *African Political Systems*. London: Oxford University Press.

Fuller, A.
1961 *Buarij, Portrait of a Lebanese Muslim Village.* Cambridge, Mass.: Harvard University Press.

Fyzee, A. A. A.
1955 *Outlines of Muhammadan Law.* London: Oxford University Press.

Galal, M.
1937 "Essai d'observations sur les rites funeraires en Egypte actuelle." *Revue des Etudes Islamiques,* p. 131 seq.

Gautier, E. F.
1923 *Le Sahara.* Paris: Payot.

Gellner, Ernest.
1962 "Concepts and Society." *Transactions of the Fifth World Congress of Sociology,* I:153–83. Washington, D.C.
1963 "Saints of the Atlas," in *Mediterranean Countrymen,* pp. 145–57. J. Pitt-Rivers, ed. Paris: Mouton.

Gerofi, R.
1953 "Michaux-Bellaire." *Tingu: Bulletin de la Société d'Histoire et d'Archéologie de Tanger,* 1:79–85.

Gibb, H. A. R., and Harold Bowen.
1950 *Islamic Society and the West,* Vol. I, Part I. London: Oxford University Press.

Gluckman, M.
1952 *Rituals of Rebellion in South East Africa.* Manchester: University Press.

Goichon, A.-M.
1927 *La vie féminine au Mzab, étude de sociologie musulmane,* 2 vols. (1927–31), I. With preface by William Marçais. Paris: Geuthner.

Granott, A.
1952 *The Land System in Palestine.* London: Eyre and Spottiswoode.

Granqvist, H.
1931 *Marriage Conditions in a Palestinian Village.* Helsingfors: Centraltryckereit.

Grant, Elihu.
1907 *The Peasantry of Palestine.* New York: The Pilgrim Press.

Harfouche, J. K.
1965 *Social Structure of Low-Income Families in Lebanon.* Beirut: Khayats.

Harik, I.

1965 "The Iqta System in Lebanon: A Comparative Political View." *Middle East Journal,* 19:405–22.

Hart, David M.

1954 "An Ethnographic Survey of the Rifian Tribe of Aith Waryaghar." *Tamuda* II, 1:51–86.

1957 "An 'Amara in the Central Rif: the Annual Pilgrimage to Sidi Bu Khiyar." *Tamuda* V, 2:239–45.

1958 "Emilio Blanco Izaga and the Berbers of the Central Rif." *Tamuda* VI, 2:171–237.

1962 "The Social Structure of the Rgibat Bedouins of the Western Sahara." *Middle East Journal,* XVI, 4:512–27.

Hess, Clyde, and Herbert Bodman.

1954 "Confessionalism and Feudality in Lebanese Politics." *Middle East Journal,* 8:10–26.

Hitti, P. K.

1957 *Lebanon in History.* New York: Macmillan.

1960 *History of the Arabs.* New York: Macmillan.

Hottinger, Arnold.

1961 "Zu ama and Parties in the Lebanese Crisis of 1958." *Middle East Journal,* 15.

Huguet, J.

1899 "Dans le Sud-Algérien." *Bull. Soc. Géogr. Paris,* 7 sér., 20:285–303.

1903 "Les Soffs." *Rev. Éc. Anthrop. Paris,* 13:94–99.

Hurewitz, J. C.

1953 *Middle East Dilemmas.* Published for the Council on Foreign Relations. New York: Harper & Row.

Ibn Khaldoun.

1958 *The Muqaddimah: An Introduction to History,* 3 vols., I. (Trans. from the Arabic by Franz Rosenthal.) New York: Bollingen Foundation.

Israel Ministry for Foreign Affairs.

1958 *The Arabs in Israel.* Jerusalem: The Government Printer.

Izaga, Emilio Blanco.

1935 *Conferencia sobre Derecho Consuetudinario Rifeño.* Unpublished.

Jessup, H. H.

1910 *Fifty Three Years in Syria,* 2 vols. New York: Fleming H. Revell Co.

Johnson-Crosbie.

1930 *Report of a Committee on the Economic Conditions of Agri-*

culturists in Palestine and the Fiscal Measures of Government in Relation thereto. Government of Palestine.

Johnstone, T. M.
1969 "The Languages of the Middle East," in *Peoples and Cultures of the Middle East*, Vol. I, Louise Sweet, ed. New York: Natural History Press.

Julien, Ch.-A.
1952 *Histoire de L'Afrique du Nord, de la conquête arabe à 1830*, 2nd ed. rev. by Roger Le Tourneau. Paris: Payot.

Khalaf, S., and Emile Shwayri.
1966 "Family Firms and Industrial Development: The Lebanese Case." *Economic Development and Cultural Change*, pp. 59–69.

Klein, F. A.
1883 "Life, Habits, and Customs of the Fallahin of Palestine." *Palestine Exploration Fund, Quarterly Statement*, 41–48. London: The Society Office; R. Bentley & Son.

Kroeber, A. L.
1948 *Anthropology.* New York. Harcourt, Brace and World.

Lacouture, J., and S. Lacouture.
1958 *Egypt in Transition.* (Trans. by J. and S. Lacouture) London: Methuen.

Lambton, Ann K. S.
1969 "Islamic Society in Persia," in *Peoples and Cultures of the Middle East*, Vol. I, Louise Sweet, ed. New York: Natural History Press.

Landall, J.
1961 "Elections in Lebanon." *Western Political Quarterly*, 14:120–47.

Landau, J. M.
1953 *Parliaments and Parties in Egypt.* Tel Aviv: Israel Publishing House.

Lesne, Marcel.
1959 *Histoire d'un Groupement Berbère: les Zemmour.* Thèse complémentaire pour le doctorat des lettres présentée à la Faculté de Lettres et Sciences Humaines à Paris.

Lewis, Bernard.
1950 *The Arabs in History.* London: Hutchinson.
1963 *Istanbul and the Civilization of the Ottoman Empire.* Norman: University of Oklahoma Press.

Macalister, R. A. S., and E. W. G. Masterman.
1905 "Occasional Papers on the Modern Inhabitants of Palestine. A History of the Doings of the Fellahin during the First Half of

the Nineteenth Century, from Native Sources." *Palestine Exploration Fund, Quarterly Statement.* Published at the Fund's Office, London.

Maldonado, Eduardo.

1952 *El Rogui.* Tetuan: Instituto General Franco.

1955 *Retazos de Historia Marroqui.* Tetuan: Instituto General Franco.

Masqueray, Emile.

1879 *Chronique d'Abou Zakaria.* Translated with a commentary by Emile Masqueray. Alger: Aillaud.

1886 *Formation des cités chez les populations sédentaires de l'Algérie.* Paris: Leroux.

Mercier, Marcel.

1922 *La civilisation urbaine au Mzab.* Alger: Pfister.

1927 *Etude sur le waqf abadhite et ses applications au Mzab.* Alger: Carbonel.

Meyer, A. J.

1959 *Middle Eastern Capitalism: Nine Essays.* Cambridge, Mass.: Harvard University Press.

Michaux-Bellaire, E.

1918 *Villes et Tribus du Maroc.* Paris: Leroux.

Mohsen, Safia K.

1967 "Aspects of the Legal Status of Women Among Awlad 'Ali." *Anthropological Quarterly,* 40:153-66.

Montagne, R.

1930 *Les Berbères et le Makhzen.* Paris: Alcan.

1931 *La Vie Sociale et Politique des Berbères.* Paris: Editions du Comite de l'Afrique Française.

Morand, Marcel.

1910 *Etudes de droit musulman algérien.* Alger: Jourdan.

Morier, J.

1818 *Second Journey through Persia.* London: Longman, Hurst, Rees, Orme, and Brown.

Motylinski, A. de C.

1885a *Guerara depuis sa fondation.* Alger: Jourdan.

1885b *Les livres de la secte abadhite.* An annotated bibliography. Alger: Fontana.

1908 "Chronique d'Ibn Saghir sur les imams de Tahert." Texte et traduction. *Act. XIV Int. Orient. Congr.,* III:3-132. Paris: Leroux.

Murphy, Robert F.

1964 "Social Distance and the Veil." *American Anthropologist,* 66:1257-74.

Nader, L.
   1965 "Communication between Village and City in the Modern Middle East." *Human Organization,* 24:21–24.
Nevo, N. n.d. "Shikma: A Moshav in the Western Negev." Stencil.
Oliphant, Laurence.
   1887 *Haifa or Life in Modern Palestine.* New York: Harper & Row.
Olmstead, A. T.
   1960 *History of the Persian Empire.* Chicago: University of Chicago Press.
Patai, Raphael.
   1949 "Musha'a Tenure and Co-operation in Palestine." *American Anthropologist,* 51:436–45.
Pelly, L.
   1879 *The Miracle of Husain.* London.
Peters, Emrys L.
   1960 "The Proliferation of Segments in the Lineage of the Bedouin of Cyrenaica." *Journal of the Royal Anthropological Institute,* 90.29–53.
   1963 "Aspects of Rank and Status among Muslims in a Lebanese Village," in *Mediterranean Countrymen,* J. Pitt-Rivers, ed. Paris: Mouton.
Pitt-Rivers, J., ed.
   1963 *Mediterranean Countrymen.* Paris: Mouton.
Poliak, A. N.
   1940 *History of Land Relations in Egypt, Syria and Palestine at the End of the Middle Ages and in Modern Times.* Jerusalem: Ever (in Hebrew).
Polk, W. R.
   1963 *The Opening of South Lebanon.* Cambridge, Mass.: Harvard University Press.
Post, George E.
   1891 "Essays on the Sects and Nationalities of Syria and Palestine." *Palestine Exploration Fund, Quarterly Statement,* pp. 99–147. London: The Society's Office; R. Bentley & Son.
Prawer, Joshua.
   1963 *A History of the Latin Kingdom of Jerusalem.* Vol. 1, *The Crusades and the First Kingdom.* Jerusalem: Bialik Institute (in Hebrew).
Qubain, Fahim I.
   1961 *Crisis in Lebanon.* Washington: Middle East Institute.
Redfield, Robert.

414 Peoples and Cultures of the Middle East

1960 *Peasant Society and Culture.* Chicago: University of Chicago Press.

Robin, Nil-Joseph.

1884 *Le Mzab et son annexion à la France.* Alger: Jourdan.

Robinson, E., and E. Smith.

1841 *Biblical Researches in Palestine, Mount Sinai and Arabia Petraea.* 3 vols. London: John Murray.

Robinson, R. D.

1949 Unpublished letters to the Institute of Current World Affairs. New York. No. 37, Sept. 5.

Rosenfeld, Henry.

1957 "Analysis of Marriage and Marriage Statistics in a Moslem-Christian Arab Village." *International Archives of Ethnography,* 48:32–62.

1958 "Processes of Structural Change within the Arab Village Extended Family." *American Anthropologist,* 60:1127–39.

1959a "Social Changes in an Arab Village." *New Outlook,* II: 6 and 7:37–42, 14–25.

1959b "Changes in the Occupational Structure of an Arab Village." *Mibiphnim,* 22:71–83 (in Hebrew).

1960 "On Determinants of the Status of Arab Village Women." *Man,* 40:66–70.

1961 "A Cultural Program for the Arab Villages." *New Outlook:* IV:3, 36–49.

1964 "From Peasantry to Wage Labor and Residual Peasantry: The Transformation of an Arab Village," in *Process and Pattern in Culture—Essays in Honor of Julian Steward.* Chicago: Aldine.

Salibi, K.

1965 *The Modern History of Lebanon.* London: Weidenfeld & Nicolson.

Salim, M. S.

1955 *Economic and Political Organization of Echchbaysh, A Marsh Village Community in South Iraq.* University of London doctoral thesis. Published 1962 as *Marsh Dwellers of The Euphrates Delta.* London: Athlone Press.

Sayigh, Y. A.

1962 *Entrepreneurs of Lebanon.* Cambridge, Mass.: Harvard University Press.

Shimoni, J.

1947 *The Arabs of Palestine.* Tel-Aviv: Am Oved (in Hebrew).

Sjoberg, Gideon.

1952 "Folk and 'Feudal' Societies." *American Journal of Sociology,* 58:231–39.

Slane, Baron MacGuckin de, trans.

1852 *Histoire des Berbères et des dynasties musulmanes de l'Afrique septentrionale,* par Ibn Khaldoun. Translation of *Kitab al 'Ibar* (Cairo) by Baron MacGuckin de Slane, 4 vols. (1853–56), I. Alger, Presses du Gouvernment. Reprinted (1927) in 5 vols. edited by Paul Casanova. Paris: Geuthner.

Stirling, A. P.[aul]

1958 "Religious Change in Republican Turkey." *Middle East Journal* (Autumn).

1960 "A Death and a Youth Club: Feuding in a Turkish Village." *Anthropological Quarterly,* 33:51–75.

1965 *Turkish Village.* London: Weidenfeld and Nicolson, Ltd.

Swartz, M., V. Turner, and A. Tuden.

1966 *Political Anthropology.* Chicago: Aldine.

Sweet, Louise E.

1965 "Camel Raiding of North Arabian Bedouin: A Mechanism of Ecological Adaptation." *American Anthropologist,* 67:1132–50.

Talmon, Y.

1952 "Social Differentiation in Cooperative Villages." *British Journal of Sociology,* Vol. IV: 339–57.

Tannous, A. I.

1949 "The Village in the National Life of the Lebanon." *Middle East Journal,* Vol. 3, no. 2.

Tawney, R. H.

1926 *Religion and the Rise of Capitalism. A Historical Study.* London: Murray.

Touma, T.

1958 *Un Village de montagne au Liban: Hadeth el Jobbe.* Paris: Mouton.

Toynbee, Arnold.

1922 *The Western Question in Greece and Turkey.* London: Constable and Co., Ltd.

Vigourus, L.

1945 "L'émigration mozabite dans les villes du Tell Algérien." *Trav. Inst. Rech. sahar.,* 3:87–102.

Villiers, Alan.

1948 "Some Aspects of the Arab Dhow Trade." *Middle East Journal,* 2:399–416.

Volney, M.C.-F.

1798 *Travels through Egypt and Syria in the Years 1783, 1784 and*

1785. 2 vols. New York: Printed by J. Tiebout for E. Duyckinck & Co.

Von Grunebaum, G. E.
  1951 *Muhammadan Festivals*. New York: Schuman.

Waschitz, J.
  1947 *The Arabs in Palestine*. Tel-Aviv: Siphriat Poalim (in Hebrew).

Weber, Max.
  1922 *Wirtschaft und Gesellschaft*, 3 vols., II. *Grundriss der Sozial-ökonomik*, III. Abt. Tübingen: Mohr.

Weingrod, Alex.
  1962 "Reciprocal Change: A Case Study of a Moroccan Immigrant Village in Israel." *American Anthropologist*, 64:115–31.
  1962 "Administered Communities: Some Characteristics of New Immigrant Villages in Israel." *Economic Development and Cultural Change*, II.

Westermarck, Edward.
  1926 *Ritual and Belief in Morocco*. 2 vols. London: Macmillan.

Weulersse, J.
  1946 *Paysans de Syrie et du Proche-Orient*. Paris: Gallimard.

Williams, H. H., and J. R. Williams.
  1965 "The Extended Family as a Vehicle of Culture Change." *Human Organization*, 24:59–64.

Wilson, C. T.
  1906 *Peasant Life in The Holy Land*. London: John Murray.

Wolf, Eric R.
  1955 "Types of Latin American Peasantry: A Preliminary Discussion." *American Anthropologist*, 57:452–71.

Yawkey, David.
  1961 *Fertility Differences in a Modernizing Country: A Survey of Lebanese Couples*. Princeton: Princeton University Press.

Zeys, E.
  1886 *Législation mozabite, son origine, ses sources, son présent, son avenir*. Alger: Jourdan.

Ziadeh, N.
  1960 "The Lebanese Elections, 1960." *Middle East Journal*, 14:367–81.